NORTH CAROLINA STUDIES IN THE
ROMANCE LANGUAGES AND LITERATURES
Number 275

INDISCERNIBLE COUNTERPARTS

THE INVENTION OF THE TEXT IN
FRENCH CLASSICAL DRAMA

UNIVERSITY OF NORTH CAROLINA AT CHAPEL HILL

DEPARTMENT OF ROMANCE LANGUAGES

NORTH CAROLINA STUDIES
IN THE ROMANCE LANGUAGES AND LITERATURES

Founder: URBAN TIGNER HOLMES

Editor: CAROL L. SHERMAN

Distributed by:

UNIVERSITY OF NORTH CAROLINA PRESS

CHAPEL HILL
North Carolina 27515-2288
U.S.A.

INDISCERNIBLE COUNTERPARTS

THE INVENTION OF THE TEXT IN FRENCH CLASSICAL DRAMA

BY

CHRISTOPHER BRAIDER

CHAPEL HILL

NORTH CAROLINA STUDIES IN THE ROMANCE
LANGUAGES AND LITERATURES
U.N.C. DEPARTMENT OF ROMANCE LANGUAGES

2002

Library of Congress Cataloging-in-Publication Data

Braider, Christopher, 1950-
  Indiscernible counterparts: the invention of the text in French classical drama / by
Christopher Braider.
    p. cm. – (North Carolina studies in the Romance languages and literatures; no. 275).
    Includes bibliographical references.
    ISBN 0-8078-9279-3 (pbk.)
    1. French drama – 17th century – History and criticism.   I. Title.   II. Series.

PQ526.B67 2002
842'.409–dc21   2002029996

Cover design: Heidi Perov

ISBN 0-8078-9279-3

IMPRESO EN ESPAÑA

PRINTED IN SPAIN

DEPÓSITO LEGAL: V. 5.023 - 2002

ARTES GRÁFICAS SOLER, S. L. - LA OLIVERETA, 28 - 46018 VALENCIA

To Jessica,
in the hope that her pleasure in reading
this book
may measure even half the love
her father felt
in writing it for her.

TABLE OF CONTENTS

	Page
LIST OF FIGURES	11
ACKNOWLEDGEMENTS	13
INTRODUCTION. INDISCERNIBLE COUNTERPARTS: THE ANTITHETICAL TEXT OF FRENCH CLASSICAL DRAMA	15
1. *CET HYMEN DIFFÉRÉ*: THE FIGURATION OF AUTHORITY IN CORNEILLE'S *LE CID*	53
2. THE POETICS OF EQUIVOCATION: *HORACE, CINNA, RODOGUNE*	100
3. THE TWIN TEXT OF IDENTITY: FRENCH DOUBLES OF PLAUTUS' *AMPHITRUO*	156
4. THE AGENCY OF THE LETTER IN THE UNCONSCIOUS, OR REASON SINCE MOLIÈRE: THE STAGING OF NAMES IN *L'ECOLE DES FEMMES*	205
5. THE PROFESSION OF HYPOCRISY: TRUTH AND PERFORMANCE IN *TARTUFFE* AND *DOM JUAN*	258
6. MEDEA'S POISON: THE WORK OF HISTORY IN THE TEXT OF RACINE'S *PHÈDRE*	322
BIBLIOGRAPHY	377

LIST OF FIGURES

Figure   *Page*

1   Rembrandt van Rijn, *Belshazzar's Feast.* Oil on canvas. Courtesy of
    the National Gallery, London. Photo: National Gallery   73

2   Set for Molière's *La Princesse d'Elide.* Engraving from André Féli-
    bien, *Les Plaisirs de l'Ile enchantée* (Paris, 1673), following page 20   83

3   Nicolas Poussin, *Judgment of Solomon.* Musée National du Louvre,
    Paris. Credit: Alinari/Art Resource, NY   90

4   Diego Velázquez, *Las Meninas.* Museo del Prado, Madrid. Credit:
    Alinari/Art Resource, NY   93

5   Hyacinthe Rimbaud, *Louis XIV en habit de sacré.* Musée National
    du Louvre, Paris. Credit: Alinari/Art Resource, NY   217

6   *La Colère.* Engraved illustration from Charles La Brun, *Conférence
    sur l'expression générale et particulière des passions* (1698; Verona,
    1751). By permission of the Houghton Library, Harvard University   274

7   Rubens workshop, *Perseus and Andromeda.* Oil on canvas. Staatli-
    che Museen zu Berlin–Preussischer Kulturbesitz, Gemäldegalerie.
    Photo: Jörg P. Anders   353

ACKNOWLEDGEMENTS

THE writing of this book was in many ways a private affair—a domestic colloquy with a body of poems I love, and with the family and friends whose boundless forebearance attended the book's long gestation. In particular, Daniel Shine worked hard to humanize my prose—a contribution the more remarkable given his attachment to Milton, a writer whose syntactical and rhetorical excesses beggar even my own. Meanwhile, my wife Helen worked hard to humanize *me*, a far more intractable task than the one Daniel faced.

I have nonetheless incurred more public debts and seize the chance to acknowledge them. First and foremost, my heartfelt thanks to Peter Spear and Merrill Lessley, formerly Dean and Associate Dean of the College of Arts and Sciences at the University of Colorado, Boulder, who made it possible to devote an entire year of sabbatical leave to completing this project. Deep gratitude is also due to Harriet Stone and Helen Harrison, whose shrewd comments on the manuscript made the book far better than it could have been without their judicious help, and above all to Carol Sherman, without whose editorial care there would have been no book at all. I have greatly benefited from the responses of colleagues at other institutions (the University of Pittsburgh, Boston College, Harvard University, the University of California at Berkeley) kind enough to invite me to share portions of my research with them in the form of public lectures. Finally, chapter 1, "*Cet Hymen différé*: The Figuration of Authority in Corneille's *Le Cid*," is an enlarged and updated version of an article that originally appeared in *Representations* 54 (Spring 1996). Thanks accordingly go to the University of California Press and to the Regents of the University of California for their permission to reproduce that work here.

INDISCERNIBLE COUNTERPARTS: THE ANTITHETICAL
TEXT OF FRENCH CLASSICAL DRAMA

> Jamais tu ne me regardes là où je te vois.
>
> –Jacques Lacan

THE following book argues that, in the dual sense rhetoric licenses, French classical drama "invents," that is, both creates and discovers, the critical object contemporary theory calls "the text." [1] This thesis pays tribute to the degree to which classical dramatists, and in particular the three greatest of them, Corneille, Molière, and Racine, succeed in forging what remains the basic paradigm of French literary grandeur. It is by now a commonplace that the plays of classical France achieve an unprecedented scenic perfection: whatever else they may be, the comedies, tragi-comedies, pastorals, martyr plays, and lyric tragedies of the Cornelian, Moliéresque, and Racinian stage are *playable* to a degree unknown before. [2] Nevertheless, what distinguishes classical drama is in the first instance its unique awareness of its *literary* properties: the canny

---

[1] The base sense of the term "invention" in classical rhetoric denotes an inventorial "finding" rather than the imaginative creation or fabrication current today. See, e.g., Cicero, *De partitione oratoria* 31. The dual (what Shakespeare might call "cross-coupled") notion of "invention" exploited here informs the place Joel Fineman assigns "repetition" in conditioning the Shakespearean sense of person and subjectivity. See *Shakespeare's Perjured Eye: The Invention of Poetic Subjectivity in the Sonnets* (Berkeley: University of California Press, 1986) 47.

[2] See Jacques Schérer, *La Dramaturgie classique en France* (1950; rpt. Paris: Nizet, 1986), Hélène Baby & Alain Viala, "Naissance de la modernité théâtrale (1600-1650)," in Alain Viala (ed.), *Le théâtre en France des origines à nos jours* (Paris: Presses Universitaires de France, 1997) 177-93, and Georges Forestier, *Essai de génétique théâtrale: Corneille à l'œuvre* (Paris: Klincksieck, 1996).

excavation of its resources as the site, instrument, and product of a concerted act of *writing*. French classical dramatists are indeed exquisitely sensitive to drama's nature and powers not merely as a script or blueprint for theatrical performance, but above all as a special kind of poem. The drama's ultimate meanings and effects occur less in the playhouse than in an acute (if belated) experience of the printed page–as correlates of those written words of which, for all their dramatic vividness, the ones declaimed in the theater are the mere afterimage or echo.

But the self-conscious literariness of classical drama also bears witness to the period's corollary awareness of the predicament in which even great art works stand as the occasion and counterpart of an inescapable double: the critical, and as often as not ironic, act of *reading*. In inventing the text as a vehicle of self-determining authorship, the "grands classiques" simultaneously invent the key critical insights shaping the methods we ourselves bring to bear on the poetic monuments they have left us.

Contemporary academic discourse relies heavily on the potent if inconsequent amalgam of social determinism and oppositional politics characterizing the "deconstructive" strain of critical thought. We tend to think it our business, if not our historical privilege, as feminists or new historicists, psychoanalysts or social semiologists, to grasp early modern art works *from behind*, in the perspective of the cultural or ideological coercions that produced them. This is in fact, as laid out in Roland Barthes's famous essays on the subject, what it normally means to see the works as *texts*.[3] Far from dictating the terms of our admiring appreciation, the masterpieces of the literary past are "methodological fields" whose most intimate secrets are revealed solely in the light of interpretive questions, principles, and procedures concealed from the poets who composed them. To read is to travel against the grain of deliberate authorial

---

[3] See Roland Barthes, "La mort de l'auteur" and "De l'œuvre au texte," in *Le bruissement de la langue* (Paris: Seuil, 1984) 71-80 and 81-85. See too *Critique et vérité* (Paris: Seuil, 1966), defending the then startling amalgam of structuralism, Brechtianism, and psychoanalysis in *Sur Racine* (Paris: Seuil, 1963) by decreeing Racine's radical accessibility to whatever critical "languages" each new historical moment brings to bear on his texts (6-8). For an arresting commentary on Barthes, see Joseph Margolis, *Interpretation Radical but Not Unruly: The New Puzzle of the Arts and History* (Berkeley: University of California Press, 1995), chap. 1, "Reinterpreting Interpretation."

intent, pursuing the evidence left by the deeper (and usually disreputable) determining structures of which we take the author's work to constitute the at once alienated and telltale remnant.

Depending on the theoretical framework employed, early modern texts are assigned a variety of sources. Some scholars emphasize the triumph of disembodied Cartesian intellect and the related mechanistic view of human identities and relations, a perspective linked to the Foucaldian nightmare of social power crystallized in the emergent modern State. Others stress the growing reach of the capitalist market whose invisible hand harnesses the blind gropings of material desire to the occult logic of money and the spreading reach of contract and property law. Still others expose the construction of the feminine, the non-European, and the laboring poor as a Lacanian Other simultaneously posited by and excluded from the dominant symbolic order high classical culture promulgates. [4] But whichever narrative we endorse, the net effect is the same. Seen as

---

[4] On the hegemonic modern State, see Michel Foucault, *Surveiller et punir: naissance de la prison* (Paris: Gallimard, 1975); Jean-Marie Apostolidès, *Le roi-machine: spectacle et politique au temps de Louis XIV* (Paris: Minuit, 1981) and *Le prince sacrifié: théâtre et politique au temps de Louis XIV* (Paris: Minuit, 1985); Michel Prigent, *Le Héros et l'Etat dans la tragédie de Pierre Corneille* (Paris: Presses Universitaires de France, 1986); Peter Burke, *The Fabrication of Louis XIV* (New Haven: Yale University Press, 1992); Mitchell Greenberg, *Corneille, Classicism, and the Ruses of Symmetry* (Cambridge: Cambridge University Press, 1986), *Subjectivity and Subjugation in Seventeenth-Century French Drama and Prose: The Family Romance of French Classicism* (Cambridge: Cambridge University Press, 1992), and *Canonical States, Canonical Stages: Oedipus, Othering, and Seventeenth-Century Drama* (Minneapolis: University of Minnesota Press, 1994); and, most recently, with Cartesian dualism as the central instrument, Dalia Judovitz, *The Culture of the Body: Genealogies of Modernity* (Ann Arbor: University of Michigan Press, 2001). On money, see Apostolidès's chapter on "l'univers quotidien" in *Le prince sacrifié* and Helen Harrison, *Pistoles/Paroles: Money and Language in Seventeenth-Century French Comedy* (Charlottesville, VA: Rookwood Press, 1996). On how changing economic relations modify social identities, see Domna C. Stanton, *The Aristocrat as Art: A Study of the* Honnête Homme *and the Dandy in Seventeenth- and Nineteenth-Century France* (New York: Columbia University Press, 1980), Erica Harth, *Ideology and Culture in Seventeenth-Century France* (Ithaca, NY: Cornell University Press, 1982), and Michael Moriarty, *Taste and Ideology in Seventeenth-Century France* (Cambridge: Cambridge University Press, 1988). On problems of "othering," in addition to Greenberg, where Freudian, Lacanian, and Irigarian notions of the Other play a central role, see Foucault's classic *Histoire de la folie à l'âge classique* (1961; rpt. Paris: Gallimard, 1972), Shoshana Felman, *Le scandale du corps parlant: Don Juan avec Austin, ou la séduction en deux langues* (Paris: Seuil, 1980), and Harriet Amy Stone, *Royal DisClosure: Problematics of Representation in French Classical Tragedy* (Birmingham, AL: Summa Publications, 1987).

symptoms of a main event that unfolds as by definition elsewhere, beyond the scope of aesthetic agency,[5] the plays lose the authority once enjoyed as canonical monuments to become mere documents of the larger cultural movements that condition them.

By contrast, I hope to show that what fundamentally makes classical drama, engendering just those monuments it is our habit to deface and dismantle, is an unexpected autonomy and clairvoyance that allow period dramatists to explore the constructions and elisions the culture imposes. The text of classical drama answers to a conscious authorial intent one of whose horizons is the ironic echo later readers pick up: the intentional object, the finished artifact, looks to and knowingly registers what, in theory, ought to escape it, the accusing "other" only another contrives to see. Far from being mere mystified vestiges of deeper cultural forces, the masterpieces of the classical repertoire deliberately *engage* them as themes for critical enactment. Who reads the plays with care and respect as well as adversarial zeal witnesses a remarkable rehearsal of the theses that shape current critical practice.

To be sure, classical dramatists lack the formal concepts we now use to explain and interpret the cultural past. Explicit notions of history or the unconscious ("political" or otherwise) occur only with their coinage in Hegel, Marx, and Freud. Similarly, methodical accounts of how cultures construct the categories they live by and the natural order these categories define descend from doctrines forged by our own century–structural anthropology, grammatology, gender studies, or theories of social reproduction and postmodern "play." But while early moderns lack the relevant idiom, they display the corresponding intuitions.

In chapter 1, Corneille's *Le Cid* will be found to encode a "new historicist" analysis of its relation to royal power in its own self-conscious (and tellingly ambivalent) practice of drama. In chapter 2, on Corneille's *Rodogune*, the disruption of the machinery of royal suc-

---

[5] A prime case in point is Terry Eagleton's *The Ideology of the Aesthetic* (Oxford: Blackwell, 1990), defining the aesthetic as an ideological fiction incapable of fathoming its own political unconscious. See too Pierre Bourdieu, *La distinction: critique sociale du jugement* (Paris: Minuit, 1979) and *Les règles de l'art: genèse et structure du champ littéraire* (Paris: Seuil, 1992). For an unusually subtle version, see John Guillory, *Cultural Capital: The Problem of Literary Canon Formation* (Chicago: University of Chicago Press, 1993).

cession provoked by the fact that the sons of the play's dead king are identical twins not only challenges the imbricated myths of paternity and psychic integrity subtending absolutist politics, but engenders a poetics of equivocation that exploits the condition of Derridean *différance*. Chapter 3 shows how the tension between the poetics of "imitation" inherited from the Renaissance and the neoclassical demand for poetic originality leads Rotrou's *Les Sosies* and Molière's *Amphitryon* to question the grounds of their own literary identity, rehearsing thereby the two-headed Althusserian phenomenon of "interpellation" and *méconnaissance*. Chapter 4 explores how, in deconstructing the name "Molière" it aims to bequeath to posterity, Molière's *L'Ecole des femmes* stages a proto-Lacanian critique of the modern Cartesian subject. Chapter 5 examines how, in the continuation of the violent literary quarrel *L'Ecole des femmes* provoked, Molière's *Tartuffe* and *Dom Juan* extend the problem of authorial identity to the multifarious hypocrisies concealing the scandalous performativeness of the moral, doctrinal, and social order they indict. Finally, in chapter 6, the peculiar difficulties surrounding recent interpretations of Racine's *Phèdre* are shown to originate in duplicities inherent to Racine's stature as the monumentally fixed yet perpetually reinvented polestar of French literary history. What resolves the apparent paradox of Racine's dual status is the fact that, by turning tragic irony into *mise en abyme*, the Racinian text inscribes its own unstable historicalness in a way that maps its ambiguous critical reception. The outline the plays yield of the period's historically determined truth thus maps our assumptions about where they come from. It would be wrong to suggest that the texts magically *escape* their historical moment, achieving a transcendence our theories allege to be impossible. [6] Nevertheless, in the growing if fumbling *acknowledgement* of that historicalness, they share our critical insights, expounding them with a toughness and lucidity due just to the want of the terms we use to articulate and tame them.

That this should be so reflects three things, all of which are recurrent themes presented under varying lights in each of this book's

---

[6] See Louis Montrose, "'Eliza, Queene of Shepheardes' and the Pastoral of Power," *English Literary Renaissance* 10 (1980) 153-82, for an early statement of the New Historicist thesis of non-transcendence.

six chapters. The first is the historical juncture at which French classical drama arises. To borrow a prescient metaphor from Montaigne's "Des cannibales," [7] the seventeenth century is when French writers fully digest the far-reaching consequences of the social, cosmological, and doctrinal upheavals that mark the preceding age. Descartes draws the lesson of intellectual autonomy from the skeptical challenge to traditional authority precipitated by the Reformation and ensuing wars of religion, the discovery of the "new world," and the Lucretian materialism underlying the triumph of naturalist science. [8] Moreover, while disposed in more whiggish

---

[7] Michel de Montaigne, "Des cannibales," *Essais* 1.31 (Paris: Garnier-Flammarion, 1969) 251: "J'ay peur que nous avons les yeux plus grands que le ventre, et plus de curiosité que nous n'avons de capacité." Subsequent references are by volume, essay, and page number in the text.

[8] For a classic analysis of Cartesian skepticism, see Richard H. Popkin, *The History of Scepticism from Erasmus to Spinoza*, rev. ed. (Berkeley: University of California Press, 1979). On the New World, see, beyond his essay on cannibals, Montaigne's "Des coches" (*Essais* 3.6) and "De l'expérience" (3.13). The discovery of America also generates one of the many arguments for doubt in the "Apologie de Raimond Sebond": "c'eust esté Pyrrhoniser, il y a mille ans, que de mettre en doute la science de la Cosmographie, et les opinions qui en estoient receuës d'un chacun; c'estoit heresie d'avouer des Antipodes; voilà de nostre siecle une grandeur infinie de terre ferme, non pas une isle ou une contrée particuliere, mais une partie esgale à peu près en grandeur à celle que nous cognoissons, qui vient d'estre decouverte." (2.12, 237) For recent commentaries, see Anthony Grafton (with April Shelford & Nancy Siraisi), *New Worlds, Ancient Texts: The Power of Tradition and the Shock of Discovery* (Cambridge, MA: Harvard University Press, 1992), Roland Greene, *Unrequited Conquests: Love and Empire in the Colonial Americas* (Chicago: University of Chicago Press, 1999), and Mary Baine Campbell, *Wonder & Science: Imagining Worlds in Early Modern Europe* (Ithaca, NY: Cornell University Press, 1999). On the impact of Lucretius' version of Epicurean materialism, see Ernst Cassirer's *The Individual and the Cosmos in Renaissance Philosophy*, trans. Mario Domandi (New York: Barnes & Noble, 1963), emphasizing *De rerum natura*'s contribution to the Renaissance assertion of freedom of thought, and Michel Serres, *La Naissance de la physique dans le texte de Lucrèce: Fleuves et turbulences* (Paris: Minuit, 1977), stressing how Epicurean chance (Latin *declinatio*, Greek *clinamen*) prepares the way for the anti-metaphysical picture of physical nature required for genuine physical science. However, in *The Legitimacy of the Modern Age*, trans. Robert M. Wallace (Cambridge, MA: MIT Press, 1983), Hans Blumenberg stresses the *anti*-scientific potential of Lucretian Epicureanism. The Epicurean "exhibition of the world's form as contingent" promotes humanity's power over physical nature and the self-assertive "curiosity" underlying European modernity (156). But Blumenberg also reminds us that the revelation of the world's contingency is linked to the mystic moment in Ockhamite nominalism (152-53), supplying a proof of God on the grounds of his remoteness from an utterly fallen, chance-driven world; and that the Epicurean myth of distant, uncaring gods serves a *therapeutic* function, schooling us in healing *ataraxia* by demonstrating physical nature's inanity and the corresponding

moods to grant human intellect a quasi-demiurgic potency, Descartes is also the first to apply the principles of mechanics to psychic life, producing the nightmare vision of godlike Man as soulless machine, the sleepwalking automaton that stalks the pages of the Second Meditation. [9] In destroying the closed anthropocentric cosmos of Aristotle and Ptolemy, unveiling the infinite intersideral spaces whose "eternal silence" so frightens Pascal, Copernicus's "solar hypothesis" licenses thought experiments like Cyrano's alarmingly libertine *Etats et empires de la Lune et du Soleil* or Fontenelle's more amiable *Entretiens sur la pluralité des mondes*, spelling out the anthropological implications of Copernican astronomy. [10] No French biblical commentary develops the disquieting theological impact of humanist textual scholarship as outspokenly as Spinoza's *Politico-Theological Treatise* or the revolutionary tracts of Stuart England. Still, the philological exposure of the linguistic and cultural specificity of the word of God as set forth in holy writ echoes in Simon's *Histoire critique du Vieux Testament* and Bayle's *Dictionnaire historique et critique*. [11] And with Riche-

---

emptiness of human desire (264-67). The Cassirer/Serres interpretation is taken up (if also problematized) by Jacques Lezra, *Unspeakable Subjects: The Genealogy of the Event in Early Modern Europe* (Stanford: Stanford University Press, 1997), who argues that the very forces of chance that legitimize the intellectual autonomy on which the modern subject depends also call the subject in question.

[9] René Descartes, *Œuvres philosophiques*, 3 vols., ed. Ferdinand Alquié (Paris: Garnier, 1988-92) 2.426-27. See too Pascal's remarkable development of the passage on automata in "Qu'est-ce que le moi?," *Pensées*, ed. Louis Lafuma (Paris: Seuil, 1962) fragment 688; ed. Philippe Sellier (Paris: Classiques Garnier, 1991) 567. Subsequent references to Pascal will appear in the text by fragment number in both editions.

[10] The best general account of this question is still Thomas S. Kuhn, *The Copernican Revolution: Planetary Astronomy in the Development of Western Thought* (Cambridge, MA: Harvard University Press, 1957). For the fragment in Pascal, see *Pensées,* Lafuma 201; Sellier 233.

[11] On humanist philology generally, see Anthony Grafton, *Joseph Scaliger: A Study in the History of Classical Scholarship* [Oxford: Clarendon Press, 1983-93] and *Commerce with the Classics: Ancient Books and Renaissance Readers* (Ann Arbor: University of Michigan Press, 1997). On Biblical textual criticism, see Robert Coogan, *Erasmus, Lee and the Correction of the Vulgate: The Shaking of the Foundations* (Geneva: Droz, 1992) and David Daniell, *William Tyndale: A Biography* (New Haven: Yale University Press, 1994). On Spinoza, see Leo Strauss, *Spinoza's Critique of Religion*, trans. E.M. Sinclair (New York: Schocken, 1965) and "How to Study Spinoza's *Theologico-Political Treatise*," in *Persecution and the Art of Writing* (Glencoe: The Free Press, 1952) 142-201. On Simon, see Henri Margival, *Essai sur Richard Simon et la critique biblique au 17ᵉ siècle* (1900; rpt. Geneva: Slatkine,

lieu's *Testament politique*, seconded by Naudé's *Considérations politiques sur les coups d'Etat*, the "new historicism" inspired by Machiavelli, Gucciardini, and the recovered writings of Tacitus engenders a theory of political conduct grounded in the black arts of dissimulation, prudential calculation, and the cynical pursuit of *raison d'Etat*.[12]

It is true that the seventeenth century largely inherits the transformations its leading writers expound. The trenchant political realism crystallized in the concerted manufacture of the solar person of Louis XIV consummates developments whose roots lie in modernizing energies at work in Valois France. The triumphant absolutist state that figures so prominently in scholarly assessments of the period's novelty was not merely a reaction to, but a precipitant of the civil wars the Bourbon dynasty made a merit of ending. Indeed, much of the ostensibly religious fury animating the Catholic

---

1970). On Bayle, see Ruth Whelan, *The Anatomy of Superstition: A Study of the Historical Theory and Practice of Pierre Bayle* (Oxford: Voltaire Foundation, 1989) and Thomas M. Lennon, *Reading Bayle* (Toronto: University of Toronto Press, 1999).

[12] Though attributed to the cardinal, the *Testament politique* is a pseudonymous work composed by Richelieu's secretariat. For a vivid picture of the operation of Richelieu's secretariat, see Christian Jouhaud, *La Main de Richelieu, ou le pouvoir cardinal* (Paris: Gallimard, 1990) 85-122. For Naudé, see "Pour une théorie baroque de l'action politique," Louis Marin's intro. to *Considérations politiques sur les coups d'Etat* (1639), ed. Frédérique Marin & Marie-Odile Perulli (Paris: Editions de Paris, 1988). On the Renaissance reception of Tacitus, see Grafton, *Commerce with the Classics* 204-208. As Grafton in particular would appreciate, I use the term "new historicism" ironically. The recovered Tacitus and Suetonius, together with the "modern" Machiavelli and Guicciardini, do for early moderns what new historicist Renaissance studies do for us today. Nor is it surprising to meet renewed interest in these writers in Victoria Kahn, *Rhetoric, Prudence, and Skepticism in the Renaissance* (Ithaca, NY: Cornell University Press, 1985), Albert Russell Ascoli & Victoria Kahn (eds.), *Machiavelli and the Discourse of Literature* (Ithaca, NY: Cornell University Press, 1993), John D. Lyons, *Exemplum: The Rhetoric of Example in Early Modern France and Italy* (Princeton: Princeton University Press, 1989), and Timothy Hampton, *Writing from History: The Rhetoric of Exemplarity in Renaissance Literature* (Ithaca, NY: Cornell University Press, 1990). See too Perez Zagorin, *Ways of Lying: Dissimulation, Persecution, and Conformity in Early Modern Europe* (Cambridge, MA: Harvard University Press, 1990), valuable both for its analysis of dissimulation and Machiavellian prudence and for exploring the intersections of political with religious thought, Jonathan Dollimore, *Radical Tragedy: Religion, Ideology and Power in the Drama of Shakespeare and his Contemporaries* (Chicago: University of Chicago Press, 1984), which makes a case for England like the one I make for France, and John D. Lyons, *The Tragedy of Origins: Pierre Corneille and Historical Perspective* (Stanford: Stanford University Press, 1996).

League was provoked by the crown's intermittent endorsement of religious toleration as a means of enlisting the support of Protestant merchants, jurists, and administrators in the royal effort to eradicate the entrenched political base of the traditional nobility represented by the Guise faction. What is new in the *grand siècle* is thus less amoral royal policy than the ironic *profession* of political amorality authorized by that policy's success. [13]

Nevertheless, it is only in the seventeenth century that French writers truly take in the lessons the Renaissance teaches. The demolition of Western self-conceit attending the discovery in America of whole civilizations unassimilated by the natural order as seen from Europe was a full century old even by the time Montaigne wrote about it. But the full force of the challenge registers only after Montaigne, in the *systematic* moral relativisms of seventeenth-century thought. The skeptical Montaigne confesses his inability to tell the difference between the self-reproducing truth of Nature and the

---

[13] The idea that, reinforced by the cultural conformism dictated by Richelieu's Académie, subjection to an absolutist State is a 17th-century novelty inspired by the 16th-century wars of religion is a recurrent premise of French classical studies. See, e.g., Paul Bénichou, *Morales du grand siècle* (Paris: Gallimard, 1948). For more recent versions, see Greenberg's *Corneille*, where the thesis provides an historical basis for his psychoanalytic interpretation of French classicism, and Hélène Merlin's otherwise unimpeachable appraisal of the transformation of notions of "public" and "private" in *Littérature et public en France au XVIIᵉ siècle* (Paris: Les Belles lettres, 1994), chaps. 3, "La ligne de faille du *public*," and 4, "La position critique des lettres." However, the more nuanced view endorsed here relies on Lucien Goldmann, *Le Dieu caché: Etude sur la vision tragique dans les Pensées de Pascal et dans le théâtre de Racine* (Paris: Gallimard, 1959), chap. 5, "Visions du monde et classes sociales," setting up his interpretation of the social and intellectual "foundation" of Jansenism. An important corollary of Goldmann's analysis is that, as a cultural phenomenon characteristic of 17th-century France, Jansenism expresses the social defeat sealed with the instauration of the Bourbon dynasty following the conversion of Henri IV in 1589. The Edict of Nantes of 1598, contributing one of the motives for Henri's assassination in 1610, thus has an ironic consequence. At the same time as it checks the Catholic nobility by defusing the religious tensions on which its ambitions fed, it confirms bourgeois dependence on the crown. This in turn paves the way not only for the system of *commis* by which the monarchy eventually reduces the traditional seats of bourgeois authority in the *parlements* and *cours souveraines*, but also for Louis XIV's revocation of the Edict of Nantes in 1685. The reward Protestant loyalists received for their support to the crown in its conflict with the *noblesse d'épée* sets the stage for their eventual expulsion from the *corps politique* they helped create. This points to the true source of 17th-century novelty, forming the very basis for the Huguenot émigré Bayle's *Dictionnaire historique et critique*, i.e., the pervasive sense of historical irony itself, indispensable to the full-fledged sense of history as such.

self-displacing revolutions of fallen human Custom. Yet Nature remains an essential postulate, a cosmological constant enabling him to gauge the otherwise unimaginable dislocations, the irresistible *bransle* to which he counterposes her. So it is up to Pascal, in the sardonic fragment on the presumed "unnaturalness" of youths eager to dispose of inconvenient fathers, to give doubt its characteristically modern form by administering the chiastic twist that turns Custom as "second nature" into Nature as mere "second custom." [14] And it is just here, in revealing how the values of nature, clarity, unity, and decorum classical cultural officially sets against the brute contingencies of historical life are mere transient fictions, that seventeenth-century drama comes into its own. A fitting emblem for the period is the chiasmus, the figure of transposition and inversion that Pascal deploys to radicalize Montaigne's skeptical thought. But this same figure is the master trope of contemporary drama, one by which, in the forms of baroque paradox and antithesis, dramatic irony, tragic reversals, and parallelisms of every sort, drama enacts its own critical situation.

This brings us to the second determinant of the drama's historical prescience. The critical self-consciousness of the plays of classical France arises not just from the ambient culture, but from sources intrinsic to drama itself, and for a start its status as *theater*. One way in which theater mirrors what the era sought to understand about itself lies in the pervasive fascination with the figure of the hypocrite. The hypocrite is of course a type for the dramatic actor, the Greek *hypocrites*. In Molière's villainous Tartuffe and Dom Juan, but also the heroic emperor of Corneille's *Cinna*, the terrifying Cléopâtre of his later *Rodogune*, or the tragic queen of Racine's *Phèdre*, it portrays not merely an evil proper to an age obsessed by the critical divorce of appearance and reality, but the image of the art that purports to expose that evil. Yet, as we shall see in chapter 5, in addition to stigmatizing an evil in which theater itself participates, the hypocrite also offers a model of the inner discipline on which all human agency depends.

If, in Molière, it takes nothing less than a secular miracle to foil the diabolical Tartuffe, it is because the wider phenomenon of dissimulation of which both hypocrisy and the art of acting are ver-

---

[14] Pascal, *Pensées*, Lafuma 126; Sellier 159.

sions so signally succeeds. The machinations that demand a *deus ex machina* in the person of the nameless officer representing the King in *Tartuffe*'s dénouement are the same as those that assure the triumph of *Cinna*'s emperor Auguste. The first lesson in the art of politics is enshrined in a Latin maxim cited throughout the century, in England, Italy, or Spain as frequently as France: *Qui nescit dissimulare nescit regnare*–who knows not how to dissimulate knows not how to rule. [15] In accordance with this principle, Auguste's triumph depends on mastering his face, concealing knowledge of the plot to murder him until the trap he lays for his enemies is finally sprung. But to master his face, he must master his desire for revenge: the self-control needed to direct the counterplot conditions the act of clemency by which he spares the conspirators' lives, earning the healing love that brings civil conflict to an end. Nor is the problem of the mastering of one's face the exclusive province of the stage, whether in the form of satiric comedy or the high politics of Cornelian heroism. The conduct literature devoted to *honnêteté* shows it to have been the central preoccupation of the accomplished courtier, what essentially distinguishes him from both his maladroit brothers and the tiresome bourgeois. [16] The interrelated problems of hypocrisy and dissimulation are then coterminous with those bearing on the nature of conscious action in general, in life as in its image on the stage.

But the pertinence of the question of hypocrisy points in turn to problems of deeper social and philosophic import linked to the peculiar *ontology* of the stage. As Pascal's exacerbation of Montaigne's skeptical views reminds us, doubling and disrupting the Cartesian epistemology of "clear and distinct ideas," classical no-

---

[15] Zagorin (174) traces the maxim back to the French king Louis XI as cited by his minister and historian Philippe de Comines. Zagorin discusses it in the context of the defence of mental reservation in the Spanish casuist Navarrus's commentary on "Humanae Aures," a passage from Gregory the Great's *Moralia* incorporated in Gratian's *Decretum*. For a contemporary French source for *Qui nescit*, see Naudé, *Considérations politiques sur les coups d'Etat*.

[16] Dissimulation is an essential element of *l'art de plaire* taught by the chevalier de Méré, Damien Mitton, and La Rochefoucauld. See, in addition to Harth, Moriarty, and Stanton, Norbert Elias's classic *The Civilizing Process*, trans. Edmund Jephcott (New York: Pantheon, 1982) and Marc Fumaroli's intro. to *L'Art de la conversation* (Paris: Classiques Garnier, 1997).

tions of scientific and moral knowledge rely on drawing *distinctions*. [17] The business of knowledge is learning to discriminate between true and false, right and wrong, illusion and reality; but also between thoughts and facts, words and things, images and the world images represent. Nor are these purely intellectual concerns; they govern the closely interconnected realms of aesthetics and social identities, policing the frontiers dividing tragic from comic, high from low, the nobly born "man of taste" from his ersatz bourgeois lookalike. By contrast, period drama *blurs* all such distinctions. Conceived as the ultimate "mirror of nature," a replica so perfect as to pass for nature itself, it erases the boundaries between "portraits" and "originals," supplanting the realities it purports to mime.

Whence, notably, the brilliant invention at the core of Molière's *Sganarelle, ou le cocu imaginaire*. To cite a commonplace of Molière criticism, one of the chief mechanisms of Moliéresque comedy is the *quiproquo*, the propensity to take one thing for another–"this for that." It is to the *quiproquo* that we owe the unconscious one-way dialogue in *L'Ecole des femmes* 4.2: an elaborate gag on the conventions of dramatic soliloquy in which, entering the stage while an absorbed Arnolphe utters his thoughts out loud, a notary responds as though Arnolphe's words were addressed to him. Just so, in *Sganarelle*, the protagonist is cuckolded not by another man, but by the *image* of another man: discovering his wife's infatuation with a beautifully crafted miniature portrait, the title character mistakenly infers her passion for the original. But as Molière's "imaginary cuckold" ingeniously hints, the comic device reproduces the sustaining structure of both dramatic spectacle and the classical theory of signs on which it rests. The spectator's passionate engagement with theater, the readiness to commit oneself, body and soul, to an illusion whose motives are as often as not quite other than those actuating the characters with whom we identify, is itself a *quiproquo*. And so too is representation in general, whether in the form of the words we take for ideas, the ideas we take for things, or the things

---

[17] See Bourdieu, Harth, Greenberg (*Corneille* and *Subjectivity and Subjugation*), Moriarty, and most recently Harriet Amy Stone, *The Classical Model: Literature and Knowledge in Seventeenth-Century France* (Ithaca, NY: Cornell University Press, 1996).

we take for the content of images themselves circularly taken for the words they express and the things the words portray. [18]

Theater turns out to be an inexhaustible fount of confusion and error. This produces both the comic machinery of Sganarelle's farcical misfortunes and the more heroic ironies of Racinian fate. But it also accounts for the era's profound *ambivalence* toward dramatic art. Though a golden age of drama whose major authors establish the very type of French literary greatness, the century also witnesses the *querelle du théâtre*: a controversy in which religious radicals like the Jansenist Pierre Nicole and (despite their order's massive contribution to classical stagecraft) Jesuits like Louis Cellot unite with the Gallican reactionaries of the Compagnie du Saint-Sacrement to denounce theater's infernal powers of distortion and deceit. [19] Nor are the attacks inspired solely, as Marc Fumaroli documents, by the pernicious ease with which the theatrical *faire-croire* of dramatic make-believe substitutes for *la foi*, Belief itself. [20] Implicit in the fidelity with which the deluding glass of theater registers the world's likeness is the still deeper scandal of revealing how far the social and credal order it mimics is itself mere show: a theatrical illusion as convincing if false, and yet as true *because* so falsely convincing, as the imaginary cuckoldry Molière's Sganarelle endures.

But still more decisive is an element of seventeenth-century dramaturgy that espouses the very shape of historical experience as such: the development of the classical soliloquy.

A major technical innovation, setting classical drama apart from the clumsier products of Renaissance writers like Jodelle and Garnier or indeed early seventeenth-century poets like Montchrestien, is mastery of what I have elsewhere called the "principle of immanence" informing the abbé d'Aubignac's authoritative *Pratique du*

---

[18] See Louis Marin, *La Critique du discours: sur la "Logique de Port-Royal" et les "Pensées" de Pascal* (Paris: Minuit, 1975) and "La parole mangée ou le corps divin saisi par les signes," in *La parole mangée et autres essais théologico-politiques* (Paris: Meridiens Klincksieck, 1986) 11-35.

[19] See Marc Fumaroli, "*Sacerdos sive rhetor, orator sive histrio*: rhétorique, théologie, et 'moralité du théâtre' de Corneille à Molière," in *Héros et orateurs: rhétorique et dramaturgie cornéliennes* (Geneva: Droz, 1990) 449-91.

[20] Fumaroli, "*Sacerdos sive rhetor, orator sive histrio*," 451; but also Felman, "La perversion de la promesse: Don Juan et la performance littéraire," 31-82.

théâtre. [21] Commissioned by no less a personage than cardinal Richelieu, d'Aubignac's treatise aims to bring drama into closer rational accord with its formal means as an at once verbal and spectacular work of art. And at the heart of the reform is the theory of *vraisemblance,* a protean doctrine whose chief point of application to drama lies in the poet's management of the dramatic action as it unfolds within the circumscribed space of the stage in the equally circumscribed time of the spectator's physical attendance at the playhouse.

As Aristotle teaches in the *Poetics,* drama is a form of *mimesis,* a mirror of human action distinguished by the absence of the mediating authorial voice and attendant moral commentary characteristic of epic or historical narration. [22] Where Homer and Virgil, Plutarch and Tacitus recount and interpret events expressly in their own vocal or rhetorical person, drama presents the events themselves as these occur in the space-time of direct human experience reproduced by the live occasion of scenic performance. To remain true to its formal nature and vocation, drama must so arrange the scenic spectacle as to efface all visible traces of the playwright's hand, creating the illusion of an action evolving in accordance with at once logical and existential laws internal to the action as such. [23]

True, what passes for *vraisemblable* in classical France proves exceptionally flexible and multiform. The laws in operation on the classical stage reflect parochial understandings about what constitutes psychological verisimilitude and practical plausibility, understandings thereby subject to uncontrolled historical change. But they also reflect notions of decorum, the notorious *bienséances,* indigenous to the system of dramatic genres then in force. What contemporary audiences took to be probable responded both to current assumptions about the nature of the real world theater imitates and

---

[21] François Hédelin, abbé d'Aubignac, *La Pratique du théâtre* (1657); facsimile of the Amsterdam edition of 1715 (Munich: Wilhelm Fink Verlag, 1971). Subsequent references appear by page number in the text.

[22] Aristotle, *Poetics* 1447a-1448a and, for the famous contrast between poetry and history, 1451a-1452a.

[23] As we shall see in chap. 1, the playwright's hidden hand is a figure of political as well as poetic authority. Jouhaud's analysis in *La Main de Richelieu* of how the most characteristic public sign of the great minister's power lies precisely in the *absence* of overt public demonstration directly bears on the comparably self-designating and self-concealing character of dramatic poetry.

to the peculiar proprieties prescribed for each kind of dramatic poem. Aristotle's *ethos*, a theory of character based on the repertoire of social and psychological types prevailing in classical Athens, [24] had to adapt to expectations specific to early modern France. Yet in doing so, it not only conformed to French notions of how different people act, the behavior of kings differing from that of servants or the conduct of women from that of men; it obeyed generic norms far richer and more complex than Aristotle's bipartite distinction of tragic and comic could cope with. To Aristotle's two-term division, French classicism adds the mixed form of tragi-comedy, the Italian pastoral, "heroic" comedy, the *ballet de cour* or masque, and the "low" native form of farce, each engendering a calculus of psychic probabilities expressed by a specific set of stock characters. [25]

The result is a system of distinctions of bewildering refinement. In an historic episode to which we shall return shortly, the infamous "querelle du *Cid*" pitting Corneille against the massed ranks of rival poets aligned with Richelieu's newly founded Académie Française, a major target was the heroine's projected marriage to her father's killer. What offended the playwright's critics was not however its social, psychological, or moral implausibility from the standpoint of real life; the marriage was a matter of public record, inscribed in the history that supplies Corneille's plot. The offense lay rather in the breach of decorum entailed by presenting such a thing in a *tragicomedy*, a noble action whose leading players are required to behave in appropriately heroic ways. A similar problem surrounds Racine's *Phèdre*, a tragedy, and therefore a play more noble even than Corneille's tragi-comic *Le Cid*, in which a queen destroys her royal stepson by the ignominious expedient of a calumnious lie. This act too is justified by precedent, finding a license in Euripides' *Hippolytus*. Racine feels nonetheless obliged, in the defensive preface to the published text, to explain both his classical warrant and his efforts to soften the blow by fobbing off the actual telling of the lie on the ignoble confidante Œnone in her character as Phèdre's slave. [26] Still, densely coded (and culturally relative) as the doctrine of *vraisem-*

---

[24] *Poetics* 1454a-b.

[25] See Gérard Genette, "Vraisemblance et motivation," in *Figures II* (Paris: Seuil, 1969) 71-99.

[26] Jean Racine, preface to *Phèdre*. I cite the "Intégrale" edition of the *Œuvres complètes* (Paris: Seuil, 1962) 246-47.

blance may be, its coherence *as* a doctrine ultimately derives from the formal constraint all modes of drama obey: the demand that the play unfold within the limits of its action, expressed solely and entirely through the unmediated words and deeds of its actors.

It is above all to this formal constraint that we owe the authority of the Unities, the singular French insistence not only on maintaining the tightly focused dramatic necessity of the plot, but on observing a rigid singleness of place and a narrow span of time commensurate with those in which the play is heard and seen. The unities essentially aim at securing the self-performing autonomy and integrity expected of dramatic mimesis. They are an extension of the scrupulous economy of means d'Aubignac calls for in proclaiming that the poet's "principale intention" must be to "travailler sur l'Action en tant que représentée" (33), confining what the audience learns to what is heard and seen on the stage. At *Pratique* 1.8, explaining "de quelle maniere le Poëte doit faire connoître la décoration & les Actions necessaires dans une piece de Theatre," he insists that the information required to grasp who the characters are, where the action takes place, its antecedent background, and in fact every detail of costume, mood, ethos, and décor must come from the characters alone, emerging "naturally" as a spontaneous expression of the plot. D'Aubignac is so uncompromising that he even proscribes all stage directions as the superfluous crutch of a cloddish want of art. In addition to eliminating didascalic scene descriptions ("Par exemple: Ici paroît un Temple ouvert; ici se découvre un Palais orné de diverses colonnes & superbement bâti. Ici les Acteurs se doivent asseoir en tel ordre"), the poet "doit faire parler ses Acteurs avec tant d'art, qu'il ne soit pas même necessaire de marquer la distinction des Actes & des Scenes, ni même de mettre les noms des Entreparleurs." (47-48)

The unities thus reflect and reinforce the demand for a form of dramatic representation as seamlessly self-announcing, self-explicating, and self-contained as the extra-theatrical life it imitates. But what defines that life, and therefore the live theatrical experience that assumes its shape before the assembled public in the playhouse, is its *historicalness*. The point strikes home when we pass from the conduct of the action as a whole to the soliloquy, a feature of the new drama more than any responsible for achieving the economy d'Aubignac prescribes.

Soliloquy is the product of a broader effort to naturalize the rhetorical patterns of speech characteristic of the humanist dramatic tradition that classical practice reforms. Particularly in its nobler genres, as tragedy or religious spectacle, the humanist drama of Jodelle, Garnier, and Montchrestien retains the tang of the lawyerly cask from which it is sociologically drawn–and we must indeed remember that, as a class, early modern dramatists come from (and, as in the relatively late cases of Rotrou and Corneille, often continue to inhabit) the legal and administrative circles from which the majority of non-clerical intellectuals were recruited in the early modern period. [27] Even in passages of dramatic exchange, where one might expect a more fast-paced mode of diction, we are treated to contrapuntal orations instead of seamlessly interlocking dialogue. In place of spontaneous acts of dramatic self-expression, we get set-piece displays of rhetorical virtuosity: a formal and tonal character emphasized in the French context by the typographical convention of putting the especially memorable bits (sentences, *pointes*, apologues, epigrammes) in quotation marks, prepackaged in readily citable form. [28]

In the crucial one-scene second act of Jodelle's *Didon se sacrifiant* (c. 1560), [29] the Carthaginian queen reacts to Aeneas' announced departure by letting loose a torrent of reproaches thickly ornamented with epic similes, complex mythological parallels, and insistent rhetorical questions. The speech lasts no fewer than 137 nearly uninterrupted lines–from verse 433 to verse 573, of which four (461-64) are interjected by the Chorus of Trojans. Nor does Aeneas reply even yet: Dido's sister Anne (sic) adds five angry lines before yielding to Dido once more, who proceeds to heap an addi-

---

[27] See Alain Viala, *Naissance de l'écrivain: sociologie de la littérature à l'âge classique* (Paris: Minuit, 1985). In a table (247) summarizing data on social provenance derived from contemporary censuses of *gens de lettres*, we find that 189 writers are "advocates." This is the single largest category, followed by "gentlemen" (188), "Jesuits" (163), "priests" (147), and "parliamentarians and members of courts" (103). When one recalls that "parliamentarians" are legislators and administrative officers, and that "members of courts" are legal as well as administrative officers, 292 writers come from legal circles.

[28] See Schérer, *La Dramaturgie classique* 321 and his "notice" to Montchrestien's *Hector* in *Théâtre du XVIIe siècle* 1 (Paris: Gallimard, 1975) 1152.

[29] Etienne Jodelle, *Didon se sacrifiant*, in Donald Stone, Jr. (ed.), *Four Renaissance Tragedies* (Cambridge, MA: Harvard University Press, 1966).

tional 84 on her faithless lover's head. So it is not until verse 663, a
full 230 lines after the scene has started, that Aeneas finally speaks,
whereupon he disburdens himself of 97 lines of plangent excuses
(663-759), followed ten lines later by 82 more (770-851). These in
turn give way to 103 lines (852-954) of still further ingenious invec-
tive on Dido's part, terminated only when a fainting queen withdraws into her palace—no doubt short of breath. When one consid-
ers that, during this one scene alone, Dido speaks 324 verses as
compared with the 461 a generous count allots the eponymous
heroine for the whole of Racine's *Phèdre*, the windy disproportion
is obvious. Soliloquy thus contributes to a broader effort aimed at
reining in the rhetorical set-piece for the sake of crisper dramatic
flow, a goal evinced by its tightly controlled relation to the occasioning action. Where traditional humanists treat their speeches as
an end in themselves for which the action serves largely as a pretext, classical playwrights firmly anchor them in the surrounding
plot even when the immediate function is to meditate on the action's wider mood or meaning. And what carries the change, lending soliloquy its characteristic shape and momentum, is the fact that
the meditation arises as the work of the characters themselves in
their capacity as active participants.

Soliloquy maintains an expository and exegetical function of the
sort traditional rhetoric assigned it, a recursive gesture by which the
evolving dramatic spectacle swallows its own tail in order to help
the spectator conceive the "design" and "invention" of the play as a
whole. It thereby contributes to what we might call the *mnemonic*
office of Aristotelian unity, facilitating the acquisition of a total unitary picture of the action and the dramatic and moral logic that
structures it. Moreover, in fulfilling this role, it freely draws on all of
the resources (figures, *topoi*, deliberative and forensic patterns of argument) rhetorical tradition provides. But it deviates from traditional type by its scrupulous commitment to the new, strictly immanent way of dramatic verisimilitude. Soliloquy attempts in the form
of rhetorical speech, and more especially in the form of rhetorical
hypotyposis or verbal picturing, to arrest the time of events as a reflex of the speaker's engagement in them. Where humanists indulge
in a verbal bagginess that tends to impede a plot whose thread was
in any case never strong to begin with, the new classical art observes
a ruthless discipline, bending all means to a single controlling end.

It is in this spirit that, opening act 4 of Hardy's *Scédase* (composed sometime between 1605 and 1615, but first published in 1624), the unfortunate father's return home is accomplished by a 32-line monologue full of terrible presentiments of the impending discovery of the bodies of his daughters, raped and murdered by aristocratic guests during his absence. [30] Hardy is, to be sure, a dramatist in the baroque mold, prone to tasteless violence and excess: with what his classical successors would have regarded as gross impropriety, the crime Scédase is about to discover (the rape, the murder, the tossing of the bodies down a well) has taken place on stage in the scene immediately preceding its discovery. Still, the basics of Hardy's method are already those of the more refined generation to come. With exemplary economy of means, the speech performs several tasks at once: it creates a pause for the homeward journey on which the discovery's effect depends; it exposes the father's state of mind, preparing the audience for the shock the scene both wheels into place and holds in dramatic suspense; and in exposing Scédase's emotional state, it sets the tone not only for the impending discovery, but for the play's moral and political argument as consummated in the climactic encounter with the king of Sparta, from whom the injured father will vainly plead for justice before the despairing act of suicide with which the tragedy ends.

But this is also the spirit suffusing the exemplary double game staged by the opening scene of Corneille's *Cinna*. [31] By its close, Corneille's play will present an apology for the saving transcendental authority assigned the absolutist monarch. It begins however with a stunning declaration of war against the political order whose mythic instauration in the person of the emperor Auguste it chronicles. Emilie's tortured deliberations on the course she means to pursue in avenging her father's murder during the recent Roman civil war draw on all of the might of rhetorical *enargeia*, the vivid word-

---

[30] Alexandre Hardy, *Scédase, ou l'hospitalité violée*, in *Théâtre du XVIIᵉ siècle* 1, 4.833-864.

[31] Pierre Corneille, *Cinna*, in *Œuvres complètes*, ed. Georges Couton (Paris: Gallimard, 1980-87) 1.1.1-52. For parallel commentaries, see Apostolidès, *Le prince sacrifié* 63-72; Merlin, *Littérature et public* 288-304, "*Cinna, Rodogune, Nicomède*: Le Roi et le moi," *Littératures* 37 (Fall 1997) 67-86, and "Corneille et la politique dans *Cinna, Rodogune* et *Nicomède*," *Littératures classiques* 32 (January, 1998) 41-61; and Lyons, *The Tragedy of Origins*, chap. 2, "*Cinna* and the Historical Logic of Empire."

painting of her motivating cause, not only to steel her in her vengeful resolve, but to suppress compassion for the hapless Cinna, the
lover she has chosen as the sacrificial instrument of her bloody design. Yet it is crucial that Emilie's deliberations unfold in the time
of a total action of which, for all their force, they remain a local
means, transcended by the events they set in motion. In conjuring
up, in the likeness of Seneca's *Medea*, [32] the infernal powers of
vengeful Hate, Emilie unleashes psychic energies that finally undo
her: the plot she weaves occasions the heroic self-overcoming by
which the cynical opportunist Octave is finally justified in the imperial Auguste of the play's finale. Though it takes five acts to show
it, by its scrupulous subordination to the whole, Emilie's soliloquy
brings on the dramatic fate to which her every word turns out to
lend its inexorable weight.

Soliloquy is then a precipitate of the surrounding action, induced by occurrences it advances in the very act of picturing them.
In the process, it institutes (but also registers) an entirely new relation to *time*, expressed as the dynamic tension between a solitary
ego, striving to impose an intelligible pattern on the masterless flux
of events, and the dramatic imitation of unmediated events themselves. In the Hegelian idiom of a later age, we should define this
tension as that opposing the self-defeating subjectivity of the Idea
to the overwhelming objective authority of the World—a world
changed by the partial consciousness we take of it, yet with the ironic consequence of confirming thereby its alien transcendence. If,
alongside the soliloquistic art of the English Shakespeare and the
Spanish Calderón, French classical drama occupies a vital transi-
tional place in Hegel's historical aesthetic programme, it is because
it enacts the condition Hegel theorizes as History itself.

Above all, however, drama's unique responsiveness to its historical situation stems from the third of the three determinants alluded
to earlier: its status as dramatic poetry, as *text*, and the peculiar
double consciousness this at once brings out and brings about.
John Lyons has recently argued that, far from mechanically under-
writing the cultural repression Ludovican absolutism dictates, clas-

---

[32] On Medea's centrality to Corneille's dramatic project, see Fumaroli, *Héros et
orateurs* 40-45, and Greenberg, *Corneille*, chap. 1, "Mythifying matrix: Corneille's
Médée and the birth of tragedy."

sical dramatic theory "inaugurates a certain cultural modernity." It
does so, however, less on the strength of what it says about drama
itself than "by disseminating the concepts of dramatic and literary
criticism and by transferring authority from 'authors' in the medieval sense to readers." [33] It is entirely characteristic in this regard
that the golden age of the great classical authors opens with a controversial *reading*–a reading moreover that highlights the telltale
tension between public spectacle and private intelligence.

In the preamble to his venomous *Observations* on Corneille's *Le
Cid*, touching off the virulent literary quarrel mentioned a moment
ago, Georges de Scudéry casts a valuable if unintended light on the
ambiguous link between live response to theatrical production and
critical response to theatrical texts. Goaded in part by envy at *Le
Cid*'s spectacular popular success, Scudéry launches an avalanche of
furious accusations, alleging everything from incompetent plotting
and flagrant breaches of plausibility and decorum to sexual depravity, hypocrisy, *lèse-majesté*, and plagiarism–this last buttressed by
the claim that such good things as the play contains have been lifted
verbatim from the Spanish original in Castro's *Mocedades del Cid*. [34]
Scudéry nevertheless has a problem: if the play is so self-evidently
bad, how do we explain what makes him so angry, namely, its
unprecedented appeal not only to the general public, but at court?
His solution is to claim that the play's admirers are the victims of an
optical illusion:

> Il est de certaines Pieces, comme de certains animaux qui sont
> en la Nature, qui de loin semblent des Etoiles, et qui de prés ne
> sont que des vermisseaux. Tout ce qui brille n'est pas toujours
> précieux; on voit des beautez d'illusion, comme des beautez ef-
> fectives, et souvent l'aparence du bien se fait prendre pour le
> bien mesme. Aussi ne m'estonnay-je pas beaucoup que le Peuple
> qui porte le jugement dans les yeux, se laisse tromper par celuy
> de tous les sens, le plus facile à decevoir. [35]

---

[33] John D. Lyons, *Kingdom of Disorder: The Theory of Tragedy in Classical
France* (West Lafayette: Purdue University Press, 1999) 203.

[34] Georges de Scudéry, *Observations sur Le Cid*, in Armand Gasté (ed.), *La
Querelle du Cid: Pièces et pamphlets* (Paris: H. Welter, 1899) 103-110. Jean Mairet
leveled the same accusation in "L'Autheur du vray Cid Espagnol à son Traducteur
François." See Gasté 67-68.

[35] Gasté 71.

While his motives are hardly of the purest, Scudéry works an
important distinction–that between what a play appears to be when
encountered in the unreflecting immediacy of scenic performance
and what it is subsequently revealed to be when seen "close to" [*de
prés*], in a careful reading of the actual text. The distinction over-
laps the one Stanley Fish detects at the basis of what he calls the
"aesthetic of the good physician" in the moralist literature of seventeenth-century England: the contrast setting off the "rhetorical"
manipulation of sensual passion from the "dialectical" stimulation
of critical judgment and the habits of instructive self-scrutiny such
judgment demands. [36] Scudéry's point is that theatrical illusion, the
overwhelming affective presence of dramatic action and delivery,
disables judgment by actuating sensuous appetite and unconscious
identificatory response. [37] Reading, by contrast, engages active
intelligence, sifting appearances in order to frame the careful
discriminations by which alone a work's true character is known.
Where the play as event dupes the beholder, the play as text invites
an integrally rational response; and it is in the light of this response
that *Le Cid* is finally unmasked as the dramaturgically incompetent
and morally bankrupt monstrosity it is.

But in underscoring the difference between the play as passionately experienced in the playhouse and what we discover only later
in the critical act of reading the text, Scudéry testifies to a crucial
feature of dramatic literature: how the "theatrical illusion" of the
play as staged blinds us to deeper levels of moral action, psychic investment, and historical meaning than are accessible in the moment
of performance. This both paradoxical and iconoclastic insight, so
typical of literary thought in the *grand siècle*, certainly bears on its
immediate target. As we shall see in chapter 1, for all his malevo-
lence, Scudéry is in fact right to claim that *Le Cid*'s noble semblance
conceals a profound deviation from the existing moral and social as
well as aesthetic order, evincing a dangerously hubristic sense of its
poet's personal worth. But as Scudéry's preamble suggests, the vital

---

[36] See Stanley E. Fish, *Self-Consuming Artifacts: The Experience of Seventeenth-
Century Literature* (Berkeley: University of California Press, 1972) 1-2.

[37] However ironic it may be for a playwright to sound this note, Scudéry
anticipates the renewed religious critique of theater in Nicole's *Traité de la comédie* (1665; rev. 1666 and 1667) and Bossuet's *Maximes et réflexions sur la comédie*
(1694).

thing is the disjunction between what he was able to read and what the public endorsed by flocking to performances in record numbers. It takes sharp eyes to see that *Le Cid*'s true subject is not the heroic tale of amorous self-sacrifice contemporary audiences admired, but a prideful claim to authority on the poet's behalf. Yet this is the play's ultimate aim, spelled out in the text Corneille leaves behind as the indelible record of the social as well as poetic ambitions that drive him.

But this brings me to my major point, the project made possible by the distance Scudéry's shrewd analysis brings to light. For what distinguishes classical drama is not only the new formal perfection achieved through the principle of immanence subtending its observance of the unities, its scrupulous verisimilitude, or the seamless dovetailing of soliloquy and plot. It is also the literary authority, the sense of masterful *authorship*, in which these things disclose at once their enabling origin and their ultimate referent.[38]

The feud between Scudéry and Corneille shortly engulfs the whole of literary France, including and especially the newly formed Académie Française, the political organ Richelieu devises not merely to reform, but to control the nation's cultural life.[39] It is nonetheless at bottom a feud of private authors intent on shouldering a way to the center of public attention. Confirmation of this aspect of the affair comes in Corneille's "Excuse à Ariste," a vainglorious piece of self-promotion rubbing salt into the open wound *Le Cid*'s popular success inflicts by boasting of the majesty of the poet's soaring Muse.[40] Coincident with the onset of the literary transformation

---

[38] The evolution of notions of authors and authorship is a leitmotiv of Grafton's work on humanist philology. One thread is the shift from conceptions of ahistorical *auctoritas* informing medieval compilations of authoritative "sentences" to an increasingly historical reconstruction of the social, cultural, and personal contexts by which such statements are shaped. I argue here that French classical drama reconsecrates the older *auctoritas*, but with this difference: the ultimate origin of literary authority is no longer an ahistorical God, but the historical *human* whose self-disciplined "genius" transcends the historical moment in which it lives.

[39] See Georges Couton, *Richelieu et le théâtre* (Lyon: Presses universitaires de Lyon, 1986) 17-21, Gasté's intro. to *La Querelle du Cid*, Christian Jouhaud, "Power and Literature: The Terms of the Exchange 1624-42," in Richard Burt (ed.), *The Administration of Aesthetics: Censorship, Political Criticism, and the Public Sphere* (Minneapolis: University of Minnesota Press, 1994) 34-82, and Hélène Merlin, *Public et littérature*, chaps. 5 and 6.

[40] For the text of the "Excuse à Ariste," see Gasté 63-66.

Paul Bénichou long ago felicitously called "le sacre de l'écrivain," the consecration of the writer as an autonomous source of value and truth, the quarrel thus marks the advent of a cultural institution to which French letters remain in thrall to this day: the transcendental figure of the Author conceived as a focus of quasi-theological interest and esteem.[41]

I do not claim that the classical era "invents" authors. Quite apart from championing the mandatory example of the Ancients, the French Renaissance had already engendered vernacular writers of comparable stature. As a result, the classical age inherits a series of names to reckon with (Marot, Ronsard, and Du Bellay; Rabelais, Garnier, Montaigne) even as it radically revises their standing, displacing them with a version of French literary history weighted in its own favor.[42] What *is* new however, a development synchronized with the emergence of "genius" as a central aesthetic category, is the relation between author and text.

In the Renaissance, as in the Middle Ages before it, the true object of value is the Work: what later writers revere and imitate is less Homer than the *Iliad*, less Petrarch or Ronsard than the body of

---

[41] Paul Bénichou, *Le Sacre de l'écrivain, 1750-1830: essai sur l'avènement d'un pouvoir spirituel laïque dans la France moderne* (Paris: José Corti, 1973). True, the felicitous term *sacre* is devised for the Enlightenment. However, the authoritative models for the quasi-sacramental claims later French writers make are the *grands classiques*. On the emergent institution of authorship in 17th-century France, see Viala, *Naissance de l'écrivain*, Timothy Murray, *Theatrical Legitimation: Allegories of Genius in Seventeenth-Century England and France* (Oxford: Oxford University Press, 1987), and Harrison, *Pistoles/Paroles*, chap. 1, "Sources of Income and Honor: Playwrights, Public, and Patrons."

[42] The revision is completed, with remarkable if notoriously misleading economy, in Boileau's *Art poétique*, propagating a history of French poetry whose decisive turn comes with Malherbe's perfection of the classical style:

> Enfin Malherbe vint, et, le premier en France,
> Fit sentir dans les vers une juste cadence,
> D'un mot mis en sa place enseigna le pouvoir,
> Et réduisit la muse aux règles du devoir.
> Par ce sage écrivain la langue réparée
> N'offrit plus rien de rude à l'oreille épurée.
> Les stances avec grâce apprirent à tomber,
> Et le vers sur le vers n'osa plus enjamber.
> Tout reconnut ses lois; et ce guide fidèle
> Aux auteurs de ce temps sert encor de modèle.
> Marchez donc sur ses pas; aimez sa pureté,
> Et de son tour heureux imitez la clarté. (1.131-42)

their sonnets. Though acknowledged as its producer, the poet is incidental to the poem, a convenient label identifying an achievement for which he serves as an instrument rather than a free creative source. In "Des livres," Montaigne writes at one memorable point that his favorite reading is history, prized for the light it shines on human nature in its concrete "diversity" as well as "truth":

> Les Historiens sont ma droitte bale: ils sont plaisans et aysez; et quant et quant l'homme en general, de qui je cherche la cognoissance, y paroist plus vif et plus entier qu'en nul autre lieu, la diversité et verité de ses conditions internes en gros et en destail, la varieté des moyens de son assemblage et des accidents qui le menacent.

Of particular value from this point of view are "lives," made precious not only by the incidents they record, but by the readiness with which these incidents lend themselves to personal application thanks to the practical and moral "counsels," the lessons, reflections, and sentences their relation prompts:

> Or ceux qui escrivent les vies, d'autant qu'ils s'amusent plus aux conseils qu'aux evenemens, plus à ce qui part du dedans qu'à ce qui arrive du dehors, ceux là me sont plus propres.

And since the historian who most consistently answers to this description is Plutarch, Plutarch is best of all: "Voilà pourquoy, en toutes sortes, c'est mon homme que Plutarque." (2.10, 86)

But what Montaigne means by calling Plutarch "mon homme" is not in fact the man so much as his books. A little earlier in the essay, when turning from discussion of his favorite poets (in particular, Virgil and Ariosto) to the moral writers who, in mingling "un peu plus de fruit au plaisir," teach him how to order "mes humeurs et mes conditions," books and authors' names are treated as synonyms: "les livres qui m'y servent, c'est Plutarque... et Seneque." More telling still, the "Plutarch" here referred to is a *Frenchman*–"c'est Plutarque, depuis qu'il est François." (83) To be sure, in calling Plutarch French, Montaigne employs a figure, affectionately transferring the French epithet from Amyot's translations of the *Lives* (1559) and *Moral Works* (1572) to the Greek writer now framed in

Montaigne's mother tongue. Nevertheless, what makes the figure possible is the identification of author with work–an identification underscored later in the essay when, explaining his habit of adding to the notes scrawled in the margins of his books by writing summaries of his reactions at the end of those he means to read only once, he cites what he wrote "en mon Guicciardin" and "en mon Philippe de Comines." (89-90) Gucciardini and Comines are the objects with which he stocks his library, possessions whose specification ("*mon* Guicciardin") is the more necessary when we recall both how numerous and, especially in the case of classical works, how variable were the editions from among which private libraries had to be furnished; despite the standardized texts printing made possible, there was no guarantee that Montaigne's "Guicciardin" and "Comines" were in fact quite the same as those in some other reader's collection.[43]

By contrast, with the rise of the *grands classiques*, and in particular the original *grand classique*, "le grand Corneille" himself, the relation definitively changes. Recognition of Corneille's greatness still springs from recognition of the greatness of his work: we deduce the first from the second just as we derive a cause from its effect. But derivative as acknowledgement of the cause may be, the cause as such remains primary; as in contemporary physics, or the theology with which physics increasingly contests intellectual dominance, the cause is always more "perfect" than the contingent effects that express it. Though we honor Corneille on the basis of the corpus of his plays, it is nonetheless *Corneille* we finally honor, in Corneille we *marvel*, as the condition of the works that single him out.

Whence for example, in direct answer to Montaigne's intimate possessives, the presumption underlying the first six verses of Boileau's Satire II, "A M. de Molière," where the socially groundless honorific particule the title awards the object of Boileau's praise speaks volumes to our point:

> Rare et fameux esprit, dont la fertile veine
> Ignore en écrivant le travail et la peine;
> Pour qui tient Apollon tous ses trésors ouverts,

---

[43] As Grafton reminds us, humanist scholarship's task was not merely interpreting, but *establishing* the texts public and private libraries housed.

Et qui sais à quel coin se marquent les bons vers:
Dans les combats d'esprit savant maître d'escrime,
Enseigne-moi, Molière, où tu trouves la rime.[44]

In declaring the awe inspired by the comic products of Molière's "fertile vein," Boileau designates a mysterious force of nature, an extraordinary gift before which he can only bow down in wondering (and envious) gratitude. The trigger for the wonder is both the work and the "esprit," the wit, spirit, or intelligence that infuses it: a unique (and uncanny) combination of rightness and *naturel*, of *prestesse* and precision, made all the more staggering by its unnervingly fluent rhyme. But the striking thing is that, unlike his forebears in the Renaissance, mindful of the battery of techniques made available by a rhetorical art specifically designed to answer such questions, what Boileau wants to know is not how, but *where*–"Teach me, Molière, where you find the rhyme." Nor does he expect a response: the "where" is a birthright, an innate possession situated at a level to which the respondent has all the less access in that he is himself the inscrutable source of the tokens of his genius.

But whence also, to return to Corneille, perhaps the greatest of that poet's innovations. Beyond the spectacular perfection to which he brings French drama, towering over vernacular predecessors and contemporaries alike, Corneille painstakingly elaborates his own literary Monument in the pathbreaking *Théâtre* of 1660, followed nearly a quarter of a century later by what he intended to be the definitive edition of 1682. In addition to the plays themselves, "revised and corrected by the author" in response to two generations of critics and the evolving climate of literary taste, Corneille publishes his three magisterial Discourses on dramatic art and frames each play with a critical introduction (the "examens") explaining and defending the author's practice with a view to shaping the posterity he craves. Though the work matters in the first instance on the strength of the heroic actions it portrays, the exemplary conduct of its protagonists, and the formal excellence with which it represents them, the ultimate point is what it reveals about the author himself. The dramatic poem is a kind of mask whose

---

[44] Boileau, Satire II: 1-6, in *Satires, Epîtres, Art poétique* 72.

true content lies not in what we immediately perceive, the acts and words produced on stage, but in what all of these contrive to intimate as its emanations–the Poet, Corneille himself.

The dramatic text is Janus-headed, facing two ways at once–toward the noble actions we admire, but also toward the secret contriver pulling strings offstage. This fundamental duplicity is indeed a property of the medium itself. As we have seen, the perfection of the art demands the erasure of all traces of the playwright's hand in the achievement of a form of dramatic presence in which the actors play out their own destinies as an expression of the immanent logic of the action in which they are engaged. Yet the perfection that displaces the author turns out, at another level, to reinstate him. The spectacle enjoyed in the playhouse is ultimately the correlate of something else, concealed by the art with which it overwhelms us: the author whose very absence is the conclusive sign of his mastery, a mode of presence the more inescapable for its masterly indirection.

It is in this deeper perspective that the battle with Scudéry is fought out–why indeed, to all of the other charges leveled at Le Cid, Scudéry adds plagiarism, an accusation whose unmistakable target is the Author as such in the very essence of his originary authorship. [45] But it is also the source not only of Scudéry's rhetorical strategy, at once the difficulty he faces and the shift he makes to meet it, but of the feature of classical drama that strategy reveals. What maddens Corneille's rival is the difference between what Le Cid persuades us to take it for and what it really is. But this difference cannot be unmasked in the theatrical experience the text inspires, only in an act of reading focused squarely on the text Corneille himself puts in our hands by publishing it. Yet this in turn means that the text is its own worst enemy, the key to decoding the fraud it perpetrates. The text is a sort of hypocrite, but a hypocrite one of whose properties is the propensity to give itself the lie. [46]

Despite the obstacles in their path, antithetic readings like Scudéry's come readily to hand, subjecting all classical plays to the iconoclastic assaults typified by the image of the pullulating worms Corneille's trompe-l'oeil turns into on close scrutiny. This is why the

---

[45] On the sociology of plagiarism in 17th-century France, see Viala, *Naissance de l'écrivain*, chap. 3, "Les droits contres les lois," esp. 86-93.

[46] As we shall see in chap. 5, Diderot will later make this case in "Le Paradoxe sur le comédien" and *Le Neveu de Rameau*.

history of French classical drama is in large measure the history of the critical debates it inspired. But what makes such readings possible is that the texts themselves *authorize* them, signaling their proximity at the turn of every page. Cornelian hubris prospectively endorses the critiques that lie in store for it, encoding both their imminence and their truth in the fabric of its own compositions. The texts of classical drama are antithetical primers in the art of critical double dealing, at once acknowledging secret inscription and supplying the means to ferret it out.

I hope this already suggests something of my book's wider scope. By developing the oppositional readings consciously embedded in the classics of seventeenth-century French drama, I aim to provoke a significant change in interpretive posture toward the classical repertoire, eschewing judgmental facility on behalf of something more respectful and historically more accurate. One consequence of this move–a consequence however that also turns out to be a condition–is to reassess the *grand siècle* as a whole.

To read the plays as I propose both entails and demands breaking the hold of a tenacious teleological illusion, challenging the tendency (shared by intellectual left and right alike) to interpret the century in the retrospective light of its presumed "apogee" in the absolutist culture of the court of Louis XIV. [47] The point here is not merely that the "hegemonic" moment of high classicism is a remarkably short-lived phenomenon, extending little further than from the Sun King's seizure of power in 1661 to the period of moral and political as well as intellectual and aesthetic stagnation associated with the Revocation of the Edict of Nantes in 1685. [48]

---

[47] This illusion stems from Voltaire's *Siècle de Louis XIV* (1751) and dominates traditional historiography. One of the curiosities of our current situation is that, even on the intellectual left (Foucault, Apostolidès, Greenberg, and to a lesser extent Marin), while we no longer read classical texts as, say, Antoine Adam did, we still endorse his sense of the period. For a recent counter to this tendency, see Marc Fumaroli, *Le Poète et le Roi: Jean de La Fontaine en son siècle* (Paris: Fallois, 1997), esp. the "preamble" and chap. 1, "L'Olympe et le Parnasse," arguing for La Fontaine's critical role as the ironically self-deprecating embodiment of free private expression modeled on Montaigne.

[48] Though left-wing commentators (Marin, Foucault, Apostolidès) make surprisingly little of it, defining the "temps de Louis XIV" (and "l'âge classique" generally) in monolithic terms, this is already an *acquis* in Paul Hazard's *Crise de la conscience européenne, 1680-1715* (Paris: Arthème Fayard, 1961) and Antoine Adam's *L'Age classique* (Paris: Arthaud, 1968-71).

The point is also that high classicism is the conscious product of the socio-cultural forces it seeks to dominate and contain, invisible as it seems to make them during the quarter century of its heyday. In its very triumph, it knows itself to be grounded on and therefore undermined by the unruly diversity, acts of resistance and defiance, protest and delay epitomized in the political sphere by the Frondes of 1648-52 and, in the aesthetic, by a century-long series of what Joan DeJean has styled "culture wars" of which her own example, the Quarrel of Ancients and Moderns touched off by Charles Perrault's *Siècle de Louis le Grand* in 1687, is neither the loudest nor the last. [49]

To be sure, with the publication of Chapelain's *Sentiments de L'Académie Française* in 1637, deciding the controversy surrounding Corneille's *Le Cid* in Scudéry's favor, the State exerts henceforth a degree of censorship and control unparalleled in French literary history. It is equally true that, despite the recent revival of interest in the *libertins* or Christian Jouhaud's remarkable resurrection of the *mazarinades* of the Fronde era, the French seventeenth century produces nothing like the outpouring of publicly radical speech characterizing the revolutionary decades between the outbreak of the English Civil War and the Stuart Restoration of 1660. [50] The French seventeenth century nonetheless remains an era of ceaseless cultural combat, pitting Cartesians against Thomists, *précieux* against classicists, *esprits forts* against *honnêtes gens*, *bons français* against *politiques*, clerics against dramatists, Jansenists against Jesuits, *anciens* against *modernes*–combat the more acrimonious for displacing the deeper historical conflicts the period failed squarely to face up to or resolve. Even the clearest and most authoritative

---

[49] See Joan DeJean, *Ancients against Moderns: Culture Wars and the Making of a Fin de Siècle* (Chicago: University of Chicago Press, 1997).

[50] On the English experience, see Christopher Hill, *The World Turned Upside Down: Radical Ideas in the English Revolution* (London: Maurice Temple Smith, 1972). On the contrasting case of France, see Christian Jouhaud, *Mazarinades: La Fronde des mots* (Paris: Aubier, 1985). One of Jouhaud's most telling theses (developed in the intro. and his brilliant analysis of the cardinal de Retz's mastery of the genre in chap. 4, "Propagande et action") is that the last thing to look for in *mazarinades* is coherent political philosophies. In a similar vein, see Erica Harth, *Cyrano de Bergerac and the Polemics of Modernity* (New York: Columbia University Press, 1970) 51-52 on the heavy revisions Cyrano's *Autre monde* underwent before even posthumous publication seemed possible.

exemplars of the high classical order are shaped by the conflicts we tend to allege they repress. Nor is the shaping purely "unconscious." Subversion rarely receives direct articulation: as in Scudéry, it is normally reserved for accounts of one's enemies, expressing the criminal intent behind what others write. Yet it is on everyone's mind all the same, defining the overt horizon of all writing, and nowhere more profoundly than in drama.

But the thesis of this book has still further implications, reflected in the "indiscernible counterparts" of its title. At one level, the phrase, borrowed from the aesthetician Arthur Danto, [51] recommends itself by reason of its pertinence to dramatic art. In the *Critique de l'Ecole des femmes*, staging a salon gathering to debate the merits of the earlier piece, Molière turns the scenic perspective from *L'Ecole des femmes* to the audience that watches it. The wise Uranie remarks that satires like Molière's "sont miroirs publics, où il ne faut jamais témoigner qu'on se voie; et c'est se taxer hautement d'un défaut, que se scandaliser qu'on le reprenne." [52] Molière deploys another mouthpiece to remind us that the persons on the stage are not in fact real people, only "des personnages en l'air, et des fântomes proprement," figures the poet "habille à sa fantaisie, pour réjouir les spectateurs." (217) Uranie makes the same point from a respectably Horatian angle by insisting that comic portraits "tombent directement sur les moeurs, et ne frappent les personnes que par réflexion." (207) And yet in comedy at least, as still a third character observes in arguing for the genre's superiority over the noble fictions of tragic theater, what gives the pleasure spectators look for is the *resemblance*:

> Lorsque vous peignez des héros, vous faites ce que vous voulez. Ce sont des portraits à plaisir, où l'on ne cherche point de

---

[51] Arthur Danto, *The Transfiguration of the Commonplace: A Philosophy of Art* (Cambridge, MA: Harvard University Press, 1981). Danto derives the phrase from scholastic philosophy. The problem of "indiscernibles," i.e., of entities that are in every both sensible and categorical respect identical counterparts of each other, was designed to illuminate the ideal ground of identity in what medieval philosophers called "quiddity," the demonstrative *whichness* each thing possesses as the particular thing it is regardless of what it shares with others.

[52] Molière, *Critique de l'Ecole des femmes*, in *Œuvres complètes* 207. All subsequent Molière references appear in the text by page number for prose and by act, scene, and line for verse.

ressemblance; et vous n'avez qu'à suivre les traits d'une imagination qui se donne l'essor, et qui souvent laisse le vrai pour attra-
per le merveilleux. Mais lorsque vous peignez les hommes, il faut
peindre d'après nature. On veut que ces portraits ressemblent; et
vous n'avez rien fait, si vous n'y faîtes reconnaître les gens de
votre siècle. (208)

Theater is thus a kind of painting, holding up to the society for
which it exists a mirror in which spectators discover versions—now
heroic and flattering, now satiric and ridiculous—of their own character and conduct. The enabling condition of both the resemblance
and the act of self-recognition it occasions is nevertheless a certain
difference, the dodge of dramatic "fantasy" that brings the portraits
to the stage. But as the intense negative reaction that drives Molière
to mount the *Critique*'s apology for his art attests, we find it in fact
impossible to *tell* that difference inasmuch as what we perceive by
its means is our own unvarnished selves—the self-accusing identities
Uranie counsels us to leave behind. The people the stage portrays
are indeed merely "phantoms" and illusions. Yet the point of the illusion, source of the peculiar joy it imparts, is that, in its very unreality, its fictive indirectness, it enables us to recognize what we are.
Theater's task, epitomizing representation at large, consists in developing distinctions *without* a difference, things other than those it
images that nevertheless touch us "by reflection," the indiscernible
counterparts of the fictive looking-glass.

But at another level, my title's "indiscernible counterparts" cap-
ture the medium that underlies the endless mirror effects produced
on the classical stage—the *text* to which we perpetually return in
search of the key to the puzzles theater sets.

The reductiveness and precipitance of current critical practice,
the deconstructive habits Molière's reflections on his art show to be
so perfectly redundant, arise from a fundamental mistake not only
about the nature of classical drama, but about the nature of texts in
general. Recent philosophical debates in the subfield of aesthetics
known as "ontology of art" may help us locate the error. Of particular relevance is the dilemma posed for aesthetics by two competing ontological models. One, proposed by Danto, defends the at
once intentional and historical notion of aesthetic representation
for which Danto resuscitates the scholastic formula cited in my

title. [53] The other, from the hand of Joseph Margolis, transfers the burden of sustaining artworks' identity from the works themselves to the shifting emphases laid out in the *readings* they undergo.

Danto's account opens with a thought experiment in which we are asked to tell the difference between a series of identical red squares of painted canvas. He argues that we do so *historically*, by invoking knowledge of who painted each square and of the special end in view in painting it. Though the squares are in every *sensible* respect "indiscernible counterparts," we still manage to distinguish them once we learn how each came to assume the form it shares with the others. Thus one ("Israelites Crossing the Red Sea") presents a Kierkegaardian parody of traditional canons of narrative painting–the artist portrays neither the escaping Hebrews, nor Pharaoh's pursuing chariots, but the moment when "the Israelites had already crossed over, and the Egyptians were drowned." Meanwhile, a second ("Red Square") is "a clever bit of Moscow landscape" and a third "a still-life executed by an embittered disciple of Matisse, called 'Red Table Cloth'." [54] Our capacity to tell the difference between identical objects is grounded in–and thus confirms the authority of–the intentional history of which any given work is the product: artworks *have a history*, and this history determines both their identity and the truth conditions governing our interpretations.

Against this view, Margolis marshals quite other facts, relating to interpretation itself. One may certainly draw on knowledge of the history of a work's making and the artist's intent in composing it. But even disregarding the extent to which matters of making and intent are themselves subject to interpretive construal (a Freudian psychoanalyst will conceive such questions far differently from a Marxist, a high modernist, or a post-Lacanian feminist), this is by no means the only reading we may offer. Nor is there any guarantee that we will draw like inferences from the same historical picture–even Marxists quarrel about what follows from the constructions they hold in common. So while Margolis agrees that the

---

[53] Danto, chap. 1. Later in the book, Danto develops a similar argument with reference to "conceptualist" works in which real objects (a bed, a urinal) are presented as (and thereby become) works of art discernible from the objects of which they are in strictly sensible terms indiscernible counterparts.

[54] Ibid. 1.

most salient fact about a work is that it *has a history*, that history includes not merely or even primarily the circumstances of its making, but rather those defined by its evolving uptake. Texts have histories because we *read* them otherwise—so radically that the "being"
postulated by "ontology of art" is a Protagorian flux, as mutable
and multiform as the ephemeral "men" who are its "measure." [55]

My readings of French classical drama suggest that neither view
matches the reality. Texts do have intentional histories, and these
histories do tell (and make) a difference. A major goal of this book
will accordingly be to *clarify* the drama's history, refining our grasp
of how and why the plays took the forms they did. Still, what such
histories reveal is that the texts they produce are their own "indiscernible counterparts." In the exemplary cases of Corneille, Molière, and Racine, the text is framed from the outset not only by the
will that made it, and by the historical, social, and ideological conditions that constrained that making, but by an uncanny awareness
of the oppositional readings subsequent readers have learned to detect. But this in turn suggests that the historical flux Margolis adduces is an inherent dimension of the texts on which we appear to
visit it. Texts, in this sense, *make* history, not only by providing a
register for our shifting responses to the issues they join, but by
consciously embracing the documentary status to which we presume to reduce them. As we shall see more specifically in our concluding chapter on Racine's *Phèdre*, French classical drama is at its
deepest level *about* the twists and turns of the evolving reactions to
which history has shown it to be subject. Careful attention to the
antithetical texts of the seventeenth-century canon may thus renew
our appreciation of what complex (and even more prescient) entities they are in such a way as to disclose something essential about
the nature of texts in general.

Which brings me to my epigraph. At first glance, Lacan's words
reinstate the methodological attitude I mean to unseat. Drawn from
the famous seminar on the *regard*, the sentence voices the testimony
of what (faithful in this to Freud) Lacan called "psychoanalytic
experience," the repeated encounter with patients' blindness to
their own motives and identities. It thereby articulates the fundamental psycho-ontological postulate encoded in Freudian theories

---

[55] Margolis, *Interpretation Radical but Not Unruly.*

of dreams, symbols, slips, jokes, compulsions, and *actes manqués*: that they spring from a place other than the one we are conscious of, making us visible at a point we do not acknowledge and systematically overlook. "Jamais tu ne me regardes là où je te vois," a typically dense formula we may translate as claiming that "you never look for me there where I see you" or that "you never look at what it is *in you* I see from where I look at you," if not indeed both at once.[56]

It is already striking that what Lacan proposes here as a strictly psychoanalytic insight informs the classical doctrine of Character, especially (though, as Racine in particular illustrates, by no means exclusively) in comedy. What, after all, is a *capitan* like the Matamore of Corneille's *Illusion comique* or the self-styled truth-teller, the rebarbative Alceste of Molière's *Misanthrope*, if not the at once self-deluded and self-accusing embodiment of Lacan's law? What in fact constitutes both comic and tragic characters alike, making them the playthings of the ironies the action sets in train, is the incapacity to see around their own corners, putting them at the mercy of an intelligence that escapes them.[57]

But quite apart from arguing the anticipation of a psychoanalytic truth supposed to lie beyond classical poets' grasp, the accommodation of Lacan's verdict urges a *reversal*, shifting our gaze from contemplation of our classical "other" to that other's even more interesting contemplation of ourselves. Rather than focus on exposing the presumed "unconscious" of classical drama, I invite exposure of our own in the pertinacity with which the drama fixes us in an ironic glass the more revealing for our presumption of methodic dominance at its expense. The experience I hope to transmit is humbling: the plays have seen us coming, anchoring us in the spectacle we imagine we supervise. And what enables them so to anchor us is the *text*–a text of our own making in that it is only in our reading that it reveals the depth and character of our engagement, yet a text that *makes* our making in the degree to which it prefigures our approach.

---

[56] Jacques Lacan, "La ligne et la lumière," *Les quatre concepts fondamentaux de la psychanalyse* (*Le séminaire de Jacques Lacan*, Livre XI), ed. Jacques-Alain Miller (Paris: Seuil, 1973; "Points" paper ed.) 118.

[57] We shall return to this point in various ways, especially in chap. 5 with reference to Molière's exploration of the performative nature of identities.

It is a truism of performance theory that dramatic texts are "scripts," documents whose *raison d'être* is the metamorphosis that overtakes them through the contingencies of production, delivery, and the reactions of live audiences. A play is not only the words its author writes conceived as what philosophers would call the "type" each performative "token" more or less successfully approximates; it also enfolds the token itself–its staging and what staging brings about. And yet a play is written *with a view* to performance, guiding where it can, but awaiting as it must the uncontrollable vicissitudes to which performance will subject it. But this means that, however feral and unpredictable it may be, the token *informs* the type; the Aristotelian "accident" alters the substance to which it supervenes. What more than anything marks the classical drama is its openness to the chances that must befall it, an openness paradoxically inscribed in the consciousness of its own authority as a poetic work of art.

In the preface to the first of his plays to be published, the *Précieuses ridicules* of 1659, Molière objects to being hurried into print against (he claims) his will: "C'est une chose étrange qu'on imprime les gens malgré eux! Je ne vois rien de si injuste, et je pardonnerais toute autre violence plutôt que celle-là." (100) To be sure, since the play is published (since Molière himself is "printed") by popular demand, he can only bow to higher necessity:

> comme le public est le juge absolu de ces sortes d'ouvrages, il y aurait de l'impertinence à moi de le démentir; et quand j'aurais eu la plus mauvaise opinion du monde de mes *Précieuses ridicules* avant leur représentation, je dois croire maintenant qu'elles valent quelque chose, puisque tant de gens ensemble en ont dit du bien. (100)

Still, the displacement from stage to print is fraught with danger, for it risks depriving the *Précieuses* of the features of live performance that make them seem worth publishing, exposing them to attentions the more unkind for being more acute:

> Mais comme une grande partie des grâces qu'on y a trouvées dépendent de l'action et du ton de voix, il m'importait qu'on ne les dépouillât pas de ces ornements, et je trouvais que le succès

qu'elles avaient eu dans la représentation était assez beau pour
en demeurer là. J'avais résolu, dis-je, de ne les faire voir qu'à la
chandelle [of theatrical lighting], pour ne point donner lieu à
quelqu'un de dire le proverbe, (100)

Elle est belle à la chandelle, mais le grand jour gâte tout–she is beautiful by candlelight, but the light of day spoils everything.

The text here is thus the *truth*, a truth Molière is all the more
eager to conceal owing to his awareness of how far it transcends
commital to public scrutiny.[58] But there is in the end nothing for it:
the text *will* see the light of day, revealing its true nature for all his
efforts to disguise it. Which leads him to close the preface with a
curious proleptic citation of one of his most memorably wicked creations, the eponymous hypocritical core of the later *Tartuffe*: "Mais
enfin, comme j'ai dit, on ne me laisse pas le temps de respirer, et M.
de Luynes [his publisher] veut m'aller relier de ce pas: à la bonne
heure, puisque Dieu l'a voulu." (101)

What "God" wills is of course what Molière wills too: his
protestations of reluctance barely conceal the excitement of appearing in print. With the publication of the *Précieuses*, he fulfils a desire inherent to the act of writing from the start–to achieve the status of an Author, a letter-press creature whose posterity is assured
by the fact of print. But the desire is its own catastrophe, subjecting
him to the merciless gaze latent in the text as such. Though its
disclosure must await the coming daylight of the readings to which
publication submits it, the truth that light discovers is already
there–and so are we.

---

[58] For a complementary (if different) view of Molière's sense of publication, see
Abby E. Zanger, "Paralyzing Performance: Sacrificing Theater on the Altar of Publication," *Stanford French Review* 12.2-3 (Fall/Winter 1988) 169-85.

CHAPTER 1

CET HYMEN DIFFERE: THE FIGURATION OF AUTHORITY IN CORNEILLE'S *LE CID*

W E begin where the golden age of French classicism does, moving between two scenes from plays by Pierre Corneille. Both scenes are centrally preoccupied with the nature of their art. The first, from *L'Illusion comique* (1635), opens the play to which it belongs with a staging of the stage whereby it also stages its author, and hence a claim to a certain kind of authority. The second, from *Le Cid* (1637), closes its play with another staging of the stage, but more indirectly: in a Scene of Judgment in which it appears to draw such authority as it enjoys not from its own nature and power as theater, but from what, in the period, supplies the figure of authority as such, namely, the King. The two scenes are thus at once closely linked and sharply contrasting, and not least because where one lays out the conditions grounding the "theatrical illusion" on which it rests, the second, in which this same illusion is put to morally uplifting and socially useful work, rehearses the impossibility to which its founding illusion commits it.

Further, in the curious way the second cancels the authority arrogated by the first, a variety of cultural domains powerfully intersect, tying theater to developments not only in other arts, and in particular painting, but in "natural philosophy" or science, early modern historiography, political philosophy, and even politics itself. Nor will this be without consequences for *theory*. *Le Cid*'s dénouement will occasion critical reflection on the methods we bring to studies of this kind, leading us to draw a lesson from Corneille concerning how we ought to conduct ourselves as students of literature, culture, and art.

Let us now turn to the second of our two examples: the scene
with which *Le Cid* reaches a close;[1] or rather with which it notoriously *fails* to close, thereby furnishing one of the chief articles of
impeachment at the heart of the violent *querelle* of which it was the
subject.[2]

The "tragi-comedy" of *Le Cid* opens with what looks like the
happy ending to another kind of play: a pastoral comedy in which
true love triumphs over paternal obduracy, the resistance of the pa-
triarchs yielding, after protracted struggle, to the meritorious wishes of their progeny.[3] Chimène and Rodrigue, beautiful young nobles at the court of Don Fernand, "premier Roi de Castille," have
had the good fortune (and good taste) to fall in love at a moment
when this proves congenial to their fathers' wishes. Much is made
especially of Chimène's anxiously dutiful dependence on paternal
will. An initially wide field of potential husbands has finally nar-
rowed to a choice between Rodrigue and the worthy if unlucky
Don Sanche. For fear that premature disclosure of her own wishes
might sting her touchy father's pride, prompting him to pick the
wrong man out of spite, Chimène conceals her love for Rodrigue.
The dramatic potential of the play's opening scene is only fully realized in a revision dating from 1660 incorporated in the definitive
text of 1682, where the original's direct presentation of the father's
choice becomes a narrative the exultant daughter extracts from her
governess for a second time:

Chimène

Elvire, m'as tu fait un rapport bien sincère?
Ne déguises-tu rien de ce qu'a dit mon père?

Elvire

Tous mes sens à moi-même en sont encor charmés:
Il estime Rodrigue autant que vous l'aimez,

---

[1] Since our argument concerns contemporary reception, the Pléiade *Œuvres
complètes* is indispensable, reproducing the original versions of both plays.

[2] The chief documents, including Scudéry's *Observations* and the final text of
the *Sentiments*, composed by Chapelain under Richelieu's supervision, are collected
in Gasté, *La Querelle du Cid*, cited henceforth by page number in the text. See too
Chapelain's draft of the *Sentiments*, ed. Georges Collas (Geneva: Slatkine, 1968).

[3] See Fumaroli, "Pierre Corneille, fils de son oeuvre," *Héros et orateurs* 43.

Et si je ne m'abuse à lire dans son âme,
Il vous commandera de répondre à sa flamme.

Chimène

Dis-moi donc, je te prie, une seconde fois
Ce qui te fait juger qu'il approuve mon choix.[4]

But the original makes the same general point even if by more plod-
dingly direct means. The curtain that rises on *Le Cid* drops on a
miniature romantic comedy closed when the father voices the qua-
si-miraculous coincidence of paternal and filial desires:

Don Rodrigue surtout n'a trait en son visage
Qui d'un homme de cœur ne soit la haute image,
Et sort d'une maison si féconde en guerriers
Qu'ils y prennent naissance au milieu des lauriers.
La valeur de son père, en son temps sans pareille,
Tant qu'a duré sa force a passé pour merveille,
Ses rides sur son front ont gravé ses exploits,
Et nous disent encor ce qu'il fut autrefois:
Je me promets du fils ce que j'ai vu du père,
Et ma fille en un mot peut l'aimer et me plaire.

(1.1.15-24)

And yet no sooner has this joyful issue been achieved than the
two fathers fall out. Anxious to enhance his line's chances of survival by selecting a fitting governor for his dauphin, an officer
charged with fashioning a Monarch out of a mere callow boy, the
new King finds himself confronted with a choice of his own–between the potent Don Gomès, general of his army and father to
Chimène, and the venerable if enfeebled Don Diègue, hero of an
earlier generation and father of Rodrigue. Much to the annoyance
of the younger and more vigorous Don Gomès, he chooses the older man. Goaded in no small part by the latter's haughty observation
that, right or wrong, the King has chosen, thereby ending all discussion–a defense made all the more infuriating in the 1660 edition by
the addition of the at once sententious and self-interested reminder
that "on doit ce respect au pouvoir absolu / De n'examiner rien

---

[4] For this variant, see *Œuvres complètes* 1.1488.

quand un Roi l'a voulu"–,[5] Don Gomès strikes his rival in the face.
Too infirm to avenge this mortal insult on his own, Don Diègue
commands his son to stand as his champion; and zealously as selfish
love urges the contrary, Rodrigue persuades himself that both filial
duty and personal honor outweigh the sophistries of the heart. Unhappy as it makes him, he challenges his prospective father-in-law
to a duel, and kills him.

Her lover's peer in duty as in honor, Chimène now seeks Rodrigue's death first by legal means via the King–in an encounter
(2.7) distinguished by a masterpiece of forensic hypotyposis–and
then by extra-legal means, finding in the amorous Don Sanche a
champion to avenge the shedding of her father's blood. But the
beautiful crux of the situation, the *comble* of commingled horror and
self-sacrificial nobility, is not merely that Chimène and Rodrigue go
on loving each other; their love actually grows more ardent for their
shared willingness to vanquish passion in the name of *la gloire*, personal honor as loyal members of their respective houses. The family
vendetta occasions an orgy of *générosité* in which the protagonists
immolate their own interests in order to prove worthy not only of
their fathers, but of each other. Rodrigue gives the theory in the famous speech where, meeting his beloved for the first time in the
play, he recounts his motives in killing her father:

> Réduit à te déplaire, ou souffrir un affront,
> J'ai retenu ma main, j'ai cru mon bras trop prompt,
> Je me suis accusé de trop de violence:
> Et ta beauté sans doute emportait la balance,
> Si je n'eusse opposé contre tous ses appas
> Qu'un homme sans honneur ne te méritait pas,
> Qu'après m'avoir chéri quand je vivais sans blâme,
> Qui m'aima généreux me haïrait infâme,
> Qu'écouter ton amour, obéir à sa voix,
> C'était m'en rendre indigne et diffamer ton choix.
> (3.4.893-902)

To which Chimène magnificently replies:

[5] For this addition, ibid. 1.1491.

De quoi qu'en ta faveur notre amour m'entretienne
Ma générosité doit répondre à la tienne:
Tu t'es, en m'offensant, montré digne de moi,
Je me dois par ta mort montrer digne de toi.

(3.4.939-42)

The trouble is that the inspiring sacrifice solves absolutely nothing: poised between opposing sets of irreducible yet irreconcilable
values, the play reaches stalemate. The deliciously recursive dilemma forming the play's argumentative plot and at once the treasure-
house and grammar for its elaborately chiastic verse [6] brings on the
climactic scene. Chimène calls Rodrigue to judgment before the
King; and Rodrigue, fresh from the spectacular if implausibly foreshortened annihilation of an invading Moorish army, [7] answers the
summons, kneeling at Chimène's feet to offer the sword with which
he implores her to exact revenge. But a band of his supporters, including Chimène's own champion Don Sanche, sue for clemency,
citing his martial exertions as proof of his overriding value to a state
that quite literally would not exist without the strong right arm by
which his lady's father was slain.

So it is now up to the King, and the King alone, the play's Arbiter or Leviathan, to resolve the antinomies by which his court is
simultaneously riven and defined. The solution, consummating all
the conflicting desires driving the play, lies at hand: a marriage forging the moral, psychological, aesthetic, and political unanimity that
would enable the play to end. But he cannot tie the hymeneal knot.
Operating now in the person of the monarch, the play is trapped by

---

[6] Corneille's elaborate ornament excited Scudéry's ridicule, as in the following
remarks about Don Arias, a messenger from the King "qui, a vray dire, ny vient que
pour faire des pointes sur les lauriers, et sur la foudre, et pour donner sujet au
Comte de Gormas, de pousser une partie des rodomontades, que je vous ay deja
montrees." (88)

[7] See Scudéry's hilarious synopsis of Rodrigue's day: "Et veritablement toutes
ces belles actions que fit le Cid en plusieurs annees, sont tellement assemblees par
force en cette Piece, pour la mettre dans les vint quatre heures [of the unity of
time], que les Personnages y semblent des Dieux de machine, qui tombent du Ciel
en terre: car enfin, dans le court espace d'un jour naturel, on eslit un Gouverneur
au Prince de Castille; il se fait une querelle et un combat, entre Dom Diegue et le
Comte, autre combat de Rodrigue et du Comte, un autre de Rodrigue contre les
Mores; un autre contre Dom Sanche; et le mariage se conclut, entre Rodrigue et
Chimene: je vous laisse à juger, si ne voila pas un jour bien employé, et si l'on n'au-
roit pas grand tort d'accuser tous ces personnages de paresse?" (77-78).

its own verisimilitude: the violent forces of contradiction and disorder, highlighting the contrasting virtues of honor, harmony, and obedience, are too starkly drawn against the magic of the royal verdict. [8] So the King temporizes, postponing the matter to some later date when passions will have cooled, Chimène completed the rites of mourning, and Rodrigue worked off the penalty he has incurred through a feudal equivalent of community service. Addressing himself first to Chimène, Don Fernand hands down the following sentence:

> Le temps assez souvent a rendu légitime
> Ce qui semblait d'abord ne se pouvoir sans crime.
> Rodrigue t'a gaignée, et tu dois être à lui,
> Mais quoique sa valeur t'ait conquise aujourd'hui,
> Il faudrait que je fusse ennemi de ta gloire
> Pour lui donner sitôt le prix de sa victoire.
> Cet Hymen différé ne rompt point une loi
> Qui sans marquer de temps lui destine ta foi.
> Prends un an si tu veux pour essuyer tes larmes.
> Rodrigue cependant, il faut prendre les armes.
> Après avoir vaincu les Mores sur nos bords,
> Renversé leurs desseins, repoussé leurs efforts,
> Va jusqu'en leur pays leur reporter la guerre,
> Commander mon armée et ravager leur terre.
> A ce seul nom de Cid ils trembleront d'effroi,
> Ils t'ont nommé Seigneur, et te voudront pour Roi.
>
> (5.7.1839-54)

Many things are at work here, social and political as well as dramatic and aesthetic; but the most striking is the conspicuously explicit gesture by which, at the moment of truth, the point of artistic and symbolic climax and closure, the play enacts its own deconstruction. To an ear attuned to current theoretical usage, the

---

[8] Echoing Scudéry, the *Sentiments* directs particularly potent criticisms at verisimilitude in the closing scene, and in particular the King's decision to give Chimène in marriage to her father's murderer. An important feature of the debate is the Aristotelian distinction between historical fact (all parties stipulate that, historically, Chimène did marry her father's killer) and what is *vraisemblable* in heroic fiction. See Scudéry (76-77) and *Sentiments* (365-69). See too the analysis of the problem of *vraisemblance* as raised by both *Le Cid* and La Fayette's *La Princesse de Clèves* in Genette, "Vraisemblance et motivation."

King's "Hymen différé" is almost too good to be true: a textbook case of what Jacques Derrida calls *différance*. [9] Putting off the moment of decision to which its plot inexorably brings it, the play defers the act by which its constitutive conflicts would be resolved. But the need to defer is in some sense built into the very structure of the exposition itself, if not into the structure of exposition as such. Smuggled in along the bias of symbolic displacement from the surrounding society and culture, the conflicts the play seeks to resolve emerge only on condition of a certain *différence*, without the substitutive "a": that saving symbolic difference without which the culture could not face them, the evasion of scenic representation being precisely the sign of the culture's inability to solve its problems head on.

That there was much to face is certified by the singular ferocity of the *querelle* the play provoked. [10] The extraordinary animus directed in particular at Chimène, denounced first in Georges de Scudéry's malevolent *Observations* and then in the *Sentiments de l'Académie Française*, drafted by Jean Chapelain under the watchful eye of the Académie's founding father, Richelieu, as a patricide, prostitute, and hypocrite, a monster of sexual license and filial treachery, [11] already reveals how deep was the psychic investment, for and against. Since no less a personage than the "hieroglyphic King" himself [12] postpones the moment at which all difference (however spelt) must cease, the play confesses how its temporizing symbolic equivocation condemns it to inconclusiveness and failure. If only the mask of a royal fiction allows the culture's tensions to show their face, when will the time come for them to take the vizard off, and how would we know when they had? [13]

---

[9] See Jacques Derrida, *De la grammatologie* (Paris: Minuit, 1967) 88-95 and "La différance" in *Marges de la philosophie* (Paris: Minuit, 1972) 1-29.

[10] In addition to his "notice" in *Œuvres complètes* (1.1456-66), see Couton, *Richelieu* 17-21, the intro. to Gasté, Jouhaud, "Power and Literature," and Merlin, *Public et littérature*, chaps. 5, "La querelle du *Cid*: de la république des lettres au *public*" and 6, "*Public* et publication: la querelle comme scène publique."

[11] See *Observations* 79-83, 90-95, and *Sentiments* 372-75.

[12] See Stephen Kogan, *The Hieroglyphic King: Wisdom and Idolatry in the Seventeenth-Century Masque* (Rutherford, NJ: Fairleigh Dickinson University Press, 1986).

[13] I echo Derrida's opening remarks in "La pharmacie de Platon": "Un texte n'est un texte que s'il cache au premier regard, au premier venu, la loi de sa composition et la règle de son jeu. Un texte reste d'ailleurs toujours imperceptible. La loi

But we need not be satisfied with this Derridean account. One may adduce the logic (and wider testimony) of *Le Cid*'s signal act of deferral to the essentially differential structure of the symbolisms to which we are condemned, always and in general, both by culture as such and by the forms in which cultures express themselves: what Derrida, generalizing the term to cover the entire spectrum of symbolic forms, calls *écriture* or "writing." [14] But we can also anchor it in *this* culture, at this particular point in its history, as a function of the specific modes of symbolic action that history prescribes. To read the text of Corneille's play, to read Corneille's play *as a text*, bearing the telltales of the historical moment of its making, we must first recall that it is not *simply* a text: as its functional destination not only as a work of poetic literature, but as the script for a public performance reminds us, it is also an expressly social phenomenon. Beyond what the play may have been meant for as an autonomous piece of dramatic verse, beyond what its author may have intended in fulfilment of a specific personal project or vision, is what was read into it as a reflex of reception: a reception that has left a text of its own in that of the controversy it occasioned in part as a direct reaction to its spectacular public success. [15]

It is moreover revealing as to the nature of writing itself that many features of the Cornelian project only become visible as a *reflex* of reception and response. Corneille hotly rejected the charges laid against the play: charges not only of aesthetic irregularity and dramaturgic incompetence, but of sexual perversion, political deviance, and an overweaning ambition or hubris manifested both in the conduct of his protagonists and in the notorious "Excuse à Ariste," in which the poet declines an invitation to set verses to music on the boastful grounds that his is no mere trilling lyric, but a

---

et la règle ne s'abritent pas dans l'inaccessible d'un secret, simplement elles ne se livrent jamais, au *présent*, à rien qu'on puisse rigoureusement nommer une perception. Au risque toujours et par essence de se perdre ainsi définitivement. Qui saura jamais telle disparition?" Jacques Derrida, *La dissémination* (Paris: Seuil, 1972) 71.

[14] On "écriture," particularly as generalized to yield what Derrida also calls "archi-écriture," see *De la grammatologie*, chap. 2, esp. 81-95.

[15] Though he does not discuss the *querelle* to this end, focusing rather on analogies between changes in understanding precipitated *within* the play by dramatic *peripeteia* and changes in understanding precipitated for subsequent readers by the evolving cultural history in which the play is inevitably caught up, see Lyons, *Tragedy of Origins* 8-11.

soaring *epic* Muse. The "Excuse" provoked indeed the first (and funniest) of the thirty-odd books, pamphlets, poems, and public letters generated during the year the controversy lasted: Jean Mairet's satiric "L'Autheur du vray Cid Espagnol à son Traducteur François," ridiculing the rival dramatist's grandiose claim that, Cardinal Richelieu's crucial early patronage notwithstanding, "Je ne dois qu'à moy seul toute ma Renommée." [16] And yet, illumined by their very envy and *malveillance*, his enemies may have seen more distinctly what he had written than did either Corneille or his adulating public.

We get a sense of what was at stake in the masterpiece of forensic hypotyposis mentioned a moment ago. Going before the King to demand Rodrigue's death in retribution for her father's, Chimène draws on all the verbal and gestural resources of rhetorical *enargeia* to paint a vivid picture of the murdered patriarch driving home the enormity of Rodrigue's crime: [17]

> Sire, mon père est mort, mes yeux on vu son sang
> Couler à grands bouillons de son généreux flanc,
> Ce sang qui tant de fois garantit vos murailles,
> Ce sang qui tant de fois vous gaigna des batailles,
> Ce sang qui tout sorti fume encor de courroux
> De se voir répandu pour d'autres que pour vous.
>
> (2.7.665-70)

However, in doing so she turns her own body into a living double of her father's bloody corpse:

> Il ne me parla point mais pour mieux m'émouvoir
> Son sang sur la poussière écrivait mon devoir,

---

[16] Pierre Corneille, "Excuse à Ariste," Gasté 64. For Mairet's *riposte*, Gasté 67-68. Mairet was doubtless the more sensitive to Corneille's boast in that both poets had collaborated in the group of "cinq auteurs" engaged by Richelieu to undertake the *mise en vers* of *La Comédie des Tuileries*, a verse play "invented" by Richelieu and composed under his close editorial supervision. See Couton's "notice," *Œuvres complètes* 1.1406-14 and *Richelieu* 25-31.

[17] On *enargeia* generally, see Jean Hagstrum, *The Sister Arts: The Tradition of Literary Pictorialism and English Poetry from Dryden to Gray* (Chicago: University of Chicago Press, 1958) 11-12. For *loci classici* in ancient rhetoric, see Aristotle, *Rhetoric* 3.11, Longinus, *On the Sublime* 15.2, Cicero, *Tusculan Disputations* 5.39.114, and Quintilian, *Institutio oratoria* 9.2.40-43.

Ou plutôt sa valeur, en cet état réduite,
Me parlait par sa plaie et hâtait ma poursuite.
Et pour se faire entendre au plus juste des Rois
Par cette triste bouche elle empruntait ma voix.

(2.7.685-90)

In the visceral present of dramatic events, unreflectingly experienced in the mode of Cartesian "passion" answering to the scene's rhetorical "action," [18] the speech offers an affecting spectacle of filial piety and grief. The daughter's exploitation of her vocal and physical presence on the royal stage as a means of making her dead father present to King and audience alike frames a direct appeal to a certain sentiment, indeed to a certain *sentimentality*, index of an underlying moral consensus. In its very vividness, Chimène's speech realizes the unconditional love the child "naturally" bears her progenitor and asserts the vengeful claims of honor and duty this love "naturally" commands–the proof of the play's commanding Nature being however just the dramatic expressiveness of words uttered in the apparent immediacy of scenic performance. And when we add what Chimène herself will not publicly confess until her momentous meeting with Rodrigue in 3.4, how the painful words she so "naturally" speaks cut across the love she continues to harbor for her father's killer, the effect is indeed overwhelming. Chimène gives us the perfect portrait of filial duty just because it demands the surrender of her own person formally entailed in the hypotypotic presentation of the paternal corpse.

---

[18] I allude to Descartes's *Passions de l'âme* (1649), esp. the contrast between the passive character of the "passions" and the external and internal "actions" that cause them, Article 1, "Que ce qui est passion au regard d'un sujet est toujours action à quelque autre égard," *Œuvres philosophiques* 3.951-52. This contrast is critical to Descartes's exposition in parts 1 and 2 of the physiological basis of the passions and the distinction between what we are made to feel by forces (including those of our own body) operating from "without" and the actions to which we determine ourselves from "within" by acts of rational will. But in calling the interplay of passion and action in Chimène's speech "Cartesian," I do not suggest that, decisive as it was to become for later representations of emotion, Corneille knew a text published a dozen years after *Le Cid*. Nor do I credit him at least at this stage with knowledge of so much as the *Discours de la méthode*, published in the same year as *Le Cid* (1637). The point is that (like Scudéry and Chapelain) Corneille reflects a pervasive sense of the passions on which Descartes draws to become its epitome.

To be sure, as a piece of hypotypotic rhetoric, the speech already implies, for all its dramatic immediacy, an act of composition and a related presence of mind designed, by canny play on its hearers' emotions, to provoke the *absence* of mind required to secure conviction in the cause for which the forensic picture enlists support. Yet even discounting the speech's rhetorical indirections, things are not so simple as they seem. Looked at more closely, *read* in fact as Corneille's enemies read it rather than passively experienced as the dramatic appearance in which contemporary audiences rejoiced, the speech turns out to be a dense tissue of symbolic cruxes largely concealed by the noble portrait of filial loyalty it means to be taken for.

Chief among these is the vampirelike feasting of Cornelian Fathers on their young. What we experience at the level of dramatic immediacy as exemplary self-abnegation proves at another properly uncanny. Thus we start with a transfer of epithets, a migration of the daughter's grieving sense of duty to the paternal corpse, infusing it with conscious life. Her attention fixed on the wound Rodrigue's sword has opened in her father's side, Chimène assigns *intent* to it: that with which, "pour mieux m'émouvoir / Son sang sur la poussière écrivait mon devoir." But what begins as a projection of Chimène's own commanding purpose on the inanimate corpse immediately becomes the expression of her father's *valeur*, his valor and inner value itself, which quite literally rises from the dead to *speak*: "Ou plutôt sa valeur, en cet état réduite, / Me parlait par sa plaie et hâtait ma poursuite." Further, just as the presiding figure of hypotyposis translates the speaker's physical presence into a screen on which listener and beholder project the scene her words and gestures evoke, so the paternal *valeur*, having spoken to Chimène, now *supplants* her in order to speak directly to the King. The bloody wound becomes the mouth through which the father's *valeur* ventriloquizes: "Et pour se faire entendre au plus juste des Rois / Par cette triste bouche elle empruntait ma voix."

We readily imagine what a Lacanian muse could make of all of this. Indeed, bearing in mind the feminine connotations of the term "flanc," which in period French not only designates (as here) the flank or side, but serves as a decorous metonymy for *ventre* or "womb," it is hard to resist pouncing on the intricate psycho-symbolic mechanisms legible in the text. Doubled by the daughter's

mouth, the maternal wound opened and bloodily inseminated by
Rodrigue's sword gives birth, in the paternal voice that speaks in
the daughter's place, to the phallic Identity that now demands retribution of the King. [19] However, it suffices for our present purpose
that, just beneath the surface of Chimène's dutiful self-effacement
on her father's behalf, lurks the ghost story of the father's vengeful
return, the paternal *revenant* rising in and as a radical act of filial
self-alienation. Demanding justice of the King, Chimène speaks not
merely for, but *as* her father: the father speaks in the daughter's
stead, violently usurping the seat of conscious self-expression in order to father *in* her his own desire for revenge. The dead progenitor's pursuit of Rodrigue's head replaces the daughter's orientation toward the seminal projection of which heads, swords, and
fatherly identities are alike symbolic doubles.

Which is not to deny the *sincerity* of Chimène's speech, though
Corneille's adversaries did in fact deny it, viewing in her subsequent
behavior, when enjoining Rodrigue (first at 3.4.950-54, and again,
on the brink of the hero's duel with Don Sanche, at 5.1.1511-32) to
defend the life she is honor-bound to seek, the hypocritical vitiation
of the sentiments she here piously espouses. What Scudéry and
Chapelain, champions of the normative unitary self-identity of classical, Cartesian psychology, interpret as hypocrisy is rather *ambivalence*: the doubleness they angrily denounce as a lie is the underlying *truth* of Chimène's desire. But while wrong, and even willfully
wrong, in insisting that the ambivalence shaping Chimène's speech
is and can only be fraud, they are yet entirely right in insisting on
the ambivalence itself.

We meet here a theme that marks Cornelian theater to the end,
and nowhere more powerfully than in *Horace* (1640), composed
during the sullen three-year interval following the *querelle du Cid* in
part to prove, by its exorbitant regularity, that its author can attain
the classical perfection his enemies allege is beyond him. [20] In the
monstrously unfeeling deeds of the eponymous "hero," who not

---

[19] See, e.g., Greenberg, *Corneille* and *Subjectivity and Subjugation*, esp. chap. 2,
"The grateful dead: Corneille's tragedy and the subject of history," which has much
to say about *Le Cid*. We shall focus more specifically on the Lacanian theory of
identity in chap. 4 with reference to Molière.

[20] As we shall see more particularly in chap. 2, it is remarkable how deeply
Corneille's later writings bear the stamp of the fierce reactions *Le Cid* inspired.

only massacres the more human (and ambivalent) Curiaces, a trio of brothers to whom he is tragically united by friendship and marriage, but murders his own sister because, unlike him, she defiantly asserts the primacy of the heart over the claims of national and family honor, we see precisely the *lack* of ambivalence the Observateur and Académie require of Chimène. Consumed by the will of the father whose name he bears–being indeed, as "Horace," the murderous reproduction of "le vieil Horace" himself–the son who succeeds the daughter in Corneille offers a spectacle so piteous and frightening that even the King, the monarchic embodiment of the Roman State for whose sake these horrors have been committed, recoils in dismay, prevented from putting him to death solely by the unhappy consciousness of the nation's debt to him:

> Cette énorme action faite presque à nos yeux
> Outrage la Nature, et blesse jusqu'aux Dieux.
> Un premier mouvement qui produit un tel crime
> Ne saurait lui servir d'excuse légitime,
> Les moins sévères lois en ce point sont d'accord,
> Et si nous les suivons, il est digne de mort.
> Si d'ailleurs nous voulons regarder le coupable,
> Ce crime quoique grand, énorme, inexcusable,
> Vient de la même épée et part du même bras
> Qui me fait aujourd'hui maître de deux Etats.
> Deux sceptres en ma main, Albe à Rome asservie,
> Parlent bien hautement en faveur de sa vie.
> Sans lui j'obéirais où je donne la loi,
> Et je serais Sujet où je suis deux fois Roi. [21]

What registers in *Horace* as tragedy proper because the son fails to achieve an identity distinct from the father's is just the ambivalence that, in *Le Cid*, yields the doubleness thanks to which, even as she pursues Rodrigue's death, Chimène preserves her own desire intact, fending off, in the generic hybrid of "tragi-comedy," the tragedy *tout court* at which the later play arrives. But the essential point remains in either case the same: the unconquerable resistance Cornelian sons and daughters oppose, as the fundamental condition of their nature and witness, to the fathers who define them.

---

[21] Pierre Corneille, *Horace*, in *Œuvres complètes* 5.3.1733-46.

Still, more is at stake in Corneille than the respect owed even the most tyrannical of fathers. Invoking the Horatian commonplace according to which "le Poeme de Theâtre fut inventé, pour instruire en divertissant," Scudéry reminds his readers that beneath the alluring exterior of dramatic entertainment "se deguise la Philosophie, de peur de paroistre trop austere aux yeux du monde," gilding the pills of moral instruction "afin qu'on les prenne sans repugnance, et qu'on se trouve guary presque sans avoir connu le remede." Now, Philosophy never fails

> de nous montrer sur la Scene, la vertu recompensée et le vice tousjours puni. Que si quelquefois l'on y voit les mechans prosperer, et les gens de bien persecutez, la face des choses, ne manquant point de changer, à la fin de la Representation, ne manque aussi de faire voir, le triomphe des innocens, et le suplice des coupables: et c'est ainsi qu'insensiblement, on nous imprime en l'ame l'horreur du vice, et l'amour de la vertu. (79-80)

In *Le Cid*, by contrast, everything is reversed:

> l'on y voit une fille desnaturée ne parler que de ses follies, lors qu'elle ne doit parler que de son malheur, pleindre la perte de son Amant, lors qu'elle ne doit songer qu'a celle de son pere; aimer encor ce qu'elle doit abhorrer; souffrir en mesme temps, et en mesme maison, ce meurtrier et ce pauvre corps; et pour achever son impieté, joindre sa main à celle qui dégoute encor du sang de son pere. Apres ce crime qui fait horreur, le spectateur n'a t'il pas raison, de penser qu'il va partir un coup de foudre, du ciel representé sur la Scene, pour chatier cette Danaide? Ou s'il sçait cette autre regle qui deffend d'ensanglanter le Theatre, n'a t'il pas subjet de croire, qu'aussi tost qu'elle en sera partie, un Messager viendra pour le moins, luy apprendre ce chastiment? mais cependant, ni l'un ni l'autre n'arrive; au contraire, le Roy carresse cette impudique; son vice y paroist rescompensé, la vertu semble bannie de la conclusion de ce Poeme; il est une instruction au mal, un aiguillon pour nous y pousser; et par ces fautes remarquables et dangereuses, directement opposé, aux principales Regles Dramatiques. (80)

Beyond the "criminal" evasion of filial duty in the interests of consummating a passion scandalously underwitten by the King himself is the undermining of public morality at large as embodied in the murdered symbol of moral right. The Nature touchingly asserted in the heroine's speech before the King is radically subverted by her subsequent words and deeds.

But Chimène's actions undermine not just the natural moral order on which the Observateur and Académie insist, but the political order meant to supplement moral nature by imposing its law from above. The death of the Father and ensuing triumph of unnatural vice presage the demise of the King whose office it is to guarantee both paternal right and moral law by lending them the support of raw political might. *Le Cid* is famous above all for the love story at its heart; but the love story doubles as a Fable of the State.

As the unusually precise title in the *dramatis personae* reminds us, the historical monarch at whose court the action occurs is not just any, but specifically the *first* Castilian king, a monarch charged not simply with defending, but with founding his kingdom. The family romance fuses with the drama of political foundation. [22] The catastrophic feud between the two fathers erupts, after all, from the King's choice of a governor for his son, a choice on which the monarchy itself depends: Fernand's own legitimacy, his very existence as "the first" and thus true King, hinges on transmitting the crown to a second, the father's possession being secured only by the accession of an heir. [23] It is moreover during the period of chaos provoked by the King's choice that the Moors invade the kingdom; and in the concluding scene, Fernand overlooks the wrong Rodrigue has done Chimène in killing her father not just because, in accord with feudal laws whose persistence is itself an important piece of the play's political puzzle, Rodrigue has "won" her by defeating her champion in a duel, but because Rodrigue has successfully replaced Don Gomès as commander of the royal army in the rescue of Castile. The marriage of Rodrigue and Chimène and the creation of the Castilian kingdom, first step in the historical emergence of the Christian monarchy of Spain, are facets of a single

---

[22] Merlin touches on this question in *Public et littérature*, chap. 7, "*Le Cid* et *L'amour tyrannique*: exaltation ou abaissement de la puissance particulière."

[23] For a recent analysis of the centrality of primogenitive succession to early modern conceptions not only of monarchy, but also of authorship, see Richard Goodkin, *Birth Marks: The Tragedy of Primogeniture in Pierre Corneille, Thomas Corneille, and Jean Racine* (Philadelphia: University of Pennsylvania Press, 2000).

problem, that of securing the basis of monarchy itself: a problem whose socio-political implications are all the greater given the troubled moment in French history at which *Le Cid* was composed and staged.

Ever since the publication of Voltaire's *Siècle de Louis XIV* in 1751, our understanding of the French seventeenth century has been colored by a teleological illusion fostered in the era itself by Charles Perrault's *Siècle de Louis le Grand* (1687): a poem much of whose interest lies in having triggered, through its fulsome praise of the "new" classical age over which Louis presided, the famous *querelle des anciens et des modernes*. [24] Bewitched in part by the aesthetic perfection of absolutist propaganda, the high official art enlisting Poussin, Le Brun, and Mignard, Boileau, Molière, and Racine as well as "le grand Corneille" himself, we tend to describe the political ideology of the reign of Louis XIV as though it were as inevitable, as monolithically entrenched, and as systematically representative of the *grand siècle* at large as it presented itself as being. Like the hapless Charles Stuart, who lost his kingdom because he construed divine right as a fact rather than a duty, [25] we are blinded to the factitiousness of the era's "greatness" by that of the fictions promoting it. But as Marc Fumaroli forcefully reminds us, though largely overshadowed by the towering Olympus of high official art, the Parnassus of free aesthetic creation remains populated all the same, and often by the same figures Versailles coopts in the monarch's cause. [26] Further, a growing number of scholars–John Lyons, Harriet Stone, Hélène Merlin, and, despite his psychoanalytic commitment to the primacy of a certain cultural unconscious inimical to critical perspicuousness on period poets' part, Mitchell Greenberg–have come to acknowledge that the importance of plays like *Le Cid* or the later *Horace* and *Cinna* is less the absolutist order they celebrate as "historically" won than the registration of everything that militates against it. French drama thus exhibits the political tensions more comfortably associated with Lope de Vega's

---

[24] See Hans Robert Jauss's intro. to the facsimile of Perrault's *Parallèle des anciens et des modernes* (1688-97; Munich: W. Fink, 1964) and DeJean, *Ancients against Moderns*.

[25] See Stephen Orgel, *The Illusion of Power: Political Theater in the English Renaissance* (Berkeley: University of California Press, 1975) 77-87.

[26] See Fumaroli, *Le Poète et le Roi*, chap. 1, "L'Olympe et le Parnasse."

Fuenteovejuna and Calderón's *Alcalde de Zalamea* or the fantasies of self-ratifying royal right enacted in the masques of the Stuart age.[27]

The France of *Le Cid* was not that of the *roi-soleil*, Louis XIV, uncontested master of France since the notorious *prise du pouvoir* of 1661, but that of Louis XIII, a sovereign whose footing was far more insecure than that of his magnificent son. The reign of Louis XIII lies in the shadow of the assassination of the King's father, Henri IV, founder of the Bourbon dynasty whose rise brought the disastrous civil wars of the sixteenth century to an end; and it opens with the turbulent regency of Louis's mother, Marie de' Medici, who inflicted on her dead husband's kingdom not only the odious Italian adventurer Concini, but a foreign policy favoring the Hapsburg Empire and Kingdom of Spain at French expense. Thus the France of 1637 still struggles to define its political identity. True, 1637 also witnesses the apogee of *le grand cardinal*, Richelieu, who instituted a centralized bureaucracy, eradicated Huguenot separatism, curbed the pretensions of the traditional nobility, and secured expanded French borders by cynically siding with the anti-imperial Protestant alliance in the Thirty Years War. But quite apart from the fact that it was Richelieu's historic task to *create* the framework for the absolutist state Louis's son would finally make his own, his mere existence as a source of authority distinct from his master's is a sign of the dynamic uncertainties characterizing the period: hereditary duke as well as cardinal-minister, Richelieu exemplifies the fractious nobility Corneille's Don Fernand must overcome to secure the peace of Castile.[28] Nor could even Richelieu protect France from the civil strife to which the regency of Anne d'Autriche reduced it after Louis's death in 1643: an era marked by yet another powerful minister, Mazarin, and by the *Frondes* of 1648 and 1650, insurrections that for a time threatened a revolution

---

[27] This is a major theme in Lyons's *Tragedy of Origins*. See too Stone, *The Classical Model*, chap. 1, "Frame Theory: Foucault, Rotrou, and Corneille," and Merlin, "*Cinna, Rodogune, Nicomède*: Le Roi et le moi" and "Corneille et la politique dans *Cinna, Rodogune* et *Nicomède*." Greenberg's *Canonical States, Canonical Stages* offers a valuable comparative perspective, relating Cornelian psycho-politics to Calderón and Shakespeare. This interpretation dates back to Bénichou's *Morales du grand siècle*, which identifies Cornelian heroism with the feudal individualism first Richelieu and then, following his *prise du pouvoir* in 1661, Louis XIV combated.

[28] For a wonderful study of Richelieu, see Jouhaud, *La Main de Richelieu*.

comparable to the one sealed in Britain with the beheading of Charles I in 1649.

Far from being a given of seventeenth-century French politics, absolutism, like Cartesian dualism, a philosophical creed with which it has much in common, [29] is more an unfulfillable project than a positive doctrine commanding behavior and belief. Nor is it that, as Louis Marin puts it, the "désir absolu" shaping absolutist theory encodes its own impossibility. [30] Just as dualism is defeated by the embodying mental, cultural, and historical contingencies that frame the skeptical dilemmas from which Descartes seeks to wrest objective knowledge, so the very social and political factors that make absolutism desirable prevent its achievement.

With the founding of monarchic Spain, the European model of successful nationhood since the emperor Charles V, Corneille invokes a history in which France finds the mirror of its own longings and of the dangers that block their realization. All of which gives a sharper edge to Scudéry's indignation not only at how ill-served Corneille's Don Fernand is, but at how poorly he fulfils his office *as King*. Whence the following huffy commentary on the scene in which, to force Chimène publicly to confess the private sentiments of love for Rodrigue her role as her father's avenger has heretofore compelled her to conceal, Don Fernand decides to pretend that her lover has died of wounds received in battle with the invading Moors:

> pour découvrir le crime de Chimene [her love for Rodrigue], le Roy s'y sert de la plus méchante finesse du monde, et mal gré ce que le Theatre demande de serieux en cette occasion, il fait agir ce sage Prince, comme un enfant qui seroit bien enjoué, en la quatriesme Scene du quatriesme Acte. Là, dans une action de

---

[29] Timothy J. Reiss challenges this view of the political entailments of Cartesian thought in "Descartes, the Palatinate, and the Thirty Years War: Political Theory and Political Practice" in *Baroque Topographies: Literature/History/Philosophy*, ed. Timothy Hampton, *Yale French Studies* 80 (New Haven: Yale University Press, 1991) 108-45. Reiss is right that Descartes's individualist resistance to intellectual authority democratizes thought along broadly liberal lines. Still, the centralizing and authoritarian tendencies exhibited, e.g., by the metaphor of modern, rational urban planning as contrasted with the random civic sprawl of medieval cities (*Discours, Œuvres philosophiques* 1.579), point in the opposite direction.

[30] Louis Marin, *Le portrait du roi* (Paris: Minuit, 1981) 11-13.

telle importance, ou sa justice devoit être balancée avec la victoire de Rodrigue [over the Moors], au lieu de la rendre a Chimene, qui feint de la luy demander, il s'amuse à luy faire piece; veut esprouver si elle aime son Amant; et en un mot, le Poete luy oste sa Couronne de dessus la teste pour le coiffer d'une Marote. Il devoit traiter avec plus de respect, la personne des Roys que l'on nous aprend estre sacrée; et considérer celuy cy dans le Throsne de Castille, et non pas comme sur le Theatre de Mondory. (93)

It does not matter what Corneille said he meant by *Le Cid*: the political, moral, and aesthetic anxieties contemporary audiences brought to the theater imprinted symbolic meanings as real as any the author put in the play. His depiction of antinomian love and its catalyzing impact on the court of *Le Cid*'s inescapably exemplary monarch is in every sense an unavoidably historical act. If the play ends, not with the bang of authentic climax, but with the whimper of temporizing evasion, it is because the historical issues willingly and unwillingly joined leave no choice.

But in asserting the need to interpret *Le Cid*'s "Hymen différé" as bearing an historical witness it can neither own nor deny, I want also to stress the perfect awareness with which, even as a reflex of its historical situation, the text inscribes its inability to reach closure and impose unitary order on the tensions at its base. It is easier, at this convenient historical distance, than it could have been at the time to make out where the fault lines lie: we, after all, are now able to *read* in the texts it has left us what the era itself was obliged blindly to *write*. But we will miss the point of such closure as the play does achieve, and thus the motive (should we want one) for a further, deeper deconstruction, if we fail to see how far the play has already done the work for us. It would force the issue to claim that the scene's deconstruction, its form and necessity, is what the play is consciously *for*. Nevertheless, its inevitability–that something of this sort must happen–is what it is consciously *about*. The inability to make things fit is no mere lapsus or *acte manqué*; it is the burden of what *Le Cid* fundamentally rehearses on behalf of the audience gathered in the space of collective representation that is the theater. What is more, the inability to close is conditioned, and is expressly *known* to be conditioned, by the form both of representation itself and of the consciousness with which it is confederate.

The development this historical reading suggests unfolds in two phases. One focuses on general conditions of representation in the culture that produced this particular play at this point in its history. The other bears on the more specific problem raised, in an unmistakably political register, by the terms under which such representations were *received* by the culture they served. These two phases are closely related. We have seen the *querelle*'s impact on Corneille's subsequent writing: production and reception, it is clear, inform each other at every point, and especially in an art like theater, where the text (or script) comes fully into its own only in the physical and emotional presence of a living audience. Much that I will say about the play's production will therefore engage questions of reception: how the form of the representation shapes reception, and how conditions of reception participate in the form that shapes them–a point of special interest being how both production and reception relate to the King, a figure in whom they remarkably and problematically fuse.

Still, it may help to begin by separating things out. Part of what makes *Le Cid* so compelling is how far it is exemplary of early modern theater generally, and in particular the tensions and contradictions–social, political, and ideological as well as moral and aesthetic–characterizing the peculiar perspective that frames early modern theater. But this already means that much of its interest stems from the light it sheds on the broader cultural situation theater at once reflects and mediates as a collective mode of representation, and more especially as a collective mode of that *form* of representation in which the early modern era found the model of all representation as such, namely, *picturing*.[31] So let us open the next phase of the exposition by casting an eye on an image that seems uniquely representative of the wider pictorial tradition to which dramatic art belongs.[32]

The image in question is *Belshazzar's Feast* by Rembrandt (fig. 1). It is a classic instance of what early modern images (theatrical as well as painterly) were for and did: a spirited example of Western

---

[31] On the pictorial sense of representation even in early modern theories of language, see Louis Marin, *Critique du discours*, chaps. 2 and 3. For Marin's application of the identification of picture and word to the figure of the King, see the intro. to *Le portrait du roi*.

[32] See my *Refiguring the Real: Picture and Modernity in Word and Image, 1400-1700* (Princeton: Princeton University Press, 1993). The following discussion of *Belshazzar's Feast* follows closely *Refiguring the Real* 17-19.

Figure 1. Rembrandt van Rijn, *Belshazzar's Feast.* Oil on canvas. Courtesy of the National Gallery, London. Photo: National Gallery

"history painting" in the form of a vigorously expressive treatment of the famous story of the Writing on the Wall in the Book of Daniel. The portrayal as such–the devices it deploys and persuasive force it exerts–is part of the visual message. Representing the scene, Rembrandt expounds representation itself, foregrounding art's at once minute and encyclopedic command over the world of sense: its capacity to convey the look and feel of people and things, textures and volumes, surfaces and light; its sensitivity to the intricate nuances of human individuals, so multifarious in physique and physiognomy, expression, character, and type; and even its power, despite its formal confinement within the "timeless" space of the visual moment, to seize the flight of time itself–in wine spilling from a goblet, or in the frozen attitude of the King apprehended in the very instant when, reaching out upon the feast, he catches sight of the mystic hand tracing its fatal characters on the wall.

Yet the story on which Rembrandt lavishes his gifts is remarkable for its hostility toward the art that communicates it, representing not only a classic *vanitas* motif, a Mirror for Magistrates warning of the fate awaiting all men (Dutch democrats and Bourbon or Hapsburg despots alike), but a signal episode in the career of an exemplary iconoclast: the prophet Daniel, canny nemesis of all idols and idol-worshippers. What precipitates the ruin spelled out on the wall is not just Belshazzar's tyrannical hubris, but the way, drinking sacrilegious wine from the gold and silver vessels despoiled from the House of God in Jerusalem, "the king and his lords, his wives, and his concubines... praised the gods of gold and silver, bronze, iron, wood, and stone": gods the painting itself venerates in the exhaustive care expended on the scene's densely variegated materiality. *Belshazzar's Feast* is thus something of a paradox: a spectacular *eidolon*, an idol or likeness harnessing Rembrandt's gifts in an image one of whose lessons is the destruction of images as such. The MENE MENE TEKEL UPHARSIN breaks in on Rembrandt's picture as violently as on the idolatrous revels: a mystic defacement reminding us of the numbering, weighing, and dividing by which art too is finally brought to book. [33]

---

[33] On the general background of iconoclasm, esp. in the Protestant North of Rembrandt, see Ernest B. Gilman, *Iconoclasm and Poetry in the English Reformation: Dagon Went Down* (Chicago: University of Chicago Press, 1986) and David Freedberg, *The Power of Images: Studies in the History and Theory of Response* (Chicago: University of Chicago Press, 1989).

But the teaching the picture conveys at its own expense owes its singular efficacy to the art it condemns: the representation affirms its peculiar vocation in the dramatic clarity with which it mounts the spectacle of its erasure. Nor should we overlook how the figuration of its iconomachic moral and the vainglorious exhibition of its mimetic power are intimately related in the person of its biblical hero, he whose story it indirectly tells and whose point of view it espouses in telling it: not the idolatrous Belshazzar, but the iconoclast, Daniel. Rembrandt and Daniel share far more than at first appears, and in particular their common concealment in an image in which both of them are so much in question. For what characterizes both is their common profession as *masters of illusion*, dominating the sensory world that destroys the blind Babylonian tyrant.

Rather than hide, Rembrandt *proclaims* his art, celebrating its capacity to deceive the beholder's senses. But by celebrating it, he denounces the machinery of his own deluding fiction. Nor does this essentially differ from the gesture by which, in the apocryphal stories of Susanna and Bel, Daniel exposes the false witness of the adulterous Elders or the priestly deceit by which the idol of brass and clay appears miraculously to consume the food and wine laid out for it each night. Though Daniel wields the exegetic power of the Word and the critical intelligence it imparts, the world he illumines is no different from the one Rembrandt paints. The vehicle of divine retribution is in the end all too worldly, being *politics* in the form of the rapacious Medes by whom the Babylonian monarch is overthrown: the God of Daniel's prophecies is the God of History too. [34] Exposing the lie at the source of apparent truth, Daniel, like Rembrandt, opens a window on a world of concrete causes and effects by which Belshazzar is destroyed less because he idolatrously embraces than because he is so stupidly blind to it. What is more, in addition to being a prophet, and as a condition of his prophecy, the biblical hero is also a detective and judge: forerunner, as Francis

---

[34] The intimate link between Judaism and historical thought, esp. from the 17th century on, is powerfully suggested by Yirmiyahu Yovel's recent interpretation of the historico-cultural background to Spinoza's philosophy of immanence in *The Marrano of Reason*, the first part of a 2-volume study, *Spinoza and Other Heretics* (Princeton: Princeton University Press, 1989).

Bacon liked to hint, of the "natural philosopher," prototype of the modern physical scientist. [35]

The ultimate "subject" of *Belshazzar's Feast*, both its theme or object and the viewpoint from which it is seen, is then a certain form, a certain *consciousness*, and the perspective of which this consciousness is both the product and bearer: source at once of illusion and of the critical insight that exposes this illusion in favor of a more authentic grasp of the real. It expresses a certain power, but also a certain *antinomy*, of perspective and thus of method, in which we already discern an image of our critical modernity: the faithful portrait of our own ambivalent posture before works of verbal and visual art.

A major expression of this ambivalence is Erwin Panofsky's distinction between "monuments" and "documents," a distinction whose importance in art history has been extended to the interpretation of Western culture at large by Michel Foucault, who uses it to crystallize the conceptual bifocalism without which his "archeology," as method and historical attitude, would be unthinkable. [36] And it is important precisely because it applies less to things themselves than to how we *perceive* them. One can look upon a work of art (visual, architectural, literary, philosophical, scientific) from either of two mutually exclusive points of view. One regards it as an end in itself, embraced for its own sake and on its own terms, in what Foucault calls its "volume propre," as defining or imposing its own horizon. The other regards it not for itself, but as an index of, or proxy for, the presumptive causes or determinants that lie "behind" or "beneath" it, things of which it is a sign and yet which it also displaces and covers up: the history of its author or public; the era, society, or culture that produced it; its formal conditions of

---

[35] See, e.g., Francis Bacon, *The New Organon and Related Writings*, ed. Fulton H. Anderson (Indianapolis: Bobbs-Merrill, 1960) 92. On the extraordinary legacy of the prophet Daniel in 17th-century philosophy and science generally, see my essay, "The Vindication of Susanna: Femininity and Truth in Early Modern Science and Art," in *Yearbook of Comparative and General Literature* 40 (1992) 41-58, and *Refiguring the Real* 169-70.

[36] See Erwin Panofsky, "The History of Art as a Humanistic Discipline," *Meaning in the Visual Arts* (Chicago: University of Chicago Press, 1955; Phoenix paper ed.) 10-14. For Foucault's use, see *L'archéologie du savoir* (Paris: Gallimard, 1969) 182-83. But see too Marin, *Le portrait du roi* 150-56.

possibility; the psychic energies and mechanisms that make it go. Nor do these viewpoints merely compete as complementary opposites; the one destroys the other: the document ruins the monument as which it first appears.

This insight explains a number of things, and for a start why the adduction of causes, contexts, and conditions is always to some extent experienced (and practised) as iconoclasm. It also accounts for the prosecutorial tone into which critical discourse so easily slips: interpretation as denunciation, a call to judgment–the MENE MENE TEKEL UPHARSIN of causal analysis exploding the self-ratifying delusions of art, emptying them of their ostensible, officially "intended" meanings to reveal the brute contingencies they emerge from and must conceal. Whence the marked family resemblance characterizing our most potent and prestigious procedures: Marxian materialism, Nietzschean "symptomology," Freudian analysis, figural, new historical, or feminist "deconstruction" exposing the false consciousness, repression, sublimation, or violent denial on which our monuments stand as upon feet of clay.[37]

But Panofsky's distinction also helps locate the nagging sense of betrayal in Stephen Greenblatt's curiously abortive second thoughts about the method with which he has become identified. Worrying about his inability to articulate the sense of "wonder" somehow central to our interest in literature and art, Greenblatt takes up the theme of wonder itself. Yet the remedy reproduces the malaise, turning wonder into an historical theme subjected to an increasingly reflex historical reduction: the Renaissance *Wunderkammer* exposed as yet another emblem of cultural expropriation.[38] But the point here is emphatically not that such methods are in some way wrong; on the contrary, they are the best we have. The

---

[37] The "feet of clay" metaphor also derives from Daniel, in the great idol destroyed in Nebuchadnezzar's Dream. The story figures in Pascal's typology (*Pensées*, Lafuma 329, 485; Sellier 361, 720). The relation to the famous fragment on the "imagination" of the King (Lafuma 25; Sellier 59) is obvious.

[38] See Stephen Greenblatt, "Resonance and Wonder," in *Learning to Curse: Essays in Early Modern Culture* (New York: Routledge, 1990) 161-83. See also the intro. to his *Marvelous Possessions: The Wonder of the New World* (Chicago: University of Chicago Press, 1991) 1-25, where a similar nostalgia succumbs to a like reduction.

problem rather inheres to method as such, an ineluctable concomitant of learning to know or understand. [39]

Yet we need to remember that our documents are also *monuments*, at some level accessible only to idolators: objects before which idolatry is the only appropriate posture. [40] For all his conceited blindness, Belshazzar is in one sense right after all; nor could art do without him–Rembrandt's, Daniel's, or Corneille's. Above all, we must never forget (as the painting also shows) how far the monument may enact its own documentary ruin, not only anticipating, but programmatically inviting its destruction as an integral moment of what it is and does, of what it communicates and stands for. This gesture presupposes moreover an important fact about human beings: *self-determination, and the dimension (wafer-thin as it may be) of perspicuous self-awareness it implies, is the condition of our conditioning.* And what is true of human beings is equally true of what Michael Baxandall calls those "deposits," those residues or vestiges of social acts, choices, and relationships, that are works of art. [41]

---

[39] This is the deep problem shaping the "epistemo-critical prologue" to Walter Benjamin, *The Origin of German Tragic Drama,* trans. John Osborne (London: New Left Books, 1977; Verso paper ed., 1985) 27-56. But as the source of Benjamin's epigraph, the Goethe of the *Farbenlehre,* grasped, this same problem informs not only Kant's discussion of Beauty as the hypotypotic "Symbol of Morality" (*Critique of Judgment,* section 59), but the role he grants aesthetics in mediating between the horizonlessly sensible world of scientific objectivity and the objectlessly supersensible world of the subjective experience of moral and teleological value. Nor is it a coincidence that all of this leads to a crux of contemporary theory: the Romantic notion of the Symbol and its "allegorical" deconstruction in Paul de Man's "The Rhetoric of Temporality," in *Blindness and Insight: Essays in the Rhetoric of Contemporary Criticism,* 2nd, revised ed. (Minneapolis: University of Minnesota Press, 1983) 187-228.

[40] A similar insight (or anxiety) induces Foucault to insist in the passage cited earlier that his method is not an "interpretive discipline," an "allegorical" procedure seeking "an 'other discourse'" behind or beneath the "proper volume" of the historical discourses that form its monuments (*L'archéologie du savoir* 182). It is nevertheless typical of method in general, and contemporary method in particular, that the characteristic effect of Foucaldian analysis is the exact opposite of what he claims for it: a point Derrida makes in his critique of Foucault's famous reading in *Histoire de la folie* (56-58) of the place of madness in Descartes's First Meditation. See "Cogito et histoire de la folie," *L'écriture et la différence* (Paris: Seuil, 1967; Points paper ed.) 51-97.

[41] Michael Baxandall, *Painting and Experience in Fifteenth-Century Italy* (Oxford: Oxford University Press, 1972; 2nd ed., 1988) 1. See too his strictures on "tact" in *Patterns of Intention: On the Historical Explanation of Pictures* (New Haven: Yale University Press, 1985) 1-11 and 105-37.

It is finally against this background that we should look at *Le Cid*. *Le Cid* is certainly a monument of French and (ongoing French insistence on the period's classical character to the contrary) more generally *baroque* dramatic art; in some respects it is the very essence of the thing.[42] Yet much of what makes it the monument it is–much of what makes it baroque–is just the acknowledgement of being at risk: the lucid admission of the causes, conditions, and desires to which our methods reduce it. Part, in fact, of the specific mission a baroque monument undertakes, especially of the "high," heroic sort to which *Le Cid* unmistakably belongs, is the attempt to preempt its own documentary ruin by first incorporating and then idealizing and transforming its motives.[43]

Consider the range of explosive, incorrigibly "low" and messy forces the play tries to bind up in the at once delightful and perilously improbable romance at its heart. *Le Cid* is about unabashedly carnal desire: Chimène's gloriously resonant "je me meurs" (3.4.865) on discovering Rodrigue in her presence shows as much.[44]

---

[42] The acrimonious debate about whether 17th-century France experienced a baroque continues to this day. In favor, see Jean Rousset, *La Littérature de l'âge baroque en France: Circe et le paon* (Paris: Corti, 1954), Pierre Charpentrat, *Le mirage baroque* (Paris: Minuit, 1967), Jean-François Maillard, *Essai sur l'esprit du héros baroque (1580-1640): le même et l'autre* (Paris: Nizet, 1973), John D. Lyons, *A Theatre of Disguise: Studies in French Baroque* Drama (Columbia, SC: French Literature Publications, 1978), Mitchell Greenberg, *Detours of Desire: Readings in the French Baroque* (Columbus: Ohio State University Press, 1984), Bernard Chedozeau, *Le Baroque* (Paris: Nathan, 1989), and Jean-Claude Vuillemin, *Baroquisme et théâtralité: le théâtre de Jean Rotrou* (Paris: Papers on French Seventeenth-Century Literature, 1994).

[43] See Gordon D. McGregor's shrewd remark that "history" as "sequence, a fleeting and unceasing diachrony in which the individual moment can never be fixed," is "the real enemy of Cornelian ethos, the real object of the Cornelian *entreprise* construed as an incessant, ongoing campaign," in "*Rodogune, Nicomède*, and the Status of History in Corneille," *Stanford French Review* 11 (Summer 1987) 136. This idea is also central to Lyons's *Tragedy of Origins*.

[44] The unmistakably carnal resonance of this encounter underscores the weakness of the reading of *Le Cid* recently proposed by Judovitz in *The Culture of the Body*, chap. 5, "Incorporations: Royal Power, or the Social Body in Corneille's *Le Cid*." Judovitz's thesis is that, in *Le Cid*, "the body's identity as a physical organism is consistently violated by the indiscriminate exchange of bodily parts, which are traded as currency in the service of personal glory or for the sake of the king. This disarticulation of the body as a physical organism will coincide in the play with its social reorganization and incorporation in the body politic of a monarchy whose political economy inaugurates the emergence of the absolutist state." (111) Judovitz is right about the issues the play joins. However, wed to the old idea of a hegemonic

It is also about politics, and about revenge, pitting body against soul, inner person against social persona, reason against appetite, the obligations of heredity against the promptings of the heart. It disguises none of these things, aiming rather to turn them into the cranky periodic music of the baroque *tirade*, digested and metamorphosed into the tricky, pulsing architecture of paradox and antithesis, ironic parallel and chiastic inversion. To be sure, at one level all of this is almost irresistibly comic, an amazing amalgam of high seriousness and high camp. But the insidious risk of irreverent laughter is not only part of the pleasure; it is part of the *point*–what still lends currency to Serge Doubrovsky's existential take on Corneille. [45] The play's stupendous symmetries, the lethal *pas-de-deux* in which hero and heroine choreograph each other's ruin as an act of purest, most passionate love, is utterly absurd. But that is just what makes it *heroic*: an inspiring vision of what human beings might be framed by the exposition of that vision's precarious implausibility.

Even at their most sublime, baroque monuments are equivocal things, shot through with the now poignant, now sardonic awareness of their own illusoriness. They are invariably a prey to the critical intellect alone capable of creating such elaborate contraptions. Bacon's "Of Masques and Triumphs" proves paradigmatic in this regard. The essay is essentially a meditation on the *how* of the masque: how the dances should be arranged; how the antic element should be handled; what music is most suitable; which male voices sound best; which colors show to most advantage in the candlelight by which settings and costumes are seen. But Bacon, for whom besides theater provides one of the more pertinacious models for the famous Idols of the Mind, [46] begins by making a show of contempt: "These things are but toys to come amongst such serious observations." If he writes about them at all, it is because, despite

---

Cartesian dualism committed to the service of a triumphant political absolutism, she misses how adamantly Corneille's play resists both. This same tendency informs Greenberg's analysis of the play in "The grateful dead."

[45] Serge Doubrovsky, *Corneille et la dialectique du héros* (Paris: Gallimard, 1963).

[46] See Bacon, *New Organon* 49, where he writes of the deluding power of intellectual systems: "These I call Idols of the Theater, because in my judgment all the received systems are so many stage plays representing worlds of their own creation after an unreal and scenic fashion."

their inanity, his royal masters like them, a satiric jab linked to his complaint about the one feature of masques that is real and important, the enormous sums of money they consume: "But yet, since princes will have such things, it is better they should be graced with elegancy than daubed with cost." [47] In fact the gesture of dismissal and the technical analysis of means rise from one root: he can write so cogently about how to mount masques just because, seeing them for the toys they are, he does not succumb to their spell. His disabused matter-of-factness speaks for his power to discern the rationally apprehensible, and thus eminently manipulable, causal machinery behind them.

Nor is this unique to Bacon, iconophobic both as a Protestant and as a natural scientist dedicated not just to the *observation* of nature, checking the vulgar pipedreams of human sense, habit, custom, prejudice, and vanity against the data of empirical experience, but to what he calls the *interpretation* of nature, working back from these data, taken as signs, to the underlying causal mechanisms that produce them. As commentators like Marin and Peter Burke have observed, one of the more remarkable features of the French seventeenth century's mythologizing discourse of the absolutist sovereign is the entire lucidity with which it both acknowledges and exploits its own artificiality. [48] And our own author, the Jesuit-trained Corneille himself, gives proof of a similar attitude in another, earlier play, *L'Illusion comique*.

Meant first and last as an apology for dramatic poetry, [49] the play

---

[47] "Masques and Triumphs," *The Essayes or Counsels, Civill and Morall* (1625), Essay 37, in *Francis Bacon: A Selection of His Works*, ed. Sidney Warhaft (London: Macmillan, 1965) 145.

[48] This is a major theme of Marin's *Portrait du roi*, but see too Burke, *Fabrication of Louis XIV*, chap. 1, for its careful distinction between "fabrication" as deliberate fiction, propagandistic magnification, or falsehood and "fabrication" as the construction of an ideal to which the monarch ought to rise and conform–a model indeed of what he is in his capacity *as* monarch regardless of how he conducts himself in his private person. Also see Marc Soriano, *La brosse à reluire sous Louis XIV: "L'Epître au roi" de Perrault, annotée par Racine et Boileau* (Paris: Nizet, 1989), for the sardonic delight with which the two *anciens* critique their rival *moderne*'s text for its failure to walk the fine line between flattery and boorish "flagornerie."

[49] On the general context in which such a defense seemed necessary, see Fumaroli, "Rhétorique et dramaturgie dans *L'Illusion comique*" and "*Sacerdos sive rhetor, orator sive histrio*," *Héros et orateurs* 261-87 and 449-91 respectively. For a more general view, see Jonas A. Barish, *The Antitheatrical Prejudice* (Berkeley: University of California Press, 1981).

opens as *mise en abyme*, with a specular evocation of both the marvels and the powers of the stage. The frame-plot significantly inverts the parable of the Prodigal Son: having wronged his boy, the Father, Pridamant, wanders the world in search of him to make amends. Finding no trace of his son, he is brought by a friend to a cave inhabited by a magician: the potent, faintly Moorish Alcandre, capable of causing fantastic visions to appear wherein Pridamant will discover what he needs to know. The play's opening lines, spoken by Pridamant's guide Dorante, is clearly, point for point, a representation of the theater itself:

> Ce grand Mage dont l'art commande à la nature
> N'a choisi pour palais que cette grotte obscure;
> La nuit qu'il entretient sur cet affreux séjour,
> N'ouvrant son voile épais qu'aux rayons d'un faux jour,
> De leur éclat douteux n'admet en ces lieux sombres
> Que ce qu'en peut souffrir le commerce des ombres.
> N'avancez pas, son art au pied de ce Rocher
> A mis de quoi punir qui s'en ose approcher,
> Et cette large bouche est un mur invisible,
> Où l'air en sa faveur devient inaccessible,
> Et lui fait un rempart, dont les funestes bords
> Sur un peu de poussière étalent mille morts.
>
> (1.1.1-12)

What Dorante describes here, under the staging conditions then obtaining in French "private" (as opposed to "public" or court) theater, is as yet only a project.[50] The play argues for, by presupposing, something like the setting for Molière's *Princesse d'Elide*, featured during the second day of the famous *Plaisirs de l'Ile enchantée* mounted at Versailles in 1664 (fig. 2). Corneille's implicit model is the *théâtre à l'italienne*: a perspective machine achieved by installing a proscenium arch between audience and stage, creating a picture-plane that would enable the dramatist to arrange figures and

[50] On general conditions of staging in 17th-century France, see Allardyce Nicoll, *The Development of the Theatre*, 5th ed. (New York: Harcourt, Brace, and World, 1966), chap. 6; Schérer, *Dramaturgie classique*, pt. 2, chap. 1; T.E. Lawrenson, *French Stage and Playhouse in the XVIIth Century* (New York: AMS Press, 1986), chaps. 5, 6, & 7; and Hélène Baby & Alain Viala, "L'essor de la vie théâtrale," in Viala (ed.), *Le théâtre en France* 156-59.

Figure 2. Set for Molière's *La Princesse d'Elide*. Engraving from André Félibien, *Les Plaisirs de l'Ile enchantée* (Paris, 1673), following page 20

décor to form a painterly illusion of reality, reinforced by a unified scheme of painted scenery of the type laid down by Serlio. By century's end theater of this kind will have become the norm, remaining so to our own day. But we should note that, in France as elsewhere, the agent chiefly responsible for the dissemination of the Italian stage is, as witnessed by the central place our illustration gives him in the audience, none other than the King. More specifically, it is the monarch whose reign follows that in which *L'Illusion comique* was originally produced, *le roi-soleil*, Louis XIV–a figure more than something of a perspective machine in his own right. [51] The model triumphs not through the theater itself, but through the opera, "machine" plays like Corneille's *Toison d'or* or *Andromède* composed to celebrate occasions of state, and the settings for elaborate entertainments at court, among them the *Plaisirs de l'Ile enchantée* themselves. [52]

Such is what Corneille wants, a design available only when the King is in the audience occupying the *place du Roi* or "state" defining the central projection-point on which a unified perspective scene depends. What he has actually got is far messier. For there is as yet no proscenium arch stage, only a rectangular structure, often a tennis court more or less successfully adapted for the purpose. Nor is there any perspective setting, only a décor reminiscent of the "mansions" of the medieval stage: an arrangement of multiple scenes (the magician's cave; the residence of Géronte, father of the young woman with whom Pridamant's son Clindor falls in love; the prison in which Clindor is put for the murder of his rival, Adraste; the garden of prince Florilame from the "play within a play" of Act 5) which, though covered by curtains, remain plainly in evidence throughout. [53]

---

[51] See Apostolidès, *Le roi-machine* and Marin, *Portrait du roi* 207-60.

[52] Beyond the sources mentioned in the preceding note, see Apostolidès, *Le prince sacrifié* and for the English context, Orgel, *The Illusion of Power*. On the *Plaisirs de l'Ile enchantée*, see Apostolidès, *Le roi-machine* 93-113.

[53] A similar arrangement in *Le Cid* created a good deal of confusion, at least for Scudéry and Chapelain. Thus, echoing the *Observations* (95), the *Sentiments* notes how "une mesme Scene y represente plusieurs lieux" (392). The problem is that, since all of the *lieux* (the home of the Comte de Gormas, the royal palace, etc.) are present throughout, it is not always clear to which the "neutral" space at the front of the stage is to be referred at any given moment.

Above all, there is no "invisible wall" it would be death to cross, indispensable prerequisite for setting off a perspective picture-space. The boundary between scene and audience is in fact violated by the nobility, the gaudy aristocrats seated on the stage itself, *côté cour et côté jardin*, destroying its separateness and geometric purity by making themselves part of the spectacle. This ironically posed a special problem for *Le Cid* precisely by virtue of its enormous popular success. As the actor-impresario Mondory wrote in a letter (18 January 1637) to the ubiquitous Guez de Balzac, the press at the Théâtre du Marais was so great that

> [o]n a vu seoir en corps aux bancs de ses loges ceux qu'on ne voit d'ordinaire que dans la Chambre dorée et sur les sièges des fleurs de lys. La foule a été si grande à nos portes, et notre lieu s'est trouvé si petit, que les recoins du théâtre qui servaient les autres fois comme de niches aux pages, ont été des places de faveur pour les cordons bleus et la scène y a été d'ordinaire parée de croix de chevaliers de l'ordre. [54]

A central goal of the later "Excuse à Ariste," nowhere expressly voiced yet nonetheless perfectly legible to Corneille's contemporaries, will be to monopolize the limelight of public attention, eclipsing rival poets. Just so, one of the tacit aims of *L'Illusion*'s apology for dramatic art is to get the nobles off the stage, clearing a space for that unity of vision and conception needed to impose not only a controlled illusion, but the integrity and authority of the poet's gaze–the perspective by which he defines the order of the scenic world. Nor is it for reasons of prestige alone that, at the end of the play, when the father learns the shocking news that his son has become a player, he is consoled by being informed how

> Même notre grand Roi, ce foudre de la guerre
> Dont le nom se fait craindre aux deux bouts de la terre,
> Le front ceint de lauriers daigne bien quelquefois
> Prêter l'oeil et l'oreille au Théâtre François.
>
> (5.6.1793-96)

---

[54] As cited in *Œuvres complètes* 1.1449-50.

What is invoked, alongside the *oreille* of attention to the moral music of Corneille's verse, is just that *oeil* whose presence alone allows him to achieve the perspective illusion he hopes for.

But though *L'Illusion comique* is very clear about what it wants, and about the authority it claims in the King's name–indeed as the King's counterpart, parallel, and surrogate–, it marks a certain ambivalence. The title reminds us that it is after all only an "illusion," an optical toy of the sort Bacon sneers at. More pointedly, equivocation slips into the very terms in which, at the close, Alcandre frames his praises of the art: "Cessez de vous plaindre," he tells Pridamant; "à présent le Théâtre / Est en un point si haut que chacun l'idolâtre." (5.6.1781-82) True, the verb Alcandre chooses, *idolâtrer*, is a *terme précieux*, a polite hyperbole; yet it is fork-tongued all the same. That the public should not merely enjoy and admire, but "idolize" theater implies the abject surrender of autonomous moral reason from which the Jansenist Pierre Nicole concludes that "la Comédie par sa nature est une école & un exercice de vice, puis qu'elle oblige necessairement à exciter en soi-même des passions vicieuses." [55] As we have seen, Scudéry asserts theater's moral mission against Corneille by describing how drama's noble portrayal of beautiful passion must persuade spectators to swallow the *utile* of virtue encapsulated in the *dulce* of sensuous pleasure. But if Scudéry is right that, in this way, "on se trouve guary presque sans avoir connu le remede," then the idolatrous imitation of the passions represented on the stage entails just the extinction of moral self-consciousness Nicole fears. Corneille's verb choice thus betokens an undercurrent of anxiety indissociable from the boastful assurance its hyperbole expounds.

Even Dorante's reference in the opening speech to "[c]e grand Mage dont l'art commande à la nature" suggests a disquieting trickiness. At one level, Dorante's claim that Alcandre's art "commands" nature encodes theater's powers of *imitatio naturae*. The spectacle of the fate of Pridamant's son since leaving his father's house reveals the art's special access to the truth–just that truth indeed Pridamant has vainly sought by other, less potent means. [56] Nevertheless, that art should be said not merely to render, portray, or imitate, but,

[55] Nicole, *Traité de la comédie* 42.
[56] For Pridamant's earlier efforts to acquire news of his boy, see 1.1.33-46.

precisely, to *command* nature may bring us up short. What Alcandre's magic induces us to take *for* nature is less nature *per se* than
nature as *subject to art*. This introduces a sense of deforming
coerciveness magnified in the revised version of 1660, where the
opening line speaks of "Ce Mage qui d'un mot renverse la
Nature." [57] Here again, a first reference is to theatrical representation: the "reversal of nature" Dorante alleges would in this sense
parallel the inversion produced in a mirror image, thereby alluding
to theater's status as a "mirror of nature," and thus to its powers
of imitation. But the point is also that, like a mirror, or indeed like
the catoptric and dioptric lenses, cones, and pyramids described
in Jean Dubreuil's *Perspective pratique* (1653), it functions less
by blandly reproducing than by actively twisting the reality it
mimics–an idea the more pointed when we recall that the play
opens by throwing over the presumptively "natural" relationship
between Father and Prodigal Son. [58]

As an heroic play, a "tragi-comedy" rather than a comedy pure
and simple, *Le Cid* does not question its own unifying rhetorical
"invention" in the way *L'Illusion comique* does. Still, marking the
transition from the romantic comedies with which Corneille's career begins to the great tragedies that will make him famous, *Le Cid*
unfolds against the backdrop of the sort of challenge to its own
founding perspective *L'Illusion comique* poses; and this fact suggests another explanation for its failure to reach a decisive close.
The artful contrivance behind the illusion is at odds with the claim
the illusion itself makes on our behalf: the two registers of human
experience, the sublimity aimed at and the hell it seeks to raise up
and redeem, only *seem* to fuse, a trompe-l'oeil that lives entirely in
the moment we look at it. [59]

---

[57] *Œuvres complètes* 1.1428.

[58] See Ernest B. Gilman, *The Curious Perspective: Literary and Pictorial Wit in the Seventeenth Century* (New Haven: Yale University Press, 1978). See also Anthony J. Cascardi, *The Limits of Illusion: A Critical Study of Calderón* (Ithaca, NY: Cornell University Press, 1984) for a specifically theatrical context.

[59] It is striking that, as we saw in the introduction, Scudéry opens his *Observa-
tions* with optical illusion: "Il est de certaines Pieces, comme de certains animaux qui sont en la Nature, qui de loin semblent des Etoiles, et qui de prés ne sont que des vermisseaux. Tout ce qui brille n'est pas toujours précieux; on voit des beautez d'illusion, comme des beautez effectives, et souvent l'aparence du bien se fait prendre pour le bien mesme. Aussi ne m'estonnay-je pas beaucoup que le Peuple qui

But there is a yet deeper level to *Le Cid*'s failure, bearing less on conditions of production than on those of *reception* as defined in particular by its relation to the King.

Le Cid inscribes the monarch in a number of ways. In the first place, he is a member of the *dramatis personae*. But of course the King is not just one character among others; he is the Hobbesian Arbiter without whom all would be lost: he to whom all the others turn as the only one capable of resolving the antinomies by which the action is driven, restoring the order disrupted by the conflicting schemes of honor and passion, duty and self-interest. But even in "private" theater, outside the precincts of "public" theater at court, the monarch is also a member of the audience if not in his own person, then as represented by one of his many officers. To mount a public spectacle means, by definition, to present an image to the King: a fact that inevitably colors and distorts, bending the tones and sight lines toward the one face no one can afford to overlook.

To cite an example from England, justified by the greater outspokenness of the English stage, consider the richly duplicitous "Prologue to the King's Majesty" prefacing the published text of Jonson's *Bartholomew Fair* (1614):

> Your Majesty is welcome to a Fair;
> Such place, such men, such language and such ware,
> You must expect: with these, the zealous noise
> Of your land's faction, scandalized at toys,
> As babies, hobby-horses, puppet-plays,
> And suchlike rage, whereof the petulant ways
> Yourself have known, and have been vexed with long.
> These for your sport, without particular wrong,
> Or just complaint of any private man,
> (Who of himself, or shall think well or can)
> The maker doth present: and hopes tonight
> To give you for a fairing, true delight. [60]

---

porte le jugement dans les yeux, se laisse tromper par celuy de tous les sens, le plus facile à decevoir." (71) This is also the place to cite Jean Starobinski's classic analysis of Cornelian ambivalence toward vision in *L'Oeil vivant: Corneille, Racine, La Bruyère, Rousseau, Stendhal* (1961; enlarged ed. Paris: Gallimard, 1999) 31-70.

[60] Ben Jonson, *Bartholomew Fair*, in *Five Plays*, ed. G.A. Wilkes (Oxford: Oxford University Press, 1981; World Classics paper ed., 1988) 487.

Composed for a performance at court, but preserved in the published text in part for the added luster, the prologue makes explicit Jonson's awareness of the ubiquitous royal presence: a presence that weighs heavily even if, as the title and opening line slyly hint, the poet is prepared to quibble about whether the welcome extended "the King's Majesty" also extends to the erudite paranoiac and boy-loving coprophile, James Stuart. It is to this troubled awareness that we owe the curious Article of Agreement, the ludic contract drawn up between author and audience in the Induction to the Stage bearing on the limits to be placed on the political interpretation of the play. Thus the Scrivener who appears as the poet's legal representative stipulates that, in exchange for the entertainment the author provides,

> it is finally agreed, by the aforesaid Hearers and Spectators, that they neither in themselves conceal, nor suffer by them to be concealed, any state-decipherer, or politic picklock of the scene, so solemnly ridiculous, as to search out, who was meant by the gingerbread-woman, who by the hobby-horse-man, who by the costard-monger, nay, who by their wares. Or that will pretend to affirm (on his own inspired ignorance) what Mirror for Magistrates is meant by the Justice, what great lady by the pig-woman, what concealed statesman, by the seller of mouse-traps, and so of the rest. [61]

Playful as it is, and much as it urges caution even to politic picklocks like ourselves, the passage voices an anxiety no contemporary playwright could escape. Little as Jonson's gingerbread woman, hobbyhorse man, or custardmonger may signify, the royal presence invests them with a potential for meaning to whose power the induction bears witness in the very act of disclaiming it.

But further still, as we have seen, it is the King who, by his at least implicit, virtual presence, gives the spectacle its form by providing, in the *place du Roi* or State, the projection-point defining the scenic perspective. The King is thus a *model*, a point driven home with extraordinary clarity by another period image, Nicolas Poussin's *Judgment of Solomon* (fig. 3), in which we recognize at once a representation of judgment and a sign of how far judgment

[61] *Bartholomew Fair* 492-93.

Figure 3. Nicolas Poussin, *Judgment of Solomon*. Musée National du Louvre, Paris. Credit: Alinari/Art Resource, NY

is itself a representation, the staging of a universe ordered with reference to the King, perched here at the apex of the inverted Albertian pyramid that looks back at us through the optic of the artist who composed it. [62] It is not by chance that this image illustrates what the climax of Le Cid should look like: the scene of judgment at its close, with its competing parties anchored to right and left along the base of the triangle through which the King imposes his perspective on the world, but by which he is in turn held aloft as King. King and Playwright (like, in Poussin, King and Painter) mirror and double each other in the perspective by which each is simultaneously expressed and constituted as a source of order, form, and truth.

But this last consideration suggests that the King is the playwright's *rival* as well as his image and counterpart: like the painter he resembles, the playwright defines the form he loyally if sycophantically claims to borrow from his sovereign. And of this too Poussin's *Solomon* offers an illustration. Even as it represents in the allegorically charged figure of Solomon—the type of kingly wisdom itself—the portrait of the ideal monarch presiding over his ideally ordered court, it also portrays the interior of a well-ordered psyche, the figuration of the workings of a well-ordered mind as well as of a well-ordered court.

As elaborated in the theories of the "King's two bodies" and the "sacrificial prince," [63] this doubling of the monarchic and psychological is a period commonplace, and nowhere more pointedly than in theater. In an English setting, Shakespeare's *Richard II* presents the spectacle of a king literally self-deposed by the failure to master his own impulses. In Spain we have the testimony of Calderón's *La vida es sueño*: a play remarkable not only for its strikingly Oedipal tale of a weak and unjust father overthrown by a son enthroned on the strength of a hard-won Christian Stoic self-mastery, but for its

[62] In view of the way Poussin's painting looks back through the inverted Albertian pyramid shaping its composition, see the parallel inversion in Jacques Lacan's account of the chiastic structure of our relation to images in *Les quatre concepts fondamentaux*, lectures 8, "La ligne et la lumière," and 9, "Qu'est-ce qu'un tableau?"

[63] See Ernest H. Kantorowicz, *The King's Two Bodies* (Princeton: Princeton University Press, 1957). On the relation between sovereignty and self-sacrifice, see Apostolidès, *Le prince sacrifié*, esp. 54-89. For recent commentaries, see Merlin, *Public et littérature*, chap. 7, and the essays cited in note 27 above.

initial portrait of the son himself in the allegorical guise of an
Everyman clothed in chains and animal skins as tokens of our bestial nature and the weight of the pre-gracine Law required to tame
it. In France we find Corneille's *Cinna* or the *Venceslas* of Rotrou:
plays in which what is shown to make a King is the self-governing
discipline through which the King *makes himself* by sublimating his
carnal nature as a passionate individual. The King is thus only King
so long as he holds sovereign sway over his own psychic life, dominating it in exactly the way Poussin's Solomon dominates his court.
The Arbiter is first arbiter within the confines of his own ego, adju-
dicating between the rival claims of good and evil, reason and passion, public right and private interest, altruism and *amour-propre*
emblematized by the mothers whose dispute it is the monarch's task
to resolve. [64] Poussin's *Solomon* is the portrait of the King not only
as Judge, but as personified Judgment itself: the faculty by which,
imposing order on the warring dimensions of the soul, every man is
to be ruled.

But this means that the image's celebration of the real King to
whom it offers the portrait of the ideal one as a likeness maintains a
certain ironic reserve implied in the *need* for such a likeness. Like
Jonson's prologue, it hints that the King is welcome only in his
Majesty–in a form the image itself cautiously teaches. Consider
from this viewpoint one last picture, much discussed in a variety of
contexts, Diego Velázquez's *Las Meninas* (fig. 4). [65] For among the
many things at work in this extraordinary image, this "Theology of

---

[64] Corneille's most explicit treatment of the topos is in *Cinna*, where the emper-
or Augustus legitimizes his usurpation of imperial power by sacrificing vengeful
self-interest for the sake of political harmony. But *Le Cid* offers a version of the
theme in the figure of the Infanta, obliged to sublimate her own passion for Rodrigue in the name of both friendship and royal blood.

[65] *Las Meninas* has generated an immense amount of commentary since Fou-
cault's *Les mots et les choses: une archéologie des sciences humaines* (Paris: Galli-
mard, 1966) 19-31. See John Searle, "*Las Meninas* and the Paradoxes of Pictorial
Representation," *Critical Inquiry* 6 (1980) 477-88; Joel Snyder & Ted Cohen,
"Reflections on *Las Meninas*: Paradox Lost," *Critical Inquiry* 7 (1980) 429-47; Leo
Steinberg, "Velasquez' *Las Meninas*," *October* 19 (1981) 45-54; Svetlana Alpers,
"Interpretation without Representation," *Representations* 1 (1983) 31-42; Joel Sny-
der, "*Las Meninas* and the Mirror of the Prince," *Critical Inquiry* 11 (1985) 539-72;
and Mieke Bal, *Reading Rembrandt: Beyond the Word-Image Opposition* (Cam-
bridge: Cambridge University Press, 1991), chap. 7, "Self-Reflection as a Mode of
Reading."

Figure 4. Diego Velázquez, *Las Meninas*. Museo del Prado, Madrid. Credit: Alinari/ Art Resource, NY

Painting" as one contemporary called it, [66] is a remarkable structural conflict and the cunning with which the painter turns it to his own advantage.

The picture's most striking feature is the way, this once, painter and sitter change places. As all of these eyes insistently directed our way indicate, the "subject" of the image is the one thing we cannot see in the image itself–whoever now happens to stand before it. As implied by the painter's presence inside the painting–seen in a moment of concentrated abstraction, stepping back from the canvas on the left to judge the agreement between what he paints and the person now before him–this "subject" is the sitter for the painting the artist works on: an image that, given the vantage-point from which we look at it, conceals what it depicts. Still, this hidden sitter is not and cannot be just anyone. This is no public picture, meant for a general spectatorship; it was designed to hang in the King's own private office in the royal summer quarters in the Alcázar, a smallish chamber where, occupying the whole of one wall with its lifesize proportions, it must have created a stunning trompe-l'oeil effect seamlessly continuous with the space from which it was viewed. [67] The painting exists for one pair of eyes only, those of the King, Philip IV of Spain, whose face dimly appears alongside that of his young Queen and Hapsburg cousin, Mariana of Austria, in the mirror hanging on the rear wall, beside the doorway where a court attendant already stands holding the curtain back in anticipation of an imminent royal departure.

The composition addresses an elaborate compliment to the King, pointed by Velázquez's addition, in red on the breast of his black tunic, of the Cross of the knightly order of Santiago: a mark of ennoblement bestowed by the King, over vigorous opposition by the hereditary aristocracy, precisely in virtue of his work as *pintor del rey*. [68] Velázquez as painter, as source of the extension of reality that is the picture before us, emerges in every sense as the King sees him, indeed as the King has *made* him just because the King alone, origin of the luminous order in which all things reveal their true na-

---

[66] Cited in Jonathan Brown, *Velázquez: Painter and Courtier* (New Haven: Yale University Press, 1986) 260.

[67] Ibid. 259.

[68] Ibid. 251-52.

ture and worth, perceives him for what he is. And yet, to ask a question attempts to plot the underlying geometry of the room bring to the fore, [69] in what exactly does the King's kingliness consist? What power in his sovereign persuades Velázquez to present himself as the King's creature even in the act of creation that affirms his own authority? The mirror at the back, specifying who stands before the canvas, seems to indicate that it is the inimitable King himself. But its position relative to the other objects in the room leaves it uncertain just what the mirror reflects. Is it, as the picture seems to suggest, the King in his own person, standing with us outside the painting's field of vision? Or is it, as the room's geometry also allows, the canvas on which Velázquez works? Who in fact is the true King: Philip, or the ideal *version* of Philip Velázquez forges in paint?

To put the case in the Hobbesian terms invoked earlier, who is the picture's true Arbiter or Leviathan: the sovereign it images, or the keen-eyed intellectual who invents his likeness? Is it, in an English context, James Stuart, or his Chancellor Bacon, the moralist and technocrat as well master of revels who, like the Richelieu of the reign of Louis XIII, absorbs much of the power symbolically assigned the monarch because it is in fact he, and not the King, who knows how the kingdom works? Or take, finally, the example of the archbishop of Meaux, Jacques-Bénigne Bossuet, instructing the dauphin of Louis XIV in his own nature and office by presenting him, in the *Discours sur l'histoire universelle* (1681), a "grand spectacle" in which the monarch-to-be may watch an epitome of all preceding ages unfold before his eyes according to the double pattern of the rise and fall of empires and the self-sustaining certainty of religion:

> C'est la suite de ces deux choses, je veux dire celle de la religion et celle des empires, que vous devez imprimer dans votre mémoire; et, comme la religion et le gouvernement politique sont les deux points sur lesquels roulent les choses humaines, voir ce qui regarde ces choses renfermé dans un abrégé, et en découvrir par ce moyen tout l'ordre et toute la suite, c'est comprendre dans sa pensée tout ce qu'il y a de grand parmi les

---

[69] See Snyder, "*Las Meninas* and the Mirror of the Prince."

hommes, et tenir, pour ainsi dire, le fil de toutes les affaires de l'univers.

Comme donc, en considérant une carte universelle, vous sortez du pays où vous êtes né, et du lieu qui vous renferme, pour parcourir toute la terre habitable, que vous embrassez par la pensée avec toutes ses mers et tous ses pays; ainsi, en considérant l'abrégé chronologique, vous sortez des bornes étroites de votre âge, et vous vous étendez dans tous les siècles. [70]

The passage creates some striking coincidences. Bossuet pens an historical composition whose underlying purpose consists in composing a monarch. Moreover, via the Ciceronian hypotaxis of its rhetoric, the text transforms the unfolding time of discourse into the prudential space of periodic prose. The passage thus works a metamorphosis that mirrors and reinforces the way the "grand spectacle" of the archbishop's abridgement digests the sprawl of historical process to produce the panoramic projection of a universal map, image of a triumphantly transhistorical understanding and command. "Style makes the man." In this pedagogical exhortation, a call to duty enjoining on the pupil's part a founding act of rational self-control, we meet a version of the theme of the "King's two bodies" in which the sovereign becomes himself by *surpassing* himself, liberated from the "narrow confines" of his own psyche as well as of his socio-historical situation through an act of inner vision and discipline.

But the image's origination in a mental act less on the dauphin's than on his tutor's part confirms that the form Bossuet proffers the prince as his own belongs equally to his servant: a form prince and servant share only insofar as, source of a "universal history," it is itself universal, the source in fact of universality as such, namely, the sovereign self of the rational subject. So whose perspective is this? Whose gaze does it espouse and assert: that of the fledgling sovereign it informs, or that of the canny archbishop whose magnificent Ciceronian periods contrive to shape him by imprinting this picture in his brain?

And what is true for Velázquez or Hobbes, Bacon, Richelieu, or Bossuet, is just as true for Corneille. Even as he invokes the King at

---

[70] Jacques-Bénigne Bossuet, *Discours sur l'histoire universelle*, ed. Jacques Truchet (Paris: Garnier-Flammarion, 1966) 40-41.

the end of *L'Illusion comique*, the King he conjures up is less the reigning monarch, Louis XIII, than the ideal spectator he creates by scripting his intelligence of the play.[71] Nor should it escape us that the climactic invocation of the King is prudently preceded by that of his minister Richelieu, tactfully acknowledged as one of those "dont nous voyons la sagesse profonde / Par ses illustres soins conserver tout le monde": heroic labors on behalf of the common good for which "les douceurs d'un spectacle si beau" supply "[d]e quoi se délasser d'un si pesant fardeau" (5.6.1789-92). As indeed the cardinal-duke will brutally remind our haughty poet by personally stage-managing the controversy in which *Le Cid* will be engulfed, though the monarch provides the "eye" and "ear" in which theater cites both the warrant of its legitimacy and the model for its authority, even royal favor counts for nothing without ministerial patronage. Whence the double irony in the fact that the language with which Corneille praises his sovereign, "ce foudre de la guerre / Dont le nom se fait craindre aux deux bouts de la terre," mirrors that of the empty braggart Matamore, to whom the hero is indentured when the action begins. Corneille may be forgiven a certain delicate sarcasm where the King is concerned, but only so long as the cardinal chooses to overlook it.

To return, in conclusion, to *Le Cid*: though we tend to see it as a portrait of the baroque hero, driven by the dialectic of self-definition to oppose, defiant and unconquerable, the decrees of paternal fate, it is also a Fable of the State. The "tragi-comedy" of Rodrigue and Chimène embodies the forces–in particular the divisive individualism mirrored in the contest between public good and private right the murder of Don Gomès unleashes–that "Don Fernand, premier Roi de Castille," must overcome to found the possibility of monarchy as such. By such a gesture Corneille, in the

---

[71] In "Rhétorique et dramaturgie," Fumaroli plots how, through the controlling agency of the magician-playwright Alcandre, the play artfully prepares Pridamant, as at once father of the hero and stand-in for the audience, for the defense of theater only explicitly introduced after the shocking revelation of Clindor's profession as an actor. The play thus deliberately shapes how Pridamant will understand what it shows him at its close. But Pridamant is of course hardly alone in being so manipulated if only because, as the hero's father, he serves as the representative of authority in general, and thus of the King as well. Mirrored in Pridamant, and subject therefore to the change Alcandre's persuasive art causes in the hero's father, the King is briefed in the attitude the play attributes him in its final scene.

wish-fulfilling prologue to *L'Illusion comique*, banishes the nobles from the stage, putting them in their places among the other paying members of the audience. By the same gesture Louis XIV will finally reduce both petulant aristocrats and overreaching ministers to the status of mere spectators of his performative Majesty at Versailles.

Nor can any of our examples efface what all of them imply even as they deny it: the King's status as an "illusion," a fiction, at risk, just like Rembrandt's Belshazzar, of being defaced and deposed by the very hand that draws his likeness. And it is just here that we find the deepest motive for the gesture of *différance* marked in the "Hymen différé" of *Le Cid*'s closing scene–at once the true story told by way of symbolic difference and the reason why the moment of truth has to be put off. The author Corneille, the minister Richelieu charged with policing his ambitions, and the monarch whose Spanish prototype tries to bring the action to a healing close all have a stake in how the play concludes. For Corneille, the issue is his stature as the nation's preeminent poet, the vatic genius to whom his countrymen turn to learn their ideal potential and identities. To the extent that the heroic couple transcend both carnal passion and the violent disorder paternal tyranny foments, they constitute an uplifting paradigm for the shared humanity the spectating public experiences in the mingled emotions of pity, wonder, and identificatory love. But insofar as this model asserts the autonomous authority of the poet who invented it, the ultimate object of public admiration is Corneille himself. The poet thereby simultaneously mimics and usurps the role the royal minister claims: that of the *political* genius who, in yoking the poet's self-promoting pride to the needs of the emergent state, affirms his own authority as the instrument of the national union whose symbol is the King poet and minister are alike called on to serve. Yet the consequence is a double threat not only to union itself, but above all to the sovereign in whom both parties acknowledge their Solomonic lord.

No one is ready to confront the secret *différend*, the quarrel or dispute encoded in the very form that suggests how all of the rival powers might fuse in a single identity: neither the King whose serio-comic impotence Corneille portrays nor his duplicitous servants–the parasitic artist who tells him how to look and act and think, and the wily minister who not only executes, but forges the royal policy to which even the monarch must submit. The time will come however when the truth must be faced; and given the character of the sovereign in whose reign the final reckoning occurs, the outcome will be costly indeed. In the Corneille of Louis XIII, the private ego of which poet and minister are competing avatars postpones the confrontation, exploiting the bias of symbolic difference in order to expound and explore its own nature and authority under cover of the King. In the Racine of Louis XIV, this same ego will immolate itself to appease the Moloch it has ironically helped fabricate at its own expense.

CHAPTER 2

THE POETICS OF EQUIVOCATION:
HORACE, CINNA, RODOGUNE

O UR reading of Corneille's *Le Cid* highlights a crucial feature of
French classical drama. The issues played out in the heroic
love story of Chimène and Rodrigue and the related fable of the
emergent absolutist state are doubled by the contest between two
versions of authority: that of the King, social embodiment of authority as such, and that of the Poet, one of whose roles is to in-
struct the sovereign in the nature and demands of the authority he
embodies. Composing a play commits the poet to competition with
his prince; the authority Corneille arrogates as source of a dramatic
spectacle at once mirrors and challenges that of the monarch whose
right to rule the spectacle images and asserts. But it does so at the
level, not of the spectacle itself, but of the poem the spectacle "represents." The text encodes meanings other than those played out in
the form of dramatic performance. Moving and engrossing as the
scenic action may be, the play's true reference lies elsewhere: in the
poetic "invention" and imaginative "design" that shape the events
in which both actors and audience passionately engage, and in the
duplicities of speech by which the disjunction is covertly expressed.

One way to characterize this dual reference is to relate it to the
figure identified in the introduction as the "secret contriver." Like
the royal minister he resembles, but also like the scheming courtier
in whom the minister finds his own dramatic counterpart, the poet
is what, in the broken French of German baroque drama, Walter
Benjamin calls an *Intrigant*, cousin of the Jacobean "revenger" or
"malcontent." [1] Intriguers, revengers, malcontents are of course

---

[1] See Benjamin, *Origin of German Tragic Drama* 125-28.

fomenters of plots, and to this extent the playwright's friends. Without characters like *Cinna*'s Emilie or, in a comic register, Molière's abominable Tartuffe, instigating the action by pursuing ends in conflict with the status quo, no drama would take place. But this suggests that such characters are the dramatist's doubles as well as associates. The disjunction between the dramatic spectacle and the text from which that spectacle springs reproduces the divorce between public events and the private machinations that precipitate them. As a result, the drama's most faithful witness is not the breathless public caught up in the performance, but an *éminence grise* capable of the skeptical detachment required to see *through* the action to the hidden hand that directs it: a watchful Machiavellian intelligence that shares the playwright's power of pulling the hidden strings that make other actors move to a purpose they cannot fathom or control. [2]

In Corneille's case, the allusion to an *éminence* is quite literal. As we have seen, behind the withering attacks levelled at *Le Cid*, pulling strings as imperious as those Corneille operates, was no less a personage than *Son Eminence par excellence*, cardinal Richelieu. Understanding better than anyone the hubris actuating Cornelian drama, Richelieu deployed the newly founded Académie Française to put the poet in his place, showing him just how far his ministerial hand could reach. Accordingly, in the aftermath of the *querelle*, as Corneille reinvents his dramatic art in reaction to the assaults the cardinal has orchestrated at his expense, it is Richelieu he addresses as both his true antagonist and the one authentic critic of his work. The outcome is a form of drama that, by exploiting the divorce between theatrical spectacle and the underlying text from which it issues, plays a double game in which the poet asserts his private right in defiance of the public order he appears to endorse.

An early product of Corneille's reconfigured art is the *Cinna* of 1642. Unlike what we observe in the case of the preceding season's *Horace*, to which we shall turn in a moment, a definite critical consensus has formed concerning *Cinna*'s presiding aim. In relating the

---

[2] We will return to this issue in chap. 4 with reference to the isomorphism linking *L'Ecole des femmes*'s plot-weaving and self-nominating "M. de La Souche" to his equally plotting and self-nominating author, Jean-Baptiste Poquelin, *dit* "Molière." True, Molière deploys this isomorphism to ironic effect, in part at his own expense; but the irony trades on the identification.

story of the signal act of clemency with which, pardoning the Republican conspirators plotting against his life, the emperor Auguste at once consolidates and legitimizes his hold on imperial power, the play presents a model of the "art of government" (*l'art de régner*) on which French absolutism hinges. [3] True, recent explorations of the political problem *Cinna* addresses increasingly insist on its fundamental intractability. Whence, notably, John Lyons's more nuanced account in *The Tragedy of Origins*, emphasizing the radical unprecedentedness and thus *improbability* of the sacrifice Auguste's clemency demands. [4] And it is indeed important that the lack of historical precedent shows the sacrifice Auguste performs to be a sort of *miracle*, beyond the reach of the ordinary mortals whose doings history chronicles. Nevertheless, the act's quasi miraculous nature underscores the justice of Hélène Merlin's view: that the core principle at the root of Cornelian political theory is not the natural *reason* history teaches, but rather a purely self-determined (and therefore wholly unprogrammed and unpredictable) act of *will* that, in overcoming, radically transcends mere reasoned human nature. [5] Just because it has no example, Auguste's clemency reconsecrates the combination of self-discipline and self-sacrifice enshrined in the absolutist myth of the King's Two Bodies. In contrast to his subjects, to whom private lives and private interests distinct from any public role are freely granted, the King, in his capacity as Christ's anointed surrogate, is at any rate notionally called on to make a Christlike offering of his creaturely person. What grants the Rome of *Cinna* a "true" (as opposed to problematically "real") monarch is the willing symbolic death by which the bloody usurper Octave

---

[3] See, e.g., Apostolidès, *Le prince sacrifié* 63-72.

[4] Lyons, *Tragedy of Origins*, chap. 2, "*Cinna* and the Historical Logic of Empire."

[5] See Merlin, "*Cinna* ou le transport des volontés unies," *Littérature et public* 288-304, "*Cinna, Rodogune, Nicomède*: Le Roi et le moi," and "Corneille et la politique dans *Cinna, Rodogune* et *Nicomède*." Compare Merlin's analysis of Corneille's fundamentally voluntarist sense of political justice with Charles Taylor's account of the voluntarist basis of morality in Descartes, *Sources of the Self: The Making of Modern Identity* (Cambridge, Mass.: Harvard University Press, 1989), chap. 8, "Descartes's Disengaged Reason," where the methodic practice of a reductively instrumental self-control entails a state of moral "unbelief" in whose light morality as such becomes impossible. What we get in its place is Cornelian *générosité*, a radically self-determined act of self-overcoming whose ultimate descendants are the Nietzschean and Heideggerian cult of pure Will.

transforms himself into the transcendent royal *example* of the play's dénouement–the godlike Auguste his erstwhile enemies embrace as uncontested master.

Despite the unambiguously noble example enacted at the level of performance, the *text* of the play tellingly equivocates. When the curtain rises, Auguste's chief adversary, the intractable Emilie whose father he has murdered in mounting the imperial throne, voices adamant rejection of absolutist rule. A crucial feature of this speech is the properly demonic energy with which the heroine speaks; it reads indeed like a reprise of a comparable speech from Corneille's first tragedy, *Médée* (1634), when the Colchian witch conjures up the powers of hell to sustain an act of revenge that culminates in the murder of her own children.[6] Emilie thus opens *Cinna* with a furious apostrophe addressing the contrary passions warring in her heart:

> Impatients désirs d'une illustre vengeance
> Dont la mort de mon père a formé la naissance,
> Enfants impétueux de mon ressentiment,
> Que ma douleur séduite embrasse aveuglément,
> Vous prenez sur mon âme un trop puissant empire:
> Durant quelques moments souffrez que je respire,
> Et que je considère, en l'état où je suis,
> Et ce que je hasarde, et ce que je poursuis.
> Quand je regarde Auguste au milieu de sa gloire,
> Et que vous reprochez à ma triste mémoire
> Que par sa propre main mon père massacré
> Du Trône où je le vois fait le premier degré,
> Quand vous me présentez cette sanglante image,
> La cause de ma haine, et l'effet de sa rage,
> Je m'abandonne toute à vos transports,
> Et crois pour une mort lui devoir mille morts.
>
> (1.1.1-16)

At one level, the speech portrays the cost of unbridled personal passion. The multiplicity of Emilie's "impatient desires" and the tyrannical "empire" they exert over her plans and feelings bespeak

---

[6] See *Médée, Œuvres complètes* 1.3.197-268, cited henceforth in the text by act, scene, and verse for plays and by volume and page number for prose.

the alienation her overpowering thirst for revenge inflicts. In place of the integrated ego of autonomous moral agency, we meet a slave possessed by forces she cannot control even though they emanate from her own psyche. The point powerfully emerges in the continuation, when the soliloquist's attention shifts from her instigating obsession with the cause of her rage to the love she feels for the man she has chosen as its agent:

> Au milieu toutefois d'une fureur si juste,
> J'aime encor plus Cinna, que je ne hais Auguste,
> Et je sens refroidir ce bouillant mouvement,
> Quand il faut pour le suivre exposer mon Amant.
> Oui, Cinna, contre moi moi-même je m'irrite
> Quand je songe aux dangers où je te précipite.
>
> (1.1.17-22)

Emilie ceases in many respects to be a person at all, becoming instead an automaton driven by anarchic powers of "vengeance" and "resentment" that, personified through the apostrophe she addresses them, usurp the attributes of personal identity at her expense. From this viewpoint, what agency Emilie retains is entirely passive–a state of "pain" that "blindly embraces" thoughts of revenge as the "impetuous children" the desire for Auguste's death unnaturally sires in her soul. Of particular interest here is the work of *imagination*, compulsively projecting the "bloody picture" of her butchered father on the screen of inner vision in such a way as to confuse the direction and nature of its own impact, arising as the equivocally simultaneous "cause" of Emilie's "hate" and "effect" of her "rage." Above all, amplifying the image of the unnatural "children" the spirit of vengeance breeds, is Emilie's resolve to exploit the enamored Cinna as the instrument of a violence so omnipotent that even love becomes its servant.

Nevertheless, both piteous and terrifying as the spectacle of Emilie's towering hate may be, it is also *magnificent*. The passions that possess her empower her as well, underscoring a truth the sometime *frondeur* La Rochefoucauld memorably formulates: "Il y a des héros en mal comme en bien." [7] The anarchic energies she em-

---

[7] François de La Rochefoucauld, *Maximes*, ed. Pierre Kuentz (Paris: Bordas, 1966), max. 185.

bodies ordain a voluntary discipline no less admirable for the evils they engender, to the point where her willing immolation of her lover is every bit the measure of the benign sacrifice Auguste will make. [8] For all she illustrates the forces of darkness and division whose overcoming justifies the emperor's absolute sway, the play's teleological close cannot efface the heroic character of her resistance to the order to which Auguste's climactic clemency wins even her assent.

Similarly, it is remarkable that the play's most thorough and persuasive statement of absolutist doctrine is put in the mouth of the leader of the conspiracy intent on destroying the new imperium. The statement occurs in the richly ironic episode in 2.1 when, exhausted and disillusioned by the exercise of the power he has committed so many crimes to seize, Auguste confides to Cinna and Maxime his desire to abdicate in favor of a restored Republic. Cinna replies by arguing that the private good the emperor craves would incur an unthinkable public cost:

> Si l'amour du pays doit ici prévaloir,
> C'est son bien seulement que vous devez vouloir,
> Et cette liberté qui lui semble si chère
> N'est pour Rome, Seigneur, qu'un bien imaginaire,
> Plus nuisible qu'utile, et qui n'approche pas
> De celui qu'un bon Prince apporte à ses Etats.
> Avec ordre et raison les honneurs il dispense,
> Avec discernement punit et récompense,
> Et dispose de tout en juste possesseur,
> Sans rien précipiter de peur d'un successeur.
> Mais quand le Peuple est maître, on n'agit qu'en tumulte,
> La voix de la raison jamais ne se consulte,
> Les honneurs sont vendus aux plus ambitieux,
> L'autorité est livrée aux plus séditieux.
> Ces petits Souverains qu'il fait pour une année,
> Voyant d'un temps si court leur puissance bornée,
> Des plus heureux desseins font avorter le fruit,
> De peur de le laisser à celui qui les suit.

---

[8] That Emilie's intransigence should be no less *admirable* than the sacrifice by which Auguste finally overcomes it points to the moral ambiguities attending "admiration" in French classical culture. See Christian Biet, "Plaisirs et dangers de l'admiration," *Littératures classiques* 32 (January 1998) 121-34.

Comme ils ont peu de part aux biens dont ils ordonnent,
Dans le champ du Public largement ils moissonnent,
Assurés que chacun leur pardonne aisément,
Espérant à son tour un pareil traitement.
Le pire des Etats c'est l'Etat populaire.

(2.1.499-521)[9]

Cinna espouses a view that most contemporary observers, Corneille included, would have taken for an incontestable truth. Against the background of the preceding century's wars of religion and the civil strife attending the regency of Marie de' Medici and Richelieu's consolidation of central royal power, the alternative to absolutist rule is the chaos minutely enacted in Emilie's opening soliloquy. And we further note that, following Richelieu's death later this same year and Louis XIII's in 1643, the minority of Louis XIV will witness the outbreak of the Frondes of 1648-53, where the rival private ambitions of the French *parlements* and *princes* create just the anarchy Cinna describes. But of course the conspirator's motive at this point is not the truth he voices, but his passion for Emilie. The political philosophy informing his counsel to the emperor is at odds with his dissimulated purpose in pronouncing it–namely, in accordance with the secret bargain struck with Emilie, who has set the emperor's death as the price for granting Cinna her love, to keep Auguste in power in order to justify his murder.

The duplicity to which private interest impels Cinna resurfaces moreover, in inverted form, in the next scene, when he explains to his confederate Maxime, appalled at his rejection of the chance to restore the lost Republic, that Auguste's mere abdication is not enough. Security from tyranny demands *tyrannicide*, setting a minatory example for future generations:

Octave aura donc vu ses fureurs assouvies,
Pillé jusqu'aux Autels, sacrifié nos vies,
Rempli les champs d'horreur, comblé Rome de morts,
Et sera quitte après pour l'effet d'un remords!
Quand le Ciel par nos mains à le punir s'apprête,
Un lâche repentir garantira sa tête!
C'est trop semer d'appas, et c'est trop inviter,

---

[9] See Merlin's parallel reading of this passage, *Littérature et public* 292-93.

> Par son impunité, quelque autre à l'imiter.
> Vengeons nos Citoyens, et que sa peine étonne
> Quiconque après sa mort aspire à la Couronne,
> Que le Peuple aux Tyrans ne soit plus exposé;
> S'il eût puni Sylla, César eût moins osé.
>
> (2.2.653-64)

Excerpted from its role in the play's developing plot, Cinna's articulation of the theory of tyrannicide underwrites a truth (*sic semper tyrannis*) as unexceptionable in its sphere as the one laid out in the foregoing apology for absolutism. But here again public truth is trumped by the private aim that prompts its formulation since the hero's dominant interest remains the same: to justify the murder Emilie demands as a condition for her love. The verity Cinna utters is belied by his secret intent in uttering it, becoming a falsehood all the more damnable for turning truth inside out. In the process, Cinna confirms what his earlier lies suggest: the duplicities to which all public speech is subject as a reflex of the personal passions that make us speak.

Still, the equivocations that inhabit the play's text are finally liquidated by the climactic act of clemency with which, sacrificing his natural thirst for revenge, Auguste earns even his most hostile subjects' willing consent. Yet even as Auguste's exemplary overcoming of violent passion achieves the unanimity of which absolutism emerges as both the instrument and fruit, the fact that it is presented as an *example* points a moral not only for the wider public in need of instruction in the political order France requires, but also for the King and the royal minister before whom the action is staged. True, Georges Forestier has recently reminded us that, where French Renaissance poets like Jodelle, observant of the ideological model set in treatises like Guillaume Budé's *Institution du Prince* or Jean Bodin's *Six livres de la République*, endorse the humanist notion of tragic drama as a "school for kings," the dramatists of the *grand siècle* are committed to a poetics of royal praise. [10] This is certainly true as a matter of overt public discourse, gathering momentum as the century unfolds to the point where, with the

---

[10] Georges Forestier, *Corneille: Le sens d'une dramaturgie* (Paris: SEDES, 1998) 71-77.

publication of Boileau's *Art poétique* in 1674, royal encomium has become French poetry's presiding theme.[11] However, precisely insofar as what historical example praises is less the reigning authority than the ideal with which authority identifies, it constitutes a lesson that, as such, leaves open the question of the justice of its application to the powers that be. Further, the whole thrust of Auguste's example lies in the reminder of the implicit *contract* between the sovereign and his people. Auguste's sacrificial clemency earns the equally sacrificial allegiance of his former enemies. Yet the sacrifice his enemies make is entirely conditional, an act his subjects willingly perform in return for the one the emperor undertakes in fulfilment of his public role.

What thus proves true even of an apologetic play like *Cinna* proves still more so of the earlier *Horace* (1640), the first Cornelian drama to follow the *querelle du Cid*. *Horace* is what Shakespeareans call a "problem play" set apart by the apparently insuperable difficulties we face in determining where it stands relative to the issues it joins; and the major focus of these difficulties, hotly debated to this day, is what we are to make of its eponymous hero, champion of the model kingdom of Rome, but also the fanatic murderer of his sister Camille. Should we see Horace as a brutal killer whose mar-

---

[11] *L'Art poétique*'s closing periods are notoriously emphatic on this point:

> Muses, dictez sa gloire à tous vos nourrissons.
> Son nom vaut mieux pour eux que toutes vos leçons.
> Que Corneille, pour lui rallumant son audace,
> Soit encor le Corneille et du Cid et d'Horace;
> Que Racine, enfantant des miracles nouveaux,
> De ses héros sur lui forme tous les tableaux;
> Que de son nom, chanté par la bouche des belles,
> Bensserade en tous lieux amuse les ruelles;
> Que Segrais dans l'églogue en charme les forêts;
> Que pour lui l'épigramme aiguise tous ses traits.
>
> (4.193-202)

On royal praise in 17th-century culture, esp. under Louis XIV, see Marin, *Le portrait du roi*, Apostolidès, *Le roi-machine*, Burke, *Fabrication of Louis XIV*, and Fumaroli, *Le Poète et le Roi*, chap. 1, "L'Olympe et le Parnasse." See too Marie-Odile Sweetser, "La conversion du Prince: réflexions sur la tragédie providentielle," *Papers on French Seventeenth-Century Literature* 10.19 (1983) 497-510 and "Tragic Situation and Providential Intervention: The Case for a New Concept of Tragedy in the XVIIth Century," *Seventeenth-Century French Studies* 7 (1985) 97-107, on the ideologically positive role weak or tyrannical kings play either as examples to avoid or as implicit praise of the reigning prince who (by definition) escapes such faults.

tial valor springs from a monstrous source, or is he rather an essentially *tragic* figure whose crime is the product of the insoluble dramatic predicament in which all of the characters are caught? [12] Still, deep though the uncertainty surrounding Horace may seem, it dissipates as soon as we recognize that he is in fact less a *character* acting in conformity with his intrinsic private nature than the *personification* of a certain conception of dramatic verse–a conception of which his sister personifies the opposite. "Horace," both the play and its title role, is finally about the form and aims of heroic drama in the context of the politics of ministerial reception exhibited by the controversy of *Le Cid*.

As Scudéry and Chapelain relentlessly document, *Le Cid* sins against the unities in numerous ways. For a start, the events of the day it portrays are so many and complex as to defy reasonable containment within the requisite twenty-four hours; and it is often unclear in which of the various spaces available to it (the royal palace; the *hôtel* of Don Gomès, father of Chimène; that of Don Diègue, father of Rodrigue; or the city street that connects all three) any given scene occurs. [13] In answer, with *Horace* in 1640, Corneille presents a poem that observes the classical rules with pointed severity. Drawing on a famous episode recounted in Livy's *History of Rome*, [14] the play portrays the events surrounding the conclusion of the war between the cities of Rome and Alba, rivals for hegemony in the exiguous corner of Italy they share. *Horace* rehearses the decision to choose three champions from each side to decide the issue in a duel; the election of sets of brothers to play this role, the Horatii for Rome and the Curiatii for Alba; Rome's triumph with the title character's return as the sole survivor of the fight; and then

---

[12] For a survey of critical assessments of Horace's character, see Lyons, *Tragedy of Origins* 39-40. Also see Greenberg, *Corneille*, chap. 3, "*Horace*, Classicism and female trouble," where the title character embodies the Oedipal (and therefore misogynistic) symbolic scheme informing French classical culture. Greenberg's argument is overstated in that it assumes a *classical* Corneille in lieu of a *baroque* one allegorically resisting the classical ethos Horace incarnates. Still, by identifying Corneille's "hero" with the classicism Richelieu and the Académie impose, Greenberg points in the right direction.

[13] See, e.g., Scudéry, *Observations*, Gasté, *La Querelle du Cid* 77-78 and 95, and Chapelain, *Sentiments*, ibid. 392.

[14] For the Latin text, see *Œuvres complètes* 1.835-38. For a French translation, ibid. 1.1555-60.

the tragic aftermath, when the exultant hero kills his sister for lamenting the death of her Alban fiancé, a slight to her victorious
brother's honor Corneille exacerbates by turning her lamentation
into vituperative hate. The fable from Livy thus frames an action
readily contained within the space of a natural day–the more emphatically so in that, in contrast to the several years recorded in the
Spanish model for *Le Cid*, a natural day is the interval Livy's history
reports. But Corneille also achieves absolute unity of place by confining the entire drama to a single room: the chamber in the home
of the Horatian family where Sabine (Horace's wife and sister of his
Alban opposite, Curiace) and Camille (sister to Horace and Curiace's intended bride) await the outcome of the duel. If unity is what
is wanted, unity is what we get, developed to the point of such pitiless perfection as to constitute something like parody. [15]

   More striking however than the play's formal regularity is the
moral and psychological rigor exhibited in the conduct of the hero.
As we have seen, louder even than criticism of *Le Cid*'s strictly aesthetic shortcomings was the outcry at what Scudéry and the Académie saw as the depravity of its heroine's divided loyalties, seeking
justice for her father's murder while maintaining a passionate regard for the author of the deed. In *Horace*, on the other hand, we
find a hero so consumed by duty to Father and State that he stops
at nothing to fulfil it: having killed the rival Curiaces, related
though they are to him by the bonds of both friendship and marriage, he goes on to murder his own sister when she upbraids him
for her lover's death.

   Though he casts the problem in artistic rather than moral or political terms, [16] the Corneille of the "examen" accompanying the

---

[15] See François Lasserre, *Corneille de 1638 à 1642: La crise technique d'Horace,
Cinna et Polyeucte* (Paris: Biblio 17, 1990) 55-62.

[16] On its face, the narrow grounds on which Corneille's *examen* faults the play's
ending lends color to Forestier's important (if hyperbolical) thesis about Cornelian
dramaturgy in *Essai de génétique théâtrale* and *Corneille*. Forestier concedes that
Corneille "embroiders" political themes on his tragic fables, weaving them into the
expressive verses his characters speak. But he argues that the long-cherished notion
that Corneille is a preeminently "political" dramatist is corroborated neither by
contemporary reception nor by contemporary notions of tragedy. For a spirited re-
buttal, see Merlin, "Corneille et la politique." For Forestier's response to such criticisms, see "Politique et tragédie chez Corneille, ou de la 'broderie'," *Littératures
classiques* 32 [January 1998] 63-74. Two facts show Forestier to be mistaken. When,

text published in the monumental *Théâtre* of 1660 evinces misgivings about this ending. He acknowledges indeed that all commentators "veulent que la mort de Camille en gâte la fin," and that they are right to do so even if they are rarely right as to why (1.839). He then goes on to cite two reasons for the dénouement's weakness. The first is that Camille's death is too sudden or abrupt ("momentanée") to serve as a major incident in a tragedy. Unlike the sacrificial duel to decide the issue of the war, an action of sufficient moral scope and dramatic complexity to attain "cette juste grandeur que lui demande Aristote, et qui consiste en un commencement, un milieu, et une fin," the killing of Camille

> surprend tout d'un coup; et toute la préparation que j'y ai donnée par la peinture de la vertu farouche d'Horace, et par la défense qu'il fait à sa sœur de regretter qui que ce soit, de lui, ou de son Amant, qui meure au combat, n'est point suffisante pour faire attendre un emportement si extraordinaire, et servir de commencement à cette action. (1.840)

However, the second, more telling reason concerns the way in which Camille's murder not only compromises unity of action by introducing a second major dramatic focus, but also mixes the "public" events on which the central plot turns with the merely "private" question of the sister's wrath and ensuing murder. Camille's death

> fait une action double par le second péril où tombe Horace après être sorti du premier. L'unité de péril d'un Héros dans la Tragédie fait l'unité d'action; et quand il en est garanti, la pièce est finie, si ce n'est que la sortie même de ce péril l'engage si nécessairement dans un autre, que la liaison et la continuité des deux n'en fasse qu'une action; ce qui n'arrive point ici, où Horace revient triomphant sans aucun besoin de tuer sa soeur, ni même de parler à elle, et l'action serait suffisamment terminée à sa victoire. Cette chute d'un péril en l'autre sans nécessité fait ici un effet d'autant plus mauvais, que d'un péril public, où il y va

---

in 1640, Chapelain and d'Aubignac communicate objections about the ending to Corneille, their basis is *moral* rather than technical; and even in 1660, Corneille makes no apology for Camille's murder on moral grounds, implicitly reaffirming the characterological and ethical necessity insisted on twenty years earlier.

de tout l'Etat, il tombe en un péril particulier, où il n'y va que de
sa vie; et, pour dire encore plus, d'un péril illustre, où il ne peut
succomber que glorieusement, en un péril infâme, dont il ne
peut sortir sans tache. (1.840)[17]

The play thus highlights a major source of ideological confusion
that Hélène Merlin has shown to be endemic to the age.[18] The finale undermines the attempt to strike a balance between public
good and private interest and the related effort to determine just
where the former lies in contrast to the latter. A compulsory focus
of this problem is of course the King, a private individual in whom
the public world is encouraged (or obliged) to identify the embodiment of the commonwealth of which public and private are recip-
rocal if also antithetical constituents. But another focus is the royal
minister Richelieu, a figure all the more disturbing in that, hereditary duke as well as cardinal, his private person replicates the
ambiguities attending his public identity as at once the projection
and stage manager of the royal persona he represents.[19]

Still, as noteworthy as the mature poet's second thoughts about
the abrupt "second" action introduced with Camille's murder is the
younger Corneille's refusal to change it. In a both propitiatory and
prophylactic gesture, the poet submitted the text to the cardinaline
entourage for review prior to staging it. Two members, Chapelain
and the abbé d'Aubignac, author of the *Pratique du théâtre*, the
systematic summary of classical doctrine commissioned by Richelieu as a literary pendant to the *Testament politique*, presented the
coterie's criticism of the ending. In particular, they objected that,
despite the historical license in Livy, Horace's murder of his sister
was too infamous a deed for a hero to perform. They proposed instead that Camille commit suicide by throwing herself on her brother's sword. As d'Aubignac later put it in the *Pratique*, by impaling
herself on her brother's sword, Horace's desperate sister would

---

[17] Corneille adds a third flaw in the ending: "Camille qui ne tient que le second
rang dans les trois premiers Actes, et y laisse le premier à Sabine, prend le premier
en ces deux derniers, où cette Sabine n'est plus considérable," with the result that,
"s'il y a égalité dans les Moeurs, il n'y en a point dans la Dignité des Personnages"
(1.840). But the focus here is the purely technical question of a balanced distribu-
tion of roles, not the ending's ethical propriety.

[18] This is the presiding theme of Merlin's *Littérature et public*.

[19] See Jouhaud, *La Main de Richelieu* 157-85.

have saved both the integrity of recorded history and the decorum required by the stage: "ainsi elle fût morte de la main d'Horace, & lui eût été digne de compassion, comme un malheureux Innocent, l'Histoire et le Theatre auroient été d'accord." [20] But though, according to Chapelain, Corneille seemed for a time to concede the point, he finally dug in his heels, preserving the close as first conceived even at the cost of a new controversy that, shorter-lived and more muted than the "querelle du *Cid*," nonetheless further embittered the poet's relations with the learned circle linked to the cardinal and the Académie. [21] Whatever the mature view of the author of the 1660 *Théâtre* may have been, the Corneille of 1640 insists. The hero's intransigent commitment to duty produces a murder whose poisoned fruit is the disturbingly double verdict the King issues in order to resolve the dilemma Horace's actions pose:

> Cette énorme action faite presque à nos yeux
> Outrage la Nature, et blesse jusqu'aux Dieux.
> Un premier mouvement qui produit un tel crime
> Ne saurait lui servir d'excuse légitime,
> Les moins sévères lois en ce point sont d'accord,
> Et si nous les suivons, il est digne de mort.
> Si d'ailleurs nous voulons regarder le coupable,
> Ce crime quoique grand, énorme, inexcusable,
> Vient de la même épée et part du même bras
> Qui me fait aujourd'hui maître de deux Etats.
> Deux sceptres en ma main, Albe à Rome asservie,
> Parlent bien hautement en faveur de sa vie.
> Sans lui j'obéirais où je donne la loi,
> Et je serais Sujet où je suis deux fois Roi.
>
> (5.3.1733-46)

The respectable unity the play achieves in all other respects is thus directly bound to the duality voiced by no less a figure than the sovereign of victorious Rome. This emphasizes the conflicts Corneille means for the royal Tulle to face in bringing Rome's war with Alba to an end. But, by the same token, it stresses the crisis

---

[20] D'Aubignac, *Pratique du théâtre* 59.

[21] For accounts of these transactions, see Couton's "notice," *Œuvres complètes* 1.1537 and 1.1552, and his later *Richelieu* 19-20.

confronting the *collective* body, the "corps politique," of which, as King, Tulle is the titular embodiment. Far from solving, the conclusion Corneille fixes on *poses* problems for a contemporary public that wants at once to pity the desperate sister whose fiancé has died and to admire the hero who killed him–a hero, as d'Aubignac reveals, whose role as champion of Roman hegemony demands that he remain as sadly "innocent" as the unfortunate sister who dies on his sword.

Our question then, forming the prime focus of the problems *Horace* raises, is how to *read* the play. Further, given that the new play presents itself as a model of conformity to the classical rules Richelieu and the Académie enforce, how should we read drama *in general* as Corneille here reimagines it? As it happens, the same question frames the text with which Corneille commits the poem to public scrutiny: the complex dedicatory epistle accompanying the first edition of 1641. For as François Lasserre has brilliantly argued, the dedication to the cardinal is a masterpiece of studied insolence. [22]

> Monseigneur,
>
> Je n'aurais jamais eu la témérité de présenter à Votre Eminence ce mauvais portrait d'Horace, si je n'eusse considéré qu'après tant de bienfaits que j'ai reçus d'elle, le silence où mon respect m'a retenu jusqu'à présent passerait pour ingratitude, et que quelque juste défiance que j'aie de mon travail, je dois avoir encore plus de confiance en votre bonté. C'est d'elle que je tiens tout ce que je suis; et ce n'est pas sans rougir que pour toute reconnaissance je vous fais un présent si peu digne de Vous, et si peu proportionné à ce que je vous dois. (1.833)

On the surface, nothing could be more scrupulously respectful than these opening lines. Though one may detect polite hyperbole in Corneille's claim to owe Richelieu "everything I am," nothing in these first words seems to suggest anything but the most humble gratitude. Moreover, while Corneille has more in mind than mere

---

[22] I am indebted here to Lasserre's *Corneille* 21-34. However, for a surprisingly tone-deaf reading of the *dédicace*, see Murray, *Theatrical Legitimation* 124-25, where Corneille's "measured letter of praise" is taken *à la lettre*, presenting Richelieu "as a perfect viewer and mimetic model of princely insight."

"acts of kindness," he has in fact contracted numerous debts to the
cardinal, including receipt of a pension and the granting of letters
of nobility to his father. [23] Nevertheless, the occasion for the dedication remains the publication of Corneille's first play since the
controversy of *Le Cid*, with the result that the allusion to "bien-
faits" is susceptible to ironic construction. For beyond the pension
or the honor done his father, the most signal "gift" the cardinal has
bestowed is the public humiliation suffered for the earlier play.
Once that is acknowledged, every word Corneille crafts proves
double-edged. For a start, there is the "temerity" involved in offering Richelieu this "ill-drawn" or, shifting the focus of the French
mauvais from the depiction to the original, this "ill-favored portrait
of Horace." The ambiguous reference of the adjective "mauvais"
makes it unclear just where Corneille's sin is supposed to lie. If the
portrait's illness is a defect of the portraitist's art, the professed
"temerity" connotes the poet's humble reluctance to obtrude on
His Eminence's benevolent attention. But if the fault lies in the
original, the sin becomes Corneille's audacity in presenting the cardinal with a token of such ambivalent esteem. The gift is a hero
whose demonic heartlessness is doubly compromising: in that it directly answers to the aesthetic strictures Richelieu's cat's-paws prescribe and because of Corneille's insistence on preserving his original ending in the face of the objections Chapelain and d'Aubignac
relayed to him.

The ironies latent in this first part of the dedication grow more
uncomfortably evident in the continuation, when Corneille confesses that he has failed to compose a version of the famous history
equal to Livy's characterization of it as being the noblest tale in all
antiquity:

> Je voudrais que ce qu'il [Tite-Live] a dit de l'action se pût dire
> de la peinture que j'en ai faite, non pour en tirer plus de vanité,
> mais seulement pour vous offrir quelque chose un peu moins in-
> digne de vous être offert. Le sujet était capable de plus de
> grâces s'il eût été traité d'une main plus savante, mais du moins
> il a reçu de la mienne toutes celles qu'elle était capable de lui
> donner, et qu'on pouvait raisonnablement attendre d'une Muse

---

[23] See Couton's "notice," *Œuvres complètes* 1.1554-55.

de Province, qui n'étant pas assez heureuse pour jouir souvent des regards de Votre Eminence n'a pas les mêmes lumières à se conduire qu'ont celles qui en sont continuellement éclairées. Et certes, Monseigneur, ce changement visible qu'on remarque en mes Ouvrages, depuis que j'ai l'honneur d'être à Votre Eminence, qu'est-ce autre chose qu'un effet des grandes Idées qu'elle m'inspire quand elle daigne souffrir que je lui rende mes devoirs; et à quoi peut-on attribuer ce qui s'y mêle de mauvais qu'aux teintures grossières que je reprends quand je demeure abandonné à ma propre foiblesse? (1.833-34)

The key is how we are to understand the "visible change" observed in Corneille's work "since I have had the honor to belong to Your Eminence." What shows this otherwise entirely conventional piece of flattery to be other than it appears is the antecedent; for if one asks in what the "visible change" consists, the answer can only be the immediately preceding play, Le Cid. Corneille had already written seven plays by the time he composed his at once stunningly successful and violently controversial tragi-comedy. It is however only with Le Cid, a play so popular that its producer Mondory was obliged to seat his most illustrious patrons on the stage to fit them in the theater at all, [24] that he achieves the celebrity that warrants dedicating his new play to a figure as august as the cardinal. But this means that the "effect of the great Ideas" the poet claims to owe His Eminence is just the play for which Richelieu has had him punished.

True, the ritual suggestion that such "graces" as poor Corneille has managed to bring his handling of Horace derive from his patron finds an echo in the equally ritual notion that such "ill things" as critics may detect are "crude dyes" (teintures grossières) seeping in when the poet is "abandoned" to his native "weakness." Things might have been different had he rejoiced in the privilege of inhabiting Paris rather than the provincial Rouen, where Corneille continues to reside till as late as 1662. But unlike his luckier colleagues, he is not "so fortunate as to bask regularly in Your Eminence's gaze" and has not therefore "benefited from the guiding lights enjoyed by those who are continually illuminated by it." And yet the

---

[24] Ibid. 1.1449-50.

product of Corneille's lowly "Provincial Muse," a figure in which Georges Couton is surely right to discern a sly echo of slighting remarks his metropolitan rivals have made at his expense, [25] is his most famous play to date. Rude provincial though he is, he has, in his "weakness," penned in *Le Cid* and the unamended *Horace* poems that far outshine anything the poets dancing attendance on the cardinal have accomplished. Unlearned though his hand may be, "unworthy" as he pretends to believe the gift he now makes his patron of a play nevertheless entirely constructed in accordance with the cardinal's formal scheme, he proves superior to those with whom Richelieu has chosen to surround himself. And not the least source of this superiority is a *moral* one: in the proud independence of his retreat in Rouen, he remains his own man, refusing to fawn upon his master.

Against this background, the final movement of the dedication, describing in detail the nature of Richelieu's supposedly beneficent influence, sounds a distinctly defiant note:

Il faut, Monseigneur, que tous ceux qui donnent leurs veilles au Théâtre publient hautement avec moi que nous vous devons deux obligations très signalées; l'une d'avoir ennobli le but de l'Art, l'autre de nous en avoir facilité les connaissances. Vous avez ennobli le but de l'Art, puisqu'au lieu de celui de plaire au peuple, que nous prescrivent nos Maîtres, et dont les deux plus honnêtes gens de leur siècle, Scipion et Lélie ont autrefois protesté de se contenter, vous nous avez donné celui de vous plaire et de vous divertir; et qu'ainsi nous ne rendons pas un petit service à l'Etat, puisque contribuant à vos divertissements, nous contribuons à l'entretien d'une santé qui lui est si précieuse et si nécessaire. Vous nous en avez facilité les conaissances puisque nous n'avons plus besoin d'autre étude pour les acquérir, que d'attacher nos yeux sur Votre Eminence quand elle honore de sa présence et de son attention le récit de nos Poèmes. C'est là que lisant sur son visage ce qui lui plaît, et ce qui ne lui plaît pas, nous nous instruisons avec certitude de ce qui est bon, et de ce qui est mauvais, et tirons des règles infaillibles de ce qu'il faut suivre et de ce qu'il faut éviter. C'est là que j'ai souvent appris en deux heures ce que mes livres n'eussent pu m'appren-

[25] Ibid. 1.1555.

dre en dix ans; c'est là que j'ai puisé ce qui m'a valu l'applaudis-
sement du Public, et c'est là qu'avec votre faveur j'espère puiser
assez pour être un jour une oeuvre digne de vos mains. (1.834)

The rhetorical footwork here is especially intricate. First comes
further conventional praise: dramatic poets owe Richelieu the double debt of ennobling their art and easing the way to knowledge of
it. However, on a close view, the ennoblement takes a peculiar
form, the more clearly when we notice that it deviates from the classical examples in whose name Corneille has been made to suffer.
"Our Masters," both the teachers we had in school and the best
modern authorities on dramatic art, teach that drama's highest goal
is to please "the people," a doctrine seconded by the protestations
of "the two most accomplished gentlemen" of the heroic Republican age, Scipio Africanus and Caius Laelius the Wise. [26] But Richelieu has reduced contemporaries to pleasing himself alone. Instead
of setting themselves the task of serving the wider community,
dramatists now direct their efforts exclusively to the state. In doing
so, moreover, their aim is not to offer that state a model of the principles on which it ought to rest or the ideals it ought to pursue. It is
simply to entertain the royal minister, helping to maintain "the well-
being of one who is so precious and so needful" to the current political order.

Through Richelieu's influence, the drama has ceased to play any
social role beyond that of making the cardinal happy. What then of
his contribution to knowledge of the art? Just as the mission of
French dramatists amounts henceforth to little more than diverting
the minister, so have their literary sources dwindled. In the past,
and above all in the classical past, mastering the art of drama required years of patient study, sleepless "vigils" spent poring over
ancient and modern models and acquiring that broader knowledge
of history, philosophy, and rhetoric all authorities agree a poet worthy of the name must own. [27] By contrast, Corneille and his fellows

---

[26] According to Couton (ibid., note 3), Corneille alludes to the prologue to Te-
rence's *Andria*, of which 17th-century commentators took Scipio and Laelius to be
joint authors. That Corneille should cite authorities from Republican as opposed to
both royal and imperial Rome is obviously significant.

[27] This is of course a commonplace of contemporary theory. See, e.g., d'Aubignac's *Pratique*, book 1, chap. 5, "De la maniere dont on doit s'instruire pour travailler au Poëme Dramatique."

"no longer need any study other than that of fixing our eyes on Your Eminence when you honor the recital of our Poems with your presence and attention." Rather than devote the lifetime of reading tradition calls for, it suffices to scrutinize His Eminence's face for signs of what pleases and what does not, drawing from this lesson "infallible rules" to be guided by. In studying the cardinal's face, "I have," Corneille protests, "often learned in two hours more than my books could have taught me in ten years." This is of course more flattery; but especially when set beside conventional re-minders of what learning to write truly demands, the flattery's deri-sive disproportion becomes obvious.

Further, in citing the cardinal's face as the text in which poets read the true secrets of their art, the flattery hints at the baleful sig-nificance of those eyes in whose implacable light his more "fortu-nate" rivals stand just because they remain in the capital. Skillfully coded yet unmistakable, Corneille describes an "asiatic" tyranny out of Tacitus, a despotic court whose supine inhabitants surrender all self-respect to their arbitrary lord. By contrast, in remaining, in his "weakness," far from the cardinal's gaze, drawing such inspi-ration as he can from a rude provincial muse who, denied regular attendance on her political master, falls back on honest labor devot-ed to lonely study and selfless craft, Corneille maintains the highest traditions of his art. And lest (*par miracle*) the linx-eyed minister should miss the point, Corneille adds another touch. For all he makes the politic claim that it is "there," in Richelieu's face, that he has "drawn [*puisé*] whatever has earned [him] the Public's ap-plause," what he in fact reminds the cardinal, *to* his face, is that the merit is all his own. The applause he boasts of was earned by the play that precedes the one he now dedicates–a reminder the more pointed given Corneille's rejection of Chapelain and d'Aubignac's advice to change the new play's end.

Whence, finally, the ambiguities surrounding the dedication's coda in Corneille's professed "hope" that, with the cardinal's ongo-ing help, he may "draw [*puiser*] enough to be, one day, a work wor-thy of your hands." The formula's elaborate (not to say baroque) obliqueness ("j'espère puiser assez pour être un jour une oeuvre digne de vos mains") makes its meaning more than a little puzzling. In what sense, for instance, should we read the preposition in the phrase "worthy of your hands"? Does it denote a work worthy of being (like the one now dedicated) put *into* Richelieu's hands? Or, circling back to the hyperbole identifying Richelieu as the *fons et origo* of Corneille's best writing, does it designate a poem that, inspired by the "infallible rules" gleaned from the cardinal's face, comes *from* the cardinal's hands, as a poem composed by Richelieu himself?

This first equivocation engenders others. For what does it mean to say that the poem Corneille hopes to write–a poem other than the *Horace* here put in Richelieu's hands, or the earlier *Le Cid* Richelieu's henchmen vilified–would be in effect the cardinal's work? And what, by extension, becomes of such poems as Corneille stipulates *are* in fact "worthy" of his patron's hands: the works of those happy rivals fortunate enough to dwell continually in the cardinal's presence? Is it not implied that, good as Corneille concedes they are, such poems lack the crucial qualities of which only he can boast in his very "weakness"–the honesty, courage, and originality of penning works that are the authentic products of his own rather than another's genius? Further, are not his rivals' poems *un*-worthy both of the poets who wrote them and of the tyrannical patron to whose arbitrary dictates they conform? And does this not in turn imply that it is just because he *refuses* to yield to the censorious pressure the cardinal exerts that Corneille alone proves worthy, as the one poet possessing the strength of character to remain true to his own inspiration, crude and provincial as that may be?

All of which points to one final ambiguity, focused on the word "work." What exactly is the word's complement? While, in keeping with the rhetorical context of a dedication, we have tacitly supposed it to mean the poem Corneille dedicates, the syntax also allows it to refer to the poet himself. Corneille reverts to the earlier theme of "belonging" to the cardinal and owing him "everything I am," including knowledge of the rules of the art of dramatic poetry. But is it really the mere hyperbole this suggests, or does it carry a more ironic and polemical charge, amplified by Corneille's seemingly modest confession of unworthiness? For if, like Corneille's rivals, one is not only the cardinal's man, but his "work," the product of his powerful hand, eye, and will, one is neither more nor less than his *creature*. By acknowledging his unworthiness, Corneille declares once again a fierce independence, standing apart in proud contrast to spineless rivals condemned to do their master's despotic bidding.

The fact is that, slippery and even contradictory as Corneille's meanings are, what matters is less their sense than the task of *making* sense they demand of the reader the dedication addresses. Corneille has his say, but in a medium that enables him, by deferring the moment at which his true intent is grasped, to force the cardinal to *read closely*. And what has to be read is not only the dedication in which Corneille specifies the cardinal as his reader, but above all the text the dedication puts into his hands: the play *Horace*, unchanged end and all, presented from the outset as its author's response to the fate inflicted on the earlier *Le Cid*.

At one level, Corneille's insistence on Camille's murder lends support to the case Lyons makes for the "historical doubleness" of *Horace*.[28] What indeed makes the play a *tragedy* in something approaching the strict sense favored by the modern theory of the genre descending from Hegel and Nietzsche through Lukács, Goldmann, and Benjamin is the intolerable burden that historical events lay on the people condemned to serve as at once their agents and victims.[29] This burden is expressed, for instance, by the insoluble conflict noted earlier between public good and private suffering, and thus, as the play's King himself admits, between politics and an uppercase "Nature" tellingly at odds with political right. This first opposition is then both adumbrated and intensified by that between genders, contrasting the armed men who *act* with the house-bound women who *wait*, but also pitting the takers of life against the bearers of the lives they take. The play is accordingly characterized by the multiplication of irreducible yet irreconcilable perspectives embodied by Horace and his father, Curiace and the King, Camille and Sabine, yielding what Lyons rightly calls a radical "relativism" in whose light the suffering and death the duel entails appear at once irrevocable and unredeemed.[30]

---

[28] See Lyons, *Tragedy of Origins*, chap. 1, "*Horace* and Historical Doubleness."

[29] On the contrast between early modern conceptions of tragedy and the one we use today, see Marvin Carlson, *Theories of the Theatre: A Historical and Critical Survey, from the Greeks to the Present* (Ithaca, NY: Cornell University Press, 1984) 33-36 and 38-51. In his *Origin of German Tragic Drama*, "Trauerspiel and Tragedy" (57-158), Benjamin addresses the divorce between the medieval sense of tragedy still current in the German baroque and what, since Hegel, later theorists (Nietzsche, Lukács, Goldmann) understand thereby.

[30] Lyons, *Tragedy of Origins* 48.

In this sense, even the fiercely consequent hero suffers division and loss. Monstrous as his conduct may appear, Horace is also a *victim*: the murder caused by his zealous embrace of duty is the correlate of the *self*-murder required to transform him into duty's pitiless instrument. Such is indeed, as Lyons notes, the testimony of the savage speech in which, responding to Curiace's humane ambivalence at the prospect of their duel, the exultant hero brags that the very sacrifice of human sentiment the two champions are called to make is the paradoxical measure of the honor their cities do them:

> Mourir pour le pays est un si digne sort,
> Qu'on briguerait en foule une si belle mort.
> Mais vouloir au Public immoler ce qu'on aime,
> S'attacher au combat contre un autre soi-même,
> Attaquer un parti qui prend pour défenseur
> Le frère d'une femme et l'Amant d'une sœur,
> Et, rompant tous ces nœuds s'armer pour la Patrie,
> Contre un sang qu'on voudrait racheter de sa vie,
> Une telle vertu n'appartenait qu'à nous,
> L'éclat de son grand nom lui fait peu de jaloux,
> Et peu d'hommes au cœur l'ont assez imprimée,
> Pour oser aspirer à tant de Renommée.
>
> (2.3.441-52)

Whatever its motives, and whatever the nature of the ends it will achieve, Horace's unquestioning allegiance entails the sacrifice of the hero's own humanity, an alienation the more radical and complete for the fanatical exaltation with which he rejoices in his fate.[31]

And yet pitiable though even Horace's condition may be, it cannot efface a sense of wrong that is both more and other than merely "tragic." This is in part because, unlike the sacrifices made by the unquestionably heroic Rodrigue and Chimène of *Le Cid*, the price the new play's hero is willing to pay is finally borne by others more than himself. But it is also because the gain achieved is compromised by the political *interest* involved. Consider more closely the terms in which the King pardons the "great, enormous, inexcusable" crime Horace commits in murdering his sister:

---

[31] Ibid. 49-52.

> Deux sceptres en ma main, Albe à Rome asservie,
> Parlent bien hautement en faveur de sa vie.
> Sans lui j'obéirais où je donne la loi,
> Et je serais Sujet où je suis deux fois Roi.

As the multiplication of first-person pronouns reminds us, though absolutism identifies sovereign and state, defining the one as the symbolic embodiment of the other, the only true beneficiary of the violence Horace inflicts is the private individual Tulle himself. The subjection of Alba to Rome is finally the subjection of both cities to one man–the royal "I" who now holds two sceptres instead of one, who gives the law where he would otherwise have obeyed it, who is now "twice King" where he would otherwise have borne the yoke of Subject everyone else must bear. The ultimate fruit of the sufferings of which the hero Horace is the instrument is the essentially arbitrary aggrandizement of the monarch who leaves Camille's murder unpunished.

All of which gives great emphasis to a speech Lyons rightly interprets as an emblematic summation of the tangle of contradictory viewpoints, commitments, and motives that informs the play: Sabine's request that she be allowed to expiate her husband's crime by dying in his place.[32] Sabine's speech, opening the climactic scene of judgment in which the King confronts the suppliant survivors of the day's tragic events, begins by voicing the double character of her identity as at once sibling of the dead Curiaces and wife of the man who killed them:

> Sire, écoutez Sabine, et voyez dans son âme
> Les douleurs d'une sœur, et celles d'une femme,
> Qui toute désolée à vos sacrés genoux
> Pleure pour sa famille, et craint pour son époux.
> (5.3.1595-98)

But of course, as the conjunction of spousal fear and familial grief announces, what brings her before the King is not the duel in which her brothers died, but the murder of her sister-in-law Camille. Though the "sorrows of a sister" lend phatic weight to her utter-

---

[32] For Lyons's reading of this speech, ibid. 69-70.

ance, it is initially in her character as wife that she speaks, offering her life in exchange for her husband's:

> Ce n'est pas que je veuille avec cet artifice
> Dérober un coupable au bras de la justice,
> Quoi qu'il ait fait pour vous traitez-le comme tel,
> Et punissez en moi ce noble criminel;
> De mon sang malheureux expiez tout son crime,
> Vous ne changerez point pour cela de victime,
> Ce ne sera point prendre une injuste pitié,
> Mais en sacrifier la plus chère moitié.
> Les nœuds de l'Hyménée et son amour extrême
> Font qu'il vit plus en moi, qu'il ne vit en lui-même,
> Et si vous m'accordez de mourir aujourd'hui,
> Il mourra plus en moi, qu'il ne mourrait en lui.
>
> (5.3.1599-1610)

The term "artifice" in the first line of the continuation already alerts us to the complex nature of the transaction the scene undertakes and of the attendant complexity of Sabine's own performance. A first point is the way the word underscores the extremity of the situation. Though an antithetically *"noble* criminal," Horace is nonetheless a *criminal* and must suffer for his crime. Further, much as Tulle owes him as a result of the victory he has won in the duel, the King is obliged, *as* King, to punish him for the murder to which that same victory led. The cause of justice, a cause all concerned would like to imagine is consistent with the rule of *nature*, can only be served by antithetical means: a device whose makeshift as well as unnatural character Sabine's "artifice" signals from the start.

But the word "artifice" also points to the speech itself. Sabine protests that her aim in proposing to die in Horace's place is not, as the King might suspect, to frustrate natural right by snatching the "guilty one" from the grasp of retributive justice. She does not therefore attempt, by artificial means, to rescue the antithetically "noble criminal" by inspiring a correspondingly antithetical "unjust pity" in the monarch's breast. On the contrary, she claims that his wife's death would punish Horace more severely than his own since the "bonds of matrimony," seconded by the "extreme" of conjugal "love" she supposes him to feel, dictate that "he lives more in me than in himself" and will in consequence "die more in me" than in his own person. The artifice would thus fulfil the decrees of natural justice more even than the more obviously natural expedient of putting the guilty hero to death.

And yet while the solution it would accomplish at least seems natural, just, and right, the proposal itself remains an *artifice*. Nor does Sabine deny or conceal its artificiality: though the end pursued is natural and just, the means to that end is makeshift. But then so, too, is the means Sabine employs to *justify* the course proposed. In speaking of "artifice," Sabine reminds us of the artificial nature of her speech itself. Persuasive as she hopes her words will be–indeed, precisely because they *are* persuasive–her speech designates its source in an *art* of persuasion, an art of *rhetoric*, as such at variance with the natural justice in whose name she purports to speak.

But in offering her life as a more painful and thus more just alternative to her husband's death, Sabine is actuated not merely, or even primarily, by a desire for justice; she is also animated by the loathing and the desire for revenge Horace has inspired by killing her brothers:

> La mort que je demande et qu'il faut que j'obtienne
> Augmentera sa peine, et finira la mienne.
> Sire, voyez l'excès de mes tristes ennuis,
> Et l'effroyable état où mes jours sont réduits.
> Quelle horreur d'embrasser un homme dont l'épée
> De toute ma famille a la trame coupée
> Et quelle impiété de haïr un époux
> Pour avoir bien servi les siens, l'Etat, et vous!
> Aimer un bras souillé du sang de tous mes frères!
> N'aimer pas un mari qui finit nos misères!
> Sire, délivrez-moi par un heureux trépas
> Des crimes de l'aimer, et de ne l'aimer pas.
>
> (5.3.1611-22)

In unpacking, step by step, the passions of horror and vengeful hate the sister feels for the husband she must criminally love as his wife, the "artifice" that opens by claiming to solve the problem of natural justice ends by revealing the outraged "nature" that seeks to punish Horace in the sacrificial death Sabine proposes in exchange for his life.

The fact, then, that the play denies any one sure position from which to command the meaning of events and the true character of the justice the monarch is called on to defend confirms the barbarous narrowness and excess of the nominal hero's conduct. Whether we see him as monster or victim is all one. The victory he wins for both Rome and his own undying renown as Rome's sacrificial agent is finally cancelled by the murderous *arbitrariness* of the tragic necessity for which Horace serves as a focal instrument. Nor is Horace the sole target of Sabine's demand to die. When we recall, as she herself pointedly does in verse 1618, that the ultimate beneficiary of her husband's hateful services is neither his own family ("les siens"), nor Rome ("l'Etat"), but the King ("vous"), the sacrifice by which she intends to brand Horace for ever targets the monarch at whose hand she claims a vengeful death.

Insofar as Corneille's conception of the oxymoronically "noble criminal" he has chosen for his hero walks in step with the play's painstaking formal regularity, the horrors that spring from Horace's zealous embrace of his sovereign's cause epitomize the moral as well as artistic entailments of conformity to the rules Scudéry and the Académie impose with Richelieu's approval. This in turn lends deeper color to Harriet Stone's interpretation of the royal edict with which the play formally ends. [33] Having pardoned Horace, Tulle urges Sabine to efface the overt symptoms of her distress since it is only "en séchant vos pleurs que vous vous montrerez / La véritable sœur de ceux que vous pleurez." (5.3.1768-70) He then turns to the rites of propitiation and mourning required to heal the wounds the conclusion of the war has inflicted. The last of these concerns doing justice to Camille:

> Je la plains, et pour rendre à son sort rigoureux
> Ce que peut souhaiter son esprit amoureux,
> Puisqu'en un même jour l'ardeur d'un même zèle
> Achève le Destin de son Amant, et d'elle,
> Je veux qu'en même jour témoin de leurs deux morts
> En un même tombeau voie enfermer leurs corps.
>
> (5.3.1777-82)

---

[33] Stone, *Classical Model* 55-58.

According to Stone, the King's decree that Camille and Curiace be buried in a common tomb constitutes a *mise en abyme*. As Forestier has pointed out, albeit in a more reductive spirit than the case calls for, the tragi-comic *Le Cid* is fundamentally "romantic." To this extent, despite the oppositional politics subtending its development, the play remains faithful to the original *pastoral* inspiration of Cornelian drama. Nor is it irrelevant that pastoral is a mode in which (the grim *Médée* of 1634 nothwithstanding) Corneille stubbornly persists well after other poets–Scudéry with *La Mort de César* or Mairet with *Sophonisbe*, both in 1634–make the explicitly political turn for which, ironically, Corneille himself eventually becomes famous. [34] With *Horace* then, six years late, Corneille refashions himself as France's preeminent "historical" poet committed to meditation on the political model of ancient Rome. But in the very act of completing the change, he pauses to set the price for the art he abjures at Richelieu's command. The historical agon sealed with the murders of Camille and Curiace mirrors the political agon pitting Corneille against the cardinal and his coterie. Corneille finally gives them the classical program-play they demand, and the result is the death of the pastoral couple, Camille and Curiace, who remain true to love to the end–he in the ambivalence with which he responds to the call to fight, she in the rage with which she turns on her inhuman brother in her dead lover's name. But, in exchange, the monarch for whose sake all of these horrors have been committed erects a funereal *monument* that, in honoring the murdered lovers, also honors the poet whose art they symbolize.

Horace thus becomes an allegory of the sacrifice Corneille consents to make, burying romantic drama along with the pastoral pair who are the play's central victims. The "historical doubleness" Lyons diagnoses gives way to the reflexive double gesture Stone discerns in the tragedy's self-designating close. But in converting the play into an allegory of the agonistic conditions of its own composition, Corneille goes a step further. Beyond the historical action and the political resistance that action encodes is the *text* of Cornelian drama, a text whose originality lies in the labor required to distinguish it from orthodox lookalikes by lesser hands.

---

[34]   Forestier, "Politique et tragédie" 67-68.

We return to our initial point: what truly matters in the dramatic poem, *Le Cid*, *Horace*, or any other, is in the end the *text* and how we *read* it. The dedication of *Horace* reminds us that the play's true meaning emerges not in the playhouse, where, for instance, we risk missing the pointed reference to the minister who begot its ruthless and inhuman hero on Corneille's Provincial Muse. We meet it in the quiet of the study where we enjoy the presence of mind required to pay the Machiavellian attention alone capable of sorting its deepest intentions out. What counts is less the play than its *double*, the indiscernible counterpart Corneille submits to the cardinal as the one reader astute enough to comprehend what he has written. The peculiar identity of the text of classical drama is then defined by an artful duplicity registered in the need to distinguish between the spectacle's manifest sense and a layer of intimations other than, and at times directly opposed to, the public intent that immediately meets the eye. But the critical force it derives therefrom, the ironic and oppositional potential its duplicity yields, trades just on how hard it is to *tell the difference*. As in Corneille's address to the cardinal, what we read as the overt work, performed on the public stage, and the text that travels on its back, though different, are also *the same*: each reproduces the other, verbatim, like identical twins. Our problem is therefore to learn to tell a difference where there *is* none–more precisely, to tell a difference where *telling* a difference is the at once moral, artistic, and political issue joined.

Yet this problem also forms the basis of the great claim Corneille makes for his art. By posing the question of difference, and the related need to *read* what drama turns out to be uniquely empowered to *write*, he identifies dramatic poetry's peculiar authority as a text whose business it is, *as* text, to reproduce rather than slavishly resolve the difficulties with which its action, themes, and characters engage. Given this task, what could be more fitting than to turn now to a play in which telling such an impossible difference is the crux on which the dramatic action explicitly revolves?

The play in question is Corneille's *Rodogune*, a tragedy first produced during the winter season of 1644-45, two years after Richelieu's death. What recommends this play is its commanding plot device: the fact that its pivotal characters are identical twins. In that the problem facing all of the play's protagonists, including and especially the twins themselves, is how to tell them apart, *Rodogune* enacts, at the level of its plot, precisely the difficulties encountered by a student of the occasioning poem. The play thus enables us to examine, in the form of a dramatic action, the duplicity that shapes its own dual identity as drama and as text.

Rodogune stages its own double nature, dramatizing in the process how this doubleness works and where it leads. But beyond instilling a deeper understanding of the duplicity of its text, the play teaches how, by virtue of this duplicity, it exposes dilemmas that frame the society to which it presents the tragic example of its geminated heroes. In Corneille's dedicatory epistle to *Horace*, the ironic resources available to any text are actualized by the external pressure its tyrannical recipient exerts. So too, in *Rodogune*, though the formal condition for the play's duplicity is its dual nature as drama and poem, the reason for exploiting it lies in the public on whose behalf a tragedy is performed. *Rodogune* portrays to its audience a world–as it happens, a royal court–whose very survival hangs on deciding which one of two identical claimants should ascend to its perilously vacant throne. In the process, the questions the play raises about its own identity, and thereby about not only its true intent, but the position of the poet who authors that intent, engage the cultural order of which it is an expression and yet from which it finally differs, as a mirror from the face whose likeness it projects. In questioning its own identity, *Rodogune* questions that of the society before which it is mounted–a society all the more pertinaciously implicated by the critical role notions of identity play in the system of moral, political, aesthetic, and psychological presumptions on which the play's action rests.

There are, it is true, features of the theme that the noble genre of tragedy will not touch. As we shall see in chapter 3, the Mercury and Night of the prologue to Molière's *Amphitryon* cheerfully expatiate on the distance between "real" identities and mere comic roles; and they also gossip about the questionable excesses of the Jovian master whose venereal appetites bring them on stage. By contrast, decorum forbids *Rodogune* to expose its own fictional conditions in this way. Nor can Corneille's tragedy deal openly with the messy reproductive processes of which comic sex (as opposed to tragic love) offers a salient image. The protagonists of tragedy must play it straight, condemned by generic propriety to be whoever it is they nobly are. And yet, in *Rodogune*, who the protagonists *are* is just the question, engendering the tragic dilemmas they have to face. Nor can they *choose* who to be, for they inhabit a world that has already defined their identities for them, even if in such a way as to call those identities in doubt.

Rodogune's central dramatic problem is that the two central characters, Antiochus and Séleucus, are not only brothers, and unusually loving friends, but twins. Indeed, when they first appear on stage in 1.3, they constitute a single entity. Offered (as they nobly yet fondly imagine) the choice between the woman they love and the throne to which their royal blood calls them, each spontaneously reacts with a romantic integrity mirrored in the other: each chooses the woman, ceding his brother the crown.

True, a central thrust of the ensuing action will be the brothers' tragic differentiation. Corneille's plot orchestrates a medley of fiercely rival interests: the twins' competition for the heroine's love; their mother Cléopâtre's struggle to maintain her hold on the throne; the heroine Rodogune's efforts to counter Cléopâtre on behalf of the twins' dead father Nicanor; Nicanor's pursuit of revenge from beyond the grave. The collective effect of all of these interests is to force the brothers apart. As early as act 1, though she does not reveal his name, Rodogune confesses a secret sympathy for one twin as against the other, providing in the process a theory of the mysterious "election" Marc Fumaroli identifies as being of the essence of Corneille's fundamentally pastoral conception of love:[35]

> Il est des nœuds secrets, il est des sympathies,
> Dont par le doux rapport les âmes assorties
> S'attachent l'une à l'autre, et se laissent piquer
> Par ces je ne sais quoi, qu'on ne peut expliquer.
> C'est par là que l'un d'eux obtient la préférence,
> Je crois voir l'autre encore avec indifférence,
> Mais cette indifférence est une aversion,
> Lorsque je le compare avec ma passion.
> Etrange effet d'amour! incroyable chimère!

[35] See Fumaroli, "Pierre Corneille, fils de son oeuvre," in *Héros et orateurs* 17-61. What Fumaroli also calls the "épopée du couple" (50) is the guiding thread of the entire essay. On *Rodogune*, see 51-54. On the Cornelian "dramaturgie du couple" more generally, 399-413.

> Je voudrais être à lui, si je n'aimais son frère,
> Et le plus grand des maux toutefois que je crains,
> C'est que mon triste sort me livre entre ses mains.
>
> (1.5.359-70)

The "chimerical" distinction Rodogune detects sharpens in the up-shot. When, in 2.4, the brothers react to their mother's demand that one of them kill Rodogune in exchange for the crown, Séleucus betrays a melancholy cynicism in contrast to Antiochus's hardier resilience. The contrast grows starker still in the wake of Rodogune's declaration at 3.4.1041-46 that she will marry the twin who agrees to murder his mother. Finally, in the interval between acts 4 and 5, Séleucus dies at the hands of his mother's henchmen, severing the twins' union once and for all. Nevertheless, what at once makes all of the interests possible and suspends their fulfilment till differentiation occurs is the original identity. The brothers are indiscernible counterparts, trapped by selves simultaneously fixed and unhinged by the fact of their gemination.

It is important that the initial lack of difference is not part of the version of events in Appian of Alexandria's history of the wars of Hellenistic Syria Corneille draws on for his tragic fable. It marks rather an act of free creation that, as the poet reports in the critical introduction to the text of 1660, produced "des incidents surprenants qui sont purement de mon invention et n'avaient jamais été vus au théâtre" (2.200). Whence the author's pronounced (if, in his own estimation, irrationally paternal) affection for this play above all others. [36] In view then of the author's strong feelings about the device, as of the marked originality he claims on its behalf, we may ask what moral and dramatic *difference* the twins' seminal gemination makes.

To begin with is the doubt thrown on the critical question of primogeniture determining the order of royal succession, a question

---

[36] "On m'a souvent fait une question à la cour: quel était celui de mes poèmes que j'estimais le plus; et j'ai trouvé tous ceux qui me l'ont faite si prévenus en faveur de *Cinna*, ou du *Cid*, que je n'ai jamais osé déclarer toute la tendresse que j'ai toujours eue pour celui-ci, à qui j'aurais volontiers donné mon suffrage, si je n'avais craint de manquer en quelque sorte au respect que je devais à ceux que je voyais pencher d'un autre côté. Cette préférence est peut-être en moi un effet de ces inclinations aveugles, qu'ont beaucoup de pères pour quelques-uns de leurs enfants, plus que pour les autres." (2.199-200)

related to the problem of counterparts even before Nicanor's murder at Cléopâtre's command creates the pressing need to fill a vacant throne. Though Nicanor's presumed death following the disastrous invasion of Parthia leaves Syria kingless, the state retains a
regent in the person of Nicanor's queen. But as the play repeatedly
reminds us, the people do not willingly accept female rule: a point
made first in the confidante Laonice's narrative of events that have
taken place before the start of the play (1.1.47-78); then in the
speech in which Cléopâtre explains to a horrified Laonice the
lengths to which she is driven by the *libido dominandi*, the delight
in power her tenure as regent has revealed (2.2.489-94); and a third
time when Cléopâtre justifies her past conduct to her sons (2.3.535-
38). A woman sovereign is by definition illegitimate, lacking the intrinsic authority only a male can possess: a fact that precipitates Syria's collapse following Nicanor's disappearance, forcing Cléopâtre
to replace him by marrying his brother, a second "Antiochus" we
must distinguish from Nicanor's son. [37] The lack of a male ruler
destabilizes the state, which indeed rallies only once Nicanor's
brother ascends the throne.

But no sooner has the brother taken Nicanor's place than he
proceeds to replicate Nicanor's strategic errors, launching an ill-advised counterattack whose failure leads him to suicide. It is at this
point that the Syrians learn that, though taken for dead, Nicanor is
in fact very much alive, and plans to reassume his crown with
Parthia's blessing. However, the Nicanor who returns is not the one
his kingdom lost. In addition to reclaiming his birthright, he intends to set his first wife aside in favor of a new one, his Parthian
adversary's sister Rodogune: a projected second marriage dictated
both by reasons of state, as a dynastic bond uniting the two warring
kingdoms, and by personal resentment. For whatever her motives
in marrying her husband's brother (and, as her speech to Laonice in
2.2 reveals, they are far from simple or pure), Cléopâtre's inadvertently bigamous second union has made a cuckold of him. He
means now to repay the insult with interest, not only taking a se-

---

[37] The problem of names (more precisely, homonymy) hovers over Cléopâtre as
well, whose name Corneille had intended to give the play instead of Rodogune's.
However, as he explains in the *examen* (1.199), he not only abandoned this plan,
but suppressed all mention of the queen's name in order to avoid potential confusion with the queen's notorious Egyptian namesake.

cond, younger bride, but marrying Rodogune in a ceremony he will compel Cléopâtre to attend, inflicting a public disgrace commensurate with the one he has endured. As Laonice puts it in the continuation of the narrative of antecedent events begun in 1.1, Cléopâtre's frantic excuses fall on deaf ears:

> On ne rencontre en lui qu'un juge inexorable,
> Et son amour nouveau la veut croire coupable;
> Son erreur est un crime, et pour l'en punir mieux,
> Il veut même épouser Rodogune à ses yeux,
> Arracher de son front le sacré Diadème,
> Pour ceindre une autre tête en sa présence même;
> Soit qu'ainsi sa vengeance eût plus d'indignité,
> Soit qu'ainsi cet Hymen eût plus d'autorité,
> Et qu'il assurât mieux par cette barbarie
> Aux enfants qui naîtraient le Trône de Syrie.
>
> (1.4.239-48)

Stirred by both her own resentment and the taste for power she has developed during Nicanor's absence, Cléopâtre responds with energy: her husband is murdered on the road home and Rodogune is taken hostage, forcing the King of Parthia to sue for terms. To be sure, as Cléopâtre boasts to Laonice in a speech exposing both the depth of her policy and the scope of her desire in saving the kingdom from its Parthian enemies, her complicated maneuvers have also bought *time*, "un trésor," as she calls it, "plus grand qu'on ne peut croire" (2.2.515). What she means is time to secure her own hold on power. But the respite Cléopâtre's maneuvers buy for her own ends is determined by the question of succession she hopes to turn to her advantage. What holds off the powerful forces Cléopâtre battles is that the identity of Nicanor's true heir remains unknown; and it is unknown because the candidates are twins.

Nicanor has left two sons, exactly identical in every respect save one, the order of their emergence from their mother's womb: an order that, in determining which of the two is technically the elder, also determines which is his father's heir. This in turn defines the central dramatic issue, announced by Laonice in the play's opening lines:

> Enfin ce jour pompeux, cet heureux jour nous luit,
> Qui d'un trouble si long doit dissiper la nuit,
> Ce grand jour, où l'Hymen étouffant la vengeance
> Entre le Parthe et nous remet l'intelligence,
> Affranchit la Princesse, et nous fait pour jamais
> Du motif de la guerre un lien de la paix.
> Ce grand jour est venu, mon frère, où notre Reine
> Cessant de plus tenir la Couronne incertaine
> Doit rompre aux yeux de tous son silence obstiné,
> De deux Princes gémeaux nous déclarer l'aîné;
> Et l'avantage seul d'un moment de naissance,
> Dont elle a jusqu'ici caché la connaissance,
> Mettant au plus heureux le sceptre dans la main,
> Va faire l'un Sujet, et l'autre Souverain.

> (1.1.1-14)

Cléopâtre's role, the source of her continuing power and the
unavoidable duty whose performance will finally undo her, is to distinguish one twin from the other. The glorious "day" the queen has
won for the fulfillment of her wishes is also the dramatic period, the
Aristotelian interval of twenty-four hours, in which she is required
to reveal which of her sons was born first, and thus not only which
is to rule, but which is to marry Rodogune in his father's place.

Not the least of the play's points of interest is that, while the
entire course of the action hangs on a secret the queen alone possesses, the content of that secret is never in fact known. [38]

---

[38] See Merlin, "Corneille et la politique," 49. However, in *Birth Marks*, chap. 6,
"A Sibling Rivalry over Sibling Rivalry: Pierre Corneille's *Rodogune* and Thomas
Corneille's *Persée et Démétrius*," Goodkin argues that one can in fact derive a solution of the riddle from the text. For Goodkin, insofar as Séleucus is the "brother
who would not be king," contemptuously resisting "the degrading compromises of
the present to which Antiochus has no apparent difficulty adapting" (99), he reveals
himself to possess the noble qualities Thomas Corneille's elder brother Pierre identifies with his own primogenitive right. I think this reading is overdetermined by
Goodkin's theme: the critique of primogeniture he undertakes demands an elder
brother even where the text cannot finally supply one; and his assessment of the respective moral characters of both brothers is similarly thesis-driven–Antiochus, e.g.,
must be the Father's "yes-man" (103) because he *must* be the younger (and therefore weaker and more pliant) sibling. But what if (as my own reading suggests) Antiochus's putative traffic with the paternal dictates that his "elder" proudly scorns
were in fact (as the examples of the quite similar "compromises" made by Rodrigue, Chimène, Curiace, or Nicomède would suggest) a sign of a hardy refusal to
surrender in the very act of doing what paternal law defines as the "right thing"?

Cléopâtre claims to identify Nicanor's heir on three occasions. The first is to Antiochus when, emboldened by Rodogune's confession of love for him, he makes a desperate appeal to his mother's better nature, culminating in the offer of his own life in exchange for his mistress's:

> Madame, commandez, je suis prêt d'obéir,
> Je percerai ce cœur qui vous ose trahir,
> Heureux si par ma mort je puis vous satisfaire,
> Et noyer dans mon sang toute votre colère.
>
> (4.3.1341-44)

Apparently softened by the noble sacrifice her son is prepared to make, Cléopâtre reveals the truth as it were despite herself:

> Ah, que n'a-t-elle pris, et la flamme, et le fer!
> Que bien plus aisément j'en saurais triompher!
> Vos larmes dans mon cœur ont trop d'intelligence,
> Elles ont presque éteint cette ardeur de vengeance,
> Je ne puis refuser des soupirs à vos pleurs,
> Je sens que je suis mère auprès de vos douleurs:
> C'en est fait, je me rends, et ma colère expire,
> Rodogune est à vous aussi bien que l'empire,
> Rendez grâces aux Dieux qui vous ont fait l'aîné,
> Possédez-la, régnez.
>
> (4.3.1349-58)

It is crucial however that, though the maternal tenderness Cléopâtre feigns in response to her son's noble gesture grants Antiochus what the law of primogeniture ordains ("Rodogune est à vous aussi bien que l'empire"), her words *give him to understand* that crown and princess are rightfully his without formally *saying* so. The terms she deploys are as artfully equivocal as the maternal heat she pretends to feel is artlessly spontaneous.

Cléopâtre's second declaration is to Séleucus three scenes later, and trades on Antiochus's revelation of Rodogune's love for him:

The point, more baldly, is that Cornelian heroes *fight*. If, then, the "elder" brother is the admirable one, the resilient Antiochus's claims would seem at least as good as the melancholy Séleucus's.

Cléopâtre

Le Trône était à toi par le droit de naissance,
Rodogune avec lui tombait en ta puissance,
Tu devais l'épouser, tu devais être Roi,
Mais comme ce secret n'est connu que de moi,
Je puis comme je veux tourner le droit d'aînesse,
Et donne à ton rival ton sceptre et ta Maîtresse.

Séleucus

A mon frère?

Cléopâtre

C'est lui, que j'ai nommé l'aîné.
(4.6.1419-25)

There is no equivocation in this instance. Nevertheless, by couching
Séleucus's right in a past tense ("Le Trône *était* à toi par le droit de
naissance"), she negates what she concedes. Moreover, in explaining that she has deprived Séleucus of his birthright, she reminds
him that, since the "secret" of her sons' birth is known to her alone,
she can "turn" the right of primogeniture where she likes. The
ostensibly inalienable right of birth is shown to be purely *performative*, a verdict or judicial "finding" that, as such, *counts* for true
whether it is in fact true or not. [39]
    The third and last purported discovery of the identity of
Nicanor's heir comes immediately before the dénouement, in a
public ceremony convened to conclude peace between Syria and
Parthia in the royal marriage of Rodogune and Antiochus:

Peuple qui m'écoutez, Parthes et Syriens,
Sujets du Roi son frère, ou qui fûtes les miens,
Voici de mes deux fils celui qu'un droit d'aînesse
Elève dans le Trône, et donne à la Princesse.
(5.3.1573-76)

---

[39] Merlin makes this point in "Corneille et la politique" 50-51. But see also J.L.
Austin's careful remarks on the elusive category of performatives he calls "verdic-
tives" (verdicts, findings, rulings, etc.) in *How to Do Things with Words*, 2nd ed. J.O.
Urmson and Marina Sbisà (Cambridge, Mass.: Harvard University Press, 1975)
153-55.

As it happens, this final declaration is technically true inasmuch as Séleucus is dead by the time Cléopâtre pronounces it, making the question of birthright moot. However, since news of Séleucus's murder becomes public only in the next scene, when a courtier reports the prince's dying words, the truth Cléopâtre's interlocutors *hear* is not the one she *utters*: the circumstances surrounding her single unequivocal statement of the fact of the matter makes even that a lie. Besides, as in the preceding cases, the claim to reveal Nicanor's heir is vitiated by ulterior motives. In her first declaration, Cléopâtre simulates maternal love to blind Antiochus to a desire for revenge that henceforth encompasses her son as well as Rodogune. The declaration to Séleucus in 4.6 is equally politic, designed to provoke the murder of his brother and the woman both brothers love. Now finally, in the marriage scene, in addition to concealing Séleucus's death, killed to prevent him from divulging her true intent, Antiochus's nomination covers her plan to poison bride and groom with the wedding cup she offers them.

But the fact that we never learn who Nicanor's true heir is merely underscores the centrality of a mystery only possible because, as twins, the brothers possess identities that are (and remain) in doubt. But here we begin to see how the plot device that drives the action assumes a profound symbolic as well as dramatic resonance. The already complex question of royal succession is doubled by the still more complex question of the nature of identity. As noted earlier, by virtue of their character as tragic heroes, the twins are condemned to be who they are; but who they are is a problem all the more poignant because the secret of their identity is in another's keeping. Condemned to be who they are without *knowing* who they are—worse, condemned to be who they are when what that is rests on their mother's twisted interest in shaping the truth to suit her own ambitions—[40] each must take up the identity the action as a

---

[40] As Cléopâtre puts it to Laonice, classing it among those truths of high politics concealed from mere "vulgar" eyes,

> Ne saurais-tu juger que si je nomme un Roi,
> C'est pour le commander, et combattre pour moi?
> J'en ai le choix en main avec le droit d'aînesse,
> Et puisqu'il en faut faire une aide à ma foiblesse,
> Que la guerre sans lui ne peut se rallumer,
> J'userai bien du droit que j'ai de le nommer.
>
> (2.2.493-98)

whole assigns him, whether this is his real identity or not. Nor are the twins alone in this. The obscurity that engulfs the heroes' identities intensifies an ambiguity that proliferates in all directions. The dramatic figure of twins is itself the twin of the more general figure of the *double* under whose troubling sign all of the major characters lie.

The disquieting proliferation of doubles is in part a function of family history. As we recall, the violence in the play springs from the apparent death of Nicanor. To avert the collapse of her husband's kingdom, Cléopâtre is compelled by popular discontent to marry his brother. But while her second marriage saves the kingdom, it provokes Nicanor to a vengeful second marriage of his own. Cléopâtre's murder of Nicanor echoes her husband's spiteful wish to reproduce the humiliation he has suffered by crowning her rival to her face. The vengeful hate that inspires the murder thus answers the mirror that the vindictive Nicanor had meant to force Cléopâtre to look in. But this in turn incites yet further mimicry in the hate with which, through Rodogune, the murdered Nicanor returns the fatal compliment. Cléopâtre and Nicanor are mirrors reflecting each other's likeness to infinity; the dual *renvoi* by which each amplifies the rage he or she replicates generates an escalating spiral of revenge that leaves in the end all but two of the Syrian court's six principals dead. [41]

But there is more to it than that, and in particular the *gender* warfare that structures the family conflict from beneath. We have seen how Cléopâtre's ambitions depend not only on Nicanor's absence, but on the symbolic and political extension of that absence in the uncertainty with which her sons' problematic identities cloak the issue of succession. However, beyond satisfying a mere personal ambition, the power Cléopâtre wields contests its paternal opposite: Cléopâtre's ambitions threaten the patriarchal order whose disruption makes them possible. [42]

---

[41] For the record, they are Nicanor and Cléopâtre; Nicanor's brother, Antiochus; the twins, Antiochus and Séleucus; and the title character, Rodogune.

[42] Greenberg develops a similar point in *Corneille*, chap. 6, "*Nicomède, Rodogune, Suréna*: monsters, melancholy and the end of the ancien régime" and *Subjectivity and Subjugation*, chap. 4, "*Rodogune*: sons and lovers." But his signature amalgam of psychoanalysis and Irigarian feminism overdetermines the reading. Thus, the fact that Nicanor is dead, combined with the question thrown on Oedipal suc-

Exceptionally in Cornelian drama, where potent mothers are hard to find, the fact that the heroes are twins determines the emergence of a maternal challenge to the otherwise uncontested authority of the Father. In the patriarchal culture *Rodogune* registers, the Mother is inevitably a target of ambivalence. This is certainly so in Corneille, the self-styled "father" of a body of work in which the only other mothers to be cast as major agents are Médée and *Nicomède*'s Arsinoé: figures whose conflicting roles as vessels of patrilinear descent and autonomous subjects of ambition and pride produce infanticidal projects parallel to Cléopâtre's. [43] The gemination of the sons in *Rodogune* thus authorizes a problematic maternal agency that subverts the projection of paternal identity from one generation to the next. To empower the mother as an independent center of will and desire risks transforming the authoritative male into the hapless steward of another man's seed, the impotent cuckold doubled by the rival who plants the horns of ridicule on his head. And Nicanor, we recall, is indeed a cuckold, doubled by the brother with whom Cléopâtre replaces him in the hour of public

cession by the indiscernible identities of Nicanor's sons, produces an "Amazonian" contest between Cléopâtre and Rodogune, both of whom are presented as "monstrous" descendants of Médée (*Subjectivity and Subjugation* 103-104), a figure Greenberg defines as embodying the feminine Other the male régime of "classical" Cornelian subjecthood posits as a permanent threat. (See *Corneille*, chap. 1, "Mythifying matrix: Corneille's *Médée* and the birth of tragedy.") This attractive reading underscores the unexpected power Corneille invests in female characters; the links between "subjectivity" and the process of cultural "subjugation" in which the at once psychological and political "subjects" of the Oedipal King internalize the relational identities classical absolutism assigns them; and the totalizing mechanisms by which classical culture fuses erotic, aesthetic, moral, and social themes. Still, it overlooks how the greatest "monster" in the play is neither Cléopâtre nor Rodogune, but the father Nicanor. After all, his unexpurgated will-to-power precipitates the original disappearance that brings Cléopâtre to the throne; and his "shade" dictates the matricide Rodogune names as the "price" for her hand. Further, in refusing to assent to either of the crimes required of them, the sons reject not only monstrous feminine "nature," but their vampirelike progenitor since the fruit of murder is in each case the same, the throne (and bed) their father occupied.

[43] True, the murderous designs of *Nicomède*'s Arsinoé aim to remove a stepson from the line of succession in favor of her own boy. However, the wicked stepmother deepens the paradigm in that Arsinoé's power entails unmanly abjection on the part of the royal Prusias, father of both sons. But note that when, in 2.3, Nicomède makes a masterful display of heroic irony designed to show his father the highhearted strength of character demanded of a King worthy of the name, his model in this role is the Livie of *Cinna* 4.3.

need. Behind the spectre of comic ridicule, or tragic "disgrace," lies a powerful challenge to paternity. As Cléopâtre's sole possession of the secret of her sons' identities reminds us, only the mother knows who her child's father is. Conversely, for all the symbolism of patriarchy defines the father as the "author" of his progeny's days, the only real certainty is who the mother is. Cléopâtre's secret embodies the doubt that the inescapable possibility of maternal infidelity throws on the legacy by which the father's status as Father is verified.

In *Rodogune* then the authority of the phallic Father is doubled by the Mother's, disputing not only the supremacy the former arrogates, but the very principle on which it rests. But this yields a further element of the dilemma in which the brothers are entangled. For the maternal claim that doubles the Father's is doubled in its turn. The demonic Mother who clamors for Rodogune's head in exchange for the Crown she alone can grant is countered by the no less demonic "Shade" (3.3.863) of her dead husband, a spectral agent clamoring just as loudly for the propitiatory shedding of Cléopâtre's blood.

The stand-in through whom the twins' dead father answers his double in Cléopâtre is Rodogune, cast in the role by her identity as the living representative of Nicanor's will. That she is in fact a double for Cléopâtre is stressed throughout the play. For a start, she is the second wife Nicanor planned to crown both in Cléopâtre's stead and to her face, compelling the queen to witness her own destitution in the humiliating public coronation of her substitute. But Rodogune's status as Nicanor's second bride also puts her in the mother's place relative to the sons. Corneille changes the course of events recorded in his historical sources in order to avoid the literal charge of incest by locating Nicanor's murder before rather than after marriage to Rodogune.[44] But the brothers' love for the princess

---

[44] "J'ai déguisé quelque chose de la vérité historique... Cléopâtre n'épousa Antiochus qu'en haine de ce que son mari avait épousé Rodogune chez les Parthes, et je fais qu'elle ne l'épouse que par la nécessité de ses affaires, sur un faux bruit de la mort de Démétrius, tant pour ne la faire pas méchante sans nécessité comme Ménélas dans l'*Oreste* d'Euridipe, que pour avoir lieu de feindre que Démétrius n'avait pas encore épousé Rodogune, et venait l'épouser dans son royaume pour la mieux établir en la place de l'autre, par le consentement de ses peuples, et assurer la couronne aux enfants qui naîtraient de ce mariage. Cette fiction m'était absolument nécessaire, afin qu'il fût tué avant que de l'avoir épousée, et que l'amour que ses

constitutes a virtual incest just the same: the place the sons are called to occupy is doubly their father's, as both the throne on which he sat and the conjugal bed in which he had meant to lie.

Rodogune and Cléopâtre are thus locked in a fearful symmetry whose most terrifying expression is the inverse identity of the demands each makes on the twins. Having first offered them her version of the bloody events concluded in Nicanor's murder, Cléopâtre proceeds to name the "price" she requires of the son who mounts the throne:

> Ainsi vous me rendrez l'innocence, et l'estime,
> Lorsque vous punirez la cause de mon crime.
> De cette même main qui vous a tant sauvé
> Dans son sang odieux je l'aurais lavé,
> Mais comme vous aviez votre part aux offenses,
> Je vous ai réservé votre part aux vengeances,
> Et pour ne tenir plus en suspens vos esprits,
> Si vous voulez régner, le Trône est à ce prix.
> Entre deux fils que j'aime avec même tendresse,
> Embrasser ma querelle est le seul droit d'aînesse,
> La mort de Rodogune en nommera l'aîné.
>
> (2.3.635-45)

But just so, in a later scene directly answering this one, when pressed by the brothers to reveal how they may earn her love, Rodogune sets her own "price" as the death of Cléopâtre, with a chilling ironic majesty magnified by the horror with which the twins recoil from a matricide they force her to name against her will:

> Il n'est plus temps, le mot en est lâché,
> Quand j'ai voulu me taire, en vain je l'ai tâché.
> Appelez ce devoir haine, rigueur, colère,
> Pour gagner Rodogune, il faut venger un père,
> Je me donne à ce prix. Osez me mériter,
> Et voyez qui de vous daignera m'accepter.
>
> (3.4.1041-46)

---

deux fils ont pour elle ne fît point d'horreur aux spectateurs, qui n'auraient pas manqué d'en prendre une assez forte, s'ils les eussent vus amoureux de la veuve de leur père, tant cette affection incestueuse répugne à nos moeurs." (2.202)

Cléopâtre and Rodogune are to this extent the same woman, and not least because each is an alienated double of Nicanor: Rodogune as deputy for his vengeful shade, and Cléopâtre as the usurper of the power the culture's patriarchal scheme designates as rightfully his.

And yet precisely because, whatever else she represents, Rodogune constitutes an autonomous focus of dramatic interest separate from the several roles she comes to perform, she too is doubled: by Cléopâtre of course, in the escalating face-off of hateful mirrors; but also within and for herself, as a dual being crucified by dilemmas of her own.

Like the enraged hero of *Horace* and the hate-filled Emilie of *Cinna*, Cléopâtre and Nicanor are possessed by the passions they simultaneously harbor and reflect back to their counterparts, immolating all other feelings to the obsessive desire to rule, dominate, punish, and destroy. Rodogune by contrast is an essentially divided being. The division first surfaces in her discriminatory attitude toward the twins. To Cléopâtre as to everybody else, their dead father included, the brothers are interchangeable: which one is in fact the elder and thus true heir to his father and husband for Rodogune is perfectly indifferent so long as one of them plays the part. Uniquely, then, Rodogune discerns a difference from the very start: the "secret" inclination that draws her to one of the otherwise indistinguishable brothers proves impossible to state, breathing paradoxes the baroque Corneille exploits to the full. Moreover, like the true Cornelian heroine she is, Rodogune *suppresses* her love in favor of higher duty–what she believes she owes Nicanor, dead for her sake, and regardless of her feelings for the man, or what she owes her native Parthia and the treaties that destine her to marry the elder twin. But her inclination remains real all the same, with the result that, until her confrontation with Cléopâtre in the dénouement, her public words are at perpetual odds with her true feelings and desires.

To be sure, until the climactic revelation of the queen's machinations in the dénouement, the tension between public words and private sentiments is shared with Cléopâtre. But there is a crucial difference. Cléopâtre's concealments express her political art, a power of dissimulation in which she cynically rejoices in the very first words she utters on stage, a magnificent apostrophe addressed to her own dark wiles and the all-consuming hate they serve:

Serments fallacieux, salutaire contrainte,
Que m'imposa la force, et qu'accepta ma crainte,
Heureux déguisements d'un immortel courroux,
Vains fantômes d'Etat, évanouissez-vous.
Si d'un péril pressant la terreur vous fit naître,
Avec ce péril même il vous faut disparaître,
Semblables à ces vœux dans l'orage formés,
Qu'efface un prompt oubli, quand les flots sont calmés.
Et vous qu'avec tant d'art cette feinte voilée,
Recours des impuissants, haine dissimulée,
Digne vertu des Rois, noble secret de Cour,
Eclatez, il est temps, et voici notre jour.
Montrons-nous toutes deux, non plus comme Sujettes,
Mais telle que je suis, et telle que vous êtes.

(2.1.395-408)

Rodogune's dissimulations, on the other hand, are selfless. In direct contrast to the mask with which Cléopâtre covers her real conduct, assuming a public role in the interest of the selfish ends she relentlessly pursues, Rodogune's betokens a deliberate *surrender* of self. Cléopâtre's central character trait consists in *being*, body and soul, the terrifying Machiavellian genius of her gloating soliloquies, dropping the veil to let us gauge the calculated distance between true self and public persona. When Rodogune allows a glimpse of her true feelings, we measure the magnitude of her sacrifice. The double of Cléopâtre doubles for her own divided heart, attaining union only as heroic self-abnegation. Rodogune proves true to herself only in the lucid willingness with which she accepts the alienation her part enjoins.

With this figure of alienation we return to the twins, as doubles of the doubling all the other principals suffer. That the brothers are, when the play begins, identical to the point of being perfect replicas translates their initial innocence. Reared as exiles in Egypt, far from the vicious conflicts of the Syriac court (1.1.35-38), they have not learned the art of dissimulation life at court requires; nor will either acquire it, staying true to the bitter end. However, to be at court, the quintessential arena of unscrupulous interest and heartless reason of state, is to lose innocence even if personal integrity remains intact. *Rodogune* is to this extent a double *Bildungsroman* in which the heroes are instructed in the grim realities to which their condition as royal princes calls them. The doubling which, at the start, underscores their common innocence comes then, as the action proceeds, to express the distance each twin travels in knowledge of self through knowledge of the world.

But this knowledge is *alienation*, represented in the first instance by the alternatives the brothers embody, Séleucus in turning away from the world to embrace the death his mother inflicts and Antiochus in holding fast to his love for Rodogune even at the cost of assuming his father's role as King. Each finally achieves his own authentic identity; yet authenticity demands acknowledgement of insuperable division. And of this too their status as twins is a sign. In the growing distance over which each looks toward the ever more remote image of himself his brother mirrors back, each registers, as loss, the alienated other his emergent self creates.

There is however a further point to the brothers' gemination, transcending the drama of personal identity to challenge the symbolic order that defines it. The sense of alienated loss, of unbridgeable inner division by which authentic identity is paradoxically won, springs in the first instance from the disruption of the normal, "natural" relation to the father. Were there one indisputable heir, the primogenitive machinery of succession would effect a seamless transition subsuming the legitimate elder son in his new symbolic person as the resurrected sire. Both crown and princess would then automatically pass to him alone, and he in turn would as automatically enter the father's place and assume his role. But this is just what the device of twins makes impossible; and because it is impossible, the sons find an occasion to resist their father's will, refusing the inheritance the world thrusts on them.[45] Though each is his father's (and, lest we forget, his *mother's*) son, neither wants the crown both parents fight for, desiring instead to separate what paternal law binds together. Commanded to accept both Rodogune and the throne as a single entity, each eagerly sacrifices the latter for his brother's sake in hopes of claiming the first in its stead.

Earning the right to Rodogune's affections is no simple matter if

---

[45] Note how this most Racinian of Corneille's plays anticipates the dogmatic "refus d'hériter" Barthes links with "homo racinianus," *Sur Racine* 50-52. This further attests (*pace* Greenberg) the centrality of the question put to the patriarchal order classical drama seems to reproduce.

only because, a complex being in her own right, one of her functions is to address the twins, as sons, on the symbolic Father's behalf. Like the Chimène of *Le Cid* 2.7, in a speech she at times reproduces word for word, [46] the princess offers her body as the medium
by which the dead progenitor is granted flesh and blood to enforce
his claims on the living:

> Si c'est son cœur en vous qui revit, et qui m'aime,
> Faites ce qu'il ferait, s'il vivait en lui-même,
> A ce cœur qu'il vous laisse osez prêter un bras.
> Pouvez-vous le porter, et ne l'écouter pas?
> S'il vous explique mal ce qu'il en doit attendre,
> Il emprunte ma voix pour se mieux faire entendre.
> Une seconde fois il vous le dit par moi,
> Prince, il faut le venger.
>
> (4.1.1167-74)

Like *Le Cid*, *Rodogune* is a ghost story in which a vamperlike paternal *revenant* feasts on his young, obtruding his uncanny presence
on a world that vainly tries to kill him. But in the earlier play, Rodrigue's filial piety turns "soul," "heart," "blood," and avenging
"arm" against each other in an agony of conflicting urges that
metaphorically dismember him for his father's sake. [47] In *Rodogune*,
however, the murder Nicanor requires through the heroine is cancelled out by the one Cléopâtre calls for as the price for the
crown–a point Séleucus registers in the disgust with which he reacts
to the monstrous equivalence of the demands the parents make:

> Dans mon ambition, dans l'ardeur de ma flamme,
> Je vois ce qu'est un Trône, et ce qu'est une femme,

---

[46] *Le Cid* 2.7.683-90. See our discussion in chap. 1.

[47] See *Le Cid* 1.7.293-352 for the lyric soliloquy in which, torn by the warring
demands of honor and love ("Père, maîtresse, honneur, amour"), a divided hero
breathes poignant antitheses ("Cher et cruel espoir d'une âme généreuse / Mais ensemble amoureuse, / Noble ennemi de mon plus grand bonheur / Qui fais toute ma
peine") and anguished interrogatives ("Faut-il laisser un affront impuni? / Faut-il
punir le père de Chimène?... M'est-tu donné pour venger mon honneur? / M'est-tu
donné pour perdre ma Chimène?") scanned by enumeration of his scattered facul-
ties and organs–"mon âme," "mon coeur," "mon bras," "ma flamme," "ma raison,"
"mon aveuglement," "mon honneur," "ma peine," "ma gloire," "ma mémoire," "mon
sang."

> Et jugeant par leur prix de leur possession,
> J'éteins enfin ma flamme, et mon ambition;
> Et je vous céderais l'un, et l'autre, avec joie,
> Si, dans la liberté que le Ciel me renvoie,
> La crainte de vous faire un funeste présent
> Ne me jetait dans l'âme un remords trop cuisant.
>
> (3.5.1081-90)

The brothers are entitled to reject the father's claims because the mother's savage parody negates them.

But at another level, to whose psychic depth Séleucus's visceral loathing bears witness, the father's command is rejected *in and for itself*. As Fumaroli notes, at the same time as they are both Nicanor and Cléopâtre's sons, the twins are pastoral beings. [48] Their commitment to the conventions of love poetry as against the high politics of tragedy asserts a difference otherwise lost from sight–a difference that, visible or not, has nonetheless been there from the first.

We encounter here a central element of Cornelian ethics and aesthetics, this too, like the paternal ghost resuscitated in Rodogune's speech, already met with in *Le Cid*. On one hand is *self*, the inner moral being expressed as pastoral Love: a mysterious force whose inexplicable yet irresistible truth informs Rodogune's avowal of her passion for the brother we later learn to be Antiochus. But on the other hand is a *second* self, identified with the noble "gloire" and heroic "générosité" Rodogune's intertextual twin Chimène voices when, despite her love for her father's killer, she commits herself to seeking her lover's death: "Je sais que je suis fille, et que mon père est mort." [49] This inspires still another echo of *Le Cid* in Rodogune's anguished analysis of the moral trap into which she and Antiochus have fallen:

---

[48] Fumaroli, "Pierre Corneille, fils de son oeuvre," in *Héros et orateurs* 51-52.

[49] *Le Cid* 3.3.834. The assertion of this second self is still more powerful in the revised text of 1660: "Je sais *ce que je suis*, et que mon père est mort" (1.1500). Where the original specifies Chimène's alter (super-)ego as being that of her father's loyal daughter, the revision prefers a calculated vagueness that leaves room for equivocation. Is Chimène impelled here by consciousness of what her father's death demands of his child, or is she moved by what she *owes herself* as a reflex of the noble "gloire" of a tragic heroine?

Du père mort pour moi voyez le sort étrange,
Si vous me laissez libre, il faut que je le venge,
Et mes feux dans mon âme ont beau s'en mutiner,
Ce n'est qu'à ce prix seul que je puis me donner:
Mais ce n'est pas de vous qu'il faut que je l'attende.
Votre refus est juste, autant que ma demande,
A force de respect votre amour s'est trahi.
Je voudrais vous haïr, s'il m'avait obéi,
Et je n'estime pas l'honneur d'une vengeance
Jusqu'à vouloir d'un crime être la récompense.
(4.1.1215-24)

Even as it contests the moral basis of paternal authority, the heroic self sets duty as the condition for pastoral love.

It is then to this contest rather than paternal law that we owe the binary·symmetries shaping at once the tragic dilemmas Cornelian characters face and the elaborate antitheses that structure Cornelian tragic verse. But in most other plays, Corneille's effects finally turn on the *elimination* of a division voiced solely to inspire the admiring pity with which we honor the price duty exacts, a price the protagonists willingly pay to overcome personal desire in order to deserve the love they enjoy. Here, by contrast, the division is seconded by the problem of succession in such a way as to offer a *choice* Cornelian heroism is elsewhere denied.

Like Rodogune, and like Rodrigue and Chimène before her, the twins express a readiness to sacrifice desire in the interest of duty, and even on behalf of the unheard of "amitié," the unexampled brotherly love, that binds them when the play begins. Antiochus in particular will manage to chart a painful course between the Scylla of love and the Charybdis of both fraternal and filial obligation to the very end. This is indeed what differentiates him from his twin, justifying the mysterious election Rodogune makes of him. Where Séleucus reacts to the claims of father and mother alike with an indiscriminate disgust, inducing a moral paralysis that presages his death at his mother's hand, Antiochus continues to hope and strive, looking for an exit:

La révolte, mon frère, est bien précipitée,
Quand la loi qu'elle rompt peut être rétractée,
Et c'est à nos désirs trop de témérité

De vouloir de tels biens avec facilité.
Le Ciel par les travaux veut qu'on monte à la gloire,
Pour gagner un triomphe, il faut une victoire.

(3.5.1063-68)

But unlike their models in other plays, and unlike Rodogune as well, the twins are in a position to *refuse* the duty enjoined by their parents. As a result, where their less fortunate counterparts must ultimately surrender to external force, burying their constitutive divisions in obedience to the alien identity ethically required of them, the twins hold fast to division itself. The double state of the heroic soul becomes the focus and goal, graphically rendered by the dual condition as identical twins that makes this focus possible.

Where the Cornelian norm (another paternal construct) sublimates native ambivalence to forge the self-sacrificial unity of heroism, the device of twins authorizes a stubborn insistence on ambivalence for its own sake. Further, if unity is in fact achieved in the end, it is thanks to the ambivalence Antiochus in particular maintains throughout. The trigger of the dénouement, during the ceremony of conjugal union in which Cléopâtre publicly identifies Antiochus as Nicanor's heir, is Timagène's report of Séleucus's murder, to which he adds the dying words with which the victim tries to name his killer:

Une main qui nous fut bien chère
Venge ainsi le refus d'un coup inhumain,
Régnez, et surtout, mon cher frère,
Gardez-vous de la même main.
C'est...

(5.4.1643-47)

Antiochus's moment of truth coincides with the final severance of the fraternal bond, freeing him at last to be his father's undisputed heir. Now fully King in his father's place, he is called on to serve as the Solomonic Judge, determining which of the two suspects, Cléopâtre or Rodogune, is guilty of Séleucus's death. Yet even now he hesitates. A first reason is that his brother's words are equivocal, leaving open not only the identity of his killer, but also which "inhuman blow" he has been murdered for refusing to strike. For

there are indeed two candidates for the part, the killing of Rodogune or that of his mother, thereby asserting a grim equivalence between princess and queen that Antiochus fully appreciates. But a
second reason for Antiochus's hesitation is more telling. By creating
a judicial doubt amplified by the rhetorical accusations his mother
and mistress level at each other, Séleucus's words allow him to
evade the alternatives the two women urge. By refusing to judge in
a speech whose suicidal as well as fatalistic ring reinforces the ontological thrust of the refusal it voices, Antiochus holds himself in
suspense to the end. Poised between his identity as the son he must
shortly cease to be and that of the symbolic Father he must present-
ly become, he maintains his right to be neither:

> Non, je n'écoute rien, et dans la mort d'un frère
> Je ne veux point juger entre vous, et ma mère:
> Assassinez un fils, massacrez un époux,
> Je ne veux me garder, ni d'elle, ni de vous.
> Suivons aveuglément ma triste Destinée,
> Pour m'exposer à tout achevons l'Hyménée.
> Cher frère, c'est pour moi le chemin du trépas,
> La main qui t'a percé ne m'épargnera pas,
> Je cherche à te rejoindre, et non à m'en défendre,
> Et lui veux bien donner tout lieu de me surprendre.
> Heureux, si sa fureur qui me prive de toi
> Se fait bientôt connaître, en achevant sur moi,
> Et si du Ciel trop lent à la réduire en poudre
> Son crime redoublé peut arracher le foudre.
>
> (5.4.1767-80)

Yet there is no escape from the world's ruthless identity claims.
Though Antiochus refuses to judge, preferring death to acceptance
of the role imposed on him, both Cléopâtre and Rodogune, acting
now in curious concert, insist on making him choose. The one does
so by drinking from the poisoned cup to prove its innocence, the
other by dashing it from the hero's hand to save the life his mother
hopes to take. Cléopâtre accordingly dies, pronouncing a curse all
the more troubling in that, beyond locating its object in the monstrous son she predicts Rodogune will bear, she plants a seed of
doubt as to the identity of the play's true criminal. For as she compels Antiochus to acknowledge, he alone now lives to profit from

the train of murder, treachery, and deceit that has brought him to
the throne:

> Règne, de crime en crime enfin te voilà Roi:
> Je t'ai défait d'un père, et d'un frère, et de moi.
> Puisse le Ciel tous deux vous prendre pour victimes,
> Et laisser choir sur vous les peines de mes crimes,
> Puissiez-vous ne trouver dedans votre union
> Qu'horreur, que jalousie, et que confusion,
> Et pour vous souhaiter tous les malheurs ensemble,
> Puisse naître de vous un fils qui me ressemble.

> (5.4.1817-24)

Rodogune in turn falls silent, consumed by the calamity that attends
her consummated union with the man she loves. Meanwhile, however systematically he may have spurned the poisoned patrimony to
which he is heir, Antiochus is now, and for ever, the inheritor of the
horrors that have brought him both his crown and Rodogune.
Though he does not literally die, avoiding the fate that overtakes his
at once less and more fortunate brother, Antiochus is morally dead
as a being distinct from the identity demanded by the society over
which he rules. The maternally crafted poison he escapes casts its
pall over a violent future that, with the fall of the final curtain,
clasps him in its sinister embrace.[50]

All of which is summed up in a final doubling effect, one that
turns the play's end back on its beginning to numbing ironic purpose. In the opening speech, Laonice announces the glorious day
that will both reveal the long-hidden truth and fix the interval for

---

[50] See Fumaroli, "Une dramaturgie de la liberté humaine: tragique païen et
tragique chrétien dans *Rodogune*," in *Héros et orateurs* 170-208. Fumaroli goes on
to save *Rodogune*'s grim appearances by interpreting the members of the play's central triangle (Rodogune, Cléopâtre, Antiochus) as allegories of the pagan past the
coming Christian revelation promised by the innate goodness of Rodogune and
Antiochus will ultimately redeem. But before taking this improbably typological
turn, Fumaroli provides a memorable summation of the surviving hero's state of
mind as the curtain falls: "Le meurtre de son frère porte à son point extrême sa tentation de refuser le pouvoir politique, et le conduit jusqu'à celle d'en fuir la menace
dans le suicide ou dans la mort acceptée. L'angoisse d'avoir à assumer la part de
crime que comporte l'exercice de la puissance politique va maintenant jusqu'à ef-
facer dans le cœur d'Antiochus sa timide vocation royale. Il souhaite mourir plutôt
que de régner." (201)

the dramatic action required to fulfil the promise of dawn. Laonice's speech thus lays out the unity of time whose form yields the unity of the action that Cléopâtre's death brings to a close. But the imagery of the close, as night falls on the day whose dawn opened the play, is all funereal darkness. Turning to the Parthian ambassadors and his own royal attendants, Antiochus issues his first orders as undisputed King, decreeing rites of mourning in place of the marriage he had planned:

> Oronte, je ne sais dans son funeste sort
> Qui m'afflige le plus, ou sa vie, ou sa mort,
> L'une et l'autre a pour moi des malheurs sans exemple,
> Plaignez mon infortune. Et vous, allez au Temple
> Y changer l'allégresse en un deuil sans pareil,
> La pompe Nuptiale en funèbre appareil,
> Et nous verrons après, par d'autres sacrifices,
> Si les Dieux voudront être à nos vœux plus propices.
>
> (5.4.1837-44)

The imagery of light gives way to imagery of darkness, and promised truth to gathering shades of anxiety and doubt. The ultimate fruit of the device of twins is to confirm what it has done so much to deny: the unshiftable tragic burden that condemns us to be our own alienated doubles in a world that rejects the equivocations we invoke to defend the difference that is true self.

And yet traces of a less tragic outcome persist: in the lingering memory of the autonomous Antiochus now irrevocably lost; but above all in the dramatic *poem* the play's finale now commits to our hands. The doubtful darkness that descends at the end has already sent us back to the ambiguous light that breaks on the opening scene. The cessation of the time of the action now fully consigns us to the recursive element of the writing that has occasioned it from the first. But the writing is in turn the counterpart of the several *readings* in which we seek the solution to enigmas far deeper than those we originally expected, enigmas that question the categories (of patriarchal truth, of identity and nobility) with which we initially approached them.

At the close of act 3, in a soliloquy following the unhappy dialogue in which the brothers digest the full horror of their predica-

ment, Antiochus responds to his twin's disdainful despair by making a profession of faith. Though already troubled by omens of his
brother's impending death, he puts his trust in what he naïvely con-
ceives to be the invincible twin powers of Nature and Love:

> Daignent les justes Dieux rendre vain ce présage;
> Cependant allons voir si nous vaincrons l'orage,
> Et si contre l'effort d'un si puissant courroux
> La Nature, et l'Amour voudront parler pour nous.
>
> (3.6.1127-30)

Antiochus sounds the same note two scenes later, in another soliloquy where, having received an assurance of love from Rodogune's
lips, he prepares to confront his mother in hopes of turning her
from her murderous design:

> Les plus doux de mes vœux enfin sont exaucés,
> Tu viens de vaincre, Amour, mais ce n'est pas assez.
> Si tu veux triompher en cette conjoncture,
> Après avoir vaincu, fais vaincre la Nature.
>
> (4.2.1249-52)

The problem of course is that the notions that Antiochus naïvely treats as simple and single are in fact neither. The Love and Nature whose powers he presents as working in personified concert
are irrevocably opposed to each other in Cléopâtre's furious rejoinder:

> Je fais plus maintenant, je presse, sollicite,
> Je commande, menace, et rien ne vous irrite.
> Le sceptre, dont ma main vous doit récompenser,
> N'a point de quoi vous faire un moment balancer,
> Vous ne considérez, ni lui, ni mon injure,
> L'amour étouffe en vous la voix de la Nature.
> Et je pourrais aimer des fils dénaturés!
>
> (4.3.1319-25)

Antiochus responds by conceding the distinction: "La Nature et
l'Amour ont leurs droits séparés" (4.3.1326); but the concession
emphasizes the complexities it labors to unravel. What after all is
Love if it proves separable from Nature? And what is Nature if it is

set against Love? Love, it seems, "stifles the voice of Nature," a hormonal compulsion that overrides what a mother has the natural right to expect of a dutiful son. And yet if natural duty overrides Love, what is the *nature* of its naturalness? The question gains further point when we note how, identifying the son's "natural" duty with an equally "natural" will-to-power, Cléopâtre incites acts of unnatural violence that reproduce the denaturement she accuses Love of inspiring.

Notions that at first seem so simple as to need neither qualification nor explanation, standing alone as self-announcing essences read off at a glance, are shown to be hopelessly ambiguous, signs of the inextricable tangle Antiochus labors to untie. But what then do these or indeed any words finally mean if there sense is subject to endless equivocation and doubt? What indeed if not the very equivocation and doubt that contain at once their inception and their end. The end of *Rodogune* is its beginning.[51] Where the dramatic action encourages us to turn to the unfolding spectacle as the source of light and meaning, the poem that occasions it reasserts its independent claims. Corneille remains a playwright, and a great one: the play grips us with all the perfection of its author's consummate skill.[52] Yet in the deepening darkness that falls with the final curtain, we find what Antiochus discovers: the world the play presents is an *illusion*; only the *poem* endures as lasting and real. And with the poem comes its Poet, the creative genius whose art consists in rewriting the world in accordance with a power of insight and invention uniquely his own.

This, too, is ambiguously reflected in the doubled identities of the tragedy's twin; or rather in the ambiguities that attend the tragic differentiation sealed with the willing death by which Séleucus sets Antiochus free to be a separate, fully individuated being. It is signif-

---

[51] This formula echoes the better to invert Forestier's poetological claims about Cornelian tragic dramaturgy in *Essai de génétique théâtrale*. For Forestier, the end is in the beginning in that Cornelian tragedy is guided from the outset by the goal of imparting the peculiar pleasure stimulated by a well-wrought dénouement: everything proceeds from its final cause in the waves of pity and fear provoked in the tragic close. By contrast, my reading suggests that, in the discovery of Corneille's poem at once *before* and *behind* the tragic spectacle, the end of the play leads back to the text that occasioned it.

[52] See Fumaroli, "Pierre Corneille, fils de son oeuvre" 51, where Rodogune is characterized as "une véritable somme de son théâtre."

icant that Séleucus's last words are posthumous: the dying speech Timagène reports at 5.4.1643-47, broken off when death overtakes the speaker before he can pronounce the name of the person responsible for killing him. With the murder that removes him as an *actor* in the play, leaving that role exclusively to the brother who survives him, Séleucus in effect becomes *text*: a scriptorial condition subtly underscored both by the fact that he does not live to pronounce the name of his assassin ("C'est...") and by the fact that he refers to his killer not as a person, but by synecdoche, as a *hand* ("une main"). The absence of the name emphasizes our dependence on the at once equivocal and constitutively underdetermined medium of language: just because he does not live to say it, Séleucus dramatizes how far our knowledge of the truth remains subservient to the vicissitudes of saying as such. But the resort to the synecdoche of the "hand" that cuts speech short specifies the *literary* character of the act by which Séleucus's life is taken for his brother's sake.

The figure of the "hand" is of course a ready and familiar (not to say compulsory) symbol of agency on which Corneille draws throughout not only this play, but all of his work; and this is certainly the primary sense attached to it both in Séleucus's speech and in Antiochus's response—"[l]a main qui t'a percé ne m'épargnera pas." (5.4.1674) But this general symbolism must be set beside more specific reference to the special kind of agency associated with poetry—what Corneille has in mind when he regrets in the dedicatory epistle to *Horace* that the play had not been composed by "une main plus savante" than his own, or when he writes at the epistle's close of wishing one day to produce a work undecipherably "worthy" of being *put in*, but also of *issuing from* Richelieu's hands ("une oeuvre digne de vos mains") (1.834). Though the hand Séleucus immediately intends is Cléopâtre's since it is she who takes his life in the scheme of the action, nevertheless, the ultimate agent of his murder is none other than the play's author, Corneille himself. [53] But this in turn further specifies Antiochus's condition, in-

---

[53] The ambiguous symbolism of the "hand" is of course the central motif of Jouhaud's analysis of "le pouvoir cardinal" in *La Main de Richelieu*. For a more literary treatment, relating the manual metaphor (and synecdoche) for agency to the problem of authorship, see Lezra, *Unspeakable Subjects*, chap. 4, "Cervantes's Hand."

THE POETICS OF EQUIVOCATION: HORACE, CINNA, RODOGUNE   155

flicted by the same hand that killed his twin. Condemned, as he is, to survive Séleucus, living out the tragic aftermath the play destines him to endure, he embodies the scripted performance that constitutes the indiscernible counterpart of the poem it is his fate to *represent*.

And yet, eternal performer in the tragedy of which his brother becomes the text, Antiochus can also be seen as a stand-in for the *reader*. Though it kills him, Séleucus dies *in the knowledge* of the hand that, in taking his life, also *silences* him, turning speech into an enigma it is his brother's task to unravel. But in surviving his twin, exiting the stage, as the curtain falls, to begin the life whose inscrutable promise turns out to have been the burden of the words with which the unknowing Laonice opened the play, Antiochus shows this task to be quite literally a life's work. The survival to which the dénouement condemns Antiochus is thus unceasing repetition, the eternal return of the beginning that frames his end only to send him back to the start again. But what is this if not the image of the act of reading to which we ourselves are called? The poem Corneille composes envelops us in the folds of an infinite recursion from which there can be no escape. Like the eminence whose subtle maneuvers the play at once models and counters, the poet imposes his vision and will as a destiny the more resistless for going unseen until its work has already begun anew.

CHAPTER 3

THE TWIN TEXT OF IDENTITY: FRENCH DOUBLES OF PLAUTUS' *AMPHITRUO*

A S we have seen, a central feature of the drama of the French classical era is an acute awareness of the disjunction between the moving (and rhetorically persuasive) "illusion" of theatrical performance and the often radically different meanings encoded in the dramatic poem that theater "represents." One expression of this disjunction is the emergence of a mode of critical reading specifically designed to uncover the disreputable truths the illusions of scenic portrayal conceal. This yields the basic terms of the quarrel of *Le Cid*, where Corneille's adversaries denounce not only the play's aesthetic shortcomings, but the hypocritical gap between the heroic fable performed on stage and the at once arrogant and depraved intentions inscribed in its text. Nor is Corneille the only target of such readings. Especially with the revival of the "querelle de la moralité du théâtre" in the reign of Louis XIV, producing both the five-year controversy surrounding Molière's *Tartuffe* (1664-69) and the contemporaneous "affaire des Imaginaires" (1666-67) in which Racine becomes embroiled, theater as a whole falls subject to deconstructive analysis on the pattern Corneille's case sets. [1] The "querelle du *Cid*" is then a testing ground for a style of interpretation that endures throughout the century.

---

[1] On the "querelle de la moralité du théâtre," see Apostolidès, *Le prince sacrifié* 49-53 and Fumaroli, "*Sacerdos sive rhetor, orator sive histrio,*" in *Héros et orateurs* 449-91. On "l'affaire des imaginaires," see Alain Viala, *Racine: La Stratégie du caméléon* (Paris: Seghers, 1990) 113-17 and Jean Rohou, *Jean Racine entre sa carrière, son œuvre et son Dieu* (Paris: Fayard, 1992) 227-33.

But a second expression of the divorce between drama and text, constituting the private *envers* implied by the *endroit* of critical reception, is a poetics of *equivocation* keyed to the conditions of censorship and coercion under which all seventeenth-century writers work. [2] In a society where the burden of official culture and the social order it celebrates weighs as heavily as in classical France, dramatic poetry provides a model of the prophylactic doublespeak required to shelter heterodox intent from public scrutiny. Under the jealous eye of royal, academic, and ecclesiastical authority, dramatists deploy the ironic resources latent in the inherently duplicitous nature of their medium in order to say what they mean without being strictly held to mean what they say. Whence the astonishing dedicatory epistle to cardinal Richelieu prefacing the published text of Corneille's *Horace*, a complex act of quasi-feudal homage whose hyperbolic excess converts open praise to covert blame, negating the allegiance it publicly professes. But whence, too, the shifting light in which we may read both *Horace* itself and the next year's *Cinna* either as loyal statements of the absolutism Richelieu champions or as indictments all the more infuriating for being indistinguishable from the apologetic works they counterfeit.

The result is to raise questions about the actual *identity* of the dramatic text, questions that, in *Rodogune*, reach beyond the poem itself to encompass the socio-cultural roles it simultaneously mirrors and challenges. The key to *Rodogune*'s extension of its own indiscernibly divided identity to the social world it portrays is the theme of identical twins. By derailing the machinery of primogenitive succession on which monarchy depends, the initial impossibility of telling the play's princely brothers apart engenders a tragedy that exposes the both moral and ontological alienation social identities entail. However, the high-minded nobility of tragic drama imposes limits on the play's development of such themes. In particular, monstrous as the deeds of the play's Syriac court may be, decorum forbids Corneille to explore the implied incest characterizing

---

[2] For the French context, see Jouhaud, *La Main de Richelieu* and "Power and Literature," and Merlin, *Public et littérature*. On the impact of censorship on early modern writing generally, see Strauss, "How to Study Spinoza's *Theologico-Political Treatise*," Yovel, *Marrano of Reason*, esp. chap. 4, "Marranos in Mask and a World without Transcendence: Rojas and *La Celestina*," and chap. 5, "Spinoza, the Multitude, and Dual Language," and Zagorin, *Ways of Lying*.

the twin brothers' love for their dead father's intended bride. Though Appian's history reports Nicanor's second marriage as an accomplished fact, Corneille eliminates it on the tellingly ambiguous grounds that the "affection incestueuse" Appian documents "répugne à nos moeurs," a formula that, without necessarily meaning to, leaves room for a moral relativism as repugnant to classical taste as incest itself. [3] Insofar moreover as tragedy commits the play's central romantic pair to the conventions of heroic *love* as opposed to mere farcical *sex*, the risk of incest presents an unwelcome reminder of the messy reproductive couplings of which comedy is the vehicle. So in order to tease out further the at once textual and symbolic implications of the theme of twins, we must leave the rarefied atmosphere of tragedy for the cruder element of its lowly counterpart. We now turn to a pair of comedies that share *Rodogune*'s basic plot device, Jean Rotrou's *Les Sosies* of 1636 and Molière's *Amphitryon* of 1668.

In obedience to a major tenet of classical doctrine enshrined not only in the notoriously dogmatic French espousal of Aristotle's "rules," but also in prevailing humanist paradigms of poetic creation whose hold on French literary culture remains unbroken until the great "quarrel of ancients and moderns" in the century's waning years, [4] both plays are "imitations." Both, that is to say, take an ancient model–as it happens, in Plautus' *Amphitruo*. The classical borrowing is indeed the more emphatic in this case for being abnormally literal and direct. In other plays based on classical patterns, the plot is updated to conform to modern manners and conditions. For example, "timeless" as *L'Avare*'s adaptation of *Aulularia*'s Euclio may be, Harpagon's usurious dealings meticulously document the sharp practices of contemporary Parisian moneylenders. [5] Here, by contrast, no transposition occurs; the ancient fable is preserved intact, underscoring its antique provenance.

This reflects the supernatural character of the incidents the plays represent. Recounting the inception and nativity of the legendary Hercules, the heroic demi-god Jupiter sires on a mortal

[3] Corneille, *Œuvres complètes* 2.202.
[4] See DeJean, *Ancients against Moderns*.
[5] See the editor's "notice" in the Pléiade *Œuvres complètes*, ed. Georges Couton (Paris: Gallimard, 1971) 2.511-12 and 2.1386, note 3 to p. 526.

woman, the Amphitryon story does not immediately lend itself to modernized adaptation. But we may also suspect an attempt to assert the *droit de cité* of the otherwise morally as well as aesthetically suspect form of comic drama. To this extent, the choice of an ancient model is a strategy of legitimation advancing the ambition announced in the *Critique de l'Ecole des femmes*. Responding to attacks directed at the gross improprieties to which he was accused of stooping, Molière (through his spokesman Dorante) argues that these alleged improprieties faithfully record the ludicrous human conduct it is comedy's satiric mission to portray. But he goes on to suggest that the very fidelity to human nature that comic crudity achieves makes the genre superior to the baseless heroic fictions of the "higher" mode of tragedy with which his critics implicitly compare his work:

> Car enfin, je trouve qu'il est bien plus aisé de se guinder sur de grands sentiments, de braver en vers la fortune, accuser les destins, et dire des injures aux dieux, que d'entrer comme il faut dans le ridicule des hommes, et de rendre agréablement sur le théâtre les défauts de tout le monde. Lorsque vous peignez des héros, vous faites ce que vous voulez. Ce sont des portraits à plaisir, où l'on ne cherche point de ressemblance; et vous n'avez qu'à suivre les traits d'une imagination qui se donne l'essor, et qui souvent laisse le vrai pour attraper le merveilleux. Mais lorsque vous peignez les hommes, il faut peindre d'après nature. On veut que ses portraits ressemblent; et vous n'avez rien fait, si vous n'y faites reconnaître les gens de votre siècle. En un mot, dans les pièces sérieuses, il suffit, pour n'être point blâmé, de dire des choses qui soient de bon sens et bien écrites; mais ce n'est pas assez dans les autres, il y faut plaisanter; et c'est une étrange entreprise que celle de faire rire les honnêtes gens. [6]

When therefore to the merit of "resemblance" we add the luster of an ancient pedigree, comedy may be forgiven the coarse laughter its faithful portrait of human foibles prompts; and with forgiveness comes entitlement to a place at least as respectable as the one tragedy enjoys.

---

[6] Molière, *La Critique de l'Ecole des femmes*, in *Œuvres complètes* 208. All subsequent references appear in the text by act, scene, and line numbers for verse and by page number for prose.

Still, even as it solves one problem, the imitation of classical models poses others. In particular, it raises questions of *identity* endemic to the aesthetic it obeys. As Thomas Greene memorably explains in *The Light in Troy*, the very models that at one level frame and authorize poetic creation tend at another to undermine it, engendering the dialectics of poetic *aemulatio*, the simultaneously reverent and iconoclastic reproduction of antique precedent that defines the early modern relation to the ancient past.[7] For insofar as a given work is based on a classical text, who is its true author: the contemporary poet who pens the modern text or the ancient one who composed the model on which it draws? How moreover can the new work meet a *second* demand of classical aesthetics, namely, the requirement of *originality* Jean Mairet invokes when, goaded by Corneille's vainglorious "Excuse à Ariste," he derides his rival for being the mere "translator" of the Spanish source from which *Le Cid* descends?[8] And what Mairet shows to be true of Corneille proves all the more so in Molière's case in that, in addition to imitating Plautus, he must reckon with the fact that Rotrou got there first. Molière's *Amphytrion* is thus a *double* imitation–of Plautus through the refracting medium of Rotrou's priority in the matter.

This already suggests how far the central dramatic theme engaged in all three plays is overdetermined. The basic story is in each case the same.[9] Resolved to produce a son embodying the ideal of cosmic Justice in the sublunary realm of mortal beings, the King of Olympus chooses Alcumena, wife of the noble Amphitryon. The problem is that what makes Alcumena a fitting vessel for Jupiter's seed is not only her fetching loveliness, but her exemplary *virtue*.

---

[7] Thomas M. Greene, *The Light in Troy: Imitation and Discovery in Renaissance Poetry* (New Haven: Yale University Press, 1982), esp. chap. 3, "Imitation and Anachronism," which surveys the various strategies by which Renaissance poets negotiate their relation to precursors.

[8] Jean Mairet, "L'Autheur du vray Cid Espagnol à son Traducteur François," in Gasté, *La Querelle du Cid* 67-68. The question of authorial originality is taken up in David Quint, *Origin and Originality in Renaissance Literature: Versions of the Source* (New Haven: Yale University Press, 1983).

[9] For the history of the Amphitryon legend's dramatic career from ancient Greece to the 20th century, see the intros. to the three plays presented in Charles E. Passage & James H. Mantinband, *Amphitryon: The Legend and Three Plays (Plautus, Molière, Kleist)* (Chapel Hill: University of North Carolina Press, 1974) and the concluding essay on the legend's fortunes after Kleist.

As true to her own heroic character as to her no less heroic husband, Alcumena is unassailably chaste. She cannot then, like Danaë, be won over by showers of gold; nor, like Europa or Leda, is she susceptible to the bestial sexual appetite symbolized by Jupiter's incarnations in animal form. The only way to seduce her is to *refrain* from seducing her; Jupiter must appear in the guise of her husband, as Amphitryon himself.

Moreover, to watch his back, guarding the gate to Amphitryon's house long enough for consummation with the hero's wife, Jupiter needs Mercury–but a Mercury who, to remain unrecognized in the interest of preserving his master's incognito, must in turn assume the form of Amphitryon's servant Sosia, "the twin." The device of twins sets up the comic machinery on which all three plays trade. During the interval required for Hercules' conception and (in Plautus and Rotrou at least) miraculously foreshortened gestation and birth, the human characters are caught up in a comedy of errors in which, Mercury passing for Sosia and Jupiter for Amphitryon, Sosia and Amphitryon are in turn mistaken for their alter egos. Worse yet, the confusion of identities engulfs Alcumena as well. Once her husband discovers that his double has usurped his place in the conjugal bed, he takes his wife for an adulteress, with near fatal results.

But the destabilized identities of the human principals mirror those of the poets who write the parts. To use a period term whose ambiguities speak volumes to our purpose, the problem is one of "invention"–a word that denotes both an act of free creative imagination and the more passive, inventorial process of chancing on or finding something new and original in material that is neither. [10]

---

[10] Rhetoricians identify invention as the "first" part of rhetoric since, without it, the orator would have nothing to say. This agrees with the place French theory grants it as attested by the episode of the "Cinq Auteurs," where Richelieu was held to be the true author of the *Comédie des Tuileries* because he invented its plot, leaving the hack work of the *mise en vers* to his poets (see Couton, *Richelieu* 25-31). Invention's primacy assumes greater relief when we recall that, following Aristotle's definition of drama as the representation of an *action*, classical theory regards the fable or subject as the "soul" of the art. This feeds the revisionist theses on Cornelian theater Forestier advances in *Essai de génétique théâtrale*, where the choice and development of the plot force all other features (themes, psychology, politics) to the second rank as byproducts of "disposition," "expression," and the general "embroidery" involved in giving the invention final theatrical form. Yet in the Latin authorities French classicists drew on alongside Aristotle, invention is often a mere preliminary to an art whose most essential part is the *eloquence* expressed in the

The identity of the author, and thus of the text as well, hinges on
unearthing a potential for *difference* in the model the poet reproduces, enabling Rotrou to distinguish himself from Plautus, and
Molière from Plautus and Rotrou alike.

But the problem of finding a means of distinguishing themselves from at once their Latin model and each other leads Rotrou
and Molière to other problems still. In mediating between the conflicting demands of original identity and the surrender of identity
entailed by the imitation of a classical source, they wind up posing
questions about identity in general; and these in turn raise questions about "imitation" in the other sense prescribed by classical
culture, the one Molière invokes in the *Critique de l'Ecole des femmes* when Dorante insists that comedy's focus on the "people of
one's own age" obliges the comic poet to paint "d'après nature."
True to their common source in the raucous Plautus, Rotrou and
Molière give us comic bawdry as broad as contemporary sensibili-
ties could stomach in a public place. [11] Yet the *text* of that bawdry
goes deeper than the occasioning farcical fable would suggest. In
unpacking what comic "nature" has to say about the nature of hu-

---

mise en vers Richelieu's "authors" undertook–Forestier's "broderie." Thus, in the
prologue to book 8 of the *Institutio*, Quintilian cites Cicero as saying that,

> while invention and arrangement [*dispositio*] are within the reach of any
> man of good sense, eloquence belongs to the orator alone, and conse-
> quently it was on the rules for the cultivation of eloquence that he ex-
> pended the greatest care. That he was justified in so doing is shown
> clearly by the actual name of the art of which I am speaking. For the
> verb *eloqui* means the production and communication to the audience
> of all that the speaker has conceived in his mind, and without this power
> all the preliminary accomplishments of oratory are as useless as a sword
> that is kept permanently concealed within its sheath.

(See Quintilian, *Institutio oratoria*, Loeb Classical Library, ed. & trans. H.E. Butler
[Cambridge, Mass.: Harvard University Press, 1986], bk. 8, pro. 14-16.) Quintilian's
depreciation of invention is in line with Cicero's remark that an able (though not
necessarily *gifted*) orator is one "who sees the hidden [or latent] content of each
topic and who has the topics in question neatly labeled [in memory] like storehous-
es of arguments," reminding us through the "storehouse" (*tesaurus*) metaphor that
the term "invention" relates to our modern "inventory." See Cicero, *De partitione
oratoria*, Loeb Classical Library, ed. & trans. H. Rackham (Cambridge, Mass.: Harvard University Press, 1942) 394.

[11] What that same public could tolerate in the more intimate ambience of private reading is another matter. Consider the success of the *roman libertin* (e.g.,
Sorel's *Francion*), of Tallement des Réaux and Bussy Rabutin's *historiettes*, or of the
more licentious of La Fontaine's *contes*.

man identities, the text discovers *not* "nature," but the socialized *forms of speech* by which society dictates what identities are.

1. AN ANAMORPHIC "TRAGI-COMEDY": THE DOUBLE TEXT OF PLAUTUS' *AMPHITRUO*

Plautus' *Amphitruo* opens with a prologue spoken by an intermediary on behalf of a powerful third party who remains off stage. This intermediary is the god Mercury, messenger of Jupiter, King of the gods: "JUPITER sent me and my name is MERCURY." [12] But since the character designated as "Mercury" is also an actor recruited to *play* Mercury, by "Jupiter" we understand the comic poet Plautus as well as the King of Olympus. That Mercury's business here is chiefly Plautus' rather than Jupiter's is besides established from the prologue's opening lines, presenting the preamble to a parodic contract between audience and playwright:

> Whereas all you good folks want me to make you prosper,
> and bring you fortune in your buyings and your sellings,
> and handsome profits in your business arrangements;
> and whereas you would wish, at home and overseas,
> to find prosperity in all your speculations,
> to consummate your present and your future deals
> with ample, fat returns, both now and evermore;
> and whereas you would have me bearer of good tidings
> for you and yours–reporting and announcing things
> which most redound to what is for your common good–
> (for you must know that all the gods have made Yours Truly
> responsible for messages and business deals)–
> whereas you want my blessings in these varied matters,
> and profits, everlasting and perennial–
> then kindly keep your mouths shut during the performance
> and all be fair, unbiased judges of our play!

(1-16)

---

[12] Plautus, *Amphitruo*, in *Complete Works*, ed. Paul Nixon (Cambridge, Mass.: Harvard University Press, 1937), vol. 1, v. 19. The translation is by Passage and Mantinband, which follows the original verse by verse. Subsequent citations are identified by verse number in the text.

In keeping with a technique for which its author was notorious, the play begins in the mode of Brechtian *Verfremdung*, an "alienation effect" violating the mimetic illusion mandated in the principle of immanence by which classical French theory set such store. [13] Bringing player and spectator into direct contact at the point of their real encounter in the playhouse, Plautus deploys a device the authoritative d'Aubignac especially abhorred, one he specifically associates with the ineffably bad and even potentially criminal example of Plautus himself. [14] Rather than help us forget or at least overlook the occasion of performance in order to engage our sympathies exclusively in the dramatic action, Plautus' Mercury speaks to the occasion as such, with particular reference to the competition in which the play is an entrant. The contract he announces will enjoin the audience both to silence and to equity; for in addition to watching, the spectators will, by their applause, help *judge* the play, determining its success in terms not only of the receipts Mercury

---

[13] On Plautus' use of prologues, epilogues, asides, and other mechanisms to produce Brecht-like alienation effects, see Timothy J. Moore, *The Theater of Plautus: Playing to the Audience* (Austin: University of Texas Press, 1998) and Niall W. Slater, *Plautus in Performance: The Theatre of the Mind,* 2nd ed. (Amsterdam: Harwood Academic Publishers, 2000).

[14] See d'Aubignac, *Pratique*, bk. 1, chap. 7, "Du mélange de la Representation avec la verité de l'Action Theatrale," 40-41, where Plautus' penchant for interpellating spectators is described not only as an irritant that "souvent embarrasse le sens, & détruit les graces de son Theatre," but, more stridently, as "dérèglement" and "désordre"–strong terms whose semantic range covers not merely infractions of the "rules" and dramaturgical messiness, but incivility, moral transgression, anarchy, and even madness. Note that d'Aubignac's example is none other than *Amphitruo*; and note too that the ultimate fruit of Plautus' irrational proceeding is to compel the spectator to imagine a "double man" whose words and sentiments founder in self-contradiction: "*Dans son Amphitryon* Jupiter est supposé dans la Ville de Thebes au temps de la naissance d'Hercules: & quand il paroît sous la forme d'Amphitryon, il dit aux Spectateurs: *Je suis Jupiter, & me change en Amphitryon quand il me plaît, paroissant ainsi & pour l'amour de vous,* dit-il aux Spectateurs, *afin de continuer cette Comedie & pour l'amour d'Alcmene, afin qu'elle soit reconnuë innocente.* Où l'on voit qu'il mêle l'interêt des Spectateurs avec celui des Acteurs, & fait un assemblage des Romains qui étoient presens avec des personnes que l'on suppose agir en Grece. La même faute est encore dans la Scene deuxiéme du premier Acte [verses 463-550] de la même Piece. Ce qui est certainement ridicule de feindre Jupiter & Mercure à Thebes visibles seulement à ceux du Palais, parler en Comediens dans la ville de Rome, à ceux qui les voyent sur le Theatre; c'est confondre l'intelligence des Spectateurs, en les contraignant de s'imaginer un homme double, & de distinguer en lui des sentimens & des paroles bien contraires sans aucune raison apparente."

aims to procure for the poet, but of the prize Plautus hopes to win
as author of the season's best comedy:

> Now for the favor Jupiter told me to ask.
> He wants the officers to search the theater
> from row to row and seat to seat and front to back,
> and if they find claquers for any party at all,
> they'll confiscate their togas and hold them all as bail.
> Yes, and if any parties have been lobbying
> and trying to secure the prize, either in person
> or by letter or by intermediate agent,
> or if the Aediles should be guilty of corruption,
> Jupiter says the penalty should be the same
> as that which deals with Unfair Campaign Practices.
>
> (64-74)

Thus, on "Jupiter's" behalf, the play opens with an actor, playing at being a god, who denounces other actors, playing at being an
audience. To ensure that the play receives a fair hearing, Plautus
playfully threatens to humiliate confederates of rival poets by ordering the ushers to undress them, exposing them to public ridicule by
stripping them of their togas: items designed not only to provide a
decent covering for laughable human nakedness, but to supply respectable social identities through the colors, patterns, and materi-
als by which Roman sumptuary laws (like their seventeenth-century
French counterparts) prescribed appropriate costumes for each
rank in society. [15] Nor is the concern Mercury voices limited to the
machinations of rival playwrights. Actors win prizes too, encourag-
ing the suspicion that the audience may harbor claques for players
as well as poets. Citing Jupiter as saying that it is "by merit" (*virtute*)
and not by appeal to lowly "ambition" or underhanded "perfidy"
(*non ambitione neque perfidia*) that Romans have traditionally
earned their victories in war, Mercury goes on to ask

---

[15] Harth, *Ideology and Culture* 46, and Moriarty, *Taste and Ideology* 1, touch on
the question. For a fuller view, see Alan Hunt, *Governance of the Consuming Passions: A History of Sumptuary Law* (New York: St. Martin's Press, 1996), chaps. 2,
"A Short History of Sumptuary Law," 6, "Recognizability: 'The Mingle-Mangle of
Apparel'," and 7, "Style Wars: Fashion and Class Struggle before Classes." Hunt
(31) graphs the volume of French sumptuary laws by century; at 20, the 17th far
outstrips all others. Though it has surprisingly little to say about sumptuary law,
also see Stephen Varick Dock, *Costume & Fashion in the Plays of Jean-Baptiste Poquelin Molière: A Seventeenth-Century Perspective* (Geneva: Slatkine, 1992) 8-9, 74.

Why shouldn't this apply to actors as well as others?
The prizes should be won for merit, not by claques.
Actors who act well get all the applause they need,
providing that the judges know their business.
And here's another order from my father Jove:
officials will be watching all the actors too.
If any one of them has hired claques for himself,
or hecklers either, or if anyone steals scenes,
his costume will be ripped to shreds–with him inside it!

                                                    (75-85)

As early as the prologue, Plautus issues an arresting *mise en garde*: on the occasion of a play that features two sets of twins to produce a comedy of mistaken identities, nothing is quite what it seems either on stage or in the auditorium. This is of course a joke, but a joke whose point is part of everyone's experience. As the use of claques and hecklers to cry up or down the work of players as well as poets attests, the art of theater depends not merely on the excellence of a play's poetry or performance, but on the devious manipulation of the public mind. [16] Mercury's prologue does openly what ambitious actors and playwrights attempt more covertly in a thousand perfidious ways: shape the audience's response by prejudicing its judgment in one's favor. On pain of being stripped naked, and so of being exposed as the risible creatures they "really are" beneath the civic disguise of decorous dress, the spectators are enjoined to see and hear the play as it "really is," that is, as the poet intends them to.

And yet what *does* Plautus intend? At one level, the answer could hardly be simpler: to make the spectators laugh; and Mercury's prologue is nothing if not funny. But a second function of the prologue is to prepare the audience for what it is about to watch. The preparatory work the prologue undertakes is moreover unusually needful on this occasion owing to the special scenic problems the plot creates.

A first problem is just that we have to do with *gods*, a point the prologue neatly ties to the author's contract by noting the personal interest Jupiter has in securing fair play:

---

[16] On the use of claques in Roman theater, see Moore, *Theater of Plautus* 10 and 114. The second reference relates to our passage in *Amphitruo*.

No need to wonder why great Jupiter himself
is so concerned for actors–no need to be surprised–
for Jove himself is an actor in this comedy.
What? You're surprised? As if this were a new departure,
that Jupiter himself has turned to histrionics?
Why, only last year, when the actors prayed to Jove,
right on the stage he appeared–a *Deus ex Machina*!

(86-92)

True, the allusion to the well-established device of the *deus ex machina* reminds us that conventions exist to ease the suspension of disbelief required to see mere actors as gods. Still, the gods who walk Plautus' stage are only gods *by convention* and must therefore be taken in the proper spirit to be gods at all. [17] And to complicate matters further, on this occasion, the conventional gods, once introduced, shed their divinity in order to engage with the human characters as humans themselves. Whatever else it may turn out to be about, *Amphitruo* tells the story of the inception of the hero Hercules, a demi-god Jupiter fathers on the mortal Alcumena. The fruit of the decidedly unheroic comedy for which the prologue prepares us will then be a hybrid of the human and the divine, a crossing thanks to which the ideal of Justice Hercules represents will assume an earthly form adjusted to the conditions of worldly imperfection. However, even leaving aside the ambiguities Hercules' dual state as god and man entails, the peculiar circumstances attending his nativity recall the ludicrous gropings from which even heroes proceed. For Jovian Justice to take on a human form, the divine must take on a human shape of its own, subject as such to all the vagaries of human existence, including the distortions of clouded human judgment against which Jupiter/Plautus draws up the prologue's contract.

But there is a more urgent problem still: the contrivance uniting human and divine is the confusing device of twins. As noted earlier, what makes Amphitryon's wife a worthy vessel for Jupiter's seed is

---

[17] The point is neatly made in the original, where the allusion to the *deus ex machina* is more muted and ironic. The Latin merely says that, in answer to the human actors' prayers in last year's tragedy, Jupiter "came, and helped them out." The machine he used is thus implicit in the gag, which turns on a naïvely literal interpretation of the god's descent on stage.

not only her physical beauty, but her exemplary virtue. This obliges
the god to approach her in the guise of her noble spouse, a strategy
that in turn requires the auxiliary humanation of Jupiter's factotum
Mercury, donning the likeness of Amphitryon's servant Sosia. The
primary point of these operations is of course to produce a comedy
of errors, making us laugh. But precisely because the characters'
identities are so readily mistaken, especially given the masks Roman
actors wear, concealing real faces otherwise easily distinguished, [18]
we need to pay close attention to keep everyone straight. Jupiter is
not Jupiter, nor Mercury Mercury; but then, half the time, Amphitryon is not Amphitryon either, nor Sosia Sosia. Whence the prologue's major function: to provide the information we need to sort
the players out.

But this already points to still deeper issues. As Socrates classi-
cally hints in Plato's *Symposium*, all comedy is potentially tragic: the
comic catastrophe that makes us laugh may at any moment take a
turn for the worst. [19] In Plautus' play, and both Rotrou and Molière
follow suit, only the *deus ex machina* the prologue forecasts will rescue Alcumena from the jealous rage to which Amphitryon is reduced, a rage exacerbated by the agony of being systematically mistaken as well as ridiculed by everyone around him. And it is to the
potential for tragedy infecting even this broadest of comedies that
we owe the prologue's most interesting joke.

As he is about to lay out the contract Jupiter/Plautus has drawn
up for the audience, Mercury (that is, the actor *playing* Mercury,

---

[18] On theatrical costumes in Roman theater generally, see Moore, *Theater of
Plautus* 1 and the bibliographical references in note 2. On the special problem of
costumes in *Amphitruo*, and in particular in the case of Mercury who not only enters "cum servili schema" (in a slave's outfit), but wearing a mask "identical to that
which will be worn by the actor playing Sosia," ibid. 110.

[19] Plato, *The Symposium* 223c-d. Since Socrates' interlocutors fall asleep before
he explains why a gifted tragedian must also be a gifted comedian, and vice versa,
we do not learn what he means. But if we accept Martha Nussbaum's ingenious
reconstruction of the historical context for Apollodorus' recital of an earlier report
of what he remembers of Aristodemus' version of a dialogue that took place many
years before, the essentially comic happenings *The Symposium* rehearses will indeed
turn out badly since the dialogue's two chief protagonists, Socrates and Alcibiades,
die soon after Apollodorus' account–the one committing the judicial suicide to
which he is sentenced for impiety, the other assassinated while in exile for more
strictly political crimes. See *The Fragility of Goodness: Luck and Ethics in Greek
Tragedy and Philosophy* (Cambridge: Cambridge University Press, 1986), chap. 6,
"The Speech of Alcibiades: A Reading of *The Symposium*."

who will in turn play Sosia, but speaks now in Jupiter's name on the playwright's behalf) promises a synopsis of the plot. The plot he refers to, however, is a *tragedy*: "Now for the favor that I've come to ask you for, / And then I'll tell you all about our tragedy." (50-51) No sooner is the word "tragedy" out of his mouth than he stops short in a doubletake timed to another on the audience's part. For of course, since this is Plautus, the public expects a *comedy*. But this circumstance raises problems of its own. For as Mercury reminds us, our comedy (if it is one) has gods and heroes for its protagonists, and it would be a serious breach of decorum to make a laughing matter of such material. Yet even if the stature of the play's august personnel calls for tragedy, the audience expects a comedy just the same. What is more, they *want* a comedy; and since, in addition to being paying patrons, they are also judges, it behooves all concerned to please in order to win their support. A comedy it will accordingly be despite having been written as tragedy.

Fortunately, Mercury is a god–a trickster god moreover, master of disguise, deceit, and subtle sleights-of-hand, but also, for good measure, god of rhetoric, and thus of writing too.[20] So to satisfy all parties, both Plautus, who wrote a tragedy, and the audience, which wants a comedy, he proposes to turn tragedy into comedy *without changing a single word*:

> What's wrong? Why do you frown? Because I said the play
> would be a tragedy? But I'm a god–I'll change it:
> I'll change the play from tragedy to comedy,
> if that's what you want, without a single change of lines!
> Well, yes or no? would you like that? What a dunce I am!
> As if I didn't know what you want–and me a god!
> I understand exactly what you have in mind:
> I'll scramble them and make a tragi-comedy.
> It wouldn't do to make it only comedy,
> not with gods and kings parading on the stage.
> What do you think? But wait–it has a slave part too.
> I'll make it what I said, a tragi-comedy.
>
> (52-63)

---

[20] On Mercury's (Hermes') mythological roots, functions, and attributes, see Robert Graves, *The Greek Myths* (Baltimore: Penguin Books, 1955) section 17.

In a play about twins in which gods are mistaken for men and men for gods while a true wife passes for faithless and a martial hero for a pitiful cuckold, Plautus invites us to a tragedy to be taken, word for word, as its lowly comic counterpart.

2. THE DEVICE OF TWINS AND THE HEROIC SELF IN ROTROU'S *LES SOSIES*

Whatever Plautus meant by this, we have good reason to think that his French imitators found a deeper resonance than the immediate comic context licenses.[21] A first reason is the political significance assigned the hero whose nativity the Amphitryon legend reports. Preserved in the Middle Ages as one of the Nine Worthies whose noble deeds hold up a mirror to chivalric knights, the Greek demi-god metamorphoses in the Renaissance into a prosopopeia of the modern State.[22] When Boileau turns in *L'Art poétique*'s final canto to the theme of unceasing royal praise that constitutes the fundamental burden of French verse, the persona he invokes for the reigning monarch is Alcides, the name Hercules bore in his youth in honor of his descent from the line of Amphitryon's father Alcaeus.[23]

But there is more, bearing on the legend's strictly literary potential. Like his contemporary Corneille, Rotrou in particular is a trag-

---

[21] On the evidence of Slater and Moore, they take it seriously indeed. Slater draws in appendix 4 on Zeph Stewart's hypothesis that Euripides' *Bacchae* is a source for *Amphitruo* to stress both the pointedness of *Amphitruo*'s "tragi-comedy" joke and how this testifies to the scope of Plautus' "metatheatrical" interests and ambitions. The blurring of identities and genres and the concomitant blurring of the boundaries between human and divine ultimately lead to a cosmological revolution in which "Plautus dethrones Dionysos and puts in his place the benevolent genius of comedy." (202) For Stewart's essay, see "The 'Amphitruo' of Plautus and Euripides' 'Bacchae,'" *Transactions of the American Philological Association* 89 (1958) 348-73.
[22] See Stephen Orgel, "The Example of Hercules," in Walther Killy (ed.), *Mythographie der frühen Neuzeit: Ihre Anwendung in den Künsten* (Wiesbaden: O. Harrassowitz, 1984) 25-47. Hercules' relevance to the political subtext of Molière's *Amphitryon* has also been noted by Abby Zanger, "Classical Anxiety: Performance, Perfection, and the Issue of Identity," in David Trott & Nicole Boursier (eds.), *L'Age du théâtre en France/The Age of Theatre in France* (Edmonton: Academic Printing & Publishing, 1988) 327-39.
[23] Nicolas Boileau, *L'Art poétique* 4.204. On the origins of the name Alcides (French Alcide), see Graves, *Greek Myths* 118.3.

ic as well as comic poet, leaving, beyond *Les Sosies* or the better known *Bague de l'oubli*, the noble *Venceslas* and *Cosroès*, and above all *Le Véritable Saint-Genest*, a play about a pagan actor converted by the role of a Christian martyr he is commanded to play at an imperial wedding. Rotrou's tragic interests help explain the dark mood of the prologue to his version of the theme. While the play closes with the joyous celebration that marks the miraculous birth of the hero whose inception it portrays, it opens with a menacing Juno, enraged at the humiliations to which her husband's incessant infidelities expose her. In place of Plautus' Mercury, we meet a homicidal queen of heaven, borrowed not from the comic model's portrayal of Hercules' birth, but from the tragic Seneca's rendition of that same hero's madness and death. [24] Rotrou thus takes the occasion of his prologue to remind us that the legends that report Hercules' heroic career also tell of the implacable enemy who kills him in the end.

Moreover, sorry cuckold though he may be, the Amphitryon of Rotrou's act 5 is decidedly unfunny. Marching home, as the play begins, from the destruction of an enemy army in a battle Sosie describes in graphic detail, [25] Amphitryon has already proved himself to be an accomplished killer. And the anger with which he reacts to the discovery of Alcmène's adulterous union with his alter ego assumes a frightening ferocity. When the captain of the guards objects in his wife's defense that, since she has been deceived by her husband's double, "L'honnêteté d'Alcmène est hors de tout soupçon" (5.4.1633), Amphitryon furiously replies:

---

[24] See Joseph Morello, *Jean Rotrou* (Boston: Twayne, 1980) 87.

[25] Jean Rotrou, *Les Sosies*, ed. Damien Charron (Geneva: Droz, 1980) 1.3.175-226, 230-42. (Subsequent references appear by act, scene, and verse in the text.) Note that, in keeping with what Vuillemin (*Baroquisme et théâtralité*) shows to be Rotrou's intensely self-conscious theatricality, Sosie's account of the battle takes the form of a speech to his master's wife that never occurs—*rehearsed* rather than delivered. True, the rehearsal performs the expository functions required of the speech it replaces: we learn about (even get to "see") Amphitryon's victory over Ptérèle, gleaning in the process how dangerous Sosie's master is when crossed; we get an example of Sosie's comic cowardice and mendacity; and we are clued in to our own ambiguous relation to the action, shared with the god Mercure, who spies on poor Sosie just as we do—a connection underscored by Mercure's asides, esp. at 1.3.227-30, where he interrupts Sosie's narrative in order to comment on it. Still, the instrument of all of this work remains quite *unreal* in that we get the speech's proleptic *citation* in place of the speech itself. This obviously anticipates the central theme/device of Rotrou's masterpiece, *Le Véritable Saint-Genest*.

> Elle a failli pourtant, d'une ou d'autre façon,
> S'agissant de l'honneur, l'erreur même est un crime,
> Rien ne peut que la mort rétablir son estime.
> Entrons, rompons, brisons, secondez mon dessein,
> Surprenons, s'il se peut, l'adultère en son sein.
>
> (5.4.1634-38)

But more important than the tragic note the play intermittently sounds is the problem that note betokens. The towering rage with which, literally beside himself, Amphitryon threatens to storm his own house and put all of its inhabitants to the sword expresses not only his frenzied jealousy, but profound anxieties about the grounds and nature of personal identity that surface as early as the opening verses of Juno's prologue:

> Soeur du plus grand des dieux (car ce nom seul me reste),
> Honteuse, je descends de la voûte céleste
> Et, veuve d'un époux qui ne mourra jamais,
> Le fuis, puisqu'il me fuit, et lui laisse la paix.
> Les maîtresses, enfin, l'emportent sur l'épouse,
> Elles sont les Junons, et je suis la jalouse,
> Il me prescrit la terre, et leur marque les cieux,
> Et du bras qu'il leur tend, il me pousse en ces lieux.
>
> (1.1.1-8)

Brought, as the stage directions put it, "en terre," at once down to earth and subject to a mortal element that belies her divine origin, Juno does not know what to call herself. The first name she takes, that of "sister of the greatest of the gods," though mythologically accurate since she is in fact Jupiter's sibling as well as wife, nonetheless misstates her identity. Rather than being her *true* name, it is the only one her husband's lecherous amours have left her. Further, these amours have not only shamed, but driven her from her native dwellingplace in the "celestial vault": paradoxical "widow of a spouse who will never die," if she flees her lord, it is because his incessant infidelities banish her. Nor is she merely denied her conjugal state; she has been at once displaced and multiplied by the endless succession of mistresses who have transformed the regal goddess into a scolding termagant: "They are the Junos, and I the jealous hag." Since she remains despite everything a goddess, her

descent on stage is a theophany foreshadowing the more spectacular one with which, in the dénouement, Jupiter sheds his disguise as
Amphitryon and, appearing in his own divine person, brings the
play to a happy end. However, in Juno's case, the theophanous pro-
cession marks her *alienation*: if the prologue vouchsafes the appari-
tion of a deity, it is because she has assumed a vengeful human likeness to replace the divine identity that has been usurped.

What is the case even of the Olympian Juno proves still more so
of the mortals in the play. Having first appeared in his own person
to bid the Night to stay its course in favor of their common master's
amorous intrigue, Rotrou's Mercure enters for a second time in 1.2,
"en habit et visage de Sosie." Sosie has himself just entered, sent by
Amphitryon to announce his recent victory and prepare his household to receive him. Pausing within sight of the goal, Sosie rehearses the account he intends to give of the battle, an account in which,
true to his nature as a comic servant, he will grant himself a more
distinguished part than he actually played:

> Mais consultons un peu ce qu'il faut que je die,
> Car je fuyais plus fort, au plus fort du combat,
> Et de frayeur encor le cœur au sein me bat.
> Plus leurs bras s'employaient à ce sanglant office,
> Plus mes jambes aussi se donnaient d'exercice,
> Je mesurais mes pas à l'ardeur de leurs coups,
> Et la peur m'animait, autant qu'eux le courroux.
>
> (1.3.160-66)

Then, in an aside Sosie misses, so engrossed in recalling his fright
and in composing the fabrications he means to tell that he fails to
notice Mercure's arrival, the messenger of the gods caustically observes:

> Ce menteur éternel, à soi seul imitable,
> Une fois pour le moins se trouve véritable.
>
> (1.3.167-68)

This sardonic remark is fathomlessly duplicitous. Sosie is indeed, as Mercure drily notes, an "eternal liar" whose amazing combination of cowardly buffoonery and self-serving mendaciousness
endows him with a thousand faces other than his own. And yet

Sosie's clownish prevarications are perfectly transparent not only because a god is present to unmask them, but because the donning of masks is intrinsic to his character. Sosie is in fact, as Mercure says, an "eternal liar," that is, in Mercure's primary sense, someone who always (eternally) lies. But of course, as a direct descendant of the Plautine Sosia and a stock embodiment of the timeless (and thus again "eternal") character type of which the Roman Sosia is a version, Rotrou's Sosie is *supposed* to lie. The very role he plays as "Sosie" programs him to act in the way Mercure diagnoses: from the instant he appears on stage, clothed in the garb of a comic servant, poltroonish lies are what we expect.

But this in turn gives the lie to Mercure's words even as it confirms their self-ratifying truth. In alleging Sosie to be "à soi seul imitable," Mercure implies first of all that he is "inimitable": his lies are so ceaseless and outrageous as to defy comparison; there is no one in the world quite like him. Yet at the very moment Mercure asserts that there is no one like him, Mercure himself intends to become *just* like him–to the point where no one, including his victim, will be able to tell them apart. And if we ask how this could be so, the answer is obvious: the "inimitable" Sosie, Mercure's "eternal liar," is already an imitation–of Plautus' Sosia and the stock characters to whose timeless family Sosia belongs, but above all of Mercure himself, the classical *father* of lies whose role relative to Jupiter Sosie reproduces in his capacity as servant to Amphitryon. If, in the development, Mercure succeeds in mirroring Sosie so precisely as to usurp his identity in everyone's eyes, including Sosie's own, it is not only because, as the character type to which he conforms, Sosie proves easy to imitate. It is because what Mercure imitates is a mirror of Mercure himself.

But who then is "Sosie" if, even before encountering his twin, Sosie is, *as* "Sosie," the spitting image of somebody else? At the conclusion of the scene of their first meeting, as Amphitryon's bewildered servant goes off to explain that he has failed to reach home to announce his master's return because a second Sosie has preceded him there, he imagines he has somehow misplaced the identity of which he had assumed himself to be in sole possession:

> Retirons nous plutôt. O prodige! O nature!
> Où me suis-je perdu? Quelle est cette aventure?

Qui croira ce miracle, aux mortels inconnu?
Où me suis-je laissé? Que suis-je devenu?
Comment peut un seul homme occuper double place?
Moi-même je me fuis, moi-même je me chasse,
Je porte tout ensemble, et je reçois les coups,
Je me vais éloigner, et je serai chez nous.

(1.3.451-58)

The notion of self as something one can lose, as a thing it is even possible to *mislay*, is on its face absurd. Whatever else it may be, a self is not an object (say, a suit of clothes) one might inadvertently leave behind along the way. This fact about the impalpable yet perdurable nature of selves explains the joke—and is it not *just like* Sosie to make this mistake, crassly reifying self through inability to rise above the level of crude matter to the ideal sphere to which self properly belongs? Still, that it should be just like him to think of his identity as a thing reminds us that "Sosie" is a *role*, something—and to begin with a costume or suit of clothes—entirely separable from the person who plays it. If another can usurp it, in what does "self" consist, and how do we tell we have one, assuming there is such a thing at all?

As Sosie's proliferating questions suggest, Rotrou offers few answers. Nor besides, as a comedy designed above all to suspend serious concerns in the interest of thoughtless diversion, is *Les Sosies* as responsible for answers as the higher form of tragedy would be.[26] Nevertheless, the wide-eyed intensity with which its personnel put anguished questions lends the play's intermittently tragic note distinctly Cartesian overtones that call for commentary.

There is no evidence of even an indirect Cartesian influence on Rotrou. *Les Sosies* was first staged in 1636, five years before the publication of Descartes's *Meditations* in 1641; nor did Rotrou effect significant revisions between the first edition of 1638 and the printed text of 1650, following the play's revival by the Théâtre du Marais in

---

[26] *Venceslas* makes weighty claims about royal selves, and *Cosroès* gives us a portrait of heroic integrity comparable to the one in Corneille's very similar Oriental tragedy, *Nicomède*; and *Le Véritable Saint-Genest* provokes a stirring representation of the integral Christian soul, the "true" self of the happy martyr dying in witness to his redemptive faith. For critical editions of *Venceslas* and *Cosroès*, see *Théâtre du XVIIᵉ siècle*, vol. 1.

1649. [27] But even leaving aside the to my mind more interesting question of a Rotrovian influence on Descartes, [28] we do not really need an explicit link. Though we are in the habit of seeing in Descartes the heroic innovator portrayed in the autobiographical *Discours de la méthode*, the philosopher is as representative of the era as we more comfortably conceive the poet to be. [29] That Rotrou should ask questions we normally associate with Descartes reflects the cultural context both writers inhabit–the period sometimes called the "first" seventeenth century, the age of the French baroque. And indeed, to readers sensitive to the baroque, the way in which both Rotrou and Descartes tie doubts about the nature of self to an interest in illusions, mirror effects, and indiscernible simulacra is nothing if not typical of the style. [30] But typical as such doubts may

---

[27] For *Les Sosies*'s performance and textual history, see the editor's intro.

[28] While there is no more evidence of a Rotrovian influence on Descartes than of a Cartesian influence on Rotrou, why should the first seem more dubious than the second? Despite the historical revision to which it has been subjected since Foucault's *Histoire de la folie*, the myth of philosophy's eminence as the Queen of the liberal arts and sciences dies hard.

[29] While this thesis informs Foucault's work from *Histoire de la folie* on, the effect is muted by the fact that the wider cultural "discourse" of which Descartes is portrayed as the captive exemplar is entirely *intellectual*. A similar outcome occurs in Stephen Gaukroger's *Descartes: an intellectual biography* (Oxford: Oxford University Press, 1995). Gaukroger wants to analyze the cultural genesis of Cartesian thought. However, his sense of what this entails is largely limited to a philological reconstruction of general cultural conditions uninformed by reflection on what they *mean*. This leads him, e.g., to underestimate the psychic price the culture exacts in terms both of what the philosopher conceived his work to be and of its interaction with another of Gaukroger's themes: Descartes's culturally conditioned "self-image" and the way that image shapes his philosophy. A glaring example of this weakness is Gaukroger's surprisingly perfunctory interpretation of the sequence of dreams related in the *Olympica* (106-11). For a more successful effort in the same direction, see Yovel's cultural biography of Spinoza, *The Marrano of Reason*. Here indeed the very nature not only of Spinoza's thought, but of its literary expression, something moreover Yovel sees as cosubstantial with the thought as such, is shown to depend on its conditions of possibility in the thinker's socio-cultural experience as a Jew.

[30] On the French baroque, see, in addition to Vuillemin, Rousset, *La Littérature de l'âge baroque*, Victor-Lucien Tapié, *Baroque et classicisme* (Paris: Plon, 1957) and *Le baroque* (Paris: Presses universitaires de France, 1961), Charpentrat, *Le mirage baroque*, Maillard, *Essai sur l'esprit du héros baroque*, Greenberg, *Detours of Desire*, and Christine Buci-Glucksmann, *La folie du voir: le baroque* (Paris: Galilée, 1986). Note however that talk of a French baroque remains highly controversial–a circumstance to which Vuillemin devotes a number of both lucid and pugnacious pages in *Baroquisme et théâtralité* (34-61). It goes without saying that French resistance to

be, that Rotrou should anticipate in detail the *systematic* form Descartes gives them in the *Meditations* points to a degree of deliberation that deserves comment–the more so since, performing his metaphysical experiments in the social dimension of drama rather than the private space of philosophical reflection, Rotrou pushes the problem of identity beyond the stage Descartes reaches.[31]

We may characterize what happens to the principal characters by saying that they are visited by the process of Hyperbolic Doubt.[32] When Sosie finally replies to Mercure's reiterated demands to know his name, Mercure accuses him of madness, a condition diagnosed as loss of both rational and physical sense: "O le fou! L'insensé!" (1.3.389) Sosie's response is to defend at once his sanity and his identity by appeal to the evidence of his own eyes, ears, and touch, to which he adds a capacity to distinguish between a waking state and dream:

> Mon maître Amphitryon, ses ennemis domptés,
> Ne m'a-t-il pas, du port, envoyé vers Alcmène
> Lui conter du combat la nouvelle certaine?
> N'en arrivé-je pas une lanterne à la main?
> Voilà pas le palais de ce prince thébain?
> Ne te parlé-je pas? Sais-je pas que je veille?
> Tes poings ne m'ont-ils pas étourdi cette oreille?
>
> (1.3.390-96)

---

the idea that their 17th century was anything but "classical" is intimately related to the difficulties encountered in historicizing Descartes, a figure in whom the French tend to see the very embodiment of classical "clarity."

[31] Radicalizations of Cartesian doubt turn out to have been something of a cottage industry in 17th-century France. See, e.g., Lionel Gossman, *Men and Masks: A Study of Molière* (Baltimore: The Johns Hopkins University Press, 1963), chap. 6, "Molière in His Own Time," which argues that part of Molière's significance lies in amplifying the contemporary critique of Descartes in philosophers like Mersenne and poets like Racine. We shall turn to Molière from this viewpoint later in this chapter and again in chapter 4.

[32] Gossman speaks of the *malin génie* in his discussion of Molière's *Amphitryon* (see *Men and Masks* 13-16). But note that the emergence of the *malin génie* is merely *one* of the episodes in the story of Cartesian Doubt. As Rotrou's text reminds us, the others are the skeptical revelation of the poverty of the system of "knowledge" in which we are educated; the discovery of the unreliability of sensory information; and the successive encounters with the examples of madness, dream, and the related (Quixotic) phenomenon of poetic "fantasy." The *malin génie* thus arises only as the climax of the series.

In the compass of a few lines, the passage rehearses all of the phases in the argument leading to the Cartesian cogito, save one; and that one, the climactic hypothesis of the *malin génie*, the evil genius who insidiously persuades me of an existence I do not possess, emerges a few scenes later, when Amphitryon tries to digest Sosie's account of his meeting with his twin:

> Dieux! Comme il est troublé! Cette disgrâce insigne
> Est le fatal présent de quelque main maligne,
> Quelque méchant esprit rencontré sur ses pas.
>
> (2.1.559-61)

It is important to remember, however, that, unlike their Cartesian counterpart, Rotrou's characters do not *choose* to question the grounds of their presumptively inalienable identities; as the beatings Sosie suffers at Mercure's hands stress with special pertinacity, the issue is imposed on them by external events. Accordingly, where Descartes, contemplating a merely theoretical double, entertains the cases of sensory error, madness, dream, and demonic possession only to dispel them, Sosie and Amphitryon, meeting *real* doubles, are driven on to deeper dilemmas still. What convinces Sosie that, however certain his own claim to it may be, his twin is just as entitled to the name "Sosie" is the unshakable certainty with which, countering all attempts to prove they are different, Mercure asserts they are the same. This assertion reaches a climax when Mercure demonstrates knowledge of things only Sosie could possibly know—for instance, what Sosie actually did during the battle as opposed to the heroic deeds he prepares to claim he performed, or the trophy (the cup of Amphitryon's vanquished enemy Pterelaus) contained in the sealed parcel his master has entrusted to him for Alcmène. What makes the double's knowledge not just convincing, but properly *uncanny* is the challenge to the illusion of privileged inwardness. [33]

---

[33] See Sigmund Freud's famous essay, "The 'Uncanny'," in *The Standard Edition of the Complete Psychological Works*, ed. & trans. James Strachey, in collaboration with Anna Freud & assisted by Alix Strachey & Alan Tyson (London: Hogarth, 1953-74) 17.219-56, where the figure of the double in Hoffmann's "Der Sandmann" is analyzed as exhibiting the return of the repressed and the concomitant revelation of the at once alienated and alienating logic of unconscious desire at the root of identity. But note that the challenge to privileged interiority that the double (Mercure) poses is identical to the one the *analyst* makes *ex officio*. From

Descartes discovers a proof of his existence in the inalienably inner form of knowledge that, in the cogito, survives even unanswerable doubts directed at its content. By contrast, Mercure's possession of Sosie's secrets converts the Cartesian innerness into outer performance, subject as such to imitation even where items we think of as purely private are concerned. The result is a sort of *anti*-cogito: an experience that, turning Sosie inside out, undermines confidence in the self-consciousness on which identity rests.

But in addition to Sosie's confrontation with a perfect replica, there is the evidence of Amphitryon's skeptical reaction to the nonsense that comes out of his servant's mouth when he tries to give a logical account of his experience. His explanation of how his twin convinced him of his right to be called Sosie is a study in tortured pronomial antecedence:

> Je n'ai pas cru d'abord à cet autre moi-même,
> J'ai démenti mes yeux, sur ce rapport extrême;
> Mais j'ai tant fait, enfin, que je me suis connu,
> Je me suis tout conté comme il est advenu,
> Jusques à me citer la coupe de Ptérèle;
> J'ai mon nom, mon habit, ma forme naturelle,
> Enfin je suis moi-même, et deux gouttes de lait
> N'ont pas, à mon avis, un rapport si parfait.
>
> (2.1.547-54)

And a little later, when Amphitryon asks him to explain yet again who drove him from his master's house, the tangled reference gets knottier still:

---

this standpoint, Sosie's response to Mercure's insights sheds an interesting light on the double function of what psychoanalysts are pleased to call the subject's "resistance." On one hand is resistance to the *truth* Mercure (the analyst) sees and imparts. But this is in turn doubled by the subject's resistance not merely to the truth, but to the *analyst himself*. As intolerable as (if not more intolerable than) the *content* of the analyst's insight is the *form* it takes, i.e., that of an invasion of what Lacan terms the "miraginary" space of psychic interiority. All of which is related to Lacan's analysis of Molière's *Amphitryon* in *Le Moi dans la théorie de Freud et dans la technique de la psychanalyse (1954-55)*, *Le Séminaire de Jacques Lacan*, bk. 2, ed. Jacques-Alain Miller (Paris: Seuil, 1978), lecture 21, "Sosie," 301-16–though Lacan curiously puts Amphitryon rather than Mercure in the analyst role (310). Lacan's reading turns on the hypothesis that "Sosie, c'est le moi. Et le mythe vous montre comment se comporte ce brave petit de moi de petit bonhomme comme vous et moi dans la vie de tous les jours." (306)

> Moi, ne vous dis-je pas?
> Moi, que j'ai rencontré, moi qui suis sur la porte
> Moi, qui me suis moi-même ajusté de la sorte,
> Moi, qui me suis chargé d'une grêle de coups,
> Ce moi, qui m'a parlé, ce moi qui suis chez vous.
>
> (2.1.586-90)

To be sure, Sosie's grammatical difficulties can be interpreted as indirect assurance of sole possession of his identity. Just because ordinary language cannot accommodate the meanings his experience gives his words, it throws its weight on his side in the quarrel with Mercure. But once he is persuaded of his twin's right to his identity, his words provoke, in his master's disbelief, a resistance that intensifies the dissociation Mercure causes. Already doubled by Mercure, Sosie is now *re*-doubled by the image of himself implicit in Amphitryon's refusal to believe him. For the master has ideas of his own about who Sosie is, ideas summarized in the string of ready-made insults Sosie recites in a resentful aside as the scene begins:

> Pestes, ivrognes, fous, impudents, effrontés,
> On nous donne à bon prix toutes ces qualités.
>
> (2.1.501-502)

Once committed to words, and to words commendable for their Cartesian precision ("Parlé-je à cette fois assez disertement, / En termes assez clairs, assez distinctement?") (2.1.533-34), Sosie's certainty about Mercure's usurpation of his identity merely confirms what Amphitryon already knows about him, producing a *third* Sosie answering to the unflattering image his master projects. The Cartesian picture of self is thus simultaneously enriched and complicated by a rival notion of identity as the possession not of the private person who *goes* by a name, but of those in whose power it lies to *give* or *withhold* that name, depending on what they see.[34]

---

[34] On naming in Rotrou, see Stephen C. Bold, "Ma(s)king a Name: Onomastics in Rotrou's Theater," *French Forum* 20.3 (September 1995) 279-97, drawing on François Rigolot's valuable *Poétique et Onomastique: l'exemple de la Renaissance* (Geneva: Droz, 1977), esp. the intro. But also consider the implications of J.L. Austin's theory of "speech acts." The fact that, however "proper" it may be, a name is always *given* raises questions about both propriety and reference that point in the direction of Althusser's notion of "interpellation."

In view of his haughty conduct toward his servant, it is only fair that Amphitryon should suffer a comparable fate. The master does not meet his actual twin until act 4. And what follows that encounter is a public confrontation in the presence of the captains of the hero's army, called on to judge which of the claimants to the title is the real Amphitryon–a quasi-judicial proceeding that culminates in a remarkable duet in which the antagonists produce a single narrative of the hero's victorious battle and ensuing return home, conducted in alternating hemistichs in which each seamlessly completes the other's sentences (4.4.1411-24). Still, by the time Jupiter and Amphitryon finally meet, the latter has already been repeatedly mistaken for his double, enduring the systematic misconstrual and disbelief to which he treats Sosie.

Thus, in 2.3-4, he reaches his palace only to be greeted by an Alcmène mystified at seeing him home again only minutes after leaving. One result of this encounter is Alcmène's increasingly irritated conviction that, in telling what she takes to be transparent lies, he either deliberately insults her intelligence and honor or has simply lost his mind: "Qui rend cet insensé jaloux de soi-même?" (2.4.858). But in addition to enduring the infuriating slight to his dignity in being called a liar, dreamer, madman, and impostor, this last being all the more unpalatable for equating Amphitryon with his clownish servant ("Ne m'approche pas, traître, / Suppôt d'un imposteur, valet digne du maître") (2.4.863-64), the hero learns that his wife has shared his bed with another. Amphitryon is a *cuckold*, suffering thereby a disgrace that attacks him not only in his own person, but through the identity he hopes to project in patrilinear time, as the noble father of a race of heroes like himself.[35]

<hr/>

[35] In stressing the centrality of adultery in Rotrou's *Sosies*, I side with Anne Ubersfeld, "Le double dans l'*Amphitryon* de Molière," in *Dramaturgie, langages dramatiques: Mélanges pour Jacques Schérer* (Paris: Nizet, 1986) 235-44 against André Gendre, "Le Jupiter de Rotrou et Molière ou le scandale justifié," in *La Mythologie au XVIIᵉ siècle* 177-85 and Forestier, *Esthétique de l'identité dans le théâtre français (1550-1680): Le déguisement et ses avatars* (Geneva: Droz, 1988) 562-63, who seems determined to minimize the theme in Rotrou in order to magnify its work in Molière so as to support his case concerning the malignant character of the latter's impostor god, whom he calls a "voleur d'âme" (563). As we saw a moment ago, when Rotrou's Amphitryon urges his troops to join him in storming and sacking his house, the aim is precisely to punish Alcmène's faithlessness (see 5.4.1638).

And indeed, as Mercury stresses us in the prologue to Plautus' play, confessing the moral as well as aesthetic impropriety of exposing such a character to the humbling vicissitudes of farce, for all we laugh at Amphitryon's increasingly frantic efforts to free himself from the comic snares that entangle him, he remains first and last a *hero*. This circumstance not only prepares us for the potentially tragic violence he threatens in the dénouement, but deepens the resonance of the plight he shares with Sosie. For *as* a hero, occupying a far higher and far larger place in our moral estimation, Amphitryon paradoxically depends on how others see him more even than his servant does. Alcmène makes the point with an irony the more devastating for its unconsciousness. Just before her first encounter with the true rather than Jovian Amphitryon, she voices the dual felicity of both loving and esteeming her noble husband:

> Il est vrai que l'honneur dessus l'amour l'emporte,
> Tant honnête soit-elle et tant soit-elle forte.
> De tous les beaux objets, la gloire est le plus doux,
> Aussi de tous les biens, ce bien seul est à nous.
> Les trésors sont des biens, mais il les faut défendre,
> On vante un noble sang, mais on le peut répandre,
> Ce soir emportera tel qui vit aujourd'hui,
> Et de ses jours le sort est plus maître que lui.
> La vertu, ce seul bien, de soi-même dispose,
> Elle possède tout, et donne toute chose.
>
> (2.2.635-44)

The encomium of honor with which Alcmène expresses her contentment is pure boilerplate, a textbook display of epideictic rhetoric reproducing heroic commonplaces the more predictable for fusing its epic picture of the virtuous martial soul with Stoic notions of personal integrity. [36] Like the Senecan Descartes of the *morale provisoire*, whose third maxim is

---

[36] Compare this with Moore's remarks on the ironic fate of *sententiae* in Rotrou's classical paradigm, *Theater of Plautus*, esp. 25-26 and 67-72. See also what we saw in chapter 2 regarding the title character's conflicting (yet equally mendacious) political moralizing in act 2 of *Cinna*.

de tâcher toujours plutôt à me vaincre que la fortune, et à chan-
ger mes désirs que l'ordre du monde; et généralement à croire
qu'il n'y a rien qui soit entièrement en notre pouvoir, que nos
pensées, [37]

she portrays heroic virtue as unshakable self-possession, escaping
the alienated play of worldly accident by holding fast to its own virtuous identity. A tissue of heroic clichés, the praise of heroic honor
is then yet another imitative double, albeit one justified here by the
moral standing of the speaker whose noble credentials it establishes. And yet the very triteness of Alcmène's speech points to what is
properly original in Rotrou: the praise of honor baits an ideological
trap concealed in the paralogism on which the speech turns.

Alcmène conflates the concepts of "honor," "glory," and "virtue," treating them as synonyms. In lines 637-38, she defines "glory"
as "the sweetest" of all "beautiful objects" and as the only good
that truly "belongs to us"; a distinction she also assigns virtue, identified in the closing couplet as the sole "good" that "disposes of
itself" and, in so disposing, "possesses all, and grants all things." At
one level, this conflation grounds honor in the noble virtue of
which she presents it as the infallible sign: by regarding the terms as
synonyms, she suggests that honor is a mere external register, the
form virtue takes when transposed from the noble soul to the world
of social recognition. People honor us for virtue; virtue is the cause
of the honor we enjoy; honor and virtue are therefore the same
thing conceived under complementary aspects.

But closely as we may link them, the two terms remain logically
distinct. Nor should we fail to notice that, careful as Alcmène may
be to define honor as a mere outward token of the virtue from
which it proceeds, it is nonetheless *honor* she praises, to the point
where, in her opening couplet, love itself is subordinate to it. Nor is
she simply wrong. To be esteemed, virtue must be known; what we
honor in virtue's name is its *proof*: in Amphitryon's case, the heroic
deeds in which it cashes out on the field of battle, in Alcmène's, the
domestic triumphs of wifely chastity. But as we learn not only from
the ease with which events persuade her husband of Alcmène's infidelity, but from Alcmène's own failure to discriminate between the

---

[37] Descartes, *Œuvres philosophiques* 1.595-96.

honor we pay virtue and the virtue so honored, the proof of virtue is subject to misconstruction precisely because it is external to the moral character it certifies. While virtue may in principle be invulnerable to the worldly chances that deprive us of treasure, blood, or breath of life, in practice it extends no further than the honor others bestow on the strength of outward signs as such susceptible to mistake.

Far from being cosubstantial with virtue, justifying the claim to being the only good that truly belongs to us, honor is a possession others grant in token of a virtue they cannot see. Virtuous as he may seem, once Amphitryon is perceived as a cuckold, all honor is lost; nor does heroic virtue stand the test, yielding to the murderous jealousy with which he consummates his own alienation in the dénouement. And with Amphitryon's metamorphosis from hero to raging cuckold, Alcmène in turn becomes an adulterous whore, condemned not only to suffer at her furious husband's hands, but to pay the insult back with a prideful fury of her own. Alcmène's theory of heroic virtue as the unassailable inner ground of heroic identity describes the machinery of virtue's overthrow. Exactly like the lowly Sosie, but with an *éclat* magnified by the height from which they fall, the noble couple are stripped of the identities with which they deludedly begin, driving them to a tragic end from which only a god can save them.

Rotrou's comedy turns out to be its own tragic counterpart, the more irrevocably in that, actuated by the alienated logic of heroic honor, its heroic protagonists insist on a tragic outcome. While Sosie, as a comic servant, can (as he also must) swallow the insults meted out to him, the play's noble personalities are programmed to take their comic misadventures with the utmost seriousness. They are undone by an heroic theory of identity the play destroys by robbing the heroes of selves they mistake for an inalienable possession. The theory is a social fiction, and the dramatic device of twins its deconstructive mark.

3. THE SOCIAL SELF IN MOLIÈRE'S *AMPHITRYON*

The situation in Molière is clearer in that, while his company regularly staged tragedies, and while Molière himself made occasional (and unsuccessful) forays in heroic poetry, he remains, like Plautus, an essentially comic poet condemned to play Sosie (as he did) even if he prefers to be Rodrigue. [38] Yet the situation is less clear in that, as a comic specialist, he blurs the separation of heroic nobility and ludicrous venery more thoroughly than even Rotrou. [39]

Appropriately enough given the problems surrounding fatherhood in the legend, the first complicating feature is a question of literary paternity. Written in 1667, during his convalescence from a serious illness and the nervous strain of the ongoing struggle around *Tartuffe*, *Amphitryon* is in part an attempt to enhance a badly compromised literary reputation, experimenting with lyric mea-

---

[38] Molière wrote one "comédie héroïque," the painfully unsuccessful *Dom Garcie de Navarre* (1661), in which he played the "tragic" role of the "jealous prince," and one "comédie galante," *La Princesse d'Elide*, for the "Plaisirs de l'Ile enchantée" in 1664. Neither play has earned a place in the canon.

[39] Here we see how Forestier is right as well as wrong about the contrast between the Rotrovian and Moliéresque versions of the story. In keeping with a pattern of adversarial overstatement that marks much of his work, he wants to distinguish the two plays *absolutely* whereas it would do better to say that Molière *intensifies* Rotrou's model. We note, e.g., that, in line with Forestier's characterization of Molière's Jupiter as a "voleur d'âme" intent on dispossessing Alcmène of her inner being, where Rotrou has Alcmène make the unwittingly ironic joke that she has shared her bed with no mortal other than her husband ("J'atteste de Jupin la majesté suprême / Que mon lit n'a reçu de mortel que vous-même") (2.4.835-36), Molière sharpens the impact by putting it in Jupiter's mouth. In place of the unconscious irony with which Alcmène tells the truth without knowing what she says, we get the supremely conscious irony with which Jupiter toys with his victim in a diabolically seductive speech in which he trades on his apparent humanity to shift the guilt for Alcmène's distress onto the husband she mistakes him for:

> L'époux, Alcmène, a commis tout le mal;
> C'est l'époux qu'il vous faut regarder en coupable.
> L'amant n'a point de part à ce transport brutal,
> Et de vous offenser son cœur n'est point capable...
> Haïssez, détestez l'époux,
>   J'y consens, et vous l'abandonne;
> Mais Alcmène, sauvez l'amant de ce courroux
> Qu'une telle offense vous donne.
>   (2.6.1304-07, 1319-22)

sures as opposed to the normal alexandrine and adapting a classical source. [40]

But here we meet a further complication. As noted earlier, in basing the play directly on a classical model, Molière sets himself a problem of poetic imitation: a problem, as it happens, on which he comments in the dedicatory epistle for the published text, addressed to "le Grand Condé," not only a royal prince and victor of the recent war in the Franche-Comté, but Molière's most prestigious ally in the *Tartuffe* affair. [41]

The problem of the dedication is that, *as* a dedication, it is thoroughly stereotyped:

> N'en déplaise à nos beaux esprits, je ne vois rien de plus ennuyeux que les épîtres dédicatoires; et VOTRE ALTESSE SERENISSIME trouvera bon, s'il lui plaît, que je ne suive point ici le style de ces messieurs-là, et refuse de me servir de deux ou trois misérables pensées qui ont été tournées et retournées tant de fois qu'elles sont usées de tous les côtés. (386)

Like the "miserable thoughts" Molière refuses to write, the genre of the dedication has been used up, a condition it shares with the literature of praise and flattery as a whole. In a culture like that of the court of Louis XIV, where unceasing panegyric is the rule, how does one write praise (as, despite his disclaimer, Molière proceeds to do) in such a way as to avoid mere commonplace? How does one find something capable not only of pleasing by its novelty, but of suggesting that the praise is sincere rather than rote, the measure of its sincerity being just the original twist the writer gives the ineffably cliché? [42]

---

[40] On this period in Molière's career, see Francine Mallet, *Molière* (Paris: Grasset, 1986) 122-24.

[41] See, e.g., the famous anecdote in which Condé explains to his wondering monarch why the *dévots* hate *Tartuffe* so passionately while voicing no criticism of the Italian *Scaramouche ermite*–a play the King understands to be far more irreligious than Molière's. "C'est, répondit le prince, que la comédie de Scaramouche joue le ciel et la religion, dont ces messieurs ne se soucient guère, tandis que celle de Molière les joue eux-mêmes; et c'est ce qu'ils ne peuvent souffrir." The anecdote is of course reported by Molière himself in the preface to *Tartuffe* (259). Also see more generally Mallet, *Molière*, pt. 1, chap. 7, "La Querelle du *Tartuffe*."

[42] Compare this with Boileau's experiments in the field, esp. in Epître VIII, "Au Roi," where he cleverly turns the trick by complaining that, as a satirist, he is temperamentally unfit to sing his infallibly victorious monarch's praises. On the cul-

But the problem of dedicatory praise is also the problem of literary·imitation, doubled here by the fact that the play Molière chooses to imitate has already been imitated by Rotrou. The need to find a new invention wringing something fresh out of "two or three miserable thoughts that have been turned this way and that" so often as to lose their lustre recapitulates the problem of reconciling the aesthetic of imitation classicism enjoins with the aesthetic of originality demanded of a true author. To this extent, the play meets, in the mode of literary identity, the dilemma confronted by its characters in the mode of dramatic action. How can Molière distinguish himself from someone he resembles like "deux gouttes de lait?" (2.1.785) How indeed does he even state the problem when the words that come to mind ("deux gouttes de lait") rehearse a proverb his rival has already repeated before him (*Les Sosies* 2.1.553)? The composition of Molière's play evolves in tandem with the action it directs; each new turn of phrase or twist of plot puts a fresh spin on the originals he reproduces, and each new spin on his originals turns a phrase or twists the plot.

Molière's first invention takes the form of a new prologue. Plautus gave us Mercury ringing changes on the themes of genre and the equivocally tragi-comic text, while Rotrou gave us Juno, marking the undertone of tragic *sérieux*. Molière now gives a dialogue in which comedy exposes at once a problem of means and a problem of reference: the ways in which the nature and meaning of what we see and hear is compromised by where it comes from, how it is written, and the rules that weigh on its address in the wider social environment.

The dialogue takes two voices, that of the god Mercure, entering on a cloud, and that of La Nuit, in a chariot drawn by a pair of mechanical horses. (And let us note that, like the version of Rotrou's play revived in 1649, Molière's *Amphitryon* is a "machine" play, making the most of such scenic effects as contemporary stagecraft was capable of.) In his capacity as messenger of the gods, Mercure conveys to La Nuit a "request" (in fact a command) on Jupiter's part. Whereupon the comedy of mistaken identities begins.

---

ture of flattery at the court of Louis XIV generally, see Marin, *Le portrait du roi*, Apostolidès, *Le roi-machine*, Soriano, *La brosse à reluire*, and Burke, *Fabrication of Louis XIV*.

For La Nuit fails at first to recognize Mercure, entering as he does
on a cloud rather than his customary winged feet–an iconographic
distinction he must moreover forego on this occasion in order to
pass for Sosie:

> Ah! ah! c'est vous, seigneur Mercure!
> Qui vous eût deviné, là, dans cette posture?
>
> (prologue, 5-6)

Mercure explains his unwonted appearance by adducing weariness: overcome by fatigue ("me trouvant las") owing to the "dif-
férents emplois," the uses (but also roles) to which Jupiter puts
him, he has decided to sit quietly on a cloud to await La Nuit's arrival (pro., 7-10). But the confession shocks his interlocutor:

> Vous vous moquez, Mercure, et vous n'y songez pas:
> Sied-il bien à des dieux de dire qu'ils sont las?
>
> (pro., 11-12)

Mercure replies with a question of his own, an inimitable verbal
shrug: "Les dieux sont-ils de fer?" (pro., 13) This in turn forces La
Nuit to explain herself:

> Non; mais il faut sans cesse
> Garder le *decorum* de la divinité.
> Il est de certains mots dont l'usage rabaisse
> Cette sublime qualité,
> Et que, pour leur indignité,
> Il est bon qu'aux hommes on laisse.
>
> (pro., 13-18)

To the problem of recognition posed by Mercure's entrance on
a cloud in contravention of iconographic convention the text now
adds that of the *bienséances*, of "decorum." This is a problem
Molière has met before, forming a major focus of the "querelle de
L'Ecole des femmes" from which, as we shall recall in chapter 4,
both *Tartuffe* and the violent controversy that play in turn provokes
ultimately rise. Though deeper matters were at issue, much attention fell on Molière's use of "certain words": a scandalous hanging
article ("le...") that triggered images of unmentionable female or-

gans (*le sein? le tétin? le cul? le con?*); the crude "potage" (as opposed to the more genteel "soupe") in the graphic analogy the servant Alain draws to explain the springs of male jealousy to his wife Georgette; above all, since, in the *Critique de l'Ecole des femmes*, Molière himself made so much of it, the off-color "tartes à la crème," the (by scatological implication) sperm-laden cream tarts the play's central protagonist hopes his naïve bride-to-be will think of whenever sex raises its ugly (if compulsory) head. [43]

In what amounts to an elegant as well as ludic anticipation of the sociology of speech acts laid out in Pierre Bourdieu's *Ce que parler veut dire*, La Nuit's displeasure invokes the question of the relation between words and things, but in such a way as to take it up a notch, to consideration of the social agendas to which usage conforms. [44] The gods possess a "sublime quality" that sets them apart from mere mortals, or at least from those mortals who, of the common sort, fall short of the eminence distinguishing their godlike betters at court. This "quality" in turn demands the tribute of a distinctive vocabulary. So while it may in fact be the case that even the gods lack the iron substance required to spare them lowly fatigue, not to mention disreputable human passions like lust, jealousy, envy, or hate, one must nonetheless never say so for fear of puncturing the dignity decorum demands.

Needless to say, La Nuit's priggish protests emphasize what she means to silence. For if the presumed "sublimity" of the gods (as of their courtly counterparts) is at the mercy of mere words, to what does it amount? If mere words can undo it, does anything *answer* to La Nuit's noble words, or is it a *fiction* that ceases to exist as soon as we abandon the appropriate terms for it? Mercure develops the point, challenging La Nuit's words by denouncing the unwarranted social privilege she takes for granted–a gesture that culminates in a conceptual knot in which a recalcitrant god complains of the condition inflicted on him by his own fictionality:

---

[43] For a helpful overview, see Mallet, *Molière*, pt. 1, chap. 6, "La Querelle de *L'Ecole des femmes*." For a recent, brilliant account of the wider issues engaged in the whole series of controversial plays from *L'Ecole des femmes* on, see Larry J. Norman, *The Public Mirror: Molière and the Social Commerce of Depiction* (Chicago: University of Chicago Press, 1999).

[44] Pierre Bourdieu, *Ce que parler veut dire: L'Economie des échanges linguistiques* (Paris: Fayard, 1982).

> A votre aise vous en parlez;
> Et vous avez, la belle, une chaise roulante
> Où, par deux bons chevaux, en dame nonchalante,
> Vous vous faites traîner partout où vous voulez.
>   Mais de moi ce n'est pas de même:
> Et je ne puis vouloir, dans mon destin fatal,
>   Aux poètes assez de mal
>   De leur impertinence extrême,
>   D'avoir, par une injuste loi
>   Dont on veut maintenir l'usage,
>   A chaque dieu, dans son emploi,
>   Donné quelque allure en partage,
>   Et de me laisser à pied, moi,
>   Comme un messager de village;
> Moi qui suis, comme on sait, en terre et dans les cieux,
> Le fameux messager du souverain des dieux;
>   Et qui, sans rien exagérer,
>   Par tous les emplois qu'il me donne,
>   Aurais besoin, plus que personne,
>   D'avoir de quoi me voiturer.
>
> (pro., 19-38)

Mercure here really complains of a purely fictional condition, drawing in his self-pity on the equally fictional dignity his character as Jupiter's messenger imparts. Granting the important role poets assign him, which, he protests, is surely not that of a village errand boy, he deserves a more dignified and (*pour tout dire*) less pedestrian mode of transportation–the more so when one adds the fatigues to which a messenger's duties expose him. But it is now La Nuit's turn to shrug, venturing the thought that things may not be as bad as they seem:

> Que voulez-vous faire à cela?
> Les poètes font à leur guise.
> Ce n'est pas la seule sottise
> Qu'on voit faire à ces messieurs-là.
> Mais contre eux toutefois votre âme à tort s'irrite,
> Et vos ailes aux pieds sont un don de leurs soins.
>
> (pro., 39-44)

To which consoling thought Mercure testily replies:

Oui; mais, pour aller plus vite,
Est-ce qu'on s'en lasse moins?
(pro., 45-46)

It is worth pausing to survey the ground Molière has already covered. For all the charming palaver conducted in the text's witty lyric measures, Mercure has still not come to the point. The business of the prologue (substituting here, in accord with the play's classical example, for Molière's customary agonistic *scène d'exposition*) is to fill in the background for the plot and the dramatic issue it joins, matters indeed to which the characters turn in a moment:

Laissons cela, seigneur Mercure,
Et sachons de quoi il s'agit.
(pro., 47-48)

But in place of a normal exposition we get an inspired impromptu on the theme of theatrical gods that recalls a number of leading issues contested in the literary wars in which the play marks a truce. The weary messenger–Mercure, a character however who will shortly double as his twin Sosie, the role played by Molière–takes a spell of hard-earned rest before resuming the office that has become so onerous to him. Nevertheless, a lot of interesting work gets done in the process. In exploring its own conditions as dramatic poetry, the prologue questions the force we are to assign the words, figures, and conventions that compose the poetry and through which it works the dramatic illusion to which the audience has already succumbed unawares. [45]

A major feature of drama is poetic fiction: what we see and hear on the stage is a phantasmatic double we take for real in place of the real itself. [46] To achieve this effect, emphasized here by the way the characters discuss their own fictive unreality, the poet draws on

---

[45] See Zanger's related comments in "Classical Anxiety: Performance, Perfection, and the Issue of Identity" on *Amphitryon* as a performative allegory of the malaise attending the classical demand of theatrical "illusion."

[46] As we saw in our introduction, Molière himself makes the point with considerable (if ultimately fruitless) care in the *Critique de l'Ecole des femmes*. See Norman, *Public Mirror*, chap. 1, "Uranie and the 'General Thesis'."

the reality he displaces. What commits us to the fiction, even as the play cheerfully expatiates on its own status *as* fiction, is in part the fact that, fictional as they may be, the characters *really talk*, engaged in at once garrulous and quarrelsome debate. But what convinces us is also a certain *truth to type*, a conventional truth in turn keyed to certain shared understandings about the world (of types, or "characters") to which the play both refers and belongs.

Mercure, for instance, is a god; but he is also "Sosie." As such, he answers, in both the divine community he comes from and the human setting in which he obtrudes, to the type of a "valet," a character one of whose elements is colorful complaint. And an aspect of the color is an otherwise indecorous use of words–just what La Nuit reproves in scolding him for confessing to lowly lassitude. Part of the art and therefore a source of the peculiar pleasure associated with this scene consists then in working colloquial usage into its intricate lyric verse: the trenchant "les dieux sont-ils de fer" or the shrugging "oui; mais" that introduces the crypto-proverbial "pour aller plus vite, / Est-ce qu'on s'en lasse moins?" La Nuit, meanwhile, is a *prude*: the snotty Latin "*decorum*" (italicized in the original) with which she reproves Mercure for confessing weariness and the precious turns of phrase and grammatical constructions ("qui vous eût deviné là, dans cette posture?" "sied-il bien à des dieux de dire qu'ils sont las?" "il est de certains mots dont l'usage rabaisse") skillfully draw the portrait–a canny resource for the actor playing the role, in which we recognize the kind of person La Nuit portrays.

And yet part of the truth we recognize, part of the knowledge about personal kinds on which the play trades, is precisely the knowledge of *roles*. *As* a prude, for example, La Nuit is the kind of person whose character note is to pretend to be another kind: the essence of the prude is not the virtue he or she proclaims, but the insufferable combination of prurience and hypocrisy behind the display of scandalized shock. Thus, in the development, as Mercure lays out the play's premise by delivering Jupiter's request that La Nuit slow her natural course to give their master time to enjoy Alcmène's favors to the full, La Nuit bridles at the seediness of the employment to which she is asked to stoop. But what offends her is less the sexual act itself than its *form*. That Jupiter should, in Mercure's words, "s'humaniser pour des beautés mortelles," deploying "cent tours ingénieux / Pour mettre à bout les plus cruelles" (pro., 56-58), is vexing enough. But worse is Jupiter's well-documented tendency to undermine both human and divine alibis for erotic passion by assuming a bestial shape in which the grossly physical reality of sexual congress is brought explicitly to light:

> Passe encore de le voir, de ce sublime étage,
> Dans celui des hommes venir,
> Prendre tous les transports que leur cœur peut fournir,
> Et se faire à leur badinage,
> Si, dans les changements où son humeur l'engage,
> A la nature humaine il s'en voulait tenir.
> Mais de voir Jupiter taureau,
> Serpent, cygne, ou quelque autre chose,
> Je ne trouve point cela beau.
> Et ne m'étonne pas si parfois on en cause.
>
> (pro., 93-102)

To which of course is added the role she herself is called to play, deflating her conceit by associating her with Jupiter's shameful doings:

> Voilà sans doute un bel emploi
> Que le grand Jupiter m'apprête!
> Et l'on donne un nom fort honnête
> Au service qu'il veut de moi!
>
> (pro., 120-23)

Of course, La Nuit's complaint at being treated like a pandar (save the name!) merely prompts Mercure's ironic rejoinder, this too part of the colloquial color the valet's role licenses. As he reminds her, what Jupiter requests is a service she has performed for illicit lovers from time immemorial; nor has she been heard to complain about it till now:

> Hé! la, la, madame la Nuit,
> Un peu doucement, je vous prie;
> Vous avez dans le monde un bruit
> De n'être pas si renchérie.
> On vous fait confidente, en cent climats divers,

> De beaucoup de bonnes affaires;
> Et je crois, à parler à sentiments ouverts,
> Que nous ne nous en devons guère.
> (pro., 136-43)

But La Nuit's vexation also prompts the reminder of the *hierarchy* to which, like it or not, both divinities belong, leading Mercure to denounce not only La Nuit's prudery, but the social order that infects the polite idiom to which she clings:

> Pour une jeune déesse,
> Vous êtes bien du bon temps.
> Un tel emploi n'est bassesse
> Que chez les petites gens.
> Lorsque dans un haut rang on a l'heur de paraître,
> Tout ce qu'on fait est toujours bel et bon;
> Et suivant ce qu'on peut être,
> Les choses changent de nom.
> (pro., 124-31)

The prologue thus informs us of its two protagonists' roles; but it also informs us of the *origins* of those roles in prevailing relations of power and the collaborative assent such relations extort. Depending on "what we are, things change their names." Names answer to a political calculus that, in dictating what we call things, dictates our responses to them, and thereby the identities we are forced assume. Whatever her prudish pretensions, La Nuit is a pandar if Jupiter wills it. Much as she may wish to distance herself from a depraved office she is nonetheless perfectly willing to thrust on Mercure,

> Sur de pareilles matières
> Vous en savez plus que moi;
> Et, pour accepter l'emploi,
> J'en veux croire vos lumières,
> (pro. 132-35)

she is already committed by the social system to which she belongs. From the very start then, in the guise of ingeniously diverting improvisations on the themes of decorum, role-playing, poetic fiction, and names, Molière's *Amphitryon* invests the central plot device of twins with a sardonic social resonance that carries far beyond the point Rotrou reaches. Rotrou's experiments with Cartesian identity claims, deepened though they may be by recognition of the degree to which what we take our selves to be is the product of how others see us, give way to a thoroughgoing political interpretation that at once redoubles and redirects their ludic force by frankly inserting them in the social realm.[47]

When, at 1.2.309-19, Sosie first encounters his Mercurial twin on the road home to report the happy issue of his master's war, the focus of Mercure's challenge to Sosie's sense of self is a direct confrontation with the Stoic model of identity on which, in Rotrou, the Cartesian cogito and Alcmène's encomium of heroic virtue equally rest. The confrontation takes the form of a series of ever more pointed questions designed to force Sosie to identify himself not as the autonomous being it flatters him to imagine, but as an expression of his engagement in an irrevocably social world. As Sosie approaches his master's door, Mercure brings him to a halt by demanding "Who goes there?" ("Qui va là?"). "Me," Sosie warily replies, "Moi"; and when Mercure goes on to ask, naturally enough, "Qui, moi?" Sosie repeats himself, "Moi," adding *sotto voce*, "Courage, Sosie." As put here, the question of identity exceeds and, by exceeding, interrogates the Cartesian framework it appears to reproduce.[48]

In Descartes, as in the soliloquies with which, in Rotrou and Molière alike, Sosie tries to digest the challenge to sole possession of his own identity, the question of self ("Qui, moi?") looks like a philosophical matter pursued at the respondent's private bidding. Here, by contrast, it is not "I myself" who voices it, but *another*; and what that other means in asking it, the response it is calculated to elicit and thus the identity that is asked for, are correspondingly different. The sentry's challenge ("Who goes there?") is not a metaphysical question: Mercure does not want to know what "self" approaches Amphitryon's palace, still less what that self's true

---

[47] See Gossman, *Men and Masks* 10-17 and 168-81.

[48] This is a central theme not only in Gossman's chapter on *Amphitryon*, but in Lacan's lecture on "Sosie." See, too, Selma Zebouni, "L'*Amphitryon* de Molière ou l'autre du sujet," in Ralph Heyndels & Barbara Woshinsky (eds.), *L'autre au XVIIe siècle* (Tübingen: Biblio 17, 1999) 347-55.

"grounds" and inner "nature" might be; he demands a *name* conceived as the coordinate of a specific place in the social order that has *given* that name with a view to locating the person who bears it. Conversely, in replying with the exasperating tautology ("moi"), Sosie does not offer a philosophical reply; he withholds the name he knows he is asked for, challenging the other's right to demand it. When moreover, in response to Mercure's ongoing challenge, Sosie does in fact go on to speak in philosophical terms, the effect is to define philosophy as *prevarication*. Sosie's philosophical answer appears to assert a truth the coercive facts of society distort or denature by supplanting the private essence metaphysics posits with the social coordinates a name confers. His reply is nevertheless both insolently out of order and a strategy of concealment designed to avoid acknowledging the relational identity Mercure asks for.

So in answer to Sosie's reiterated "moi" in response to his renewed demand to know who he is, Mercure narrows the question's scope by unpacking some of its implicit content: "Quel est ton sort, dis-moi?" "D'être homme," Sosie replies, "et de parler." This is of course equivocation. Quibbling on the sense of the term *sort*, Sosie parries the patent force the context gives Mercure's question by offering humanist bromides. Instead of specifying the place in the social order that defines his station in life, he asserts his metaphysical "essence" as a Man endowed with the distinctive human capacity to reason as exercised in the power of speech. [49] This prompts Mercure to rephrase the question in order to compel Sosie to descend from the heights of metaphysical abstraction to the sphere of actual social relation: "Es-tu maître, ou valet?" But Sosie continues to wriggle, adding to the definition of his humanity by affirming his free will: "Comme il me prend envie." And when Mercure asks just where he thinks free will takes him, he haughtily, but also circularly, and, further, given that he travels on his master's orders, *mendaciously* adduces free will once more: "Où j'ai dessein d'aller."

By invoking the discourse of philosophy, the passage undermines philosophy's pretensions. Put in the context of the concrete

---

[49] Lacan notes the anticipatory ironies at work in this definition: "Voilà quelqu'un qui n'avait pas été aux séminaires, mais qui en a la marque de fabrique," "Sosie" 307. But he misses how far Sosie reflects (and parodies) the humanist education Molière received from the Jesuits.

social relations to which even philosophers are bound, philosophical speech is made to appear both comic and evasive–a point
Mercure drives home in the sequel when, abandoning the thrust
and parry of verbal equivocation, he resorts to the simple yet decisive expedient of physical violence. Though Sosie withholds Amphitryon's name, earning the beating Mercure threatens, he is obliged to concede the fact to which the beating testifies. Evasion must
end in belonging, and in subjection to the social forces belonging
expresses: "J'appartiens à mon maître."

Molière goes on to develop the Cartesian muddles Rotrou explores. In an aside prompted by Mercure's proof of inside knowledge only Sosie could have, a Turing Test compelling Sosie to confess Mercure's right to his identity,[50] Sosie takes the road of Hyperbolic Doubt:

> Il ne ment pas d'un mot à chaque repartie;
> Et de moi je commence à douter pour de bon.
> Près de moi, par la force, il est déjà Sosie;
> Il pourrait bien encor l'être par la raison.
> Pourtant, quand je me tâte et que je me rappelle,
> Il me semble que je suis moi.
> Où puis-je rencontrer quelque clarté fidèle,
> Pour démêler ce que je vois?
>
> (1.2.484-91)

However, as in Rotrou, rather than lead to the cogito's assertion of
self as the one certainty doubt cannot shake, the result is an anti-
cogito converting self-discovery into anxious interrogation:

> Mais si tu l'es, dis-moi qui tu veux que je sois.
> Car encor faut-il que je sois quelque chose.
>
> (1.2.511-12)

Then too, when Sosie tries to explain to his furious master what has
prevented him from preparing his household for his triumphant re-

---

[50] Pascal's "Qu'est-ce que le moi?" (*Pensées*, Lafuma 688; Sellier 567) anticipates the Turing Test to equally devastating effect. For a related if different reading of
what we might call the behavioral dilemma of identity *Amphitryon* poses, see Stone,
The Classical Model 102-11.

turn, he produces schizophrenic doubletalk worthy of his Rotrovian forebear:

> Faut-il le répéter vingt fois de même sorte?
> Moi, vous dis-je, ce moi plus robuste que moi;
> Ce moi qui s'est de force emparé de la porte;
>   Ce moi qui m'a fait filer doux;
>   Ce moi qui le seul moi veut être;
>   Ce moi de moi-même jaloux;
>   Ce moi vaillant dont le courroux
> Au moi poltron s'est fait connaître;
> Enfin ce moi qui suis chez nous;
> Ce moi qui s'est montré mon maître;
> Ce moi qui m'a roué de coups.
>
> (2.1.810-20)

In Molière, however, the schizophrenia betokens less the disorienting private experience Sosie undergoes than the doubling he endures as a reflex of his place in the social order.

We note, for instance, that the frantic gibberish Sosie talks requires a *license*: just because his story sounds so crazy even to him, he requests his master's permission (granted at 2.1.713-14) before venturing to tell it at all. But if the truth sounds like an extravagant pack of lies, it is because Sosie listens to his own words with his master's ears. The truth, or what *passes* for truth, is thus conditional on his master's consent to hear it, and still more on the master's willingness to *believe* it. And while Amphitryon's understandable refusal to believe it is based in part on its inherent implausibility, his deepest motive is what he makes less of the story itself than of the person who vouches for it. This determines the derisive form the refusal takes:

> Il faut que ce matin, à force trop de boire,
> Il s'est troublé le cerveau.
>
> (2.1.823-24)

As the rejoinder's third-person form suggests, turning Sosie into an object his master disdains to address in person, whatever Sosie says will be heard through the alienating filter of Amphitryon's prefabricated notion of who he is.

The upshot makes the point more explicit still. The dismissal of Sosie's story as the ravings of a drunk raises the problem of "other minds": in the absence of direct observation of his servant's inner, "mental" state, how can Amphitryon judge if he tells the truth? Sosie answers the question by swearing an oath:

> Je veux être pendu, si j'ai bu que de l'eau!
> A mon serment on peut m'en croire.
>
> (2.1.823-24)

The implicit argument in the second line (my oath should carry conviction just because it *is* an oath; would I swear an oath if I were lying?) draws on a speech-act theory of truth claims. An oath is a form of speech conventionally designed to underwrite the truth of what it swears to. Its meaning, what J.L. Austin would call its "force" as an "illocutionary act," that is, as an act I perform in uttering a "locution," is to confirm that the "sense" of what I say (the literal reference of my words) is true.[51] In swearing an oath, Sosie at once affirms and corrects for the autonomous private inwardness he has earlier (unsuccessfully) defended against Mercure. In *giving* his word, Sosie asserts that Amphitryon must take him *at* his word; and he must do so because, in the absence of the direct access to his servant's state of mind needed to verify by simple inspection whether he speaks truly or not, there is in the end nothing but Sosie's word for it.

Sosie's effort runs aground however as soon as we move to what Austin calls the "perlocutionary" stage, the level of the *effect* his form of words brings about. Does the oath suffice to persuade the interlocutor that the sense of the words Sosie utters is true? *In* swearing an oath (the *il*-locution), Sosie defends the truth of what he swears to: the implicit locution, "I am not drunk; this really happened." But *by* swearing an oath (a *per*-locution), does he convince

---

[51] For the definition of "illocutionary acts," refining on the more general "doctrine" of "speech acts" with a view to contrasting acts we perform "*in* saying something" (illocutions) with acts we perform "*by* saying something" (perlocutions), see Austin, *How to Do Things with Words*, lecture 8. We shall return to the special relevance of speech-act theory to Molière in chapter 5 with reference to *Tartuffe* and *Dom Juan*, when we shall also have occasion to discuss Felman's *Le Scandale du corps parlant*.

Amphitryon that what he swears to is true? The answer is no; but it is no not just because, whether Sosie swears to it or not, the story that prompts his master to say he must be drunk is too incredible to be true. Amphitryon refuses to believe the oath because the person who swears it is not to be trusted. In *giving* his word, Sosie wants to be taken *at* his word: "May I be hanged if I have drunk anything but water!" But Sosie is the kind of person who *cannot* be taken at his word–the kind of person who would in fact swear an oath to give color to a lie. [52]

Nor is Amphitryon entirely mistaken. Sosie's oath contains a grammatical ambiguity (a problem of sense) that questions what it swears to (its force). The oath, "Je veux être pendu, si j'ai bu que de l'eau," seems to mean (and means to be *taken* to mean) what my translation renders: "May I be hanged if I have drunk *anything* but water" ("*que* de l'eau"). But the conjunctive particle "que," which Sosie's desired sense bids us read as an abbreviated form of the phrase "autre chose que" or "rien que," accepts a better reading. Given the colloquial French habit of abridging two-part negative constructions by dropping the first element, the word "que" more naturally evokes the "ne... que..." construction ("only" or "nothing but") to produce an exactly opposite sense: "May I be hanged if I have drunk *nothing* but water." Taken in conjunction with knowledge of the kind of person Sosie is, the equivocal form of the oath suggests that Sosie has in fact been drinking and is therefore drunk even if the story he tells is true.

Sosie's oath thereby defeats the point of its own exercise. But in the process, it also defeats the ontological claim undergirding the epistemic procedure he recommends: the idea that his master must take him at his word because only direct access to his private mental state can determine whether he tells the truth or not. Nor is there any comfort in the irony that, as the earlier scene with Mercure has shown, drunkard and liar though Sosie may be, on *this* occasion he tells the sober truth. The irony rather accentuates the dimensions of Sosie's plight. Just because we know he tells the truth,

---

[52] Though its range of examples is quite different, see Steven Shapin's fascinating historical sociology of the adjudication of truth claims in *A Social History of Truth: Civility and Science in Seventeenth-Century England* (Chicago: University of Chicago Press, 1994).

we can appreciate more fully the tenor of his master's disbelief. Above all, we understand more clearly the perlocutionary weight of what happens next. When Sosie continues to insist that he is telling the truth, Amphitryon cuts him off with the finally unanswerable reminder of their respective social identities:

> Suis-moi, je t'impose silence.
> C'est trop fatiguer l'esprit;
> Et je suis un vrai fou d'avoir la patience
> D'écouter d'un valet les sottises qu'il dit.
>
> (2.1.835-38)

As Sosie himself puts it in the caustic aside the master's demand for obedient silence provokes,

> Tous les discours sont des sottises
> Partant d'un homme sans éclat:
> Ce seraient paroles exquises
> Si c'était un grand qui parlât.
>
> (2.1.839-42)

All of which brings us back to Sosie's earlier question in response to Mercure's usurpation of his identity: "qui veux-tu que je sois?" This is yet another equivocal formula. Though the question's literal sense is to ask "who do you *want* me to be," the idiomatic force of the verb *vouloir* produces a second meaning we may render in the form "who am I *supposed* to be?" But the literal sense counts just the same, underscoring the fact that Sosie's identity is not of his own making. To the extent indeed that we can genuinely say he has one, Sosie's self is in the giving of others, and more specifically the masters to whom it is his social fate to belong.

The theme of twins in *Amphitryon* thus transcends the challenge Rotrou addresses to the notion of self associated with Cartesian Stoicism and the essentialist metaphysics it supports, the position to which Sosie spontaneously resorts before Mercure beats him into submission. The thrust of Sosie's experience is to show how self is forged on the anvil of social coercion, an identity to which he is inextricably bound despite the alienation it incurs. Sosie is a victim of the psycho-sociological process Louis Althusser

202 INDISCERNIBLE COUNTERPARTS

calls "méconnaissance." His person is not only subject to mis-recognition, as an independent entity whose nature we merely mis-take; rather, as Mercure's usurpation of Sosie's identity makes plain, it is the product of an active *misconstruction* in which every word and deed is systematically given an alienating sense he is powerless to dispel, but to which he must nonetheless submit, as-suming it in place of the identity he wills.[53] In a movement linked to the related Althusserian phenomenon of "interpellation" or "hailing," a process, modeled on Lacan's analysis of the Symbolic, whereby individuals are called into social being by the name soci-ety assigns them,[54] Sosie is trapped by the self his betters impose. Every effort to defend a difference compounds the identity they enforce.

Nor is Sosie alone in this. Amphitryon is never treated to the name-calling (literally, "interpellation": the fact of being summoned by name) visited upon his lowly servant. Yet he too, by the close, is called a dreamer, madman, and cuckold, just as the loyal Alcmène is converted into the adulterous whore he threatens to murder. The comic misunderstandings the device of twins makes possible take a decidedly sinister turn in which we glimpse the hell of social rela-tions.

And yet for all the sinister value *Amphitryon* gets out of the Plautine theme of twins, diagnosing a social pathology the more dif-ficult to cure in that it is identical with social order as such, the play remains a comedy. In the dénouement, shedding all disguise, Jupiter descends to set everything right, "annoncé par le bruit du tonnerre, armé de son foudre, dans un nuage, sur son aigle." (3.10.1890) To be sure, the saving theophany enfolds ambiguities of its own. Jupiter appears in a divine identity the accompanying the-atrical machinery seems to establish beyond reasonable doubt: "A ces marques," he assures Amphitryon, "tu peux aisément le con-naître." (3.10.1892) But the identifying iconography recalls the pro-logue's ironic glosses on the fictional character of the iconographic conventions he invokes, undermining the identity he asserts. Still,

---

[53] For an explanation both of "méconnaissance" and of its relation to Lacan's theory of the Symbolic, see Louis Althusser, "Freud et Lacan," in *Positions (1964-1975)* (Paris: Editions sociales, 1976) 9-34.

[54] On "interpellation," see Althusser, "Les appareils idéologiques d'Etat," ibid. 110-19.

fictional or not, Jupiter's descent assures a happy ending that, in rescuing the actors from the calamitous consequences of their deeds, preserves the right of laughter.

Nevertheless, the very laughter that allows the play to end in a state of what looks like commity and happiness also authorizes the sardonic commentaries Sosie (Molière) piles up as the action rushes to a close. Thus Sosie to Mercure: "je ne vis de ma vie / Un dieu plus diable que toi" (3.9.1888-89); Sosie to Amphitryon, reminding his master that, happy ending or no, he remains a cuckold: "Le seigneur Jupiter sait dorer la pilule" (3.10.1913); or Sosie's biting curtain-line: "Sur telles affaires toujours / Le meilleur est de ne rien dire." (3.10.1942-43) The blinding light and deafening noise of the theophanous dénouement drive sinister afterthoughts to the back-ground—a gesture of repression seconded by the belittling laughter that greets the servant's mordant discontent. While the Molière that is Sosie rails at the lies that paper over the fissures at once disfigur-ing and disclosing the true order of things, the Sosie that is Molière is assured of our indulgence, conscious that his double's angry words will be heard "in character," as the harmless colorful mutter-ings of a stock valet. Yet the silence that falls with the final curtain, the "ne rien dire" that marks the passage from the spectacle just ended to that spectacle's lingering afterimage in the *text*, plants a diacritical signal of the speech it elides.

Amphitryon, we recall, is a product of the period in Molière's career dominated by the five-year conflict surrounding *Tartuffe*, a play itself responding to the critical assaults provoked six years ear-lier by *L'Ecole des femmes* (1662). Like other works composed at this time, *Le Misanthrope* (1666), *Le Médecin malgré lui* (1666), or *Le Sicilien, ou l'amour peintre* (1667), *Amphitryon* avoids the mis-take of directly commenting on its place in this wider context. Yet with a pertinacity unknown since the violent *Dom Juan* of 1665, *Amphitryon* inscribes (albeit only in passing) the ciphers that make it possible to read what its comic valet expressly leaves unsaid. The mocking veil of decorous silence Sosie drops over the scabrous deeds the play rehearses, reinforced by the leading culprit's divine stature and the heroic fruit the title character's conjugal misfortune yields, allows the public to pretend it has not heard. But what the public has not heard gets written all the same, in the text that serves as *sub*-text to Sosie's terminal silence. And what gets written is not merely Molière's challenge to the social order the concord of the play's dénouement paradoxically endorses and indicts. It is above all the fate of the self or "subject," the Cartesian ego whose surrender to the interpellative force of social relation Molière portrays. But the Cartesian subject, as defining the form the era grants personal identity and the self-determination identity claims, is just what *L'Ecole des femmes* was about. The silence that falls with *Amphitryon*'s final curtain thus points back to the play that started it all, and to which we now turn.

CHAPTER 4

THE AGENCY OF THE LETTER IN THE UNCONSCIOUS, OR REASON SINCE MOLIERE: THE STAGING OF NAMES IN *L'ECOLE DES FEMMES*

O N its face, nothing could seem more uncomplicated, more purely diverting, than Molière's *L'Ecole des femmes*. In a nameless town, Paris or some smaller, provincial city, [1] lives an arrogant eccentric possessed of the comically overdetermined name "Arnolphe," recalling the folkloric patron of cuckolds, Arnulf de Cornibont de Villars. [2] In defiance of the unlucky augury of his name, and in line with social ambitions evinced by his efforts to replace it with the noble-sounding "Monsieur de La Souche," Arnolphe announces his intention to take a wife. However, having made a name for himself as the author of satiric chronicles exposing the conjugal misfortunes of his fellow citizens, our hero means to avoid the common lot of husbands. Where other men wed blindly, condemned by lack of foresight to suffer subjection to their spouses' whims, Arnolphe has a *plan*, outlined in the *scène d'exposition* to his friend and foil, the eminently rational *honnête homme* Chrysalde.

Arnolphe has convinced himself that the best way to ensure his wife will never deceive him is to marry a woman so unschooled in the ways of the world as to be incapable of imagining delights other than those he dictates. With this end in view, he has some years passed purchased a young girl he calls Agnès from an indigent peasantwoman he mistakenly supposes to be her mother (1.1.129-34).

---

[1] The text indicates only that "La scène est dans une place de ville."
[2] See Maurice & Wilfred Drake, *Saints and Their Emblems* (1916; rpt. Detroit: Gale Research Co., 1971) 18.

The child has been raised "dans un petit couvent, loin de toute pratique" (1.1.135), according to a system of his own devising. As spelled out in a pamphlet he obliges his ward to read aloud in 3.2, *Les Maximes du mariage, ou les devoirs de la femme mariée, avec son exercice journalier*, this system demands the girl's total subservience to her mate. In addition to being held prisoner by domestics as witless as herself in a secret establishment Arnolphe maintains for the purpose, Agnès learns that a proper wife is her husband's exclusive property, denied a will of her own. Her dress must conform to his taste and pocketbook, and she is forbidden make-up, flirting, outings, gaming, visitors beyond those her husband chooses, and gifts from other men. Further, on the principle that "femme qui compose en sait plus qu'il ne faut" (1.1.94), she is even deprived of any means of *writing*:

> Dans ses meubles, dût-elle en avoir de l'ennui,
> Il ne faut écritoire, encre, papier, ni plumes:
> Le mari doit, dans les bonnes coutumes,
> Ecrire tout ce qui s'écrit chez lui.
> (3.2.780-83)

The trouble is that the young Horace, son of Arnolphe's friend Oronte, chances to see Agnès at her window and falls madly in love. Abetted by a nameless *entremetteuse*, "une vieille," so Horace reports, "d'un génie, à vrai dire, au-dessus de l'humain" (3.4.970-71), he contrives to speak with her and win her innocent heart. However, failing to link Agnès's ogrish captor, known to him only as "Monsieur de La Souche," with his father's friend Arnolphe, Horace takes counsel with our hero, who exploits these confidences to frustrate his rival's hopes. Arnolphe and Horace battle for the heroine's hand, the one aided by his incognito, the other by Love itself, for Love

> est un grand maître:
> Ce qu'on ne fut jamais, il nous enseigne à l'être;
> Et souvent de nos mœurs l'absolu changement
> Devient par ses leçons l'ouvrage d'un moment.
> (3.4.900-903)

The rivalry triggers an escalating series of plots and counterplots, ironic reversals and giddy *quiproquos*–featuring, in contravention of the *Maximes du mariage*, the penning of a letter Agnès attaches to a cobblestone she hurls at her lover's head in obedience to her captor's wishes. The climax is reached with the arrival of Horace's father and Oronte's friend Enrique, a gentleman who, driven into exile by un-named legal difficulties caused by the "envy" and "imposture" of others (5.9.1749), has spent the interval amassing a fortune in Ameri-ca. The heaven-sent pair conclude the marriage of Horace with En-rique's daughter, a nameless girl abandoned at the time of her fa-ther's flight who turns out to be none other than Agnès.

And there you have it, a comic love story told in its essentials many times before and since, and notably in Molière's own *L'Ecole des maris* of 1661. But straightforward and even trite as all this may seem, when examined closely in its text by a reader undistracted by the charm and pace of live rehearsal in the theater, the play reveals far more than its plot promises.

Such is besides the testimony of the controversy it occasioned. First staged on the Feast of St. Stephen, 26 December 1662, *L'Ecole des femmes* caps the string of successes initiated by the play with which the Illustre Théâtre marked its definitive installation in the capital, *Les Précieuses ridicules* of 1659. But in addition to securing its author's contemporary fame, *L'Ecole* provoked a violent quarrel that conditioned his literary output for years to come. Beginning with the ingeniously specular *Critique de l'Ecole des femmes* and *Impromptu de Versailles* of 1663, Molière composes no fewer than five plays whose inspiration can be traced to the debate surround-ing *L'Ecole des femmes*, including three of his greatest creations: the vengeful *Tartuffe* (1664), directing a counterattack at the notorious "cabale des dévots," the pious conspiracy Molière rightly saw be-hind the assaults to which *L'Ecole* was exposed; the even more vengeful *Dom Juan* (1665), which broadens the front to engage the moral basis of the entire social order; and finally, in the wake of *Dom Juan*'s universal condemnation, Molière's symbolic withdrawl from Parisian society in the person of Alceste at the end of *Le Mi-santhrope* in 1666.[3] Deliriously as the *esprits forts* at court or in the

---

[3] For overviews of the *querelle*, see the intro. to Georges Mongrédien's 2-vol. collection of writings produced during the controversy, *La Querelle de l'Ecole des*

cheaper seats of the *parterre* received it, the play touched off a movement of resistance whose violence signals the depth of the investment on both sides. Whence this chapter's aim: to sort out some of the motives for this resistance as these become legible in the text of the play itself. And at the heart of the case, at once the play's major theme and most signal achievement, is the Comedy of the Subject, the simultaneous *mise en scène* and *mise en cause* of the sovereign "I" of modern social experience.

A central feature of the comedy of the subject is the *name*. Names and what names inscribe, indeed the process of inscription itself, what the play insistently calls "writing" or *l'écrit*,[4] are spectacularly at issue in *L'Ecole des femmes*. Much is made of the name's grip on its bearer's identity and fate. To cite a telltale Molière title, *Le Médecin malgré lui*, names shape their owners "despite them," from a space French calls "l'insu," the zone of what in our conduct is unknowing because unknown.[5] Nor is this true merely of the

---

femmes (Paris: Marcel Didier, 1971) and Mallet, *Molière*, pt. 1, chaps. 6-8. On the general cultural environment, see Gérard Defaux, *Molière, ou les métamorphoses du comique: De la comédie morale au triomphe de la folie* (Lexington, KY: French Forum, 1980), pt. 1, chap. 1, "Situation de Molière: Théâtre et société au début du règne de Louis XIV," and Hugh Gaston Hall, *Comedy in Context: Essays on Molière* (Jackson: University of Mississippi Press, 1984). On the inner continuity shaping Molière's dramatic output from *L'Ecole des femmes* to *Le Misanthrope*, see Jacques Guicharnaud, *Molière, une aventure théâtrale: Tartuffe, Dom Juan, Le Misanthrope* (Paris: Gallimard, 1963) and Defaux's continuation. But note that Guicharnaud and Defaux's accounts of Molière's "adventure" and the metamorphoses by which it transforms the comic and its genres suppose a finally irreducible intellectual and aesthetic autonomy on the author's part—one Molière himself systematically calls in doubt. Here, by contrast, we make room for the pressure exerted by public reception on production as such. See, e.g., Norman's *Public Mirror*, which explores the multifarious ways in which Molière's role as the "painter" of public morals is transformed by the intense reaction of the public whose image he holds up in the satiric "mirror" of comic drama. Norman sums up his case in pt. 3, "Recognition," whose opening chapter bears the telling title "From Arnolphe to Alceste."

[4] Note the temporal (and thus ontological) contrast between English *writing* and French *écrit*. The latter, a nominalized past participle, emphasizes the text as *written*, and thus as the vestige of an anterior productive act. The former, however, incorporates the verbal present of an ongoing process oriented toward the future. Where an *écrit* inscribes what *was*, a *writing* points to the open-ended realm of what *will* be. We shall return to this contrast later.

[5] Important here is Vincent Descombes, *L'Inconscient malgré lui* (Paris: Minuit, 1977), which revises Lacan's linguistic theory of the unconscious by reflecting on the formal properties of speech acts. Rather than identify the unconscious with the "je n'en veux rien savoir" of repression, Descombes focuses on the much wider and

play's characters. One dimension of the meaning of names and the related theme of the *écrit* is their relevance to the author: a certain baptist, "Jean-Baptiste Poquelin," called "Molière," a figure whose fortunes echo those of his hero, the self-styled "Monsieur de La Souche," also known as "Arnolphe."

But we shall further find how, as a reflex of the problem of names, the action is determined by three women. One of them, dead long before the play begins, is *only* a name, "Angélique," mother of the lost Agnès. The second has no name at all: the old woman (she too dead) Horace assigns a "more than human genius." The third is Agnès herself, the young woman of uncertain parentage Arnolphe means for a wife. By providing the occasion for a critical counter-demonstration on the part of women, the question of names and the subject raises the cognate problems of authorship and gender. The comic catastrophe reserved for Arnolphe challenges the gendered notion of authority and the equally gendered sovereignty authority claims.

There is of course a highly developed poetics of names in period comedy generally, revealed in the stock of Pantalons and Capitaines, Scapins, Orontes, and Gorgibuses, Uranies, Martines, and Valères inherited from classical antiquity, Italian pastoral, Renaissance farce, and the *commedia dell'arte.* [6] Molière thus paid close if stylized attention to what characters are called throughout his career. It is even possible to chart his dramatic trajectory as a *function* of names, noting, for instance, how the Mascarille of the early farces, based on the Italian Mascarillo, gives way to an onomastic creature of his own mintage: the Sganarelle who, first surfacing in the *Médecin volant* of 1647, dogs his heels all the way to the *Médecin malgré lui* of 1666.

But especially dating from the sequence of plays on which he chiefly stakes his reputation, names become a signal thematic pre-

---

more fundamental field defined by everything acts of enunciation force to the background as a condition of their possibility–a field of which repression is a major constituent, but nonetheless only one of many. Thus, the "vérité d'un énoncé" is shaped by the conditions of its "énonciation" such that *only so much* proves "dicible à tel instant." To this extent, though Austin's comparable theory of speech acts is conspicuous by its absence, Descombes's book anticipates Felman's *Le Scandale du corps parlant.*

[6] For an historical overview of the poetics of names in early modern literature, see Rigolot, *Poétique et Onomastique.*

occupation. The problem of names, and in the first instance the names of *things*, is a major element of the quarrel *L'Ecole des femmes* unleashed. In the *Critique de l'Ecole des femmes*, recording the chief objections at least publicly voiced about the mother play, a major concern is the scandalous directness with which *L'Ecole*'s unexpurgated words reflect the unspeakable crudity of corporeal nature. At 2.5.571-78, reporting an interview with Horace during which Arnolphe's rival lays hold of some private object belonging to her, a shame-faced Agnès cannot bring herself to name it. The result is a hanging definite article (*le*) which, though ultimately referred to the anodyne "ruban," works on the overheated imaginations of Arnolphe and audience alike to evoke an unmentionable sexual organ.[7] Another example is Arnolphe's account to Chrysalde of just how vacuous he means his wife to be. Arnolphe supposes her to play crambo (*le corbillon*), a parlor game in which players stick counters into a wicker basket, thereby occasioning the salacious *équivoque* developed in the sequel. For Arnolphe imagines that, when asked what goes in the basket, his wife will ingenuously reply "une tarte à la crème." (1.1.99) The confection's creamy contents acquire erotic connotations of such ineffable vulgarity that the *Critique*'s witless *marquis* can find no way to explain his violent disapproval beyond endlessly repeating its source: "Y a-t-il assez de pommes en Normandie pour *tarte à la crème? Tarte à la crème*, morbleu! *tarte à la crème!*" (208)

But the play points to other unnamed things. While in the first instance a mere plot device designed to set up the dramatic reversal effected in the dénouement, Enrique's legal difficulties bespeak a pervasive social violence whose acknowledgement Molière tacitly relies on. Moreover, Enrique's abandonment of his daughter at the time of his flight implicitly refers to the practice of baby-farming, a phenomenon responsible for the death of so many children in ancien régime France as to constitute a socially licensed form of infanticide.[8] And though presented in the first instance as his own eccentric brainchild, the programme Arnolphe designs for Agnès's

---

[7] For *L'Ecole des femmes*'s notorious hanging article, see the *Critique de l'Ecole des femmes* 203.

[8] See Paul Bairoch, *Cities and Economic Development: From the Dawn of History to the Present*, trans. Christopher Braider (Chicago: University of Chicago Press, 1988) 206-207.

education illustrates the prevailing pedagogic system it parodies. Further, in the sermon with which Arnolphe prefaces Agnès's reading of the *Maximes du mariage*, reinforcing female subjection with the threat of eternal hellfire (3.2.736-37), the play associates devout morality with sneaking male self-interest: a point to which the *cabale des dévots* drew particular attention as proof positive of Molière's indecency and irreligion.[9]

But the chief focus of the theme of names falls on what they mean for Molière's characters. We see it in his first important success, the *Précieuses ridicules*, a play that, not at all coincidentally, already addresses the problem of women and the challenge they pose to the central authorial project. The root of the argument is a both social and feminine *demand* expressed in the title characters' desire to transform their humdrum if comfortably respectable bourgeois existence into the flowery speech and towering passion of literary adventure and its social facsimile in upper-class life. At once the instrument and token of this desire is a *change of names*: the heroines try to rid themselves of the stereotypically provincial Madelon and Cathos with which their fathers have saddled them in favor of new names redolent of poetry and romance.[10] "Hé! de grâce, mon père," cries Madelon in scene 4, "défaites-vous de ces noms étranges, et nous appelez autrement." Her father is for the occasion a curiously un-Pantalon-like Gorgibus, identified in the *dramatis personae* as a "bon bourgeois" who, unlike the *gentilhomme* of the late *comédie-ballet*, harbors no pretensions to gentility requiring a proper name like "Monsieur Jourdain." Confronted by his daughter's demand that he forsake "ces noms étranges," he angrily retorts: "Comment, ces noms étranges? Ne sont-ce pas vos noms de baptême?" Madelon haughtily replies:

> Mon Dieu, que vous êtes vulgaire! Pour moi, un de mes étonnements, c'est que vous ayez pu faire une fille si spirituelle que

---

[9] Set on by the Compagnie du Saint-Sacrement, Charles Robinet's *Panégyrique de l'Ecole des femmes ou Conversations comiques sur les œuvres de M. de Molière* (1663) leads the charge on this point. See Mallet, *Molière* 88-89. Also see Hall, *Comedy in Context*, chaps. 8, "Parody in *L'Ecole des femmes*," and 9, "Some Background to *Tartuffe*."

[10] Part of the joke here is that, though they look feminine, the *précieuses* new names are in fact masculine. "Aminte," e.g., derived from the Italian "Aminta," belongs to the eponymous hero of Tasso's famous pastoral comedy.

> moi. A-t-on jamais parlé dans le beau style de Cathos ni de
> Madelon, et ne m'avouerez-vous pas que ce serait assez d'un de
> ces noms pour décrier le plus beau roman du monde?

To which her cousin Cathos adds:

> Il est vrai, mon oncle, qu'une oreille un peu délicate pâtit fu-
> rieusement à entendre prononcer ces mots-là; et le nom de
> Polixène que ma cousine a choisi, et celui d'Aminte que je me
> suis donné, ont une grâce dont il faut que vous demeuriez d'ac-
> cord. (103)

An ear sensitive to gender overtones will detect an unpleasant
fatuousness. We sense on Molière's part, at this still vulnerable moment in his career, an unseemly desire to insinuate himself into the
public's good graces at the *précieuses'* expense: a triangulation-game
cementing the union of author and audience in a derisive pointing
at a feminine third. [11] Yet much as Molière invites us to jeer at his
protagonists, the project they pursue is no laughing matter. In rejecting their given names, Madelon and Cathos initiate a resistance
that, speaking of the doomed Pyrrhus of Racine's *Andromaque*,
Roland Barthes calls a "refus d'hériter," the rejection of a cultural
legacy. [12] Especially in a society as rigidly stratified as that of seventeenth-century France, names are never innocent. The name "Jean-
Baptiste Poquelin," for one, tells us a great deal about its bearer:
that he is French; that he is Christian, and surely Catholic; that he is
by birth bourgeois, destined to reproduce his father's station in
life–his father's caste, profession, and lineal ambitions. And turning
to Poquelin family history, we note that "Jean-Baptiste" was not
Molière's original Christian name. Baptised simply "Jean," as his father's namesake, on 15 January 1622, he was subsequently renamed
"Jean-Baptiste" so that a younger brother could become "Jean,"
thereby presumably doubling the chances that the paternal "Jean
Poquelin" would survive. [13] To reject the name is then to reject the
moral, familial, and social identity that name inscribes. And what

---

[11] On the anthropology of triangulation, see René Girard, *La Violence et le sacré*
(Paris: Grasset, 1972) and *Le Bouc émissaire* (Paris: Grasset, 1982).
[12] Barthes, *Sur Racine* 50-52.
[13] See Mallet, *Molière* 17-18.

else indeed is the testimony of the romantic plot the *précieuses* concoct in tandem with their new heroic names? Despite its comic inadequacy, their desire to live the life described in novels and, by that means, to reinvent the identity laid down in their given names contests their place in the inherited order of things.

Such is also the force of the name by which Arnolphe means henceforth to be known, "Monsieur de la Souche." Like the *précieuses*, Arnolphe rejects the bourgeois "Arnolphe" in favor of a name ennobled in the first instance by a syntactical coupling of the honorific "Monsieur" with the particule of nobility and the definite article of proprietary place. [14] But beyond betraying the hero's hunger for a more satisfying social identity, the renaming engages a project of authorship. As "Monsieur de La Souche," Arnolphe intends to forge not just a personal, but, as a necessary means to that end, an intergenerational identity as, precisely, the author of a *family*. Further, drawing on the agricultural use of the word "souche" to denote the root stock on which vines or fruit trees are grafted, the family Arnolphe has in mind will be distinguished as "de bonne et vieille souche," of ancient and illustrious ancestry. Arnolphe's aristocratic pretensions blind him to a less appealing horticultural sense of the word "souche," equivalent to "tronçon," the stump left when a tree is cut down. But the underlying plan is clear. To anchor himself in social space along the lines staked out in the form of his new name, Arnolphe must project himself forward in lineal time as the progenitive root the viticultural "souche" connotes.

---

[14] In forging the name "M. de La Souche," Molière lampooned not only onomastic pretension in general, but a highly specific instance. As Mallet reports (*Molière* 81), when Chrysalde teases Arnolphe by citing the example of a certain "Gros-Pierre," he aims at the "grand" Pierre Corneille's younger brother Thomas, who had recently taken the name Chrysalde lampoons:

> Quel abus de quitter le vrai nom de ses pères,
> Pour en vouloir prendre un bâti sur des chimères!
> De la plupart des gens c'est la démangeaison;
> Et, sans vous embrasser dans la comparaison,
> Je sais un paysan qu'on appelait Gros-Pierre,
> Qui, n'ayant pour tout bien qu'un seul quartier de terre,
> Y fit tout à l'entour faire un fossé bourbeux,
> Et de monsieur de l'Isle en prit le nom pompeux.
> (1.1.175-82)

This doubtless contributed to the role the Corneille circle played in the early stages of the furious controversy by which Molière was soon engulfed.

This explains why the revelation of his project takes place precisely now, in the present performatively recapitulated by the expository scene in which Arnolphe lays out his plan. The marriage has had to wait till Agnès is of marriageable, that is to say, childbearing age. Another secret, parallel to that surrounding Agnès's paternity, emerges as crucial to the play's dual plot: the anonymous child has become a woman, achieving a bodily maturation announced by certain unmentionable physical symptoms that show her to be ready to bear the son to whom Arnolphe may leave the name "de La Souche." The acquisition of an heir is in fact essential if Arnolphe is to secure the title he craves. What after all is a *souche* that bears no fruit? And what is a dynastic name that has no posterity to which it may be conveyed?

But even this fails to give the full measure of the ambition behind Arnolphe's new name. For the name's ultimate meaning is less what it says about its bearer's identity construed as the immediate content of the name itself than the claim it makes on the larger world before which it projects him. The point emerges with peculiar force in a passage in *L'Art de Penser* or *Logique de Port-Royal* (1683) in which the Jansenist logicians Antoine Arnauld and Pierre Nicole relate the name to the exemplary problem of portraits. [15]

The context for the discussion of portraits is the effort to tame the slippery family of tropes by reducing them to a special case of the general class of signs, of which the *Logique* has earlier cited names as the norm. [16] Logically considered, a portrait is an analogue in which we recognize the original by taking what we see in the image in place of what we would otherwise see in the actual face. Though it portrays one, a portrait is not itself a face, but rather a kind of metaphor, standing *as* the face for which it figures in that face's absence. And yet the portrait's analogical relation to its original is in the end no different from the mode of reference met in a name in that, on closer scrutiny, both portrait and name turn out to be *representations*.

[15] See Antoine Arnauld & Pierre Nicole, *L'Art de penser*, ed. Bruno Baron von Freytag Löringhoff & Herbert E. Brekle (Stuttgart-Bad Cannstatt: Friedrich Frommann Verlag, 1967), pt. 2, chap. 14, "Des Propositions où l'on donne aux signes le nom des choses" (2.129-33).

[16] See pt. 2, chap. 1, "Des Mots dans leur rapport aux Propositions," esp. 2.92-93. But see also pt. 1, chap. 1, "Des idées selon leur nature & leur origine," esp. 1.31-33, where Arnauld and Nicole combat Hobbesian theses about thought's dependence on words and the related arbitrariness of our names for things.

As the authors put it, citing a generic royal name for which that of the reigning monarch serves as an obvious alternative, "Le portrait de César, c'est César": the portrait of Louis is Louis. [17] Confronted with a portrait, the natural question is not "Whom does it portray" or "Who is it like" but "Who *is* that?" And the answer is the *name*, "César" or "Louis." Portrait and name are exact equivalents in that each stands for the other in an identical relation to the person both signify, a person indeed both *represent* as the basis of their function as signs. True, in the portrait, the sign reproduces the representation that grounds it: it is the name "César" or "Louis" in the form of an image. By contrast, in the name as such, the relation between sign and referent seems more indirect because the representation connecting the two remains implicit; it emerges not in the sign itself, but in an accompanying mental act in which, responding to the name, we evoke the referent as an "idea." But an "idea" is itself an image or portrait: to hear and understand the name "César" or "Louis" is to *see* César or Louis in the mental picture the name evokes. The apparent difference between portrait and name is thereby liquidated by their common insertion in a circular series of substitutions: the name evokes an idea that portrays a person whose likeness is in turn identified by a name. [18]

Yet the equivalence of portrait and name reveals more about names than the *Logique* acknowledges. [19] After all, not just *anyone* gets a portrait painted. To be portrayed, even if only in the form of

---

[17] Pt. 2, chap. 14 (2.130). Note, however, that I cite here Marin's abbreviated version of the original in *Le portrait du roi* 16. As I point out in "Image and *Imaginaire*" in Molière's *Sganarelle, ou Le Cocu imaginaire*," forthcoming in *PMLA*, the logicians actually describe what one will normally *say* of a portrait ("l'on dira sans preparation & sans façon d'un portrait, de Caesar, que c'est Caesar"). While this makes a difference to a full analysis of the passage in question, which Marin reads a little carelessly, the ultimate goal is indeed the one Marin characterizes: to exhibit what Arnauld and Nicole take to be the unequivocal clarity and distinctness names and portraits share.

[18] This doctrine of "ideas" is the thesis defended against Hobbes in *L'Art de penser*'s opening argument (pt. 1, chaps. 1-2). Nor (despite the theological interests dictating the form their logic takes) is the doctrine at all peculiar to Arnauld and Nicole; it is common to early modern philosophers of all persuasions. See W.J.T. Mitchell, *Iconology: Image, Text, Ideology* (Chicago: University of Chicago Press, 1986) chaps. 1, "What Is an Image?" and 5, "Eye and Ear: Edmund Burke and the Politics of Sensibility," esp. 121-25.

[19] It also reveals more about the nature of "ideas," and in particular their *imaginary* character–the point I explore in "Image and *Imaginaire*."

an "idea," one must have a name and thus the recognizable identity a name both supposes and confers. This points to a Hegelian insight, elaborated with specific reference to Molière's era, the age of Louis XIV and the culture of flattery (*Schmeichelei*) Hegel takes for one of its hallmarks. [20] According to Hegel, the essence of a name lies in its *propriety*: it designates one person alone, he for whom it is the true and "proper" name. However, this propriety does not inhere to the name itself, but is instead granted by those who acknowledge the bearer's exclusive right to it. Rather than merely denoting a particular identity, it actively *constitutes* the unique individual to whom it belongs:

> [I]t is in the name alone that the distinction of the individual from every one else is not imagined but is actually made by all. By having a name the individual passes for a pure individual not merely in his own consciousness of himself, but in the consciousness of all. [21]

This is in fact why the *Logique* chooses the example it does. "César" ("Louis") is not just any name: belonging to the King, it is that name than which no other is more proper, as denoting an identity than which no other is more individual or unique. But this in turn reveals the deeper reason for conceiving the name as equivalent to a portrait: the portrait of Louis is Louis because, *as* Louis, its subject already possesses "in the consciousness of all" the unique identity both name and portrait grant. The portrait of Louis is Louis because Louis is his own portrait.

To see more clearly the mechanism at work here, we turn to a canonical exemplar, Hyacinthe Rigaud's portrait of *Louis XIV en habit de sacré* (fig. 5). The first and most obvious thing in this portrait is the man who posed for it. The painting is valued first and last on the strength of a likeness whose immediate purpose is to answer the question: "Who is Louis?" In reply, the portrait provides his very image, Louis himself. But in answering the question, the painting further intimates that we have heard the name "Louis" and

---

[20] See Georg Wilhelm Friedrich Hegel, *The Phenomenology of Mind*, trans. George Lichtheim (New York: Harper & Row, 1967) 524-34. Marin makes a point of the reference to the court of Louis XIV. See *Le portrait du roi* 15.

[21] Hegel, *Phenomenology* 533.

Figure 5. Hyacinthe Rimbaud, *Louis XIV en habit de sacré.* Musée National du
Louvre, Paris. Credit: Alinari/Art Resource, NY

that, as a result, the name already has a content: the original epitomized by his likeness. To record Louis's portrait for public inspection supposes a stature that warrants and even *demands* portraiture.
A portrait is no mere tautology. As faithfully as it replicates, it necessarily magnifies its subject; the image that inscribes thereby en-
larges the identity it portrays.

What is already true in the present of representation, the *hic et
nunc* of the image as such, becomes more evident when we recall
that, by recording, the portrait *preserves* its poser's likeness. In line
with what Louis Marin calls the "wonder of representation" analyzed in Alberti's *De pictura* of 1435, inaugurating modern Western
thought about images, in recording what he saw in the moment of
portraying him, the painter *re*-presents its subject: in space, by
standing for him in his physical absence; but above all in *time*, according him an immortality denied the natural person. [22] In showing us who Louis *is*, the image reminds us who he *was*, awarding a
posthumous identity that survives the present of portrayal. Or
rather, since the present of portrayal, of the painting Rigaud has left
us, encompasses not only the moment when it was painted, but that
later moment when we behold it, it grants an immortality whose
form is the self-perpetuating present of the image itself.

So even leaving aside the particulars of Rigaud's portrait of the
king–the flattering grandeur of Louis's costume and appointments;
the genteel majesty of his pose and the commanding self-assurance
of his gaze; the virile leg of the gentleman dancer in which we sense
the conqueror's martial stride [23]–the bare fact of portrayal accords
an identity (and thus a name) that transcends the contingent cir-
cumstancialness of resemblance. More precisely, it imbues the contingent and circumstancial with an undying grandeur the picture's
formal majesty pretends merely to mimic. This last point is reinforced by the picture's recursively *performative* force. Rigaud paints
Louis's portrait because he is the king; to this extent, the portrait
indexes a stature the king already has *as king*. But conversely, *by*
portraying him, Rigaud grants the stature he records. Whence the

---

[22] Marin, *Le portrait du roi* 9-10; Leon Battista Alberti, *De pictura* 2:25; *On
Painting*, ed. and parallel tr. Cecil Grayson (London: Phaidon, 1972) 60-61.

[23] For comparable remarks, see Abby E. Zanger, *Scenes from the Marriage of
Louis XIV: Nuptial Fictions and the Making of Absolutist Power* (Stanford: Stanford
University Press, 1997) 32-33.

image's service in the propagandistic enterprise Peter Burke has termed the "fabrication of Louis XIV." [24] The image creates the monarch it resembles by the claim it makes on posterity in the form of his very likeness.

But there is still more. For who is the source of Rigaud's *Portrait of Louis XIV*? In one sense, given the painting's performative aspect, the source is obviously the portraitist Rigaud. It is he who observes and reproduces Louis's likeness, and he who magnifies the stature the portrait implies by adding the ostensive signs of Louis's grandeur. Yet the poser brings more than his bare likeness to the business. Especially when, as here, the artist has been commissioned to paint no less a personage than the king, there are always at least two parties to the transaction of which a portrait is the result: the painter and the subject. [25] A likeness requires the painterly gaze that takes down and enhances the original's traits. But opposite that gaze, and meeting it, is a *second*: that of the poser looking back. If the portraitist's work is well and truly done, if it succeeds not only on disinterestedly aesthetic grounds, but from the intensely interested viewpoint of the person who pays for it, the effect is what we have in Rigaud: not just an image of Louis passively surrendered to our inspection, but *Louis himself* majestically inspecting us in turn. As the majestic directness and authority of the sovereign's look is there to remind us, to gaze upon Rigaud's portrait of Louis is to fall under the gaze with which Louis returns our look, projecting *through* Rigaud the self-determined assertion of his own identity.

Yet even this is incomplete. As the recursive time of the image suggests, the portrait's ultimate destination is that later moment when it will be seen. Like the royal gaze it renders, Rigaud's picture projects itself into the field of our beholding where alone it truly realizes what it aims to. We ourselves as beholders finally actualize Louis's sovereign identity by registering our consciousness of falling

---

[24] Burke, *Fabrication of Louis XIV*; but see too (among many comparable studies) Marin's classic *Portrait du roi* and Apostolidès, *Le roi-machine*.

[25] This has become a focus of early modern art history. For a classic pioneering study, see Baxandall, *Painting and Experience*, chap. 1, "Conditions of Trade." For a particularly hard-nosed analysis in this vein, see Svetlana Alpers, *Rembrandt's Enterprise: The Studio and the Market* (Chicago: University of Chicago Press, 1988), esp. chaps. 3, "A Master in the Studio," and 4, "Freedom, Art, and Money."

under his commanding gaze. The portrait takes place as an extension not only of Louis's authoritative identity, but of the *scene* in which, as Hegel puts it, that identity is at once imagined and made real as the product of "the consciousness of all," to wit, the absolutist court. As Hegel writes in the continuation of the passage cited above, as an expression of the will to power implicit in the claim to the "independent self-existence" a proper name supplies, the "individualistic self-consciousness" becomes a *monarch*:

> By its name, then, the monarch becomes absolutely detached from every one, exclusive and solitary, and in virtue of it is unique as an atom that cannot communicate any part of its essential nature, and has no equal. This name is... the actual reality which universal power has inherently within itself: through the name the power is the monarch. Conversely he, this particular individual, thereby knows himself, this individual self, to be the universal power, knows that the nobles not only are ready and prepared for the service of the state-authority [he embodies], but are grouped as an ornamental setting round the throne, and that they are for ever telling him who sits thereon what he is. [26]

Whence the portrait's function: to extort an act of recognition and surrender that, in pretending to acknowledge, in fact *achieves* the identity Louis's gaze asserts as the expression of his name.

This sheds light on a symptomatic moment in Arnolphe's performance. In 3.2, setting the stage for the scandalous sermon that culminates in the reading of the *Maximes du mariage*, Arnolphe orders Agnès to set her work aside and fix her eye on his face while he speaks:

> Levez un peu la tête, et tournez le visage:
> (*Mettant le doigt sur son front.*)
> Là, regardez-moi là durant cet entretien;
> Et jusqu'au moindre mot, imprimez-le-vous bien.
> (3.2.676-78)

He then delivers a compendium of gender stereotypes destined to impress on his ward their respective roles in the marriage he now describes:

---

[26] Hegel, *Phenomenology* 533-34.

Le mariage, Agnès, n'est pas un badinage:
A d'austères devoirs le rang de femme engage;
Et vous n'y montez pas, à ce que je prétends,
Pour être libertine et prendre du bon temps.
Votre sexe n'est là que pour la dépendance:
Du côté de la barbe est la toute-puissance.
Bien qu'on soit deux moitiés de la société,
Ces deux moitiés pourtant n'ont point d'égalité:
L'une est moitié suprême, et l'autre subalterne;
L'une en tout est soumise à l'autre qui gouverne;
Et ce que le soldat, dans son devoir instruit,
Montre d'obéissance au chef qui le conduit,
Le valet à son maître, un enfant à son père,
A son supérieur le moindre petit frère,
N'approche point encor de la docilité,
Et de l'obéissance, et de l'humilité,
Et du profond respect où la femme doit être
Pour son mari, son chef, son seigneur, et son maître.

(3.2.695-712)

The sermon Arnolphe pronounces and the reading it prepares play out themes Hegel develops in a section of the *Phenomenology* that anticipates the later passage on the logic of the name: the master-slave dialectic. [27] The task in which Arnolphe schools his bride-to-be is that of actively realizing his identity as husband by first realizing her own as wife. Imprinting the lesson in her memory ("imprimez-le-vous bien"), she internalizes her own servile character in order to internalize and thereby constitute the mastery he claims for himself. But the key to the operation lies less in the lesson *per se* than in the face-to-face encounter (Arnolphe's "entretien") that enforces it. True, driven by a compulsive self-betrayal we shall analyze later, Arnolphe undermines his own objective by directing Agnès's attention to his forehead, site of the cuckold's horns he means to avoid. But the conscious intent is clear: to turn his face into an effigy comparable to the one Rigaud composes for his sovereign, *Louis le grand*. What Agnès is meant to see is the austere effulgence of Arnolphe's *gaze* in whose light she will perceive herself as the abject dependent before whom Arnolphe reigns supreme.

---

[27] Ibid. 229-40.

In Rigaud's portrait of the king, of which the pseudo-likeness Arnolphe presents to Agnès is a counterpart and parody, we discover the ideal to which all portraits aspire: the form not just of identity ("c'est Louis"), but of the power of sovereign self-representation on which identity depends. This reflects what Arnolphe wants in choosing a new and proper name. The immediate target of the demand he makes is of course Agnès, enacted in the crudely (and therefore comically) literal vis-à-vis in which he compels her to rehearse the abjection the *Maximes* prescribe for her. But Agnès is finally a synecdoche for the wider world of which she is part. Her role is to accord in the domestic sphere the identity Arnolphe projects before the general public in the name "Monsieur de la Souche," an identity that, to be realized, must exist not only for Arnolphe and his abject wife, but "in the consciousness of all." But by the centrality they give the gaze in at once determining and projecting the sovereign identity advanced in the form of the name, both Rigaud's portrait and its Arnolphian parody indicate something further: the nature of the *agency* of which name, portrait, and gaze are alike expressions. What defines Louis in Rigaud's portrait is Louis's embodiment of the ideal of conscious subjecthood. Rigaud's likeness of the king doubles as an image of the Cartesian ego, beneficiary of the dualist severance of mind and body that Descartes presents as both a major finding and an enabling condition of rational reflection and the methodic "search for truth." [28]

Consider the following passage from the *Discours de la méthode*, outlining the content of Descartes's unpublished treatise on the physical universe, *Le Monde*:

> J'ai eu dessein d'y comprendre tout ce que je pensais savoir, avant que de l'écrire, touchant la nature des choses matérielles. Mais, tout de même que les peintres, ne pouvant également bien représenter dans un tableau plat toutes les diverses faces d'un corps solide, en choisissent une des principales qu'ils mettent seule vers le jour, et ombrageant les autres, ne les font paraître qu'en tant qu'on les peut voir en la regardant: ainsi, craignant de

---

[28] The following discussion is a heavily abbreviated version of the one I undertake in *Hercules at the Crossroads: Baroque Self-Invention and Historical Truth in Art*, chap. 5, "Imaginary Selves: The Trial of Identity in Descartes, Cyrano, and Pascal," currently circulating among learned presses.

ne pouvoir mettre en mon discours tout ce que j'avais en la pensée, j'entrepris seulement d'y exposer bien amplement ce que je
concevais de la lumière; puis, à son occasion, d'y ajouter quelque
chose du Soleil et des étoiles fixes, à cause qu'elle en procède
presque toute; des cieux, à cause qu'ils la transmettent; des
planètes, des comètes et de la terre, à cause qu'elles la font
réfléchir; et en particulier de tous les corps qui sont sur la terre, à
cause qu'ils sont ou colorés, ou transparents, ou lumineux; et enfin de l'homme, à cause qu'il en est le spectateur. [29]

The passage addresses a problem of exposition. Given the cogito's picture of human understanding as an act of mental vision divorced from all bodily influences, and among them those attending
human language and communication, Descartes's difficulty is to convey in writing "everything I thought I had learned, before writing it,
touching on the nature of material things." The problem is how to
convey his physical system *as a whole*–both *in* its entirety and *as* an
entirety–to people who have not yet discovered it for themselves. [30]
How does one transmit, in the inevitably flattening because se-
quential medium of discourse, what is by its very nature comprehen-
sible only volumetrically, as a complete and universal system? The
solution flows from the analogy. Just as painters choose one face of a
given object, causing others to appear "only so far as they can be
seen while looking at the first," so Descartes begins with *light*, proceeding from there, by a chain of pseudo-causal inferences, to discuss the sun and stars because they produce it; the heavens, because
they transmit it; planets, comets, and the earth, because they reflect
it; then the various bodies on the earth inasmuch as light illumines
them; and so on down to Man, "because he is its spectator."

Yet it is striking how, by virtue of its place at the end of the passage, where the exposition reaches its both logical and causal
culmination, the figure of Man as "spectator" turns out to have
structured the development from the start. The passage on *Le*

---

[29] René Descartes, *Discours de la méthode*, in *Œuvres philosophiques*, 3 vols., ed.
Ferdinand Alquié (Paris: Garnier, 1988-92) 1.614-15.

[30] In the 6th part of the *Discours*, Descartes reminds us indeed that "on ne
saurait si bien concevoir une chose et la rendre sienne, lorsqu'on l'apprend de
quelque autre, que lorsqu'on l'invente soi-même," ibid. 1.641. The need to discover
("invent") knowledge for oneself defines the expository dilemma the 5th part describes.

Monde concludes where it begins: with the Cartesian ego whose concerted act of vision converts light into the cosmic spectacle the text unfolds before our eyes. The structure of Cartesian science as an emergent rational whole anticipates the movement of the metaphysics that supplies its theory. In the *Méditations métaphysiques*, the progress of hyperbolic doubt culminates in the self whose thinking turns out to have been its condition of possibility all along. Just so, *Le Monde*'s exhibition of the universal system of nature folds back on the rational spectator whose activity *makes* the spectacle to which both the system and its mental source owe their authority. But the crucial point is that the spectator makes a spectacle that reveals him as its source only because of the *form* he gives it. The spectator is a product of the picture he produces, an origin implicit in the structure of representation as such. If science is possible, it is on the basis of our rational power to divorce ourselves as "minds" from the spectacle of nature as a condition for there *being* such a spectacle. If nature offers the purchase knowledge requires, it is because human beings are capable of detaching themselves by means for which painters provide a model.

This yields one final facet of Arnolphe's enterprise. During the introductory debate with his friend Chrysalde, Arnolphe at one point uses the prestigious Cartesian word "method" to describe his matrimonial programme. In immediate context, the word is laughably pretentious, evincing Arnolphe's conceited refusal to listen to reason. When Chrysalde renews his earlier urging that conjugal misfortunes are "coups du hasard" (1.1.13), unavoidable blows of chance it is foolish to take to heart, Arnolphe replies:

> Pressez-moi de me joindre à femme autre que sotte,
> Prêchez, patrocinez jusqu'à la Pentecôte;
> Vous serez ébahi, quand vous serez au bout,
> Que vous ne m'aurez rien persuadé du tout.

Chrysalde

Je ne vous dis plus mot.

Arnolphe

Chacun a sa méthode.
En femme, comme en tout, je veux suivre ma mode.

(1.1.117-24)

The grandiloquent *méthode* is deflated by the rhymed link to the ephemeral *mode*, put in the feminine of passing fashion rather than the masculine of a concerted means. Arnolphe's "method" is then a mere fad, craze, or hobbyhorse.[31] Yet the word hints at something important about the nature and scope of his ambition, an intimation underscored in a later speech extorted by the catastrophe Chrysalde prophesies. Grappling with the fact that, for all his efforts to prevent it, Agnès has given her heart to Horace, Arnolphe voices not only disappointed love and wounded pride, but frustrated *ingenuity*:

> J'enrage de trouver cette place usurpée,
> Et j'enrage de voir ma prudence trompée...
> Ciel! puisque pour un choix j'ai tant philosophé,
> Faut-il de ses appas m'être si fort coiffé!
>
> (3.5.988-89, 994-95)

The whole point has been to avert Chrysalde's "coups du hasard" by anticipating them. In arranging his marriage, Arnolphe has deployed a prudential calculus modeled on the mental attitude Descartes's *Discours* associates with science, a posture of detachment on which he dilates in the soliloquy marking the onset of the final dramatic crisis:

> En sage philosophe on m'a vu, vingt années,
> Contempler des maris les tristes destinées,
> Et m'instruire avec soin de tous les accidents

---

[31] The canonical account of "mode" or fashion in the *grand siècle* is Jean de La Bruyère, *Les Caractères ou les moeurs de ce siècle*, "De la Mode." I use the Pléiade text, ed. Julien Benda (Paris: Gallimard, 1951). Following Montaigne, La Bruyère puts the section on fashion in a strategically sensitive position. Thus, it comes immediately after the increasingly skeptical sections on "l'Homme" and "Jugements" and just before the eminently Montaignesque "De Quelques Usages." The latter in turn opens on portrayal of the proper (but mostly *im*-proper) way of inculcating redeeming moral teachings from the pulpit ("De la Chaire") preceding the final section, "Des Esprits forts," where the moralist takes on the full ontological challenge posed to Christian orthodoxy by skeptical Wits emboldened by the ever widening spectacle of cultural change and cultural relativism for which fashion supplies the well-timed topical model. Arnolphe's "méthode/mode" rhyme thus cuts deep indeed. For a contemporary English counterpart, see Campbell's brilliant account (*Wonder & Science*, chap. 7) of the Puritan John Bulwer's *Anthropometamorphosis*, a diatribe denouncing fashion's power to dissolve human nature itself.

Qui font dans le malheur tomber les plus prudents:
Des disgrâces d'autrui, profitant dans mon âme,
J'ai cherché les moyens, voulant prendre une femme,
De pouvoir garantir mon front de tous affronts,
Et le tirer de pair d'avec les autres fronts;
Pour ce noble dessein j'ai cru mettre en pratique
Tout ce que peut trouver l'humaine politique;
Et, comme si du sort il était arrêté
Que nul homme ici-bas n'en serait exempté,
Après l'expérience et toutes les lumières,
Que j'ai pu m'acquérir sur de telles matières,
Après vingt ans et plus de méditation
Pour me conduire en tout avec précaution,
De tant d'autres maris j'aurais quitter la trace,
Pour me trouver après dans la même disgrâce!

(4.7.1188-1205)

Rather than commit himself to marriage like another man, Arnolphe has spent twenty years standing apart from the spectacle of marital relations in order to observe and record the experience of his fellows.[32] From this experience, carefully if satirically digested in his comic chronicles, he has extrapolated a set of rules designed to preempt the future and secure a "place" from which fate or fortune can never dislodge him precisely because it is grounded in intellectual mastery of the machinery governing conjugal affairs. Chrysalde's argument, also drawn from experience, is that since no man ever has achieved the absolute security Arnolphe craves, no man ever will: a stoic empiricism, skeptical and relaxed, counseling acceptance of what Lucretius' great philosophical poem, the *De rerum natura*, presents as the ineluctable "nature of things." Like the

---

[32] See Pierre Force, *Molière ou Le Prix des choses: morale, économie et comédie* (Paris: Nathan, 1994), chaps. 1, "Scepticisme et comédie," and 2, "Le refus de l'échange." Force examines many of the questions engaged here, and in particular how, in arrogating the methodical viewpoint of what we might call the "transcendental" spectator for whom the world is a pure "object," a gesture that entails precisely what Force calls a "refusal of exchange," i.e., a refusal to circulate in a world of *other* "subjects" in whose eyes one becomes an object in turn, Molière's protagonists (Arnolphe, but also Orgon, Dom Juan, Alceste, Harpagon) ironically confirm their enthrallment. For an analysis of the mechanisms of this enthrallment at work in contemporary society, as of their impact on Molière himself, see Norman, *Public Mirror*.

THE AGENCY OF THE LETTER IN THE UNCONSCIOUS 227

Cartesian rationalist he is, Arnolphe draws the opposite moral from the same body of facts: if no man ever has succeeded in what he proposes, it is because none has ever gone about it the right way. He thus breathes the can-do spirit infusing Descartes's faith in what disciplined human reason can achieve.[33]

The question posed by Arnolphe's project bears then on the conditions of successful agency: how may we guide events where we will? Arnolphe's answer is "method" and what method at once supposes and secures: the distance from events needed to convert them into an instructive spectacle. As he puts it in reply to Chrysalde's worries about the wisdom of marrying after writing so many satires about the conjugal estate,

> Enfin, ce sont partout des sujets de satire;
> Et, comme spectateur, ne puis-je pas en rire?
>
> (1.1.43-44)

Arnolphe is the transcendental spectator who, in Descartes as in Rigaud's *Louis XIV*, is empowered by his remoteness from the spectacle on which he acts to supervise and, by supervising, change a world to which he would otherwise be in thrall. And the ultimate fruit of the change is a radical act of self-fashioning,[34] shaping the world so as to impose on it the stamp of the identity inscribed in his new (and "proper") name.

A token of the complex recursiveness of what *L'Ecole des femmes* engages is that the project of self-fashioning linked to the hero's name mirrors an exactly similar project on the author's part. To be sure, Molière is nothing if not discreet about it. In the preface to *Les Précieuses ridicules*, marking his début as a published author, he makes a show of cheerful reluctance, adducing his appearance in print to public demand and piratical publishers:

---

[33] Compare this with the initial characterization of methodic reasoning in Descartes's *Discours*. See *Œuvres philosophiques* 1.568.

[34] I invoke the now classic notion proposed in Stephen Greenblatt, *Renaissance Self-Fashioning: From More to Shakespeare* (Chicago: University of Chicago Press, 1980). This too has of course its Cartesian echo in the Stoic self-fashioning Descartes performs in framing his "morale provisoire." See *Œuvres philosophiques* 1.591-98.

C'est une chose étrange qu'on imprime les gens malgré eux! Je ne vois rien de si injuste, et je pardonnerais toute autre violence plutôt que celle-là.

Ce n'est pas que je veuille faire ici l'auteur modeste, et mépriser par honneur ma comédie. J'offenserais mal à propos tout Paris, si je l'accusais d'avoir pu applaudir à une sottise: comme le public est le juge absolu de ces sortes d'ouvrages, il y aurait de l'impertinence à moi de le démentir; et quand j'aurais eu la plus mauvaise opinion du monde de mes *Précieuses ridicules* avant leur représentation, je dois croire maintenant qu'elles valent quelque chose, puisque tant de gens ensemble en ont dit du bien. (100)

Nor moreover, in light of period ideology and taste, are his authorial ambitions unproblematic. Eager as the public may be to read as well as see his work, he remains a *comic* author practising a "low" form incapable of awarding the status tragic authorship confers. To make matters worse, unlike Corneille or Racine, tragic poets who write for the stage without actually dirtying their hands on it, Molière's reputation largely rests on his accomplishments as both actor and director. Molière's dubious standing as a comic writer is thus compounded by his persistence in an activity notorious for being not only socially, but theologically suspect, as attested by the newly revived *querelle de la moralité du théâtre* of which *Tartuffe* is a major document and by the exclusion of actors and actresses from participation in the rites of the Church in the archdiocese of Paris. [35] Given then both his genre and his profession, the claim to

---

[35] See Georges Mongrédien, *La Vie quotidienne des comédiens au temps de Molière* (Paris: Hachette, 1966), pt. 1, chaps. 1, "L'Eglise et les comédiens," and 2, "L'Opinion publique et les comédiens." Note that, in the unfolding *querelle de la moralité du théâtre*, especially in the wake of the outrage *Tartuffe* provoked, Molière becomes a prime target. In Nicole's *Traité de la comédie* (1665; rev. 1666 and 1667), tragic poets like Corneille emerge as unwitting tools of the diabolical passions on which even noble tragedy feeds. In Molière, we meet the Devil himself. Thus, in a pamphlet attacking *Tartuffe* cited in Molière's first petition to the King on the play's behalf, Pierre Roullé denounces the comic poet as "ce démon vêtu de chair et habillé en homme; un libertin, un impie digne d'un supplice exemplaire." (258) (For an abridged text of Roullé's pamphlet, see the Pléiade *Œuvres complètes* 1.1143-44.) In a document to which we shall return in chapter 5 as offering the most acute as well as violent attack Molière endured, *Observations sur une comédie de Molière intitulée le Festin de Pierre* (1665), the Sieur de Rochemont makes the same charge, calling the poet "homme et Demon tout ensemble; *un Diable incarné* comme luy-mesme se definit." Georges Mongrédien (ed.), *Comédies et pamphlets sur Molière* (Paris: Nizet, 1986) 90.

authority constitutes a scandalous breach of decorum: it was simply not *bienséant* to nourish the pretentions he did. This seems indeed to have been one of the motives behind the *querelle* provoked by *L'Ecole des femmes*, reflected in the personal animus feeding the attacks he underwent: to punish him for usurping a station to which he was not entitled.[36]

Yet problematic as it may be, the project of authorship and the deeper project of self-identification it promotes shape his theatrical practice at every level. An obvious example is the abandonment of the prose of the early farces in favor of the ennobling numbers of alexandrine verse. And there is the evidence of the incautiously hubristic manifesto assigned the *Critique*'s Dorante, defending not only *L'Ecole*, but comedy in general on the grounds of its superiority to the "high" form of tragedy itself:

> Car enfin, je trouve qu'il est bien plus aisé de se guinder sur de grands sentiments, de braver en vers la fortune, accuser les destins, et dire des injures aux dieux, que d'entrer comme il faut dans le ridicule des hommes, et de rendre agréablement sur le théâtre les défauts de tout le monde. Lorsque vous peignez des héros, vous faites ce que vous voulez. Ce sont des portraits à plaisir, où l'on ne cherche point de ressemblance; et vous n'avez qu'à suivre les traits d'une imagination qui se donne l'essor, et qui souvent laisse le vrai pour attraper le merveilleux. Mais lorsque vous peignez les hommes, il faut peindre d'après nature. On veut que ces portraits ressemblent; et vous n'avez rien fait, si vous n'y faites reconnaître les gens de votre siècle. (208)[37]

---

[36] The controversy's tone is intensely personal throughout, but two particularly pungent examples are Edme Boursault's *Le Portrait du peintre* (1663) and Jean Donneau de Visé's *Zélinde ou la Véritable Critique de l'Ecole des femmes* (1663). A major presumption among Molière's adversaries, at once moral, aesthetic, and social in character, is voiced in Philippe de La Croix's *La Guerre comique*: "Molière auteur! il n'y a que de la superficie et du jeu. Sa présomption est insupportable; il se méconnaît depuis qu'on court à quatre ou cinq farces qu'il a dérobées de tous côtés." As cited in Pléiade *Œuvres complètes* 1.1140. Note however that *La Guerre comique* defends Molière (the name of the speaker just cited is "de la Rancune"). See Norman's discussion of both this text and the related question of Molière's "oddly precarious" standing as an author both then and now, *Public Mirror* 26-34.

[37] The sharp-eyed as well as sharp-tongued Donneau makes Molière pay for Dorante's manifesto in *Lettre sur les affaires du théâtre*: "[Elomire, the insulting anagramme Donneau invariably uses for Molière] dit qu'il peint d'après nature; cependant, quoique nous voyons bien des jaloux, nous en voyons peu qui ressemblent à

But the project of self-identification emerges not only in the use of verse or the natural fidelity claimed for satiric portraiture; it also surfaces in Molière's conversion of the traditional farce, whether French or modeled on the Italian *commedia dell'arte*, into the *comédie de caractère*.[38] This shift is accompanied by the development of an argumentative plot, a self-conscious architectonic keyed to his adaptation of a classical device: the preliminary *agon* with which Plautus sets out the central moral issue the play develops and arbitrates. The dramatic unity of the action is thus intensified by a thematic unity signaled as early as the opening scene in an introductory debate that becomes a hallmark of Moliéresque dramaturgy.

This thematic unity is in turn deepened by Molière's *directorial* control. The Illustre Théâtre was famous for its professionalism. Contemporary witnesses report how each "oeillade" was exactly

---

Arnolphe, c'est pourquoi il se devrait donner encore plus de gloire, et dire qu'il peint d'après son imagination; mais comme elle ne lui peut représenter des héros, je suis assuré qu'il ne nous en fera jamais voir s'ils ne sont jaloux [a jab at Molière's unsuccessful *Dom Garcie de Navarre ou le prince jaloux*]. Ce sont là les grands sentiments qu'il leur inspire, et la jalousie est tout ce qui les fait agir depuis le commencement jusqu'à la fin de ses pièces sérieuses, aussi bien que de ses comiques, et puisqu'il y met si peu de différence, je ne sais pas pourquoi il assure que les pièces comiques doivent l'emporter sur les sérieuses." As cited in Pléiade *Œuvres complètes* 1.1111.

[38] This is a venerable insight. In Gossman's *Men and Masks*, the move from farce to moral comedy enables Molière to deepen themes (narcissistic self-deception, opportunistic self-concealment, or self-protective dissimulation in the face of arbitrary force) merely latent in the lesser form. In Guicharnaud, the sophisticated turn Molière's career takes with the *Précieuses* and *L'Ecole des femmes* provides the engine for the "aventure théâtrale" that issues in the masterpieces he produces from *Le Misanthrope* on. Defaux's *Métamorphoses du comique* presupposes the same principle. And so it continues down to W.D. Howarth, *Molière: A Playwright and His Audience* (Cambridge: Cambridge University Press, 1982), esp. chaps. 4, "The legacy of farce," 5, "Comedy and character," and 6, "Laughter and 'le rire dans l' âme'," Peter Hampshire Nurse, *Molière and the Comic Spirit* (Geneva: Droz, 1991), chaps. 4, "The evolution of farce: *La Jalousie du Barbouillé* to *George Dandin*," and 5, "Towards 'la grande comédie': *L'Ecole des femmes*," or Jürgen Grimm, *Molière en son temps* (Paris: Biblio 17, 1993), chap. B, "Le Théâtre de Molière: les phases d'évolution, ses formes, ses thèmes." But see Yves Kermanac'h, *Molière ou la double tentation* (Paris: Galilée, 1980), which cites the "conviction" that one may "passer, par gradation, de la farce à la comédie de caractères" as the first critical prejudice to be overcome to understand Molière (23). Since Kermanac'h finally succumbs to another venerable "temptation," that of psychologizing Molière's work (see chap. 4, "La vie et l'oeuvre ou les deux tentations de Molière"), he himself does not make the most of the opportunity he opens up.

timed, how each step was precisely counted and placed. [39] In the *Impromptu de Versailles*, retaliating for attacks launched by his competitors at the Hôtel de Bourgogne, Molière turns a spotlight on Montfleury, star of the rival troupe. The immediate thrust of Molière's mockery is Montfleury's Falstaffian girth. When Montfleury plays a monarch, one meets

> un roi qui soit gros et gras comme quatre; un roi, morbleu! qui soit entripaillé comme il faut; un roi d'une vaste circonférence, et qui puisse remplir un trône de la belle manière. La belle chose qu'un roi d'une taille galante! (215)

If what amuses Molière is Montfleury's obesity, what *offends* him as both poet and director is his indiscipline. The part is literally shaped to suit the player. Worse, the planetary influence of Montfleury's massive belly extends to the orotund pomposity with which he recites his lines. Though we cannot exactly picture Montfleury's technique, we sense the kind of thing Molière makes fun of when he turns from his rival's bulk to mimicking his acting style:

> il faut dire les choses avec emphase. Ecoutez-moi. (*Il contrefait Montfleury...*)
> Te le dirai-je, Araspe? etc.
> Voyez-vous cette posture? Remarquez bien cela. Là, appuyez comme il faut le dernier vers. Voilà ce qui attire l'approbation, et fait faire le brouhaha. (215-16)

Where, in the rival company, poet and director bend to suit their narcissistic actors' every whim, in Molière's, each detail of timing,

---

[39] See Mallet, *Molière*, pt. 4, chap. 3, "L'acteur-auteur," esp. 369-70, where she records contemporary testimonials to the professional discipline Molière the director imposed on his company, and in particular the following from the preface to the 1682 edition of Molière's plays: "Un coup d'oeil, un pas, un geste, tout y était observé avec une exactitude qui avait été inconnue jusque-là sur les théâtres de Paris." (For the full preface, see the Pléiade *Œuvres complètes* 1.996-1002.) One of the most interesting as well as surprising testimonials comes from Donneau's pen, in a passage in the 3rd part of his *Nouvelles nouvelles* (1663) otherwise notable for its derisive dismissal of Molière. Thus, in the midst of a thoroughgoing criticism of *L'Ecole des femmes*, he nevertheless concedes that "Jamais comédie ne fut si bien représentée, ni avec tant d'art, chaque acteur sait combien il y doit faire de pas, et toutes ces oeillades sont comptées." Pléiade *Œuvres complètes* 1.1021.

blocking, delivery, and byplay fuses in a single dominant conception structured by the director's reading of the text.

However, both the thematic unity achieved through the Plautine *agon* and the professional discipline Molière imposed as a director ultimately refer to his most fundamental innovation. For integral to the conversion of farce into polished moral comedy is the abandonment of the traditional scenario in favor of a predetermined dramatic script. During the early year's of his troupe's existence, in addition to acting, Molière served as the company's scenarist, drawing up the *canevas*, the basic plotline on which the actors would then improvise (or "embroider") not only their *jeux de scènes*, but their lines. [40] But beginning with *La Jalousie du Barbouillé* and *Le Médecin volant* of the late 1640s, and more especially dating from Molière's first verse play, *L'Etourdi ou les contretemps* of 1655, the scenario becomes a dramatic poem. Where before the actors were free to invent their own parts within the limits of the scenario, the poet now lays down a fixed text the players learn by heart, reciting it word for word. And the words they recite are of course Molière's, projecting his presiding vision and intent.

We note how the conduct of *L'Ecole*'s central character mirrors Molière's own complex theatrical practice. We have already seen that Arnolphe is a satiric author. This contributes indeed to his dilemma, leading Chrysalde to object to his friend's marital plans in part owing to the *name* Arnolphe has made for himself by publishing the misfortunes of his fellow citizens:

> Mais quand je crains pour vous, c'est cette raillerie
> Dont cent pauvres maris ont souffert la furie:
> Car enfin vous savez qu'il n'est grands, ni petits,
> Que de votre critique on ait vus garantis;
> Que vos plus grands plaisirs sont, partout où vous êtes,
> De faire cent éclats des intrigues secrètes...
>
> (1.1.15-20)

Arnolphe's comic destiny is presented from the outset as a consequence of a literary activity he shares with his author–one moreover that, as Larry Norman explains in a study to which I am deeply in-

---

[40] See Couton's introduction to Molière's first surviving farces, *La Jalousie du Barbouillé* and *Le Médecin volant*, in the Pléiade *Œuvres complètes* 1.3-5.

debted, Molière's enemies made an explicit issue in the controversy *L'Ecole des femmes* touched off.[41] As the poet Donneau de Visé puts it in his *Lettre sur les affaires du théâtre*, "Ceux qui jouent tout le monde, doivent, sans murmurer, souffrir que l'on les attaque, puisqu'ils en fournissent le sujet, et qu'on ne fait que leur rendre ce qu'ils prêtent aux autres."[42] It is not just that, like another man, Molière offers fodder for satire; in a role reversal reflected in the title of one of the most vicious attacks he endured, Boursault's *Le Portrait du peintre*, he has made himself a target by mocking those who now mock him in return.[43]

But Arnolphe resembles Molière in being an actor as well as author. There is the comedy he performs for his rival Horace, pretending to be a loyal family friend seconding the young man's efforts to outwit the hateful "Monsieur de La Souche." Conversely, with Agnès, he acts the authoritative part of "Monsieur de La Souche," cutting a masterful figure quite different from the role reality gives him as "Arnolphe." Arnolphe plays in fact so many parts that it is finally impossible to tell when he is acting and when not.[44] In a soliloquy late in the play, following the discovery of Agnès's love for Horace, Arnolphe declares his overwhelming love for his ward:

> De quel œil la traîtresse a soutenu ma vue!
> De tout ce qu'elle a fait elle n'est point émue;
> Et, bien qu'elle me mette à deux doigts du trépas,
> On dirait, à la voir, qu'elle n'y touche pas.
> Plus, en la regardant, je la voyais tranquille,
> Plus je sentais en moi s'échauffer une bile;
> Et ces bouillants transports dont s'enflammait mon cœur
> Y semblaient redoubler mon amoureuse ardeur.
> J'étais aigri, fâché, désespéré contre elle;

---

[41] Norman, *The Public Mirror.*

[42] Donneau, *Lettre sur les affaires du théâtre*, as cited in the Pléiade *Œuvres complètes* 1.1113.

[43] For an abridged text of Boursault's *Portrait du peintre*, see Pléiade *Œuvres complètes* 1.1050-67. For a complete version, see the Slatkine rpt. of the 19th-century ed. by "le Bibliophile Jacob" (Geneva: Slatkine, 1969).

[44] Though he makes only passing reference to *L'Ecole des femmes*, this kind of confusion is a presiding theme of Gossman's *Men and Masks*. We can also relate Arnolphe's problem to Diderot's commentary on the ontology of acting in "Le paradoxe sur le comédien" and *Le Neveu de Rameau*. We shall discuss the relevance of Diderot's views more specifically in chapter 5.

Et cependant jamais je ne la vis si belle,
Jamais ses yeux aux miens n'ont paru si perçants,
Jamais je n'eus pour eux des désirs si pressants;
Et je sens là-dedans qu'il faudra que je crève,
Si de mon triste sort la disgrâce s'achève.

(4.1.1012-25)

But is it *love* he voices here? The context of a soliloquy, invoking the convention of undisguised private speech, encourages us to think so, as does the monologue's place in the evolving plot. For it is only now that he knows he can lose Agnès, revealing an autonomy his egotism has concealed, that something like true love is possible. But for that very reason, what Arnolphe calls "love" may merely be the shattered image of the *amour-propre* that has driven him from the start. Even "love" is *de la comédie*, a part he plays in the service of wounded vanity.

But beyond resembling Molière in being a satiric author and actor, Arnolphe plays a part in a comedy he directs as well as writes. Having scripted events in which he takes the leading role, Arnolphe rehearses others in the parts he assigns to them. The most explicit example is the scene in which he walks his servants Alain and Georgette through the responses they are to make should his rival try to gain entrance to his house. Arnolphe drills them in their "leçon" (4.4.1103), a theatrical term denoting both what has to be learned (a "lesson") and a *reading*—how one's lines are to be delivered as an expression of their motivating subtext:

Arnolphe

S'il venait doucement: "Alain, mon pauvre cœur,
Par un peu de secours soulage ma langueur."

Alain

Vous êtes un sot.

Arnolphe, à Georgette

        Bon. "Georgette, ma mignonne,
Tu me parais si douce et si bonne personne…"

Georgette

Vous êtes un nigaud.

Arnolphe, à Alain

Bon. "Quel mal trouves-tu
Dans un dessein honnête et tout plein de vertu?"

Alain

Vous êtes un fripon.

Arnolphe, à Georgette

Fort bien. "Ma mort est sûre,
Si tu ne prends pitié des peines que j'endure."

Georgette

Vous êtes un benêt, un impudent.

(4.4.1106-14)

But the sharpest example of Arnolphe's directorial activity comes in the scene of the *Maximes*. Presented at 3.2.744 as the work of some anonymous "good soul" who is nonetheless patently Arnolphe himself, the *Maximes* forms a blueprint for the future. By compelling Agnès to read it aloud as a "lesson" she must get "by heart" (3.2.740), he rehearses her for the role she is to play in the comedy of conjugal life. Thus even as Molière's literary creation, a character he not only wrote, but "created" in the special French sense of being the first actor to play the part, Arnolphe turns out to be his author's counterpart. All of which is condensed in the ambition the two most signally share, the desire for a new name: in Arnolphe's case, the noble "Monsieur de La Souche," and in Molière's the name "Molière" itself.

"Molière" is of course the stage name he took as part of his professionalization, reflecting at once the pseudonymity demanded by the socially suspect nature of his chosen métier and the quasi-ritualistic character of his induction into the embattled, semi-secret world of players. [45] And it doubtless also reflects that subtle dis-

---

[45] On the enigmatic origin of the name "Molière," see Jean-Léonor Le Gallois, Sieur de Grimarest's *Vie de M. de Molière* (1705). Having recounted how Molière's troupe was formed, Grimarest writes that "[c]e fut alors que Molière prit ce nom qu'il a toujours porté depuis. Mais lorsqu'on lui a demandé ce qui l'avait engagé à prendre celui-là plutôt qu'un autre, jamais il n'en a voulu dire la raison, même à ses

INDISCERNIBLE COUNTERPARTS

placement of identity by which, as a condition of the profession of
acting, the actor ceases to be quite anyone at all. But the change
of name further bespeaks what it makes possible: the replacement of
the name he was given by the one he set out to forge for himself. In
this sense, even more than the Pierre Corneille of Marc Fumaroli's
Héros et orateurs, it is Molière who deserves the right to be called
"fils de son oeuvre." [46]

I have argued elsewhere how a symbolic change of name betokens, in the autobiographical version of the great Illumination of 10
November 1619 Descartes offers in the *Discours*, the *self-engendering* character of Cartesian science. At the logical turn of the pi-
caresque Descent that led him from the collège de la Flèche to the
scene of the outbreak of the Thirty Years War, the Father of modern science, René Descartes, withdraws into the womblike *poêle* of
his winter quarters on the road between the army and the imperial
court. And there he floats in the amniotic medium of pure thought
until, having glimpsed the synoptic form of the Method and everything it will enable him to achieve, he resurfaces quite literally "re-
born"–*rené* as "Descartes," the authoritative creator of modern science. [47] Though Molière's ambition may not be quite so hubristic as
the philosopher's, the general project is the same. By converting
Renaissance farce and Italianate comedy into the medium of his
own distinctive mode of literary expression, the poet turns the
bourgeois tapistry-maker's son Jean-Baptiste Poquelin into the inimitable comic Genius. The exact similarity of Molière and Arnolphe's identity projects frames *L'Ecole des femmes*'s special testimony. For what is ultimately at stake in the very play that
consummated Molière's self-nomination as an author is the status of
the enterprise itself, one whose fundamental impossibility the play
makes it its business to rehearse.

In a soliloquy at the end of act 3 digesting the defeat of his strat-
agems, Arnolphe determines to confront Agnès with knowledge of

---

meilleurs amis." As reproduced in *Œuvres complètes* 14. Needless to say, the mystery surrounding Molière's choice of stage name confirms its momentousness. On
the marginal world of actors, see Mongrédien, *La Vie quotidienne*, pt. 3, chap. 4,
"Les comédiens en famille."

[46] Fumaroli, "Pierre Corneille, fils de son oeuvre," in *Héros et orateurs* 17-61.

[47] I argue out the symbolism of Descartes's name at length in the chapter of
Hercules at the Crossroads cited earlier.

the love letter she has perfidiously sent his rival: "Je veux entrer un peu, mais seulement pour voir / Quelle est sa contenance après un trait si noir." (3.5.1002-03) However, even before leaving the stage, he curiously undercuts his own resolve, closing the soliloquy with a plaintive prayer:

> Ciel, faites que mon front soit exempt de disgrâce;
> Ou bien, s'il est écrit qu'il faille que j'y passe,
> Donnez-moi tout au moins, pour de tels accidents,
> La constance qu'on voit à de certaines gens!
>
> (3.5.1004-07)

To begin with, as the protagonist experiences it in the immediacy of the comic action, this prayer marks the humbling of the Cartesian hubris informing the hero's conduct to this point. With an ironic echo of the Lucretian stoicism Chrysalde voiced in the opening scene, Arnolphe confesses the powerlessness his friend has preached from the start. But the prayer is also a *mise en abyme*. Like the Mercure of the introductory dialogue in *Amphitryon*, complaining of the poetic convention that makes him travel on foot like a village errand boy, Arnolphe here dimly senses his true identity as a fictional character. For it *is* in fact "written" that he suffer a cuckold's fate, and by the actor, director, and poet who plays his part. Arnolphe's prayer marks the uncanny moment when the autonomous agent the hero has arrogantly taken himself to be encounters his fundamental subjection to the text that scripts his lot.

As hinted at the outset, the text or *écrit* is a pervasive figure throughout the play.[48] The clearest examples are the writings that circulate on the stage itself: the *Maximes du mariage* Agnès reads in 3.2; the "tablettes" or notebooks Arnolphe takes from his pocket in order to write down Horace's story of the ridiculous older man who holds Horace's love prisoner, only to discover that he is himself the man in question (1.4.306-307); the love letter Agnès sends Horace despite the maxim that outlaws it. The texts physically brought on

---

[48] For another analysis of the presence of the printed word in Molière's theater, see Zanger, "Paralyzing Performance." Note however that, as discussed in our intro., Zanger is concerned with what she takes to be the fundamentally repressive experience of publication, and thus with images of the play as printed word *outside* the precincts of theater itself. By contrast, our focus here is with the image of written and printed words within the play as such.

stage are doubled by others the play alludes to: the "doux écrits" Arnolphe associates with the "cercle" and "ruelle" (1.1.88-89), code names for the *salons* presided over by literary ladies epito- mized by the odious "femme qui compose" anathematized in Ag- nès's schooling (1.1.94); the letters Horace otherwise needlessly notes he and Arnolphe have *not* exchanged since last meeting (1.4.264); the womanly "verses," "romances," "letters," and "love notes" at which Arnolphe jeers when the illusion of absolute con- trol over Agnès is at its height (2.2.244-47); the marriage contract that the notary comes to draw up in 4.2; the *leçon* Alain and Geor- gette rehearse in 4.4. But whatever their form, all of these writings point to the master script evoked in Arnolphe's prayer: the text of the play itself. The question is, what difference does this make? What new dimension does the play derive from its evocation of the authorial text that controls the actors fates?

Drawing attention to the artful fiction on which the play is based, the author's emergence as the godlike contriver who pulls the strings that make the protagonists move *à leur insu* demonstrates Molière's mastery of the playwright's craft. The *mise en abyme* is to this extent an act of self-advertisement integral to the identity pro- ject the poet shares with his hero. Yet something deeper stirs in Arnolphe's prayer. Though we as readers see how the hero's fleeting glimpse of the author's hand unmasks the play's artifactual nature, from Arnolphe's standpoint the distress that prompts the prayer is *real*. The hero's anguished intuition of the concerted intelligence be- hind his comic entanglement is then not merely artful; it sketches a relation that reaches beyond the fiction to embrace us all. The alien hand that pens the supporting script becomes a figure for the con- straining Other that forms the ground of identity as such.

The figure of the other, and the challenge it will eventually put to the identity claims the play makes on its author's behalf, is fore- cast in the peculiar difficulties surrounding Arnolphe's new name. Quite apart from the semantic vicissitudes latent in the word "souche," countering the wished-for "root stock" with the humili- ating "stump," it is important that we only learn of the name's exis- tence because Chrysalde cannot remember it. [49] Offering ironic con- gratulations on his friend's success in producing a bride whose

---

[49] Though he does not comment on the content of Arnolphe's chosen name, Norman offers a comparable analysis of its comic fate in *Public Mirror* 147-49.

innocence exceeds his wildest expectations, Chrysalde reverts to old habits:

Chrysalde

Je me réjouis fort, seigneur Arnolphe...

Arnolphe

Bon!
Me voulez-vous toujours appeler de ce nom?

Chrysalde

Ah! malgré que j'en aie, il me vient à la bouche,
Et jamais je ne songe à Monsieur de La Souche.

(1.1.165-68)

However hard one tries, it is not enough to give oneself a name; others must use it too. And a whole dimension of comic byplay in *L'Ecole des femmes* is just the fact that nobody gets it right. The greatest offender is Horace; in the scene in which he first shares his budding romance with Arnolphe, he utters his rival's name only to *mangle* it:

Horace

Mais peut-être il n'est pas que vous n'ayez bien vu
Ce jeune astre d'amour de tant d'attraits pourvu:
C'est Agnès qu'on l'appelle.

Arnolphe, à part

Ah! je crève!

Horace

Pour l'homme,
C'est, je crois, de La Zousse, ou Source, qu'on le nomme.

(1.4.325-28)

To be sure, the misunderstanding keeps Arnolphe's hopes alive: Horace remains in the dark to his rival's true identity just because he does not know his "proper" name. But it is also clear that

Arnolphe's schemes are put at risk by their onomastic eccentricity. As Hegel would have prophesied, albeit in an ironic vein he would have despised,[50] the sovereign person for whom Arnolphe coins a new name exists first and last in other people's mouths.

But the relation to others is inscribed at a still deeper level, as a reflex of identity's essentially *imaginary* character in the strict technical sense Jacques Lacan gives the term.[51] This is already implicit in the relevance of the portrait. The desire to impose the identity claimed in a name is equivalent to the desire to become one's own effigy–as Hegel puts it, to achieve in and for oneself the identity one imagines one has for others, an identity moreover one can *only* have for others in that only they can confer it in the form in which one imagines it. Identity is to this extent a mirage whose hold on our imagination springs from the source of the human sense of self in what Lacan calls the "mirror stage" of psychic development: the moment when the child first encounters its ego ("moi") in the jubilant apprehension of its image in a mirror.[52] The mirror image is of course properly *inane*,[53] a trick of light relative to a blank reflecting surface. It also enfolds a fundamental *error*, inviting us to identify ourselves with–to identify ourselves *as*–what optics shows to be the at once external and inverted object met in the glass. This empty and inverted copy nonetheless forms the blueprint of what we take ourselves to be. In the process, it grounds identity in an alienation all the more complete for encompassing *in* us a viewpoint *on* us that cannot be our own, belonging to those others for whom alone we are genuinely visible in the form we imagine.

---

[50] For an expression of Hegel's symptomatic dislike of "the so-called *Irony*" with which Romantics like Friedrich Schlegel obtained comparable effects, see his *Introductory Lectures on Aesthetics*, trans. Bernard Bosanquet, ed. Michael Inwood (London: Penguin Books, 1993), chap. 4, "Historical Deduction of the True Idea of Art in Modern Philosophy," 70-75.

[51] The "imaginary" is of course a perennial Lacanian theme, but see in particular (besides the "mirror stage" essay referred to below) the sequence of lectures on "La topique de l'imaginaire" in Jacques Lacan, *Les Ecrits techniques de Freud (1953-54), Le Séminaire de Jacques Lacan*, bk. 1, ed. Jacques-Alain Miller (Paris: Seuil, 1975) 87-182.

[52] See Jacques Lacan, "Le stade du miroir comme formateur de la fonction du Je telle qu'elle nous est révélée dans l'expérience psychanalytique," in *Ecrits* 1 (Paris: Seuil, 1966; "Points" paper ed.) 89-97.

[53] Ibid. 89.

What is true of self in the spatial form of an image becomes all the more so when we consider its temporal dimension as a *project*. Like Rigaud's portrait of the king, the image of self referred to as "me" is perceived in the first instance as a *present*: I inspect my self (my image) in the same way I inspect the portrait of the sovereign in whose image I model myself. And yet, as our analysis of Rigaud's painting shows, the realization of this present lies in the *future*, at that later moment when a *beholder* will give it its name. This produces what Lacan defines as the fundamental tense of self's imaginary identity: the future perfect. [54] The tense is future in that who I am (or, like Arnolphe or Molière, claim to be) awaits the confirmation others must give even in my own eyes, as counterparts of the ideal other I project myself as being. But it is perfect in that what I imagine is the *fulfillment* of the project that I am: I identify myself as what I imagine I will have become once others concede the identity I claim. In choosing a name he demands that others recognize, Arnolphe (Molière) doubly commits himself to the imaginary: by asserting an original that is the inverted copy of what an alien eye alone perceives; and by binding himself to a self that inhabits a future he can only imagine as "perfect," and thus in the form of a past the future as such can never reproduce.

But identity's imaginary character arises above all from a dialectic the image of self as sovereign simultaneously incorporates and conceals: the dialectic of image and beholder on which the constitution of sovereign self-existence depends. By inscribing the beholder whose acknowledgement of falling under the portrait's gaze actualizes that gaze as an expression of the beholder's subjection to the self-determined identity the portrait asserts, the image presents a *second* self screened by the sovereignty that meets us at first glance. In place of the identity the gaze images lies another that escapes it while remaining available to others just the same. [55]

This is Molière's own situation in the controversy *L'Ecole des femmes* provoked. It informs the striking reversal of perspective to which we owe the *Critique*: the criss-cross displacement by which,

---

[54] See "Zeitlich-Entwickelungsgeschichte," *Les Ecrits techniques de Freud*, esp. 180-82.

[55] For examples of what this can lead to, see Louis Marin, "Le corps glorieux du Roi et son portrait," in *La parole mangée* 195-250 and Zanger, *Scenes from the Marriage of Louis XIV*, chap. 1, "Liminal Images."

removing the public from the relative security of its place in the *parterre* or *loges*, Molière retaliates for the humiliating spectacle his adversaries have made of him.[56] The same logic shapes *L'Impromptu de Versailles*. This second play represents a fictional rehearsal for still a third play, commissioned by no less an authority than the king to answer Molière's enemies among rival players and poets, in the *cabale des dévots*, and at court. A highpoint comes when, in his dual role as director and actor, Molière both shows his colleague La Grange how the part of a "marquis ridicule" is to be played and plays that of the duc de La Feuillade, the courtier who imagined he was the model for the *Critique*'s idiot *marquis*, witlessly repeating the offending "tarte à la crème."[57]

But the *Impromptu* administers a further twist to its author's perspective by portraying a Molière beset by unruly actors who not only misplay their parts and complain of lack of rehearsal time, but criticize the whole conception of the play. A crisis is reached when Molière's partner and mother-in-law, Madeleine Béjart, interrupts the proceedings to protest that he treats their company's rivals far too leniently (222). In addition to responding to his enemies by putting them on the stage, Molière gives his own version of Boursault's *Portrait du peintre*, of which indeed he makes explicit issue when

---

[56] I again cite Norman's *Public Mirror*, esp. pt. 2, "Recognition."

[57] *L'Impromptu* 218. The heart of the scene runs as follows, internal quotes setting off the text of the play Molière's company rehearses from that in which they rehearse it: "*La Grange*: 'Bonjour, marquis.' *Molière*: Mon Dieu! ce n'est point là le ton d'un marquis; il faut le prendre un peu plus haut; et la plupart de ces messieurs affectent une manière de parler particulière, pour se distinguer du commun: Bonjour, marquis. Recommencez. *La Grange*: 'Bonjours, marquis.' *Molière*: 'Ah! marquis, ton serviteur.' *La Grange*: 'Que fais-tu?' *Molière*: 'Parbleu! tu vois; j'attends que tous ces messieurs aient débouché la porte, pour présenter là mon visage.' *La Grange*: 'Têtebleu! quelle foule! Je n'ai garde de m'y aller frotter, et j'aime mieux entrer des derniers.' *Molière*: 'Il y a là vingt gens qui sont fort assurés de n'entrer point, et qui ne laissent pas de se presser, et d'occuper toutes les avenues de la porte.' *La Grange*: 'Crions nos deux noms à l'huissier, afin qu'il nous appelle.' *Molière*: 'Cela est bon pour toi; mais pour moi, je ne veux pas être joué par Molière.' *La Grange*: 'Je pense pourtant, marquis, que c'est toi qu'il joue dans la Critique.' *Molière*: 'Moi? Je suis ton valet; c'est toi-même en propre personne.' *La Grange*: 'Ah! ma foi, tu es bon de m'appliquer ton personnage.' *Molière*: 'Parbleu! je te trouve plaisant de me donner ce qui t'appartient.' *La Grange, riant*: 'Ah! ah! ah! cela est drôle.' *Molière, riant*: 'Ah! ah! ah! cela est bouffon.' *La Grange*: 'Quoi! tu veux soutenir que ce n'est pas toi qu'on joue dans le marquis de la Critique?' *Molière*: 'Il est vrai, c'est moi. Détestable, morbleu! Détestable! tarte à la crème! C'est moi, c'est moi, assurément, c'est moi.'"

"Mademoiselle Béjart" disrupts the rehearsal. In answer to Boursault's "portrait," the *Impromptu* presents the painter's *self*-portrait
as others portray him: a prophylactic act of self-mockery in which
the poet preempts what hostile beholders will see as ironic self-betrayal.

Molière's contribution to the controversy surrounding *L'Ecole
des femmes* deliberately exploits the compulsion by which his hero
reveals the delusion inherent in his commitment to his imaginary
self. This yields the central feature of Arnolphe's conduct in the
play: not only the degree to which he is deceived about his own motives and character, but how *patent* his self-deceptions are. We have
already seen an example in the introductory debate with Chrysalde,
where the *méthode* he brings to choosing a mate is exposed as the
mere mania intimated by the rhyming feminine *mode*. Then there is
the transparent mystery with which he cloaks his identity as the
"good soul" who authored the *Maximes*, unmasking in the process
the ignoble stratagem behind the supposed immutable truths defining conjugal roles and the threat of eternal hellfire that lends those
truths muscle. But we see it above all in Arnolphe's soliloquies, a series of nine speeches that progressively expose a solipsistic alienation at work from the start.

The first is a triumph of projection in which the hero mocks
Chrysalde for his own *ridicule*. Replying to Chrysalde's irritation at
his stubbornness, Arnolphe marvels at how infatuated people are
with their own view of things: "Chose étrange de voir comme avec
passion / Un chacun est chaussé de son opinion." (1.1.197-98) Two
scenes later, self-congratulatory gloating over Agnès's *naïveté* leads
to ill-advised jeering at female learning and letters:

> Héroïnes du temps, mesdames les savantes,
> Pousseuses de tendresse et de beaux sentiments,
> Je défie à la fois tous vos vers, vos romans,
> Vos lettres, billets doux, toute votre science,
> De valoir cette honnête et pudique ignorance.
> (1.3.244-48)

Two things strike us here: the unseemly logic that links the virtuous
epithets "honnête" and "pudique" to his ward's appalling "ignorance"; and the strange emphasis Arnolphe's words acquire as an

apostrophe haranguing visionary enemies lodged in his own obsession.

But the ludicrous overconfidence of Arnolphe's second soliloquy has evaporared by the end of the very next scene, following the
revelation of Horace's love for Agnès. His dismay is mitigated only
by his rival's foolish indiscretion in confiding the news to him:

> Avec quelle imprudence et quelle hâte extrême
> Il m'est venu conter cette affaire à moi-même!
> Bien que mon autre nom le tienne dans l'erreur,
> Etourdi montra-t-il jamais tant de fureur?
>
> (1.4.359-62)

But the relief is short-lived, yielding on mature reflection to the
misgivings voiced in Arnolphe's fourth soliloquy, where it occurs to
him that Agnès may not be the *naïve* he thought. Having vainly
sought out Horace in order to learn just how far his relations with
Agnès have developed, Arnolphe remarks that it is probably just as
well that he failed to find him:

> Il m'est, lorsque j'y pense, avantageux sans doute
> D'avoir perdu mes pas, et pu manquer sa route:
> Car enfin de mon cœur le trouble impérieux
> N'eût pu se renfermer tout entier à ses yeux;
> Il eût fait éclater l'ennui qui me dévore,
> Et je ne voudrais pas qu'il sût ce qu'il ignore,
> Mais je ne suis pas homme à gober le morceau,
> Et laisser un champ libre aux vœux du damoiseau.
> J'en veux rompre le cours, et, sans tarder, apprendre
> Jusqu'où l'intelligence entre eux a pu s'étendre.
>
> (2.1.371-80)

In 3.3, following the scene of the *Maximes*, Arnolphe is again
convinced he has nothing to fear:

> Je ne puis faire mieux que d'en faire ma femme.
> Ainsi que je voudrai je tournerai cette âme;
> Comme un morceau de cire entre mes mains elle est,
> Et je puis lui donner la forme qui me plaît.
>
> (3.3.808-811)

But his elation sets up the catastrophe that befalls him when his rival reveals Agnès's love for him by reading Arnolphe the letter she has sent. This leads to the soliloquy (3.5.977-1007) cited earlier in which the hero not only bemoans his baffled "prudence" and "philosophy," but expresses the first stirrings of a love directly tied to the belated acknowledgement of his ward's invincible autonomy. The result, following the disastrous failure of his attempt to bully her in the interval between acts 3 and 4, is a complete reversal of their respective positions, culminating in the desperate passion voiced in Arnolphe's seventh soliloquy (4.1.1012-25).

By the close of this soliloquy, wounded vanity, and in particular the vexing idea that he will have reared the perfect bride only to lose her to the "jeune fou dont elle s'amourache" (4.1.1032), gets him up in arms once more. The speech accordingly concludes with threats:

> Non, parbleu! non, parbleu! Petit sot, mon ami,
> Vous aurez beau tourner, ou j'y perdrai mes peines,
> Ou je rendrai, ma foi, vos espérances vaines,
> Et de moi tout à fait vous ne vous rirez point.
>
> (4.1.1035-38)

Arnolphe's last-ditch militancy carries over to his penultimate soliloquy in 4.5, where he furiously reviews the counter-measures he has taken to frustrate the young lovers. However, by his final monologue, though he still hopes at least to prevent Horace from carrying Agnès off, he is compelled to admit that "cruel fate" (*bourreau de destin*) (4.7.1206) has defeated all his schemes. There remains nothing but to lament the twenty-years waste of ingenious effort sacrificed to the "noble design" that now conclusively lies in ruins.

Arnolphe's increasingly frantic deliberations form a hall of mirrors: the more deeply events drive him into himself, the more completely he is divorced not only from the world he tries to dominate, but from his own identity. The epitome of the process is a famous joke, when the soliloquy begun in the preceding scene spills over into the virtuoso 22-line one-way dialogue with the notary at 4.2.1039-1060. "Se croyant seul, et sans voir ni entendre le notaire," Arnolphe casts about for a means of rescuing his schemes from the threatened wreck. In keeping with convention, his inner thoughts

take the form of an act of private speech presenting solitary consciousness as inner colloquy. However, on this occasion, the soliloquist's private thoughts are overheard by another, who responds
without missing a beat as though the words were addressed to him.
The result is not merely comic play on a shopworn dramatic trick,
but a portrait of alienation all the starker for defamiliarizing the
theatrical trope it manipulates. The notary's presence turns the conventional soliloquy into the disturbing spectacle of a man so lost in
the labyrinths of his own mind as to talk to himself out loud. Just
when the embittered hero imagines himself most alone, and when
the supporting convention encourages the audience to imagine him
most at one with his "inner" self, he is in fact most thoroughly exposed to ironic notice, turning psychic "innerness" inside out. But
this merely makes explicit what we have seen from the start. The
one-way dialogue's portrait of alienation is the logical term of an
ironic self-defeat the audience has witnessed since the expository
scene. The Cartesian spectator Molière's protagonist imagines himself to be has made a spectacle of himself in the imaginary act of
stage-managing the spectacle of others. The very effort to impose
his self-made identity as "Monsieur de La Souche" confirms, *malgré
lui*, the identity he inherits as "Arnolphe."

The prayer the hero pronounces in the *mise en abyme*, evoking
the authorial hand to which his status as a fictional character subjects him, announces then a wider condition that is not fictional at
all. The prayer depicts identity as an act of faith grounded in, and
therefore undermined by, the paranoid insight inspiring the fear of
that *breach* of faith of which a cuckold's horns are the emblem.
Arnolphe's fate embodies the nightmarish underside of the ambition driving the identity claims of which both the sovereign and the
Cartesian ego are counterparts: the process by which we are delivered to others who, in seeing what we are, conclusively make what
it is they see, thereby revealing their primacy as sources of our identities.

Arnolphe is thus the instrument of a project to which he remains necessarily blind as an expression of what that project shows
him to be. And the essential form of this project is what Molière's
text calls the *écrit*; but the *écrit* not only as the sign of the author
Molière, whose pen composed it, but also as the counterpart of that
more general other by whom Arnolphe's fate and identity are alike

determined, as indeed are Molière's own. Which brings us to our final point: the role played, in relation to the *écrit*, by the other *par excellence*, the *women* through whose agency Molière's *écrit* engineers Arnolphe's exemplary undoing; women moreover whose agency is linked to a singular *absence*, as figures of what we have called *l'insu* through which, in Molière's hands, Arnolphe stage manages his own defeat.

The first of these women is the nameless go-between who enables Horace to meet Agnès even before the play begins. We note that, at 3.4.973, Horace pronounces her dead by the time we learn of her contribution. Without her, the young lovers would not have spoken, with the result that there would have been no action, and thus no play. Yet when the curtain rises, she is no longer of the world whose shape she has helped determine. The fact that she is dead lends a surprising weight to Horace's characterization of her as a "certaine vieille... / D'un génie, à vrai dire, au-dessus de l'humain." (3.4.970-71) True, in view of Horace's own rather low-flying intellect, we cannot take this estimation at face value. The old woman's supernatural character is nonetheless vouched for by the second female agent, she too dead when the play begins, Agnès's mother Angélique. The mother's name is not evoked until the very last scene; but when it is at last pronounced, it is in conjunction with Oronte's disclosure of her daughter's true identity, key to the dénouement: "La fille qu'autrefois de l'aimable Angélique, / Sous des liens secrets, eut le seigneur Enrique." (5.9.1736-37) But even before disclosing her name, the play invokes her presiding spirit in the speech with which, addressing his brother-in-law Chrysalde, Agnès's father Enrique sets the table for the final revelation:

> Aussitôt qu'à mes yeux je vous ai vu paraître,
> Quand on ne m'eût rien dit, j'aurais su vous connaître.
> Je vous vois tous les traits de cette aimable sœur
> Dont l'hymen autrefois m'avait fait possesseur;
> Et je serais heureux si la Parque cruelle
> M'eût laissé ramener cette épouse fidèle,
> Pour jouir avec moi des sensibles douceurs
> De revoir tous les siens après nos longs malheurs.
> Mais, puisque du destin la fatale puissance
> Nous prive pour jamais de sa chère présence,

Tâchons de nous résoudre, et de nous contenter
Du seul fruit amoureux qui m'en est pu rester.

(5.7.1652-63)

While lamenting the absence of his beloved, pointedly "faithful" wife, Enrique weaves a tissue of associations that overcome her
loss. Angélique, as a mortal "presence," may be no more, but she
projects herself on stage just the same: in the tender, pious regret
with which her husband honors her memory; in the "loving fruit,"
the long-lost daughter, he has returned to reclaim; but also in the
person of her brother Chrysalde, whose features so clearly reproduce her own as to make his identity plain even had no one
uttered his name. True to the celestial connotation of her own
name, the dead Angélique watches over her daughter like the attendant angels the Canon of the Mass assigns the saintly patroness
whose baptismal name Agnès bears: according to *La Légende dorée*,
the noble Roman girl martyred for refusing to wed the pagan
groom her tyrannical father chooses. [58] Further, though we only
learn it now that Enrique observes the likeness, Angélique's image
has been before us from the first, preserved in the brother who
serves as a living counterpart set against Arnolphe as early as the
opening scene. Symbolically identified moreover not only with
tutelary angels, but with the "Parque" or Fate whose cruel decree
has cut her mortal life short, Angélique orchestrates the action from
beyond the grave, ensuring her daughter's marriage to the man she
loves.

The mother Angélique and the aged go-between are thus the
play's decisive agents, in virtual combat with Arnolphe throughout.
Why then place them under the sign of absence underscored by
death? Or to put the case the other way around, why give them
with a purely *textual* presence, as Horace's nameless "vieille" and
Enrique's regretted "Angélique"?

To cite a commonplace of cultural criticism, the Cartesian subject of which Arnolphe serves as the parodic exemplar is implicitly
male. True, in elaborating, through the cogito, the dualist theory of
conscious identity, Descartes seems to rule gender out as a critical

---

[58] On St. Agnes's legend, see Jacques de Voragine, *La Légende dorée*, ed. &
trans. J.-B. M. Roze (Paris: Edouard Rouveyre, 1902) 1.191-97.

determinant of mind. For if mind is divorced from body, it is logically independent of the corporeal vessel it happens to inhabit. It is here that, as Erica Harth chronicles, certain women, the notorious "Cartésiennes," found a license for intellectual ambitions the era otherwise thwarted by denying women any education beyond the one appropriate to the domestic role alotted them and by denying them any right of authorship beyond that linked to the minor genres of private letters and prose romance. [59] And we note in passing the light this sheds on the seventh of Arnolphe's *Maximes du mariage*, forbidding a wife's possession of writing implements. Once again, parody turns out to reproduce the norm. Yet for all the cogito licenses female intellectual ambitions, the Cartesian ego remains intimately because tacitly male. Indeed, by asserting the radical distinction of mind and body, the cogito implicitly defends the male principle on which the ego rests by insulating it from its contaminating feminine other.

Such is besides the point of Descartes's late *Passions de l'âme*, a psychological treatise responding, as it happens, to queries from a female correspondent, Elizabeth of Bohemia, Princess Palatine. [60] The aim of Descartes's theory of the passions is not merely the scientific one of understanding how the human psyche works; it is above all to *neutralize* emotions that, though inherently separate from the mind, nevertheless get at it through the body that mind is obliged to occupy. And while, symptomatically, Descartes has little to say about it, chief among these troubling "affections of the body" is the *sexual*. [61] Sexual

---

[59] See Erica Harth, *Cartesian Women: Versions and Subversions of Rational Discourse in the Old Régime* (Ithaca, NY: Cornell University Press, 1992). See, too, Joan DeJean's *Ancients against Moderns* and her earlier work on 17th-century romance, *Tender Geographies: Women and the Origins of the Novel in France* (New York: Columbia University Press, 1991).

[60] For the text of the *Passions de l'âme*, see Descartes, *Œuvres philosophiques* 3.951-1103. On its origins in the author's correspondence with Elizabeth, Princess Palatine, see 3.941.

[61] The phrase, "affections of the body," is Spinoza's. Though Cartesian in his devotion to "geometric" method and his unwavering commitment to "reason" as the sole guide to philosophical inquiry, Spinoza was a monist rigorously opposed to Descartes's distinction of mind and body. For him indeed, mind and body were the same thing seen under complementary "attributes"–now that of "thought," and now that of the body whose "affections" *move* thought. Still, though non-Cartesian in rejecting dualism, Spinoza remains Cartesian in that the point of acknowledging monism is the knowledge (and thus *self*-knowledge) it yields–a knowledge that in turn enables us to control and, as a means to that end, in some sense divorce

desire is a disturbance the female produces in the male, disrupting rational thought by subjecting it to the cravings of its corporeal other. To think in a way capable of scientific truth demands sidelining the feminine presence that threatens to derange it. This too is encoded in Arnolphe's marital project. What he aims for is marriage without risk, the possibility of reproductive (and recreational) sex without passion and the troubling lack from which passion springs: a desire as such bound to another one cannot control, desired in her separateness as the autonomous agent of desires of her own. As epitomized by Arnolphe's scheme for a happy because dispassionate conjugal state, the subject is thus founded on the repression of the feminine. If then two of our play's three primary agents are absences, it is because, *as* absences, they embody the elision they elude and defeat: uncanny *revenantes* marking the inevitable "return of the repressed" by which Arnolphe is undone just because he represses them.

All of which is related to the third and most potent female agent, Agnès. And it is related further to the *form* Agnès's agency takes: "love" of course, Horace's "great teacher," representing the instructive ruses of sexual desire; but especially an *écrit* in the shape of the letter she hurls from the window of the room in which Arnolphe incarcerates her.

We recall that the Arnolphian soliloquy that contains the ironic prayer "s'il est écrit" is provoked by Agnès's letter. More precisely, it is provoked by a *reading* of her letter. Since the letter is addressed to Horace, Arnolphe only knows about it because his clueless rival shares it with him, inopportunely rejoicing in the ingenuity with which his love-inspired mistress has outwitted the despotic Monsieur de La Souche. Having revealed the fact of the letter, Horace proceeds to read it aloud so that both Arnolphe and the audience may hear it. But the reading also stresses both the letter's status as *writing* and the *absence* that makes writing at once necessary and possible: necessary because, imprisoned in Arnolphe's house, Agnès has no other means of communicating with her lover; but also possible because it is in the absence of *both* males, the one who impris-

---

thought from corporeal "affection." The fruit of this divorce is the mysterious "amor dei intellectualis" in which we achieve not only the most perfect form of knowledge available to human beings, but that perfect freedom from bodily "affection" Descartes tries to lay at the very basis of thought as such.

ons and the one who fills her with desire, that she can say *in* writing what she truly *means*. [62] The reading of the letter underscores the conditions under which Agnès literally *makes herself heard*; and this is what we conditionally hear her say:

Horace lit

> Je veux vous écrire, et je suis bien en peine par où je m'y prendrai. J'ai des pensées que je désirerais que vous sussiez; mais je ne sais comment faire pour les dire, et je me défie de mes paroles. Comme je commence à connaître qu'on m'a toujours tenue dans l'ignorance, j'ai peur de mettre quelque chose qui ne soit pas bien, d'en dire plus que je ne devrais. En vérité, je ne sais ce que vous m'avez fait; mais je sens que je suis fâchée à mourir de ce qu'on me fait faire contre vous, que j'aurai toutes les peines du monde à me passer de vous, et que je serais bien aise d'être à vous. Peut-être qu'il y a du mal à dire cela; mais enfin je ne puis m'en empêcher de le dire, et je voudrais que cela se pût faire sans qu'il y en eût. On me dit fort que tous les jeunes hommes sont des trompeurs, qu'il ne les faut point écouter, et que tout ce que vous me dites n'est que pour m'abuser; mais je vous assure que je n'ai pu encore me figurer cela de vous, et je suis si touchée de vos paroles, que je ne saurais croire qu'elles soient menteuses. Dites-moi franchement ce qui en est; car enfin, comme je suis sans malice, vous auriez le plus grand tort du monde si vous me trompiez; et je pense que j'en mourrais de déplaisir. (3.4, between verses 947 and 948)

Agnès's letter, a form of mediated speech to which, in its writer's's absence, Horace lends a voice and Arnolphe an ear, is crucial on two counts. First, just because it *is* a letter, physically circulating beyond her reach, the author cannot control the reading. [63] As a re-

---

[62] The fact that Agnès is empowered by the absence from one's recipient writing entails recalls Derrida's famous analysis of the decontextualizing "origin" of the *écrit* in "signature événement contexte," in *Marges de la philosophie* 367-93. But it also recalls Strauss's theses about the nature of writing under conditions of censorship in *Persecution and the Art of Writing*. This provides an occasion to note that Strauss's theories promote an intensely ironic, differential style of reading as ingenious and as problematic as Derrida's. See, e.g., Yovel's "Note on Strauss's Insight and Its Limits" for students of Spinoza in *Marrano of Reason* 150-52.

[63] See similar points made in Tzvetan Todorov's poetological analysis of Laclos's *Les Liaisons dangereuses* in *Littérature et signification* (Paris: Larousse, 1967), chap. 1, "Le sens des lettres," and in Janet Gurkin Altman, *Epistolarity: Approaches to a Form* (Columbus: Ohio State University Press, 1982).

sult, it conveys Agnès's love both to its intended recipient and to the one person from whom she most wants to conceal it. This in turn provokes the spasm of jealous rage that provides the initial motive for Arnolphe's soliloquy. But a second reason for the letter's importance is the way it reveals for the first time in the play Agnès's status as an autonomous subject, a status of which writing is at once a sign and vehicle. It is then worth reading the letter closely, resisting the temptation to write it off as a mere plot device in order to see just what gets written.

We note for a start that it is in prose: the letter abandons the stylized verse in force everywhere else in the play, approximating the language of everyday life. This relates to its remarkable simplicity, shifting the weight from the artfulness of saying to the content of what is said. True, there is an art to the letter's artlessness. Agnès twice resorts to the bland intensive *bien* ("je suis bien en peine," "je serais bien aise"), a stylistic fault made more audible by use of the equally bland moral adjective: "j'ai peur de mettre quelque chose qui ne soit pas bien." She relies heavily on cliché, this too repeated: "j'aurai toutes les peines du monde à me passer de vous," "vous auriez le plus grand tort du monde si vous me trompiez," "je suis fâchée à mourir de ce qu'on me fait faire contre vous," "je pense que j'en mourrais de déplaisir." Combined with the repetitions, the crudeness of her usage shows her straining at the limits of a childishly inadequate vocabulary: beyond being both repetitious and cliché, "fâchée à mourir" and "mourir de déplaisir" bespeak petulance rather than pain or passion. The letter's style is thus *characteristic*, a model–indeed a literary stereotype–of adolescent speech. [64] But the very inadequacy of Agnès's diction emphasizes the unaffected labor of putting her thoughts on paper as honestly and directly as she can: a labor to which she herself draws attention in insisting on how hard it is to find the words required to make her meaning plain and her feelings known.

This leads to a further point: the letter expresses Agnès's painstaking *thoughts*, things she can think and therefore say precisely because neither of the males competing for her hand is there to bully or distract her. And what she *thinks* is capital. While indirectly ac-

---

[64] Compare Agnès's letter from this point of view with those of Sophie Volange in *Les Liaisons dangereuses*.

knowledging her return of the love Horace claims to feel, she is nevertheless cautious about expressing it: "En vérité, je ne sais ce que vous m'avez fait; mais je sens que je suis fâchée à mourir de ce qu'on me fait faire contre vous, que j'aurai toutes les peines du monde à me passer de vous, et que je serais bien aise d'être à vous." Similarly, she carefully discriminates between what she wishes to be the case and what may in fact be so. She reports for instance that people (the impersonal *on*, by which of course we understand Arnolphe) have told her "que tous les jeunes hommes sont des trompeurs" and "que tout ce que vous me dites n'est que pour m'abuser." But while she assures Horace that she cannot bring herself to believe it of him, this is not because she knows it is not true, but only because the words he has spoken make her *feel* that it cannot be true: "je suis si touchée de vos paroles, que je ne saurais croire qu'elles soient menteuses." This not only leaves it open whether his professions of love are honest or not; it induces her to request his frank assurance that they *are* true, reminding him the while of the wrong he would do in abusing her own good faith: "car enfin, comme je suis sans malice, vous auriez le plus grand tort du monde si vous me trompiez."

All of which brings us back to the point at which Agnès herself begins: the belated discovery of having been kept in ignorance. Unlike either of the men who claim to love her, both of whom presume absolute certainty about the state of their own feelings and the content of their own minds, Agnès distrusts not only her words, but the thoughts and emotions they express. It is then not merely a matter of finding the right words to convey what she feels; it is a matter of being clear about the nature of her feelings themselves. Having come as near voicing love as she honestly can, she immediately confesses that, so far as she knows, there may well be "du mal à dire cela." If she does still say it, it is because she cannot help it ("je ne puis m'en empêcher") and, above all, because, whatever the truth of the matter may be, she would like for there to be no wrong it ("je voudrais que cela se pût faire sans qu'il y en eût"). For all its deficiencies, the letter is a paragon of careful truth, all the more moving for acknowledging potential depths of error and self-deception for which the writer cannot honestly answer.

It is precisely the exemplary lucidity with which, in stark contrast to Arnolphe's own elaborate self-deceptions, Agnès holds fast to such truth as she can in the midst of the passions of desire, hope, fear, and doubt that most disturbs her captor. Arnolphe's response is as always overdetermined; from where he stands, the letter's virtues can only be seen as diabolical deceit:

> Quoi! pour une innocente un esprit si présent!
> Elle a feint d'être telle à mes yeux, la traitresse,
> Ou le diable à son âme a soufflé cette adresse.
>
> (3.5.979-981)

Given the twenty years of ingenious effort he has expended to prevent it, how else if not by demonic inspiration could she have acquired the self-knowledge and resolve the letter displays? [65] But though the discovery is overdetermined, as much a product of its appearance "à mes yeux" as the helpless "sotte" the new diabolical Agnès supplants, Arnolphe nonetheless responds to something real. He reacts indeed to *the real itself* conceived as what breaks through the otherwise seamless projections of the imaginary–a radical other the benighted hero can only see as endowed with the uncanniness his invocation of the devil perfectly captures.

The soliloquy recording the shock with which Arnolphe absorbs Agnès's letter ("Enfin me voilà mort de ce funeste écrit") (3.5.982) closes act 3: the act that, in classical dramaturgy, presents the *péripétie*, the sudden reversal that knots up the central dramatic crisis whose "catastrophe" in act 4 brings on the dénouement of act 5. This is followed by the major intermission when, as pledged toward the speech's close, Arnolphe confronts Agnès to see if she can face him as the perfidious devil her letter reveals her to be. When the curtain rises on act 4, Arnolphe returns to the stage, frantically pacing up and down as he tries to rally his scattered spirits. For Agnès has indeed faced him, giving back the challenge addressed to her. Arnolphe's first words sum it up: "J'ai peine, je l'avoue, à demeurer en place." (4.1.1008)

The effect is of course one of comic contrast: the militant determination with which he left the stage has evaporated in the interval,

---

[65] We detect here a final irony at Descartes's expense: Arnolphe invokes something like his philosophical model's *malin génie* to help him cope with the wreck of his version of the Cartesian enterprise. Of course, a further irony is that Molière himself will shortly be identified with the supernatural agent Arnolphe alleges must lie behind Agnès's "perfidious" intelligence.

giving way to the manic pacing and feverish speech with which the new act begins. But the joke makes a deeper point. As attested by the new name he has meant to take, alluding to the root stock on which he intended to graft the family "de La Souche," Arnolphe's aim (shared, *mutatis mutandis*, with his Cartesian model) has been to *root himself to the spot*: to achieve the perdurable identity of which lineage is the temporal expression, overcoming time, change, death itself in the name passed on to his descendants. Now, in the wake of his failure to outface Agnès, an Agnès moreover who, as her letter shows, has beaten him at his own game as both a writer and a self, Arnolphe is literally uprooted–the toppled stump of the man he imagined himself to be. But what is true of Arnolphe is true also of the sovereign subject, the Cartesian ego of which Molière's unhappy protagonist is the comic embodiment. To the extent that, in Descartes, the discourse of self that frames the cogito lays claim to timeless certainty, it is here shown to be an *illusion*. It cannot "stay in place" because it cannot, any more than Arnolphe, arrest the time of the world of which it is part. And the agent of this demonstration is the woman on whose repression the project crucially stands: the incarnate other whose uncanny familiar presence has been there from the first, denied and travestied though it may be.

The Arnolphian comedy of the subject ends where in any case it has to as a comedy: with the overthrow of the hubristic project of the sovereign ego modeled in the name. And the project is overthrown by what it represses: by women, embodiment, passion, time–figures of the fears and desires that, when the play opens, Arnolphe imagines he has overcome. We have seen, in his prayer, Arnolphe wonder "s'il est écrit." It *is* written. But, more than that, it is *writing*: the evolving trace of an unknown hand that composes the fate of all concerned. But this brings us to a final question. Granted that it is writing, the process of literary "invention" that works through the words and deeds of the characters engrossed in the unfolding action, to whom does it belong? Whose creative hand and designing intelligence does it disclose?

A short answer would be "Molière." But what we have seen of Molière's own historical predicament suggests that this would have to be a *superhuman* Molière "d'un génie, à vrai dire, au-dessus de l'humain": an angelic go-between or messenger shuttling between the world portrayed on stage and another world whose absence is the condition for its inscription—a "real" world whose unmentionable, not to say "diabolical" irruption in the play so offended Molière's contemporaries. But this already indicates the inadequacy of the short answer. Rather than "Molière," the uncanny source is writing itself and the activity that, *as* writing, it addresses: the *reading* now reaching an end. These two in concert author Arnolphe's fate from a place to which the poet himself has in the end no clearer access than his unfortunate stand-in.

Let us call this source the *unconscious*, the inscrutable yet fundamental other by which each of us is finally guided: something available only mediately, in the traces it leaves for those who learn to read them. Whence the leading reference in this chapter's title: the famous essay in which Lacan develops the linguistic idea at the bottom of Freud's seminal masterpiece, *The Interpretation of Dreams*. One consequence of our reading of *L'Ecole des femmes* is to show it to be a tissue of symptomatic acts, a network of allusions, echoes, metaphors, and parallels tying names to identities, selves to gender, models to authorities in such a way as to weave a plot whose outcome points emphatically beyond anything either the characters or their author can recognize or control. Like Freudian dreamwork, it is a patchwork of symbolic substitutions, analogical displacements, and screening condensations by which insights, fears, and desires removed from conscious acknowledgement filter to the surface on condition of remaining *méconnus*—accommodated to a "manifest" content that conceals even as it discloses, that reveals only on condition of deforming the "latent" meanings stored within. But if this is so, if dreams, slips, jokes, compulsions, and actes manqués form a kind of allegory in which the unconscious encodes messages despite our efforts to "school" or censor it, it is because, as Lacan urges, the unconscious is language itself. But language here is not *spoken*, the words that "spontaneously" spring from the characters' mouths; it is, rather, *writing*, penning hidden messages in anticipation of the later moment when they may at last be read for what they are. [66]

---

[66] Jacques Lacan, "L'instance de la lettre dans l'inconscient ou la raison depuis Freud," *Ecrits* 1.249-89.

Arnolphe, the sovereign subject, is perpetually betrayed by his own words: the name he hopes to secure by renouncing his given one; the *Maximes* of which, for all he tries to conceal the fact in the interest of converting his strategic precepts into immutable truths, he is nonetheless transparently the wholly mutable author; the self-inflating reference to "method" and his claim to the authority of a Cartesian "spectator" disengaged from the spectacle of the fellow beings whose conduct he reduces to prudential rules. And he betrays himself by his every deed as well: all of those scripted and therefore blindly automatic acts by which, for all the self-determined spontaneity he imagines he exercises, he unerringly hastens the very fate he means to escape. But then so do we all, a fact of which only one character seems fully aware in her unknowing complicity with the angelic mother and the superhuman crone who watch over her: the Agnès of the letter, carefully acknowledging what she cannot know but may reveal just the same *à son insu*.

CHAPTER 5

THE PROFESSION OF HYPOCRISY: TRUTH AND
PERFORMANCE IN *TARTUFFE* AND *DOM JUAN*

T HE ultimate focus of this chapter is the most inscrutable work
in Molière's corpus, the moody *Dom Juan* of 1665. We shall try
our hand at unraveling the play's classic puzzles. Why, for example,
as outraged contemporaries pertinaciously demanded, is the only
consistent opponent to the title character's atheism the farcical
Sganarelle, whose faith in God, the Devil, and the afterlife is ex-
ceeded only by his superstitious belief in werewolves and the bo-
geyman? [1] Or how should we take the legendary seducer himself: as
the epitome of an evil darker than the one tradition bequeaths or as
a proto-Romantic ironist like the hero of the Mozart/Da Ponte

---

[1] The Sieur de Rochemont makes the point in his *Observations sur une comédie
de Molière intitulée Le Festin de Pierre* (1665). The list of *Dom Juan*'s satanic impi-
eties includes "une Religieuse débauchée, et dont l'on publie la prostitution, un
Pauvre à qui l'on donne l'aumosne, à condition de renier Dieu; un Libertin qui se-
duit autant de filles qu'il en rencontre; un Enfant qui se moque de son Pere et qui
souhaite sa mort; un Impie qui raille le Ciel, et qui se rit de ses foudres; un Athée
qui reduit toute la Foy à deux et deux sont quatre, et quatre et quatre sont huit."
But Rochemont really hits his stride when he gets to the role of Sganarelle, characterized as "un Extravagant qui raisonne crotesquement de Dieu, et qui par une
cheute affectée *casse le nez à ses argumens*; un Valet infame fait au badinage de son
Maistre, dont toute la creance aboutit au Moine-Bouru; *car pourveu que l'on croye le
Moine-Bouru, tout va bien, le reste n'est que bagatelle*; un Demon qui se mesle dans
toutes les Scenes, et qui repand sur le Theatre les plus noires fumées de l'Enfer; et
enfin un Moliere pire que tout cela, habillé en Sganarelle, qui se moque de Dieu et
du Diable, qui joüe le Ciel et l'Enfer, qui souffle le chaud et le froid, qui confond la
vertu et le vice, qui croit et ne croit pas, qui pleure et qui rit, qui reprend et qui approuve, qui est Censeur et Athée, qui est hypocrite et libertin, qui est homme et Demon tout ensemble: *un Diable incarné*, comme luy-mesme se definit." Mongrédien,
Comédies et pamphlets sur Molière 89-90.

opera? But to solve *Dom Juan*'s enigmas, we must come at them by way of the play that at once foreshadowed and superseded it, the fiercely contested *Tartuffe* of 1664-69.

A first reason is the remarkable continuity of Molière's output from *L'Ecole des femmes* of 1662 to the final version of *Tartuffe*, staged by hardwon royal license in 1669. *Dom Juan* is an episode in the period of intense creative experiment during which Molière perfects his distinctive contribution to French theater, the fullblown *comédie de caractère* of which, for his friend Boileau as for later scholars, the next year's *Misanthrope* (1666) marks the triumph. [2] But grasping this continuity requires dispelling a teleological illusion endemic to the circular perspective of literary history. Since our interest in the plays that precede is predicated on the masterpieces to follow, the latter seem to *cause* the former in just the way a dramatic dénouement induces the turns of plot that bring it about. [3] And the source of this inverted causality is the poet's self-determined *genius*, the transcendent *je ne sais quoi* of which the masterpieces form the expressive monuments.

By contrast, I propose to explore the essential *adventitiousness* of Molière's creative process. It is important, for instance, that in

---

[2] Guicharnaud, *Molière, une aventure théâtrale*. Though Guicharnaud pioneers reading the plays in terms of their scenic "destination" as *works of theater*, he leaves questions of reception quite aside, focusing on the text alone as the correlate of a mental *mise en scène*. This autonomy encourages a finalism of the kind Defaux's *Molière, ou les métamorphoses du comique* endorses, albeit nuanced by a livelier sense of theater's implication in the society to which it ministers. Thus, the traditions of "moral comedy" with which Molière begins reach their logical catastrophe in *Dom Juan*, where the poet's efforts to tell an unvarnished local truth bring the lightning bolts of contemporary resistance on his head. The attendant "remise en question" of the comic "norm" entails the "end of comic innocence" in *Le Misanthrope*, seen as the play in which Molière discovers at last the "comic wisdom" of *l'universelle comédie* whose archetypes are Erasmus's *Praise of Folly*, the humane skepticism of Montaigne, and the *roman rabelaisien*. Similarly, despite its intense engagement with contemporary response, Norman's *Public Mirror* makes the same assumption about *Le Misanthrope*'s retrospective priority (see, e.g., chap. 11, "From Arnolphe to Alceste"). For Boileau's comparable assessment, see *L'Art poétique* 3.393-400, where Molière is notoriously identified as "l'auteur du Misanthrope."

[3] Forestier's *Essai de génétique théâtrale* supplies a fascinating case history of this process of circular constitution. The author maps Corneille's "démarche créatrice," demonstrating how all features of Cornelian dramaturgy are systematically deduced from their formal and teleological end in the "sublime" experience of pity, fear, and admiration inspired by the heroic confrontations of the tragic close. This determines not only the structure of his book, but his picture of the essence of Corneille's genius, i.e., the "esthétique du sublime" laid out in his final chapter.

the ironic self-portrait inscribed in the features of *L'Ecole*'s Arnolphe, Molière himself undermines the self-determined creative autonomy critical tradition alleges. We also note the sheer untidiness of the sequence in which *Dom Juan* stands. Though construed as a stage on the road from *L'Ecole* to *Le Misanthrope*, *Tartuffe* still hangs in the balance three years after the latter's début. Indeed, incorporating two major rewrites, including a change of title that alters both the central character's name and *état civil*,[4] *Tartuffe*'s genesis spans four major works beyond *Le Misanthrope* and *Dom Juan*: *Le Médecin malgré lui* of 1666 and *Amphitryon*, *Georges Dandin*, and *L'Avare*, all in 1668. *Dom Juan* meanwhile, shut down a mere fifteen performances into its run, was banished from the public stage till its revival in 1841.[5] Far from contributing to a central line of development, *Dom Juan* is a mutant, an evolutionary deadend; nor will Molière write anything remotely like it again. The fundamental engine of Molière's development is neither the inner coherence of the dramatic work, nor his maturing genius, but the brute contingencies of evolving public *response* and the interests and anxieties that response betokens. *Dom Juan* is the upshot of public uptake, an inspired improvisation reacting to the implacable violence of public reception.

But there is a second reason for coming at *Dom Juan* through *Tartuffe*. The fact is not made explicit until act 5, when the title character announces to his scandalized servant his climactic embrace of the aptly named "profession" of a hypocrite. The play is nonetheless guided from the start by a theme it shares with *Tartuffe*: the theme, precisely, of *hypocrisy*. The theme of hypocrisy, of concealment and simulation, of *dis*-simulation and pretence, points most obviously toward the infamous "cabale des dévots," the pious conspiracy directed by the Compagnie du Saint-Sacrement whose composite portrait in *Tartuffe* Molière now reprises as a preliminary to sending Dom Juan to hell. But as Molière's adversaries were quick to retort, hypocrisy also points to the poet's *own* "profession": the

---

[4] See the "notice" in the Pléiade *Œuvres complètes* 1.842-47. Note in particular how, in the second version, before reverting to type in the text we possess today, the hypocritical director of conscience "Tartuffe" becomes a sword-bearing gentleman named "Panulphe."

[5] Ibid. 2.3-8. It is striking that, even with the restoration of the original text in 1819, the play remains unstaged for two more decades.

art of theatrical acting whose practitioner, the French *comédien* or Greek *hypocrites*, is the simulator par excellence. Hypocrisy in this wider sense already suggests the scope of the issues joined. For one thing, what happens when, as a professional liar and hypocrite, the actor is called on to mimic a hypocrite *proper*, a person whose character is a simulation in its own right? What moreover distinguishes mere acting from hypocrisy when the essence of both is a make-believe that apes belief itself, the Faith in whose name both sides in the debate pretend to speak? [6]

The theme of hypocrisy thus bears on the complex nature of *performance*, a term whose semantic range proves as elusive as hypocrisy's own. In particular, as Shoshana Felman argues, it illuminates the set of problems endemic to what J.L. Austin liked ironically to call the "doctrine" of performative utterances underlying the theory of speech acts. [7] *Tartuffe* and *Dom Juan* anticipate Austin's critique of the traditional philosophical presumption that language is defined above all by correspondence between what utterances claim and "the truth" of actual states of affairs. Taken together with the fact that "falsehood" (honest error as well as lies) alters the states of affairs from which it deviates, hypocrisy's strategic nature underscores how far language shapes the world philosophy prefers to see it as reporting. As Felman puts it, "truth is an act," both deed and performance, changing what it purports to represent.[8] So for all these reasons we begin with *Tartuffe*. More precisely, we begin where *Tartuffe* will end–in the problematic dénouement by which it magnifies the conflicts it tries to resolve.

---

[6] See Fumaroli, "*Sacerdos sive rhetor, orator sive histrio*," in *Héros et orateurs* 451; but also see Felman, *Le scandale du corps parlant*, "La perversion de la promesse: Don Juan et la performance littéraire," 31-80. Though lacking both the philological (Fumaroli) and theoretical (Felman) equipment developed in the interval, J.D. Hubert, *Molière and the Comedy of Intellect* (Berkeley: University of California Press, 1962), chap. 10, "Hypocrisy as Spectacle," and Gossman, *Men and Masks*, explore this dilemma.

[7] Austin, *How to Do Things with Words*. On the irony in Austin's use of the term "doctrine," see Felman's brilliant analysis of the serio-comic playfulness of his style generally, *Le scandale du corps parlant*, "Au-delà du principe de félicité: la performance de l'humour," 160-86.

[8] Felman, *Le scandale du corps parlant* 219.

262 INDISCERNIBLE COUNTERPARTS

1. TRUTH AND PERFORMANCE: *TARTUFFE*

Tartuffe reaches its catastrophe with the villain's vindictive entry at the start of the final scene. As many have noted, Tartuffe's victim, the bourgeois patriarch Orgon, is the impotent toy of his own childish *amour-propre*, a petulant mother's boy as incapable of imposing his will on others as of controlling his own narcissistic impulses.[9] The impostor's success springs from Orgon's blindness to the gap between the flattering mirage of moral mastery Tartuffe presents him and the self-deceiving weakness evinced by his abject failure to govern his dependents: his prudish mother, Mme Pernelle; his young second wife, Elmire; his feisty servant, Dorine; his spoiled (and witless) children, Damis and Mariane. Truth does finally dawn, but only with Orgon's apparent eviction from the home he has recklessly deeded to Tartuffe: a fate compounded by impending arrest for concealing incriminating political papers entrusted to him by a friend and foolishly conveyed to his treacherous parasite. Nor is this a purely personal tragedy. Orgon's private overthrow subverts the system of natural rights (property and marital rights; rights of contract and inheritance; the right to bestow one's children in marriage as one sees fit; the right to command obedience of dependent servants) his household symbolizes.[10]

---

[9] See Gossman, *Men and Masks*, chap. 4, "Le Tartuffe," and Greenberg, *Subjectivity and Subjugation*, chap. 5, "Molière's *Tartuffe* and the scandal of insight." Both writers relate Tartuffe's exploitation of Orgon's narcissistic self-idolatry to the larger question of the *royal* self-idolatry the finale at once connives in and implicitly denounces. Gossman puts the case trenchantly: "The defeat of the false idol thus goes hand in hand with the triumph of the true one" (143), but is reluctant to overstate it, suggesting that "Molière's conscious purpose had been to satirize the negative force of opposition to absolutism" (144), leaving the critique of absolutism itself to later, 18th-century writers. Greenberg shares Gossman's view that the critique of absolutist idolatry *Tartuffe* encodes was not consciously framed, but in order to assert that the "scandal" the play constitutes derives precisely from the *unconscious* character of its insight–and indeed from its (unintended) insight into the work of the unconscious as such. It is however noteworthy that much recent French research, and in particular Merlin's *Public et littérature* and Fumaroli's *Le Poète et le Roi*, encourages us to assign a greater role to conscious influences.

[10] See Apostolidès, *Le prince sacrifié* 173-81, which describes *Tartuffe*'s dénouement as enacting a "retour du roi" specifically designed to restabilize legal and economic relations destabilized by processes of exchange symbolized by Orgon's "unnatural" conveyance of his property. Also valuable is Fumaroli, who describes

THE PROFESSION OF HYPOCRISY

If Orgon is nonetheless spared the end he so richly deserves, it is only by a sort of miracle, a *deus ex machina* operated in the name (if not the person) of the King, endowed for the occasion with literally godlike powers. As the court officer sent on the King's behalf puts it in explaining how, against all likelihood, it is in fact Tartuffe and not Orgon he has come arrest,

> Nous vivons sous un prince ennemi de la fraude,
> Un prince dont les yeux se font jour dans les cœurs,
> Et que ne peut tromper tout l'art des imposteurs.
> D'un fin discernement sa grande âme pourvue
> Sur les choses toujours jette une droite vue;
> Chez elle jamais rien ne surprend trop d'accès,
> Et sa ferme raison ne tombe en nul excès.
> Il donne aux gens de bien une gloire immortelle;
> Mais sans aveuglement il fait briller ce zèle,
> Et l'amour pour les vrais ne ferme point son cœur
> A tout ce que les faux doivent donner d'horreur.
>
> (5.7.1906-16)

Unlike Orgon, blind plaything of vanity and passion, the King deploys a panoptic power of vision that penetrates all places and all hearts. By the undimmed light of "reason" that, dissolving the fount of error and illusion in internal "excess," defeats external "fraud" and "imposture," the King shares the benevolent ubiquity and omnipotence of the God whose annointed surrogate he is, restoring the natural order the diabolical deceiver disrupts.[11]

The play's implausible ending in part reflects pure comic convention. In line with the moral office prescribed in its preface, *Tartuffe* proposes a satiric "portrait" of the "vices" and "foibles" (*ridicules*) of the age (256); and as the *Critique de L'Ecole des*

---

the dénouement's judicial vindication of socio-economic right thus: "Après avoir montré la fertilité du théâtre comme mimésis libératrice de la société laïque, Molière va en faire l'épiphanie de la puissance royale, émanation de cette société et garant public de son bien commun," *Héros et orateurs* 489. See too Greenberg, *Subjectivity and Subjugation* 116-18, allowing, however, for the modifications Greenberg's psychoanalytic interests entail.

[11] The King's godlike stature is of course a period truism, explored in Kantorowicz, *The King's Two Bodies*, and Apostolidès, *Le roi-machine* 11-13 and *Le prince sacrifié*, chap. 1, "Le roi sacré." The idea also informs Fumaroli's characterization of *Tartuffe*'s dénouement.

femmes asserts, this requires knowing laughter grounded in "resemblance." (208) "Resemblance" in turn dictates conformity to generic *vraisemblance*, presenting characters and actions adapted to the ethos or decorum of dramatic type. Yet it also invokes a calculus of probabilities based on *real* human conduct, motives, and relations. As comedy, the play must end happily. But because, as Aristotle reminds us, comedy portrays people like ourselves only "worse," [12] the play's personnel are condemned to endure a disaster from which only something uncompromised by the prevailing comic element can save them. The finale's *deus ex machina* thus reconciles the conflicting demands of comic realism and comic happiness.

But convention is here reinforced by the occasion for the initial, three-act version of the play. The original *Tartuffe* highlighted a spectacular series of royal entertainments, the famous "Plaisirs de l'Ile enchantée" of May 1664, celebrating the official installation of the court of Louis XIV in the palace of Versailles. [13] Beyond accomplishing its generic mission as a "public mirror" delineating the vices of the age, it was expressly designed as a tribute to the great Sun King whose theatrical apotheosis it helped enact. In counterpoint to the unfolding catastrophe overtaking its bourgeois household, the play presents a comic theory of the genesis of the absolutist State, exploiting its conventional ending to demonstrate both why the nation needs a monarch and why that monarch must be *absolute*. As absolute, the monarch is absolved of mere (intrinsically comic if potentially tragic) humanity so as to serve as an impartial arbiter and judge. The King symbolically incarnates the nation he rules; but he also stands *above* that nation in order to escape the play of interests, emotions, and passionate sectarian prejudices that both shape and distort national life. Molière converts the comic necessity of the close into the political apology the circumstances of *Tartuffe*'s original performance call for: the happy ending doubles as the still happier advent of Ludovican France.

Whence Marc Fumaroli's characterization of *Tartuffe*'s dénoue-

---

[12] Aristotle, *Poetics* 1449a.
[13] See Apostolidès, *Le roi-machine*, pt. 1, chap. 5. Our chief contemporary source is André Félibien's *Les Plaisirs de l'Ile enchantée* (1664). Couton reproduces Félibien's text in the Pléiade *Œuvres complètes* 1.749-829.

ment as a "lay liturgy" of State.[14] The finale recapitulates the ritual annointment whose model is the rite of consecration in the Catholic mass. As Louis Marin explains, the sacramental repetition of Christ's words from the Last Supper, "Ceci est mon corps," exactly parallels the legendary utterance from which Louis's royal authority springs: "L'état, c'est moi."[15] In the mass, both when and as the officiant priest pronounces them, the performative words of consecration *effect* the miracle of transubstantiation, turning the eucharistic bread into the sacred body whose redemptive sacrifice the ritual reenacts. Moreover, as a "mystery" belief in which identifies the community of believers, Christ's real presence in the eucharist renews his covenant with the faithful, reincorporating the congregants in the body of his Church. Just so, in saying "l'état, c'est moi," Louis not only announces, but *constitutes* the perspicuous national order whose name he takes: the anarchic social energies of everyday life are at once bound up and redeemed in Louis's consecratory embodiment of the state. In pledging allegiance to the monarch who intervenes on behalf of Orgon's beleaguered family, *Tartuffe*'s finale reconsecrates both Louis's royal person and the state Louis embodies. In the godlike terms in which the court officer invokes the King in whose name he speaks, the dénouement performs a ritual showing forth, a quasi-eucharistic monstration, that institutes the social order incarnated by the monarch before whom it occurs.

However, given the dénouement's character as ritual monstration, it is all the more telling that many things are sublimated or concealed. We note, for example, the severely truncated version of the nation the play portrays. In contemporary usage, the term *nation* chiefly referred to the three estates, the nobility, clergy, and such members of *la roture* or commons as by their economic, administrative, or intellectual functions impinged on public notice.[16] The word's meaning thus excluded the great mass of the population, denoted by the pejorative "petit peuple" or "populace." Accordingly, in place of the laboring millions whose very humanity

---

[14] Fumaroli, *Héros et orateurs* 490.
[15] See Marin, *Le portrait du roi* 14-19.
[16] Apostolidès, *Le roi-machine* 20-22.

official culture tended to call in doubt, [17] we get the feisty and clear-sighted, but nonetheless devoted *domestique* Dorine: a demotic *bonne enfant* whose popular good sense is finally subordinate to the bourgeois family whose interests she unconditionally espouses. Nor do we learn where Orgon's property comes from. Though Orgon is no parasite like Tartuffe, his wealth remains entirely abstract, a *don du ciel* cut off from its material source in concrete social practice. [18]

But ideologically more privileged figures are also conspicuous by their absence, and for a start the monarch himself. The King's absence from the stage is in part mandated by decorum. Though a monarch may participate, as Louis himself notably did, in other kinds of spectacle, and in particular in a *ballet de cour* or masque, [19] he cannot with propriety appear in a satiric comedy depicting life among the lower orders. Besides, the occasion of *Tartuffe*'s pre-miere already places him in the audience, adding a physical impe-diment to the question of *bienséance*. So the King is represented on stage by the character the dramatis personae calls the "exempt," a nameless official relieved from normal service in order to deputize for a superior in the chain of command. But the King's absence thereby draws attention to the *representational* character of the social order. Just as the sovereign stands for the state he ritually personates, so is he in turn represented *in* the state as an expres-sion of his absolute sovereignty. In this sense, the *exempt* is not only nameless, but selfless. It is not he, but the King who acts, and all the more incontrovertibly in that the monarch's agency operates

---

[17] See La Bruyère, *Les Caractères*, "De l'Homme," character 128: "L'on voit cer-tains animaux farouches, des mâles et des femelles, répandus par la campagne, noirs, livides et tout brûlés de soleil, attachés à la terre qu'ils fouillent et qu'ils re-muent avec une opiniâtreté invincible; ils ont comme une voix articulée, et quand ils se lèvent sur leurs pieds, ils montrent une face humaine, et en effet ils sont des hommes; ils se retirent la nuit dans des tanières où ils vivent de pain noir, d'eau et de racine; ils épargnent aux autres hommes la peine de semer, de labourer et de re-cueillir pour vivre, et méritent ainsi de ne pas manquer de ce pain qu'ils ont semé."

[18] An index of how classical culture mystifies the material sources of wealth is the fact that, though Harrison's *Pistoles/Paroles* finds many illuminating things to say about *spending* and *distributing* money, discussions of *making* money are almost entirely confined to the dealings of players and writers. Thus, while we have chap-ters on the "sources of income and honor" available to authors and actors, on the "value of discourse," or on the "demystification of expenditure," there is little if any hint of the generation of wealth in the larger society.

[19] See Apostolidès's discussion of *ballets de cour* in *Le roi-machine* 59-65.

through a system of automatized intermediaries who do his bidding as a reflex of the numenous royal will. That the King should be left out is integral to the rite the play enacts, a direct function of the power it assigns him. But there are still other omissions, and in particular one signaled by a curious and, to my knowledge, hitherto unnoticed fact.

In the narrative accounting for the play's unlikely happy ending, the *exempt* explains how Tartuffe has been undone by his own overreaching machinations. In presenting himself to the authorities to denounce Orgon and claim his property, he disclosed his true identity as a notorious criminal for whom the tireless royal eye has been watching:

> Venant vous accuser, il s'est trahi lui-même,
> Et, par un juste trait de l'équité suprême,
> S'est découvert au prince un fourbe renommé,
> Dont sous un autre nom il était informé;
> Et c'est un long détail d'actions toutes noires
> Dont on pourrait former des volumes d'histoires.
>
> (5.7.1921-26)

The *exempt*'s narrative highlights a theodicical irony: the villain accomplishes his own ruin in trying to compass that of the misguided *père de famille* whose cause the King espouses. In the process, he precipitates what his malefactions otherwise subvert, the spectacular exhibition of the political *telos* whose vindication in the finale restores the natural order. Tartuffe's actions recall those of *Cinna's* Emilie, whose plot to overthrow Auguste's fledgling empire ultimately justifies the tyrant against whom she rebels. But here we meet the curious point: whoever Tartuffe is, it is not "Tartuffe." The renown he has earned as "un fourbe renommé" comes to him "under another name." The name the play gives him is an *alias*, supplanting the one by which the authorities know him. But what that other, presumably true name is we do not learn since the *exempt* does not pronounce it. In the moment of ritual monstration where his anonymous deputy shows the King as the teleological guarantor of the state, we discover a certain *mystery*: that surrounding the true identity of the title character known to us as "Tartuffe."

This mystery has a name of its own: it is a "mystère d'état," an item of knowledge the state withholds from public scrutiny "par raison d'état," on behalf of the body politic and all it secures. [20] The secrecy figured in the villain's name preserves the confidentiality in which the state cloaks its apparatus to assure its efficacy; and what indeed undoes Tartuffe is ignorance of the royal eye that tracks his every move. But state secrets also protect the ritual identity, the ritual *mask*, required to maintain public obedience to political authority. Whence the ambiguity surrounding the notorious maxim of statecraft that the great Jesuit casuist Navarrus attributes to Louis XIV's namesake, Louis XI: "Qui nescit dissimulare nescit regnare," who knows not how to dissimulate knows not how to rule. [21] As alleged, notably, by opponents of the Society of Jesus and political absolutism alike, the maxim offers cynical counsel arrestingly apposite to the subject of Molière's play: political success depends on concealing interests, motives, and identities that would not survive the light of day. But the maxim is further linked to the theme of princely "sacrifice" we have met in earlier chapters: the legal fiction of the King's Two Bodies, the principle of royal gemination on which absolutism rests. [22]

In this latter perspective, the mystery surrounding Tartuffe's real name instances the secret knowledge the King spares his people, enabling them to get on with the happy, productive lives whose disruption Orgon's private catastrophe illustrates. But by the same token, the mystery marks the gap between the public image both play and state present and the state's true nature: a gap inhabited by the secret operatives behind the secular miracle Molière's spectacle foregrounds. In the very gesture by which the *exempt* reveals the truth, confirming the natural rights and relations on which social order depends, we meet a blank that is nothing less than the truth about "Tartuffe." Whoever "Tartuffe" may *really* be is elided precisely insofar as the play reproduces the limits of public knowledge reason of state dictates. The private impostor mirrors the *political*

---

[20] For introductions to the doctrine of "reason of state," see Friedrich Meinecke, *Machiavellianism, the Doctrine of Raison d'Etat and Its Place in Modern History*, trans. Douglas Scott (New Haven: Yale University Press, 1957), Etienne Thuau, *Raison d'Etat et pensée politique à l'époque de Richelieu* (Paris: Armand Colin, 1966), and William Farr Church, *Richelieu and Reason of State* (Princeton: Princeton University Press, 1973).
[21] See Zagorin, *Ways of Lying* 174.
[22] See note 11.

imposture that masks the means by which the state brings him to justice.

There is much to dwell on here, but of particular relevance is how the ersatz mystery of state Molière makes of Tartuffe's name does double duty. The royal propaganda featured in the comedy's close intersects with polemical aims more immediately Molière's own: aims he associates with the monarch insofar as he suggests they share a common enemy. Just because he is not named, or more precisely, just because he is at once *un-* and *re-*named in the gesture by which the play unmasks him, the "fourbe renommé" comes to stand for something else, something kept as carefully off stage as the identity of the villain who gives the play its name.

As we have noted, Molière's chief personal motive for *Tartuffe* was the vicious polemic provoked by the play with which the great period of theatrical experiment begins, *L'Ecole des femmes*. *Tartuffe* was indeed the third in a series of plays in which Molière publicly responds to the violent attacks *L'Ecole*'s success brought on his head. The first was the *Critique de L'Ecole des femmes*, staging a salon debate refuting allegations of artistic impropriety and the related charge of indecent morals. The *Critique* was then followed by *L'Impromptu de Versailles*, commissioned by the King himself as a rejoinder to rival poets and Molière's theatrical competitors at the Hôtel de Bourgogne: Edme Boursault, whose attempt to turn the satiric tables on Molière in the *Portrait du peintre* was repaid by a vicious counter-portrait in which a stammering victim deforms his own name; the competition's leading actor Montfleury, whose ham acting style Molière mercilessly mimics; and the Corneille brothers, especially Thomas, the self-styled "Monsieur de L'Isle" directly targeted by *L'Ecole*'s "Monsieur de La Souche." [23]

But it is with *Tartuffe* that Molière turns (here too reportedly with royal encouragement) on his most implacable and dangerous enemies, the "cabale des dévots" formed by the Compagnie du Saint-Sacrement: a pious fifth column infiltrating lay society in order to restore proper public morals and a Catholic orthodoxy undermined by both growing secularism and competing exponents of Christian renewal. [24] In addition to attacking widespread blasphemy,

---

[23] See Mallet, *Molière* 81.

[24] For a suprisingly apologetic history of the Compagnie du Saint-Sacrement, see Raoul Allier, *La Cabale des dévots* (1902; rpt. Geneva: Slatkine, 1970).

inattendance at church, and the sources of moral laxity (theater-going, costly dress, sumptuous dinner parties, *salon* chit-chat) cat-alogued by Orgon's mother, the humorlessly intolerant Mme Per-nelle, the Compagnie dogged the doctrinal foes of Gallican right-mindedness: Protestant heretics in whose face they wave the standard of the Holy Sacrament, the Catholic mass with the central mystery of Christ's real presence reaffirmed at the Council of Trent; the moral relaxation encouraged by Jesuit casuistry in its efforts to reconcile the strict letter of Church teaching with the practical complexities of daily life; and the calvinizing rigorism of French Jansenists, critical of the Compagnie's own unseemly traffic with sec-ular authority.[25] The accusation Molière implicitly makes in the per-son of Tartuffe, one that, though indirect, escaped none of his con-temporaries, is that, for all their overt piety, the Compagnie is a mere faction like any other, guilty of just what Jansenists claimed: a hypo-critical thirst for power advancing hidden interests whose gross wordliness is evinced precisely by the Compagnie's access to po-litical power.

All of these things are reflected in the famous anecdote includ-ed in the preface to the text of 1669, reporting a conversation be-tween the King and *le grand Condé*. A week after *Tartuffe* was banned for the first time,

> on représenta devant la cour une pièce intitulée *Scaramouche er-mite*: et le roi, en sortant, dit au grand prince: "Je voudrais bien savoir pourquoi les gens qui se scandalisent si fort de la comédie de Molière ne disent mot de celle de *Scaramouche?*", à quoi le

---

[25] Marie-Florine Bruneau analyzes the link between Jansenist unworldliness and "modernity" in *Racine: Le jansénisme et la modernité* (Paris: Corti, 1986). See esp. chaps. 1, "L'absolutisme théologique," 3, "Théologie politique et discours politique moderne," and 5, "Le jansénisme entre la théologie et l'affirmation de soi. La raison et l'historiographie." Drawing on Blumenberg's interpretation of the neo-gnostic cosmology of late-medieval nominalism in *Legitimacy of the Modern Age*, she de-scribes how the "theological absolutism" and unbending *contemptus mundi* of Bar-cos, Saint-Cyran, and Pascal paradoxically mandates both political absolutism (an irrevocably fallen world demands a Hobbist overlord) and a radical individualism in spiritual matters (as a social institution, the ecclesiastical hierarchy commands *per se* no more, if also no less, obedience than the State, regulating our disorderly bod-ies while leaving our souls free to pursue their independent search for communion with God). Bruneau's analysis thus updates Lucien Goldmann's *Le Dieu caché*, pt. 2, on the social and intellectual "foundation" of the "tragic vision" of Jansenism conceived as a harbinger of dialectical materialism.

prince répondit: "La raison de cela, c'est que la comédie de *Scaramouche* joue le ciel et la religion, dont ces messieurs-là ne se soucient point: mais celle de Molière les joue eux-mêmes; c'est ce qu'ils ne peuvent souffrir." (258)

So *Tartuffe* was from the start about something other than what it expressly stages; but so too was its fierce reception at devout hands. While Molière's adversaries protest their submission to God's will, from the poet's standpoint, they pursue private appetites concealed from the public eye. In terms of *Tartuffe*'s dénouement, and recalling the sage Uranie's remark in the *Critique* concerning those who foolishly convict themselves of the faults whose comic portrayal they decry (207), *Tartuffe* is about self-denouncing enemies known to King and public alike "under another name," as the president Lamoignon, the prince de Conti, or archbishop Bossuet.

This leads to a further point. Though the attack was immediately directed at Molière as "un démon incarné" condemned to everlasting hellfire, the controversy provided a pretext for reviving the dormant "querelle de la moralité du théâtre" provisionally laid to rest a generation earlier by Richelieu and Louis XIII. The issues surrounding Molière personally quickly engulf theater as a whole, of which Molière himself henceforth becomes the most clearly visible symbol. [26] This was in part a renewal of ancient Christian prejudice, one of the few issues on which both Catholic and Protestant commentators could agree. [27] As religious authorities had urged from the early Fathers down to the Counter-Reformation's Carlo Borromeo and the Calvinist Prynne, the essence of theater is an art of lies, pretence, deceit whose hellish nature is revealed just by its power to persuade a gullible public of fictional beliefs inimical to the purity of Faith. But it was also motivated by the new self-confi-

---

[26] See Mallet, *Molière*, pt. 1, chap. 7, "La Querelle du *Tartuffe*" and Fumaroli, *Héros et orateurs* 485-91. In an encomium of "Louis XIV le plus glorieux de tous les rois du monde" (1664), the curate Pierre Roullé disdains to call Molière by name, citing him simply as "[u]n homme, ou plutôt un démon vêtu de chair et habillé en homme" (Pléiade *Œuvres complètes* 1.1143).

[27] Barish, *Antitheatrical Prejudice*, demonstrates the ecumenism pious Christians achieve on this point. See too Fumaroli, savoring the ironic unanimity that leads the Calvinist William Prynne's *Histriomastix* (1631) to cite the same encyclopedic range of early Church authorities as the Counter-Reformation's St. Carlo Borromeo (*Héros et orateurs* 452-53).

dence of the lay civilization of which, as Richelieu grasped, theater is the most prestigious exponent. The very polish theatrical production achieves, purging the stage of the vulgar "license" that characterizes French drama before the reforms the cardinal's Academy undertakes, reinforces its corrupting influence.

Consider the following passage from the Jansenist Pierre Nicole's *Traité de la comédie*. According to Nicole, theater

> est un métier où des hommes & des femmes representent des passions de haine, de colere, d'ambition, de vengeance, & principalement d'amour. Il faut qu'ils les expriment le plus naturellement, & le plus vivement qu'il leur est possible; & ils ne le sçauroient faire s'ils ne les excitent en quelque sorte en eux-mêmes, & si leur ame ne se les imprime, pour les exprimer exterieurement par les gestes, & par les paroles. Il faut donc que ceux qui representent une passion d'amour en soient en quelque sorte touchez pendant qu'ils la representent. Or il ne faut pas s'imaginer que l'on puisse effacer de son esprit cette impression qu'on y a excitée volontairement, & qu'elle ne laisse pas en nous une grande disposition à cette même passion qu'on a bien voulu ressentir. Ainsi la Comédie par sa nature est une école & un exercice de vice, puis qu'elle oblige necessairement à exciter en soi-même des passions vicieuses. Que si l'on considère que toute la vie des Comediens est occupée dans cet exercice: qu'ils la passent tout entiere à apprendre en particulier, ou à repeter entr'eux, ou à representer devant des spectateurs, l'image de quelque vice; qu'ils n'ont presque autre chose dans l'esprit que ces folies; on verra facilement qu'il est impossible d'allier ce métier avec la pureté de nôtre Religion. [28]

A first point is that Nicole targets theater in its most noble form: the passions he catalogues (hate, anger, ambition, vengeance, above all love) are preeminently symptoms of heroic tragedy. We are then in the realm of Corneille's *Le Cid*, a play the focus of heat-

---

[28] Nicole, *Traité de la comédie* 41-42. See Apostolidès's commentary (*Le prince sacrifié* 49-50) on a comparable passage later in the *Traité* concerning the impact actors produce on the audience: "[l]e diable se contente aussi quelquefois de remplir la memoire de ces images, sans passer plus avant, & sans en former encore aucune tentation sensible; mais ensuite après un long temps il les excite & les réveille, sans même qu'on se souvienne comment elles y sont entrées, afin de leur faire porter des fruits de mort, *ut fructificent morti*." (47)

THE PROFESSION OF HYPOCRISY

ed censure precisely owing to what observers took to be the cynical bait-and-switch that allows Chimène to conceal an unnatural desire for her father's murderer behind the mask of noble sacrifice. Beyond furnishing a worldly distraction from the care of the soul that ought to be a Christian's unique concern, theater panders to appetites all the more reprehensible for the idealized forms of speech and conduct with which players and poets disguise them. The new-found decorum and respectability that enable "even women" to attend the public playhouse without fear of blame or scandal [29] is fresh proof of the art's diabolical subtlety.

But more telling than this standard objection is Nicole's analysis of the *craft* involved. Whatever its conscious moral aim, persuasive performance demands that actors "express" the passions in which drama trades "in the most natural and lively way they can," a goal achieved by reproducing the external "gestures" and "words" that communicate the inner state of the "mind" or "soul." At one level, this requires mastering the psycho-physical machinery of emotion described in Descartes's *Passions de l'âme*. The profession of acting incorporates a physical discipline exactly comparable to the Cartesian system of expression the academic artist Charles LeBrun lays out in his famous *Conférence sur l'expression générale et particulière* and the physiognomic studies illustrating its findings (fig. 6). Like the successful painter, the actor relates each passion to the precise physical movements the natural mechanics of emotion transmit to the bodily vessel through which emotion operates. [30]

However, as a painter rather than actor, LeBrun maintains a critical mental distance from what he represents. In portraying the passions, he commits their motions to a medium detached from his own body, depicting without feeling them. This spares him the risk of undergoing the mechanical action whose physical symptoms he delineates. By contrast, for the actor, expressive aims and expressive medium are the same: the very body that conveys emotion reproduces the movements it imitates. This leads Nicole to insist that, in or-

---

[29] See Mongrédien, *Vie quotidienne des comédiens*, pt. 1, chaps. 1 and 2.
[30] On the physiological expression of the passions, see Descartes, *Passions de l'âme*, pt. 2, arts. 96-136, in *Œuvres philosophiques* 3.1027-52. On artistic applications of Descartes's theory, see Norman Bryson, *Word and Image: French Painting of the Ancien Régime* (Cambridge: Cambridge University Press, 1981), chap. 2, "The Legible Body: LeBrun."

Figure 6. *La Colère.* Engraved illustration from Charles Le Brun, *Conféren-ce sur l'expression générale et particulière des passions* (1698; Verona, 1751). By permission of the Houghton Library, Harvard University

der to express the passions "in the most natural and lively way they can," actors have no choice but to "excite" them in their own hearts, causing the soul to "imprint them" in its own substance. The nature of their calling exposes actors to a curious process of mechanical reaction: the reproduction of the words and gestures that communicate the passions to the public provokes a corresponding internal change by which the soul contracts the feelings it portrays. By an iron law of psychic mechanics, the voluntary portrayal of emotion has the involuntary consequence of inscribing that emotion in the soul: *ex*-pression becomes *im*-pression, producing a "disposition to the very passion one has consented to feel," a disposition it is otiose even to "imagine one may efface from the mind." Worse yet, rather than mitigating passion's hold on the mind, the discipline of acting compounds the contagion. The labor of memorization and apprenticeship necessary to perfect the actor's craft locks its practitioners into ceaseless communion with the "vices" it is their job to represent. Their "entire life" thus revolves around the passions: "they spend the whole of it in learning the image of some vice in private, or in rehearsing it together, or in representing it before spectators," with the result that "they have almost nothing but such follies in mind." Whether unwittingly or with malice aforethought, theater is of necessity a "school" for vice, spawning feelings inimical to the "purity of our Religion."

What is true even of the noble tragedies Nicole has in mind is all the more so of Moliéresque comedy since, deprived of the tendentious alibis of heroic fiction, its nature is more transparent. In the "public mirror" defense he invokes throughout the controversies of *L'Ecole des femmes* and *Tartuffe*, Molière may pretend to ridicule the "vices of the age" in order that, by laughing at, we may recognize ourselves in them and reform our conduct accordingly; his plays nonetheless encourage a moral laxity whose measure is just the indulgent laughter they inspire. This is why, for the *dévots* and their *mondain* allies, off-color jokes like *L'Ecole*'s "tarte à la crème" or obscenely dangling masculine article ("le...") inevitably turn into the derisive caricature of proper morals contained in Arnolphe's parodic homily on the duties of a wife. And this is also why, in the person of *Tartuffe*'s devout "impostor," Molière perversely attributes theater's vices to theater's enemies themselves, a satanic inversion in which both theater and the poet reveal their true diabolical face.

The charge has a certain justice. Molière complains in the preface of the double bind his adversaries put him in. According to the *dévots*, one proof of his irreligion is the mere fact of putting the language of faith in a hypocrite's mouth. In the first seduction scene, the comic effect turns on the burlesque fusion of Tartuffe's adulterous desires with the conventions of prayer, turning two-faced praise of the Creator into lascivious praise of the carnal creature:

> L'amour qui nous attache aux beautés éternelles
> N'étouffe pas en nous l'amour des temporelles;
> Nos sens facilement peuvent être charmés
> Des ouvrages parfaits que le ciel a formés.
> Ses attraits réfléchis brillent dans vos pareilles;
> Mais il étale en vous ses plus rares merveilles;
> Il a sur votre face épanché des beautés
> Dont les yeux sont surpris et les cœurs transportés;
> Et je n'ai pu vous voir, parfaite créature,
> Sans admirer en vous l'auteur de la nature.
>
> (3.3.933-42)

More egregious still is the second seduction scene, where lust's espousal of the idiom of faith implicates the Gallican Compagnie in the casuistical practices tarring ultramontane Jesuits:

> *Tartuffe*
>
> Si ce n'est que le ciel qu'à mes vœux on oppose,
> Lever un tel obstacle est à moi peu de chose;
> Et cela ne doit pas retenir votre cœur.

> *Elmire*
>
> Mais des arrêts du ciel on nous fait tant de peur!

> *Tartuffe*
>
> Je puis vous dissiper ces craintes ridicules,
> Madame, et je sais l'art de lever les scrupules.
> Le ciel défend, de vrai, certains contentements,
> Mais on trouve avec lui des accommodements.
> Selon divers besoins, il est une science
> D'étendre les liens de notre conscience,
> Et de rectifier le mal de l'action

Avec la pureté de notre intention.
De ces secrets, madame, on saura vous instruire;
Vous n'avez seulement qu'à vous laisser conduire.
Contentez mon désir, et n'ayez point d'effroi;
Je vous réponds de tout, et prends le mal sur moi.

(4.5.1481-96)

Molière counters the accusation by asking how else he could have proceeded?

On me reproche d'avoir mis des termes de piété dans la bouche de mon imposteur. Hé! pouvais-je m'en empêcher, pour bien représenter le caractère d'un hypocrite? Il suffit, ce me semble, que je fasse connaître les motifs criminels qui lui font dire les choses; et que j'en aie retranché les termes consacrés, dont on aurait eu peine à lui entendre faire un mauvais usage. – Mais il débite au quatrième acte une morale pernicieuse. – Mais cette morale est-elle quelque chose dont tout le monde n'eût les oreilles rebattues? Dit-elle rien de nouveau dans ma comédie? Et peut-on craindre que des choses si généralement détestées fassent quelque impression dans les esprits? Que je les rende dangereuses en les faisant monter sur le théâtre; qu'elles reçoivent quelque autorité de la bouche d'un scélérat? (256-57)

The hypocrite just *is* the Tartuffe-like creature who misappropriates the idiom of virtue for base private ends. The question then is not the terms the character uses, but what is intended by them. Though true and false *dévots* employ the same words, they do not mean the same thing; and it is the meaning, not the words, that Molière targets. It is thus unjust to condemn him for making Tartuffe speak as he does since this is the only way to picture a vice whose exposure is all the more needful given the pious mask it wears, erasing the line between true and false the play loyally claims to restore.

However, Molière's defense raises more problems than it solves. For a start, the double bind of which the poet complains exactly mirrors the one he crafts for the *dévots*. This is the sting in the tail of Uranie's account of comic portraits in the *Critique de L'Ecole des femmes*, adapting the classic Horatian distinction between the satire of "men" and that of "manners":

> Ces sortes de satires tombent directement sur les mœurs, et ne frappent les personnes que par réflexion. N'allons point nous appliquer nous-mêmes les traits d'une censure générale; et profitons de la leçon, si nous pouvons, sans faire semblant qu'on parle à nous. Toutes les peintures ridicules qu'on expose sur les théâtres doivent être regardées sans chagrin de tout le monde. Ce sont miroirs publics, où il ne faut jamais témoigner qu'on se voie; et c'est se taxer hautement d'un défaut, que se scandaliser qu'on le reprenne. (207)

In accord with the reflexive logic Uranie outlines, devout protest ratifies the alleged calumny since only a *faux dévot* would take umbrage at seeing another exposed on stage: the profession of scandalized shock convicts Molière's critics of the hypocrisy *Tartuffe* portrays. But what is this if not a rhetorical trap designed to reduce the pious to the helpless silence they allege to be Molière's objective from the first? Similarly, Molière's distinction between the words his character speaks and how he means them intensifies the question it brushes aside. We note, for instance, that while he says his play is animated by respect for "true" devotion, the only spokesperson for this elusive quality is no *dévot* at all, but the worldly *honnête homme* Cléante. Nor should it escape us that Cléante's praise of true piety is not only hedged by careful disclaimers of competence in theological matters, but is syntactically subordinate to the one skill he *does* feel competent to own, the power to tell a hypocrite when he sees one:

> Je ne suis point, mon frère, un docteur révéré;
> Et le savoir chez moi n'est pas tout retiré.
> Mais, un en mot, je sais, pour toute ma science,
> Du faux avec le vrai faire la différence.
> Et comme je ne vois nul genre de héros
> Qui soient plus à priser que les parfaits dévots,
> Aucune chose au monde et plus noble et plus belle
> Que la sainte ferveur d'un véritable zèle;
> Aussi ne vois-je rien qui soit plus odieux
> Que le dehors plâtré d'un zèle spécieux,
> Que ces francs charlatans, que ces dévots de place,
> De qui la sacrilège et trompeuse grimace
> Abuse impunément, et se joue, à leur gré,
> De ce qu'ont les mortels de plus saint et sacré.
>
> (1.5.351-64)

To be sure, in view of the misgivings surrounding even the reverent portrayal of saintly martyrs on the stage, leading the theorist Jules de la Mesnardière to proscribe martyr plays as inimical to tragic art,[31] decorum forbids the introduction of holy persons in comedy. But entrusting the defense of true piety to Cléante confirms the accusation the device counters: the comic stage leaves no room for devotion, exiling it to the fringes of ordinary secular intercourse comedy mimics. In the continuation of his efforts to reason with Orgon, Cléante cites a number of examples of genuinely pious men, stressing as one common feature a notably un-*cabale*-like reluctance to judge other people's conduct:

> Ils ne censurent point toutes nos actions,
> Ils trouvent trop d'orgueil dans ces corrections:
> Et, laissant la fierté des paroles aux autres,
> C'est par leurs actions qu'ils reprennent les nôtres.
> L'apparence du mal a chez eux peu d'appui,
> Et leur âme est portée à juger bien d'autrui.
> Point de cabale en eux, point d'intrigues à suivre;
> On les voit, pour tous soins, se mêler de bien vivre.
>
> (1.5.391-98)

And he further notes that people the more readily acknowledge their piety for their tractable *politesse*. The truly devout are then those whose piety conforms to the canons of good manners and good taste to which lay life confines it:

> Ce titre par aucun ne leur est débattu;
> Ce ne sont point du tout fanfarons de vertu;
> On ne voit point en eux ce faste insupportable,
> Et leur dévotion est humaine, est traitable.
>
> (1.5.387-90)

But the limits to which Molière's putative defense of true devotion condemns that elusive quantity appears most clearly in the dénouement where, under cover of resolving the legal issue between

---

[31] Jean de La Mesnardière, *La Poëtique* (1639; Paris: Antoine Sommaville, 1640) 109. On the general debate surrounding the "comédie de dévotion," see Couton's "notice" to Corneille's *Polyeucte*, in *Œuvres complètes* 1.1628-33.

Tartuffe and Orgon, the play submits the poet's dispute with his pious enemies to royal arbitration. Consider again how the dénouement works. A quasi-liturgical consecration of the King, the scene not only recalls who the sovereign is, but *praises* him for so being: in addition to performing his Majesty's bidding, the *exempt* extols that majesty's source in Louis's wisdom, justice, and unstinting love for his people. This too conforms to accepted proprieties: though motivated by the King's dramatic role as the *deus ex machina* required to achieve a happy ending, panegyric is the only idiom in which a reigning prince *can* be invoked. This produces a degree of equivocation in that the figure the *exempt* extols in such extravagant terms is the royal persona rather than the concrete individual whose service as *deus ex machina* remains an inherently implausible dramatic convention. And the text further equivocates in recalling the absolutist myth of the King's Two Bodies, a doctrine that mediates the gap between public role and private person by positing a princely gemination and the heroic sacrifice it enjoins. But the play's equivocation is also a resource: by praising the King for being what the *exempt* so fulsomely praises him for being, it attempts at a deeper level to school him in the symbolic identity he truly possesses only insofar as he rises to the occasion for which the play lauds him.

We return to the finale's complex performativeness and the way this structures the action from the start. The dénouement reproduces the rite of consecration by which both King and state are constituted in the royal dictum, "l'état, c'est moi." In the process, however, it unpacks the godlike attributes the King both owns and acquires as a circular condition of the transubstantiation of which he is the vehicle and beneficiary. But this in turn enables Molière to define the King's position in his quarrel with the *dévots*. Because the play's Louis is so godlike, penetrating Tartuffe's identity, well known to him "under another name" as the *cabale* that besets his loyal poet, he further recognizes his own best interest and his associated duties *as prince*. What shows the King to be the King the play praises him for being is his defense of the state as that secular space the *dévots* perfidiously subvert.

This relates to a point implicit in what we have already seen: Orgon and family are a microcosm of the nation Louis personifies. [32] The identification is based in the first instance on the typological convention linking Father and King, and thus Nature and Law. But convention is reinforced by topical parallels. Not only does Tartuffe stand for the *cabale* directed by the Compagnie du Saint-Sacrement whose powerful influence at court during this early stage of his personal reign Louis resented; Tartuffe's ally in his efforts to control Orgon, the blind and intolerant Mme Pernelle, strikingly resembles the dowager Queen, the belatedly pious Anne d'Autriche, whose death in 1666 helps clear the way for the play's entry into the public repertoire. Orgon is thus an image of the King as he is, only "worse": a minatory comic double for the "better" King the dénouement shows Louis to be. The threat Tartuffe embodies hangs over the King himself as well as his kingdom, the two being by ritual conflation one and the same. The play enlists the monarch's support in a struggle biographical allusion portrays as his own.

The binding element is *theater*. As Fumaroli points out, the dénouement is the last in a series of *mises en abyme* whose key lies in the second seduction scene (4.5), where Orgon's loyal wife allows the impostor to make love to her in the presence of her husband hidden beneath a table to overhear what passes. [33] In the transgendered person of Elmire, whose name defiantly encodes the insulting anagramme "Elomire" of Donneau de Visé's *Zélinde*, [34] the heroine fulfils for her spouse the office the play as a whole performs for the King. Picking up another hint encoded in the heroine's name, the Old French for physician (*mire*) attested by "Le vilein mire," the *fabliau* on which *Le Médecin malgré lui* is based, the task assigned Molière's female double is *therapeutic*. And the

---

[32] See esp. Fumaroli, *Héros et orateurs* 488-91, but this point also informs Gossman and Greenberg's readings of the play.

[33] Fumaroli, *Héros et orateurs* 488-91.

[34] The character Oriane launches the distorted name in scene 3. See Jean Donneau de Visé, *Zélinde ou La Véritable Critique de l'Ecole des femmes*, rpt. in Georges Mongrédien (ed.), *La Querelle de l'Ecole des femmes* 1.18. The name stuck, figuring in parodies and attacks down to Le Boulanger de Chalussay's *Elomire hypocondre ou les médecins vengez* (1670). Molière retaliates in *L'Impromtu de Versailles*. Mlle de Brie mentions "une pièce contre Molière, que les grands comédiens [the Hôtel de Bourgogne] vont jouer," and Molière replies, "Il est vrai, on me l'a voulu lire; et c'est un nommé Br... Brou... Broussaut qui l'a faite." (220) It is tempting to infer that poor Brousault was targeted because he stammered.

instrument she deploys to a therapeutic end is the *mirror* inscribed in the verbs *mirer* and *admirer*: a device whose power to reveal its patient's face provokes the admiring wonder Aristotle took to be the beginning of knowledge and wisdom.[35]

Elmire's name also recalls the Lacanian phenomenon of *mirage*.[36] It is important from this viewpoint that the second seduction scene turns on a pretence. Tartuffe's first attempt on Elmire's honor provokes an immediate rebuff, reinforced by ironic blackmail: Elmire promises to conceal Tartuffe's indiscretion on condition that he renounce her daughter's hand in marriage (3.3). By contrast, Elmire invites the second attempt by feigning the desire Tartuffe wishes. Her therapeutic work ambiguously preys on a narcissistic self-approbation as deluded as Orgon's own, inducing her victim to lower the guard naturally raised by her earlier rejection. Further, the cure she administers to her husband relies on the same idolatrous *amour-propre* that Tartuffe exploits to swindle him of wife, wealth, and good name.[37] But in her case, the mirage acts as a

---

[35] Aristotle, *Metaphysics* 982b. Descartes makes the same point in the *Passions de l'âme*, pt. 2, art. 75, "A quoi sert particulièrement l'admiration."

[36] "Mirage" is the objective correlative of "l'imaginaire"; more generally, "mirage" is the *world itself* in that the projections, transferences, and symbolic substitutions, condensations, and displacements "l'imaginaire" continuously operates form the medium through which we inhabit the world at all. What we might call Elmire's "experiment" with Orgon's "experience" (in French the two words are the same) represents a proto-Lacanian reinterpretation of two major *topoi* of early modern letters: "life is a stage" and "life is a dream." Or rather, if "life is a stage," thereby enabling theater both to mirror and to manipulate it as efficiently as Elmire does, it is because, thanks to the mechanisms psychoanalysis describes, "life" is quite literally "a dream." See Lacan's *Le Moi*, lecture 21, "Sosie," 301-16 and the whole development in *Les quatre concepts fondamentaux*. The machinery of unconscious repetition (lectures 2-5) leads to the "anamorphic" properties of vision and "le regard" as the internalized (and therefore imaginary) yet indigestibly alien token ("le petit objet *a*") by which the Real makes its presence known (6-9). This leads in turn to the phenomena of transference, resistance, and drive at once registered and precipitated by the "presence of the analyst" (10-15); to the constitution of the subject in the "field of the Other" and the twin processes of alienation and "anaphisis," i.e., the experience of "fading" or "disappearance" that reveal self's character as mirage (16-17); and finally, following a discussion of the *counter*-transference at work in psychoanalytic interpretation (18-19), to what all of this proves not only about self, but about *analysis*, i.e., what the whole development *presupposes*: "en toi plus que toi." (20)

[37] Both Gossman and Greenberg speak to this, as to its corollary: the irony with which Orgon's "false" idol is replaced by a "true" one.

Galenic counter-poison, killing the toxin by exposing it to a surfeit of its own substance. Orgon's confrontation with the humiliating spectacle of his shame breaks through his narcissistic defenses to restore the psychic clarity Tartuffe's gross flattery clouds. But in turning the image of the invasive foreign body into the antigen that mobilizes self-love in its own defense, she demonstrates the self-correcting powers theater grants the secular order it typifies. Theater mends the world by replicating it. In the process, it institutes a homeostatic autonomy that eliminates the need to which religion arrogates the exclusive right to minister. In the profane perspective the scene implicitly espouses on theater's behalf, religion is either politely sidelined, and thereby rendered harmlessly "human" and "tractable," or it assumes the likeness of the pious parasite who feeds on its secular host.

The *dévots* are thus quite right to suspect Molière's motives, alleging a duplicitousness that gives the lie to the comic *bonhommie* that meets us at first glance. But the interpretive problems this raises engage far more than conscious motives. They speak to the very nature of theatrical art, anticipating an idea that Denis Diderot develops a century later in the chameleonlike person of the Neveu de Rameau.

By the time the Neveu comments on it in the 1780s, *Tartuffe* is already firmly lodged in the canon, so much so as initially to appear as one in a series of "classics" whose formal perfection and high-minded moral purpose are taken for granted. This in fact gives the Neveu's commentary its peculiar bite as a generational settling of accounts with the *grands classiques* to whose authoritative example Diderot elsewhere suggests their epigones in his own time are slavishly in thrall. [38] Still, mixed as Diderot's motives may be, the Neveu's interpretation is arresting. For the Neveu does not claim that classic works like *Tartuffe* do not deserve the stature accorded them; he claims rather that they have been systematically *misread*

---

[38] In comparing English and French acting styles, the dialogue's first speaker explains how actors' performances are conditioned by national verse forms. This indirectly characterizes the not only metric, but emotional and thematic bondage poets share with the actors who perform their plays. We shall return to this issue in chap. 6. See Denis Diderot, "Paradoxe sur le comédien," in *Paradoxe sur le comédien, précédé des Entretiens sur le Fils naturel,* ed. Raymond Laubreaux (Paris: Flammarion, 1981) 126-27. Subsequent references appear in the text.

precisely on the score of the moral rectitude their canonic status obliges us to impute them.

The dialogue's right-minded narrator, a person the text ironically designates as "Moi," is led at one point to observe that, for all his folly, venality, and inconsequence, his interlocutor is at times a shrewd judge of character:

> J'étais quelquefois surpris de la justesse des observations de ce fou, sur les hommes et sur les caractères; et je le lui témoignai.
>
> C'est, me répondit-il, qu'on tire parti de la mauvaise compagnie, comme du libertinage. On est dédommagé de la perte de son innocence, par celle de ses préjugés. Dans la société des méchants, où le vice se montre à masque levé, on apprend à les connaître. Et puis j'ai un peu lu.
>
> MOI. –Qu'avez-vous lu?
>
> LUI. –J'ai lu et je lis et relis sans cesse Théophraste, La Bruyère et Molière.
>
> MOI. –Ce sont d'excellents livres.
>
> LUI. –Ils sont bien meilleurs qu'on ne pense; mais qui est-ce qui sait les lire?
>
> MOI. –Tout le monde, selon la mesure de son esprit.
>
> LUI. –Presque personne. Pourriez-vous me dire ce qu'on y cherche?
>
> MOI. –L'amusement et l'instruction.
>
> LUI. –Mais quelle instruction; car c'est là le point?
>
> MOI. –La connaissance de ses devoirs; l'amour de la vertu; la haine du vice.
>
> LUI. –Moi, j'y recueille tout ce qu'il faut faire, et tout ce qu'il ne faut pas dire. Ainsi quand je lis L'Avare, je me dis: sois avare, si tu veux; mais garde-toi de parler comme l'avare. Quand je lis le Tartuffe, je me dis: sois hypocrite, si tu veux; mais ne parle pas comme l'hypocrite. Garde des vices qui te sont utiles; mais n'en aie ni le ton ni les apparences qui te rendraient ridicule. Pour se garantir de ce ton, de ces apparences, il faut les connaître. Or, ces auteurs en ont fait des peintures excellentes. Je suis moi et je reste ce que je suis; mais j'agis et je parle comme il convient. [39]

Like the accomplished actor, musician, mime, and (when need arises) hypocrite he is, the Neveu underscores a technical dilemma

---

[39] Denis Diderot, Le Neveu de Rameau, ed. Jean-Claude Bonnet (Paris: Flammarion, 1983) 91-92. Subsequent references appear in the text.

at the heart of *Tartuffe*. Especially given the universally endorsed conventions of theatrical mimesis, the classical demand for "truth to nature" conceived as the indiscernible replica of the world the-ater represents, how does one portray a hypocrite? As the Neveu reminds us, the essence of the hypocrite is to *pass undetected*: the *true* hypocrite, the sinister genuine article, is indistinguishable from the role he or she plays. It is then in the nature of a Tartuffe, like the actor who both plays and resembles him, to be taken *à la lettre*, as and for the virtuous other he counterfeits.

This produces the Neveu's counter-canonical reading. The re-markable thing about Molière's Tartuffe is that he *fails* to pass undetected; it is in fact all too obvious that Tartuffe is an impostor. This is indeed what makes Tartuffe "ridiculous." It is also why we laugh at his victim Orgon. Confronted with Orgon's astonishing fail-ure to see Tartuffe for what he is, a frustrated Cléante does not *argue* the point since it is perfectly self-evident; Orgon's own description of his first meeting with Tartuffe, offered as evidence of the para-site's unparalleled piety, could not speak more plainly to the case:

> Ah! Si vous aviez vu comme j'en fis rencontre,
> Vous auriez pris pour lui l'amitié que je montre.
> Chaque jour à l'église il venait, d'un air doux,
> Tout vis-à-vis de moi se mettre à deux genoux.
> Il attirait les yeux de l'assemblée entière
> Par l'ardeur dont au ciel il poussait sa prière;
> Il faisait des soupirs, de grands élancements,
> Et baisait humblement la terre à tous moments;
> Et, lorsque je sortais, il me devançait vite
> Pour m'aller, à la porte, offrir de l'eau bénite.
>
> (1.5.281-90)

Tartuffe's strategic placement "tout vis-à-vis de moi," ostenta-tiously kneeling in a posture that ambiguously suggests devoted worship *of* as well as *before* Orgon; the melodramatic "ejaculations" and prostrations that obtrude on everyone's notice; his pointed haste in scurrying ahead of Orgon to sprinkle holy water on his head: all infallibly mark the theatrical and therefore hypocritical character of the impostor's conduct. Whence Cléante's helpless dis-may at Orgon's obstinate refusal to acknowledge what could not be more transparent:

Hé quoi! Vous ne ferez nulle distinction
Entre l'hypocrisie et la dévotion?
Vous les voulez traiter d'un semblable langage,
Et rendre même honneur au masque qu'au visage;
Egaler l'artifice à la sincérité,
Confondre l'apparence avec la vérité,
Estimer le fantôme autant que la personne,
Et la fausse monnaie à l'égal de la bonne?

(1.5.331-38)

But this is in turn just what, from the Neveu's point of view, makes Tartuffe's self-denouncing *comédie* so instructive. Everything that makes his conduct so blatant as to provoke derision at both Tartuffe and Orgon's expense illustrates what a hypocrite must avoid. In his extravagant performance in the role of a *dévot*, Tartuffe falls into the trap of merely *playing the hypocrite*. Far then from revealing what a hypocrite looks like and how we might distinguish one from the virtuous personage he or she pretends to be, Tartuffe shows what hypocrites should *not* look like, namely, the hypocrites they are.

The Neveu's counter-canonical reading has an important corollary, however. As we have seen, Molière protests his innocence of impiety: far from portraying true devotion as mere hypocrisy, he aims to teach us how to tell the two apart, unmasking the evil for the public good. But as the Neveu insidiously hints, the true conduct of a true hypocrite *cannot* be unmasked. If Tartuffe's hypocrisy is so transparent as to convict his victim of willful self-deceit, Molière cannot mean to depict a *genuine* hypocrite at all, but rather a botched copy so obvious only Orgon could be fooled. What Molière presents in the guise of a true is in fact a *false* hypocrite, and Molière is *himself* a hypocrite to pretend otherwise. [40]

---

[40] Once again, Rochement nails it: "Certes, il faut avouër que Moliere est luy-mesme un Tartuffe achevé par un veritable Hypocrite, et qu'il ressemble à ces Comediens dont parle Seneque, qui corrompoient de son temps les mœurs, sous pretexte de les reformer, et qui, sous couleur de reprendre le vice, l'insinuoient adroitement dans les esprits." And a little later: "Certes, c'est bien à faire à Moliere de parler de la devotion, avec laquelle il a si peu de commerce et qu'il n'a jamais connuë ny par pratique ny par theorie. L'hypocrite et le devot ont une mesme aparence, ce n'est qu'une mesme chose dans le public, il n'y a que l'interieur qui les distingue, et afin *de ne point laisser d'equivoque, et d'oster tout ce qui peut confondre*

This is of course a paradox of the sort to which Diderot was addicted, a deliberately perverse idea calculated to puzzle and shock; one moreover he kept carefully under wraps since the dialogue remained unpublished until Goethe's German translation of 1805, twenty years after the author's death. Nor do I think that Diderot seriously intends us to convict Molière of the hypocrisy the Neveu alleges. The point rather is to uncover a deeper and more pervasive phenomenon of which hypocrisy is a special case: the radical intransparency of human acts and motives that an accomplished hypocrite exploits. If hypocrisy is possible, it is because, in real life as in theater, it is in the nature of human relations that all we ever know of other people is how they behave. This is indeed what makes theater so persuasive, leading Molière and Diderot's contemporaries to conceive it as the most perfect kind of mimesis, capturing the very form of human experience. But this also means that the "real life" theater imitates is *itself* theatrical, as intractably elusive and equivocal as the hypocrisy Molière and Diderot invoke as its model.

The case the Neveu makes bears on the account of the art of acting Diderot offers in another dialogue, the *Paradoxe sur le comédien*. The first speaker begins by challenging naïve assumptions about acting the general public shares with Nicole. Nicole takes it for granted that a "natural" and "lively" portrait of the passions in which theater traffics demands that actors "excite" them in their own hearts. This prompts the mechanical reversal by which players actively acquire the emotions of hate, anger, ambition, vengeance, or love they represent, losing their own voluntary identities by absorption in their roles. The medium of this transformation is what Diderot's period calls "sensibility": to give a truly convincing picture of the passions, actors must *feel* them since what spectators witness (the words actors speak; their tones of voice; their gestures, movements, countenances) is the automatized *expression* of such feelings.

Against this view, the first speaker elaborates the paradox of the dialogue's title. Supported by colorful anecdotes from backstage life, and most memorably one in which, unnoticed by the audience,

---

le bien et le mal [a citation of Molière's first petition to the King], il devoit faire voir ce que le Devot fait en secret, aussi-bien que l'hypocrite." Mongrédien (ed.), *Comédies et pamphlets sur Molière* 85, 87-88.

a pair of actors conduct a furious quarrel in the midst of performing a love scene (142-44), he argues that the actors who most persuade us of the truth of what they perform are in fact those who
feel the least. Among "les premières qualités" that make an accomplished player is the *insensibility* required for disciplined self-
observation and self-control:

> je lui veux beaucoup de jugement; il me faut dans cet homme un
> spectateur froid et tranquille; j'en exige, par conséquent, de la
> pénétration et nulle sensibilité, l'art de tout imiter, ou, ce qui re-
> vient au même, une égale aptitude à toutes sortes de caractères et
> de rôles. (127-28)

If spectators are moved, it is just because the actors who move them
are not:

> Nous sentons, nous; eux, ils observent, étudient et peignent...
> La sensibilité n'est guère la qualité d'un grand génie. Il aimera la
> justice; mais il exercera cette vertu sans en recueillir la douceur.
> Ce n'est pas son cœur, c'est sa tête qui fait tout. A la moindre
> circonstance inopinée, l'homme sensible la perd; il ne sera ni
> un grand roi, ni un grand ministre, ni un grand capitaine, ni un
> grand avocat, ni un grand médecin. Remplissez la salle du spec-
> tacle de ces pleureurs-là, mais ne m'en placez aucun sur la scène.
> (131)

What we take for a faithful image of real life is the product of a
profound misprision grounded in the actor's power to manipulate
our responses to what we see and hear; and this is possible only insofar as actors remain detached, coldly calculating the effect their
words, gestures, expressions, and tones have on the assembled audience:

> Les larmes du comédien descendent de son cerveau; celles de
> l'homme sensible montent de son cœur: ce sont les entrailles qui
> troublent sans mesure la tête de l'homme sensible; c'est la tête
> du comédien qui porte quelquefois un trouble passager dans ses
> entrailles; il pleure comme un prêtre incrédule qui prêche la Pas-
> sion; comme un séducteur aux genoux d'une femme qu'il n'aime
> pas, mais qu'il veut tromper; comme un gueux dans la rue ou à

la porte d'une église, qui vous injurie lorsqu'il désespère de vous toucher; ou comme une courtisane qui ne sent rien, mais qui se pâme entre vos bras. (133-34)

This departure from natural expectations is not just a matter of technique; it reveals the very nature of theatrical "truth." However closely it resembles life outside the playhouse, "ce qu'on appelle au théâtre *être vrai*" remains crucially different. Were theater in fact to show us "les choses comme elles sont en nature," instead of "truth," we would get the merely *banal*: "Le vrai en ce sens ne serait que le commun." Rather than being convinced and moved, we would be put off:

> Une femme malheureuse, et vraiment malheureuse, pleure et ne vous touche point: il y a pis, c'est qu'un trait léger qui la défigure vous fait rire; c'est qu'un accent qui lui est propre dissone à votre oreille et vous blesse; c'est qu'un mouvement qui lui est habituel vous montre sa douleur ignoble et maussade; c'est que les passions outrées sont presque toutes sujettes à des grimaces que l'artiste sans goût copie servilement, mais que le grand artiste évite. (137)

Far from conforming to natural truth, what audiences savor as "true" is "la conformité des actions, des discours, de la figure, de la voix, du mouvement, du geste, avec un modèle idéal imaginé par le poète, et souvent exagéré par le comédien." (137) Instead of what we take for life as it *is* we get life as it *should* be, life as we *want* it to be, heightened, magnified, clarified to satisfy the desire to escape the graceless clutter of common experience that sends us to the theater in the first place. Like Molière's Orgon, we are moved and convinced to the precise extent that theater persuades us of a truth we are all the more ready to believe because it *flatters* us:

> Nous voulons qu'au plus fort des tourments l'homme garde le caractère d'homme, la dignité de son espèce. Quel est l'effet de cet effort héroïque? de distraire de la douleur et de la tempérer. Nous voulons que cette femme tombe avec décence, avec mollesse, et que ce héros meure comme le gladiateur ancien, au milieu de l'arène, aux applaudissements du cirque, avec grâce, avec noblesse, dans une attitude élégante et pittoresque. Qui est-ce

qui remplira notre attente? Sera-ce l'athlète que la douleur sub-
jugue et que la sensibilité décompose? Ou l'athlète académisé
qui se possède et pratique les leçons de la gymnastique en ren-
dant le dernier soupir? Le gladiateur ancien, comme un grand
comédien, un grand comédien, ainsi que le gladiateur ancien, ne
meurent pas comme on meurt sur un lit, mais sont tenus de nous
jouer une autre mort pour nous plaire, et le spectateur délicat
sentirait que la vérité nue, l'action dénuée de tout apprêt serait
mesquine et contrasterait avec la poésie du reste. (137-38)

The idealized "exaggerations" of theatrical truth serve the *communicative* function required to ensure that spectators understand
what the actor portrays, and thus what they are to believe in. Austin
makes the point in a paper on "pretending" one of whose aims is to
challenge a behaviorist theory of feeling or emotion (and thereby,
more broadly, of personal identity) that minimizes the distinction
between "acting" in the broad sense of doing or behaving and "being" construed as what one is, really or genuinely, regardless of how
one acts. Austin imagines the case of a man called on to pretend to
be angry. [41] Such a man may well be the kind of person who keeps
his emotions to himself: rather than break out in self-evidently chol-
eric symptoms (raising his voice, scowling, stamping his foot), he
more naturally *smothers* his feelings, seeking revenge in an icy irony
all the more satisfying for eluding its target's notice. In order then
to pretend to be angry, such a man would not act the way he does

---

[41] J.L. Austin, "Pretending," *Philosophical Papers*, 2nd ed., J.O. Urmson & G.J.
Warnock (Oxford: Oxford University Press, 1970) 253-71. Note that while Austin's
immediate target is behaviorism, he does not endorse a simple-minded "mentalist"
alternative. The point rather is the impossibility of drawing the kind of hard-and-
fast line both sides in the mentalism/behaviorism debate want to. This explains
what Felman gets wrong in her otherwise brilliant extrapolations from Austin's theory of performatives. In acknowledging that truth is always "an act" in the sense of
a *doing* or *making*, we are not thereby committed to the punning conclusion that it
is *just* "an act"–simulation, illusion, pretence. As suggested by a paper on "Truth"
(ibid. 117-33) Felman does not discuss in her book, and again in *How to Do Things
with Words* (140-47), Austin urges us to distinguish between what we might call
"local" and "general" uses of the term: the meaning of the word "truth," and thus
the conditions we must satisfy in order to claim we *have* it, is always a local function
of context and purpose. Felman sins against the underlying "doctrine" in two ways:
first by generalizing; second, *in* generalizing, by *hypostasizing*, i.e., by speaking (as,
to be fair, French grammar obliges her to) of "*the* truth," "*la* vérité." This does not
correct the complementary errors of positivists and idealists; it *reproduces* it.

when *truly* so, for this would defeat the point of the exercise. Even setting aside the question of whether his audience is to be *convinced* of what he pretends, pretending to be angry means conveying at least what it is he pretends; and this in turn requires expressing or, more precisely, *signifying* what the feeling is–by raising his voice, scowling, stamping his foot.

Performance must be larger than life as a reflex of the communicative act that enables witnesses to tell what it is they witness. In this sense, the self-denouncing excess Orgon describes in relating his first meeting with Tartuffe reproduces the performance the impostor's role demands. As the Neveu reminds us, a successful hypocrite would never reveal his hand in this way. But by the same token, we would not know that he *was* a hypocrite and would therefore fail to draw the distinctions that are so obvious to Orgon's brother-in-law. To convey Tartuffe's hypocrisy, the actor must then overdo it in just the way Orgon describes, giving us the *square* of simulated devotion needed to recognize simulation as such. Such is moreover the testimony of the textual history of Molière's play itself. Rewriting *Tartuffe* at least twice before giving it the form in which we know it today, Molière expanded the original version mounted at Versailles in 1664, inserting two full acts of disambiguating exposition before allowing the title character on stage at all.[42]

All of this confirms the insight the first speaker promotes from the start. The passage contrasting the audience's overactive sensibility with the cold calculation acting demands concludes with a curious equivocation. Whereas, on stage, the "insensible" actor's "head does everything," the "man of sensibility" *loses* his "at the least unexpected circumstance." As a result, the latter "will be neither a great king, nor a great minister, nor a great captain, nor a great advocate, nor a great doctor. Fill the auditorium with cry-babies like that, but don't put any of them on the stage." Read one way, the passage draws a parallel between what it takes to be a great actor and what it takes to be a great *anything*: in whatever realm, greatness demands a cool head; the man who fails to master his emotions

---

[42] For a concise account of *Tartuffe*'s composition history, which is coterminous with that of the quarrel the play provoked, see Couton's "notice" in the Pléiade *Œuvres complètes* 834-47.

fails to master events as greatness must. However, the context makes it unclear what *part* we are to understand the "man of sensibility" to play. The syntax suggests it is his role outside the theater, as a *real* king, minister, captain, advocate, or physician: it is a question of what it takes to *be* rather than *play* a king or minister. On the other hand, the general context suggests not a real role, but a *performance*; the copula ("il ne sera") would then denote not "being," but "playing"–he will not *be* in the sense of *being taken for* the great man whose part he simulates.

The syntactical ambiguity that allows the second reading underscores the parallel discovered in the first. Since being and acting demand the same skill, being just *is* acting by another name; and indeed, a few lines later, this is exactly where Diderot takes us in a second parallel, ironically embroidering on the metaphor of the "great stage of the world":

> Dans la grande comédie, la comédie du monde, celle à laquelle j'en reviens toujours, toutes les âmes chaudes occupent le théâtre; tous les hommes de génie sont au parterre. Les premiers s'appellent des fous; les seconds, qui s'occupent à copier leurs folies, s'appellent des sages. C'est l'œil du sage qui saisit le ridicule de tant de personnages divers, qui le peint, et qui vous fait rire et de ces fâcheux originaux dont vous avez été la victime, et de vous-même. C'est lui qui vous observait, et qui traçait la copie comique et du fâcheux et de votre supplice. (131-32)

The Neveu's revisionist reading of *Tartuffe* draws the same moral. By arguing that the play is just the school for hypocrites the *dévots* claim, the Neveu grounds theatrical mimesis in the "comedy" of life itself. Hypocrisy and theater fuse in trading on the equivocally social character of human motives and identities. The Neveu goes on to observe that what "wounds" pious right-mindedness, offending public taste as well as morality, or better, the public taste we commonly take in morality's place, is less vice itself than the "air" and "tone" that give it away:

> Le vice ne blesse les hommes que par intervalle. Les caractères apparents du vice les blessent du matin au soir. Peut-être vaudrait-il mieux être un insolent que d'en avoir la physionomie; l'insolent de caractère n'insulte que de temps en temps; l'insolent de phsyionomie insulte toujours. (92)

This equivocal remark can also be read in two ways. A first denounces the hypocrisy infecting society as a whole construed as a masquerade in which what we praise or blame, value or revile, is never truth, but only *show*. A more generous reading adduces the dilemma Molière faces in dealing with hypocrisy itself: how does one portray a thing whose very nature consists in passing for something else? But the more generous reading proves the more radical. For if we are incapable of telling the difference between truth and simulation, it is because there is in the end no difference to tell. The "truth" and "nature" that, in the superficially more caustic interpretation of the Neveu's remark, seem concealed by social masquerade turn out, in the second, to be masquerade themselves. The "truth" of "nature" is its alienation in the truthless ground of performative social being.

Here at last we meet the central dilemma *Tartuffe* addresses, the social condition it tries to diagnose and cure only endlessly to reproduce its symptoms in the savage controversies that envelop it. What saves the play, making it even in its own day the monument Diderot's Neveu defaces, is an obstinate *act of faith*, this too enacted in its ambiguous dénouement. [43] If both the play and (albeit only within the performative limits of the finale) the attendant quarrel with the *dévots* come to an end, it is thanks to the monarch's intervention on his poet's behalf. The judicial gesture by which, in the person of the *exempt*, the King distinguishes with all the authority of absolute sovereignty between the bourgeois householder and the odious parasite is the same as that by which he discriminates between rival parties all the more difficult to tell apart in that each accuses the other of the hypocrisy to which social circumstance reduces both alike.

Molière's act of faith is moreover reflected in the comedy's formal as well as moral properties. The exclusive focus on Orgon's family assures a rigorous unity of place expressed in the adoption of a single scene throughout, the public chamber at the boundary between private home and public street where the family receives visitors. [44] Unity of time is achieved in the growing domestic crisis that,

---

[43] Compare with the role of *fides* in Lacan's "Sosie."
[44] Much could be made of the ambiguities of this threshold between "public" and "private" in light of Merlin's *Public et littérature*.

in galvanizing resistance to Tartuffe's extortions, precipitates the seizure of Orgon's property whose execution brings on the close. Above all is the unity of action embodied in the seamless dovetailing of time and place in the cathartic convulsion overtaking Orgon's family and in the symbolic identification of nation and household, father and monarch, theater and state, fusing comic text and social subtext in the happy ending comic convention mandates. Whatever else it may be, *Tartuffe* is a well-wrought play, exuding classical regularity in every aspect of structure, plot, and design.

And yet just because everything depends on an act of faith, a comic sacrament that rescues the situation only insofar as the participants credit it, the play remains at the mercy of events it cannot control. In particular, it submits the issue to the judgment of a King who proved unequal to the task to which the absolutist propaganda Molière rehearses calls him the more emphatically because absolutism left no alternative. All-seeing and all-mighty as Molière paints him, Louis was as powerless to force a decision as the competing parties that awaited his verdict. Louis did grant Molière a handsome pension and adopted the Illustre Théâtre as the royal company. Nevertheless, he left his loyal poet twisting in the wind for the full five years it took to grant the royal privilege that ended the quarrel once and for all.

The ultimate outcome of *Tartuffe* is thus a betrayal all the more bitter for the sacrifice Molière makes on the King's behalf. Especially when compared with the proud Cornelian model of dramatic authorship, there is something almost infantile in the supplicatory gesture with which the comic poet throws himself at the feet of the sovereign he helps constitute. But by the same token, the King is guilty of *breach of contract*. The loyal sacrifice the poet makes, entailing not only self-abasement, but the self-censorship observed in everything the play leaves out of the picture drawn of Louis's state, demands a return. As Hobbes specifically calls it in articulating the absolutist theory to which Corneille's *Cinna* draws Richelieu's attention, the voluntary "renunciation" of personal power expects an answering sacrifice on the King's part in order to engender the symbolic body that gives the state its redemptive form.[45] But this is just

---

[45] Thomas Hobbes, *Leviathan* (London: Everyman, 1914), chaps. 14-15.

what Molière fails to obtain even as he surrenders the means of doing anything about it.

2. TRUTH AS PERFORMANCE: DOM JUAN

We now come to *Dom Juan*, staged in February 1665, nine months after *Tartuffe*'s rancorous début and four years before its canonization in the form we enjoy today. As noted earlier, the explicit link between the two plays does not emerge until act 5. Yet *Dom Juan* explores the same ground from the first, but with this crucial difference. In *Tartuffe*, the hypocrite's exposure liquidates the threat to the moral and social order whose faithful embrace is enacted in the self-censoring regularity consummated in the play's sacramental dénouement. In the new play, the exposure *compounds* the problems the play raises, producing an uncontrollable symbolic outpouring deepened by a finale that, instead of solving, multiplies the dilemmas to which it responds. And as we might expect, the most obvious signs of *Dom Juan*'s problematic status are its enigmatic *artistic* properties, the trenchant irregularities of its overall plot and design.

Though composed at the apogee of French classicism, it is hard to imagine a less classical play than this. The action's crowded incidents exert tremendous pressure on the unity of time; looked at closely, *Dom Juan* far exceeds the natural span of twenty-four hours classical doctrine prescribes. With the Stone Guest's arrival for dinner at the end of act 4 in answer to the taunting invitation Dom Juan extends on first visiting his tomb, the play has already completed a feverish day. Beyond two meetings with the statue of the murdered Commander, we witness seduction scenes and philosophical debates; encounters with peasants, a beggar, and an unpaid shopkeeper; angry confrontations with a jilted mistress, her vengeful brothers, and the don's indignant father; a failed abduction, a boatwreck, and a swordfight with bandits.[46] Still, the title character's destruction only takes place when he returns to the

---

[46] These last are narrated rather than witnessed, but for our present purpose it amounts to the same.

Commander's tomb, keeping the dinner date the statue issues during their second meeting. Though the pace of events disguises the fact, act 5 telescopes an entire *second* day within the five scenes alotted it.

But the most striking result of *Dom Juan*'s busy plot is abandonment of all semblance of unity of place. Especially dating from the *Précieuses ridicules*, the formal perfection displayed in the use of verse, the framing *agon*, and the scrupulously economical development of the plot is undergirded by confinement to a single set. In *L'Ecole*, we have the street before Arnolphe's house; in *Tartuffe*, Orgon's public reception room; in *Le Misanthrope*, the *salon* of Alceste's faithless mistress Célimène. The rule is thus a scenic unity as absolute as in the tragedies of Racine. *Dom Juan* by contrast exhibits a restless scenic multiplicity. Act 1 takes place before a palace in the town to which the hero retires after jilting Done Elvire. Act 2 moves to open country by the sea, where the seducer consorts with gullible peasants following his rescue from the wreck that foils his efforts to kidnap a young bride. Though the stage directions indicate only one scene for act 3, the forest through which don and servant flee mounted pursuers, we can in fact distinguish three: the road they follow through the woods; the crossroads where they meet a beggar from whom they ask directions; and the tomb of the Commander. Act 4 takes us to the apartment in which, testily demanding supper, Dom Juan receives a series of importunate visitors: the hapless shopkeeper M. Dimanche; Done Elvire in the veil of a novitiate nun; his angry father, reminding him of his moral duties as a gentleman; and the Stone Guest. Finally, in act 5, we move to open countryside once more before returning to the Commander's tomb for the supernatural dénouement.

Despite its sprawling episodes and shifting locales, the action retains a fierce coherence, hammering at Dom Juan's moral character while marching him to his inexorable fate. Yet as attested by the final act's weirdly foreshortened transition from the moralist portrait of hypocrisy in scenes 1 through 3 to the supernatural climax in scenes 4 and 5, the plot is governed less by natural probability than by a kind of *dreamwork* indexed by the deep metaphorical resonance of the spaces in which it moves: city, country, ocean, forest, crossroads, tomb. Mixing scenes of social satire and burlesque with ghostly visitations and metaphysical colloquy, *Dom Juan* is preeminently a play of *mind*, or rather of mind's unconscious underside. While the ferocious unity of action counterbalances the overthrow of the unities of time and place, the plot is driven by symbolic compulsions as blindly mechanical as the stone automaton by which "heaven" works the desolate miracle of the close.

A telling symptom of the complexities *Dom Juan*'s compulsions generate is a bit of text we normally might not read, the stage direction for the title character's speech in 5.3 to his jilted mistress's brother. Echoing the lame excuses given Done Elvire four acts earlier (1.3), Dom Juan refuses Dom Carlos's demand that he restore his sister's honor by marrying her. Sensible though he claims to be of the justice of the proposed remedy, he insists that "le ciel s'y oppose directement." For in the interval since setting the rendezvous for the present encounter back in 3.4, Dom Juan has undergone a conversion that enjoins a radical "change of life," committing him to conduct of the utmost "austerity" required to "corriger désormais... tous les dérèglements criminels où m'a porté le feu d'une aveugle jeunesse." For all its rightness in mere human terms, marriage constitutes a carnal indulgence incommensurate with the penitential rigor "la voix du ciel" ordains (308-309). Needless to say, the reasons Dom Juan adduces are mendacious. He has in fact experienced no conversion; his motive is rather cessation of desire (briefly rekindled, to be sure, by the spectacle of a tearfully earnest Done Elvire in the veil of a novitiate nun in 4.6), coupled with the role of *dévot* he now plays to elude the increasingly inconvenient consequences of his misdeeds. So he delivers his speech in what the direction calls "un ton hypocrite." Since he does not mean what he says, he adopts the tone insincerity calls for: that of a man who merely simulates the pious sentiments he declares.

Still, innocuous as the direction seems, it poses puzzling questions. The first is why Molière gives it all, especially in view of the absence of comparable devices in *Tartuffe*. The obvious answer is as a guide to the actor who plays the part, and to the reader expected to approximate live performance. In delivering the lines, the player must convey the distinction between the dramatic *text*, the actual words the don pronounces, and the *subtext* that makes him say what the verbal surface reports. In terms of Austin's doctrine of

298 INDISCERNIBLE COUNTERPARTS

speech acts, a theory whose special relevance to this play Felman emphasizes, [47] the actor must help us hear both the "sense" of Dom Juan's words, their literal meaning, and the verbal act he performs in uttering them–the quite different "force" his words acquire as a function of his true intent. [48] Distinguishing these things proves all the more difficult in the present instance in that Dom Juan's excuse is a case of what Austin calls "etiolated" or, more pungently, "parasitic" speech. [49] It is not just that, in conformity with and indeed as an aggravation of their fictive place in a *drama*, Dom Juan's words are not "serious," uttered "in play" rather than "in earnest"; they constitute a speech act that lives off *other* speech acts. In rejecting Dom Carlos's demand (Dom Juan's *surface* speech act) on the grounds of atonement for his youthful crimes, he performs a *second* speech act: that of declaring a conversion inspired by the "voice of heaven" whose opposition to the expected marriage he regretfully transmits. But of course his true intent is yet a *third* speech act: that of lying in order to evade the marital entanglements on which his mistress's brother insists, and to which he is moreover committed by still other words, namely, the promise of undying love with which he initially seduced Don Elvire.

All of this defines the actor's task: to find the tone of voice required to make Dom Juan's intricate duplicity audible: a vocal performance reinforced on stage by gesture and facial expression, and perhaps even a change of costume, replacing the beplumed and beribboned scarlet and gold of a *grand seigneur* with the quasi-ecclesiastical black borrowed from the Tartuffe to whom the scene alludes. The actor's job is besides all the more difficult in that, though he is called on to *play* a hypocrite, he is not (we hope) *himself* a hypocrite. The speech the direction frames is thus at least triply "parasitic": the speaker pretends to reject pretend demands by playing a character who cloaks his true motives in a bogus declaration of penitent faith.

But the answer to this initial question raises another. For the hypocritical speech the direction frames is not the first of its kind;

---

[47] Felman, *Le Scandale du corps parlant*, esp. "La perversion de la promesse: Don Juan et la performance littéraire," 31-80.
[48] See Austin, *How to Do Things with Words* 94-108.
[49] Ibid. 22.

that honor goes to the words addressed to Dom Juan's father two scenes earlier (5.1). The final act opens indeed with a *coup de théâtre* motivated by the supernatural visit of the Stone Guest at the end of act 4. As the curtain rises on the scene immediately following the statue's visit, Dom Louis voices astonished joy:

> Quoi! Mon fils, serait-il possible que la bonté du ciel eût exaucé mes vœux? ce que vous me dites est-il bien vrai? ne m'abusez-vous point d'un faux espoir, et puis-je prendre quelque assurance sur la nouveauté surprenante d'une telle conversion?

Whereupon his perfidious son repeats the avowal made in the *entr'acte*:

> Oui, vous me voyez revenu de toutes mes erreurs; je ne suis plus le même d'hier soir, et le ciel, tout d'un coup, a fait en moi un changement qui va surprendre tout le monde. Il a touché mon âme et dessillé mes yeux; et je regarde avec horreur le long aveuglement où j'ai été, et les désordres criminels de la vie que j'ai menée. J'en repasse dans mon esprit toutes les abominations, et m'étonne comme le ciel les a pu souffrir si longtemps, et n'a pas vingt fois, sur ma tête, laissé tomber les coups de sa justice redoutable. Je vois les grâces que sa bonté m'a faites en ne me punissant point de mes crimes; et je prétends en profiter comme je dois, faire éclater aux yeux du monde un soudain changement de vie, réparer par là le scandale de mes actions passées, et m'efforcer d'en obtenir du ciel une pleine rémission. C'est à quoi je vais travailler; et je vous prie, monsieur, de vouloir bien contribuer à ce dessein, et de m'aider vous-même à faire choix d'une personne qui me serve de guide, et sous la conduite de qui je puisse marcher sûrement dans le chemin où je m'en vais entrer. (307)

The father's jubilant exit is then followed in 5.2 by a second *coup de théâtre* when Dom Juan sneeringly reveals to a flabbergasted Sganarelle that, despite the disturbing testimony of the Stone Guest, his professed conversion is a sham:

> *Sganarelle*
>
> Ah! monsieur, que j'ai de joie de vous voir converti! Il y a longtemps que j'attendais cela; et voilà, grâce au ciel, tous mes souhaits accomplis.

Dom Juan

La peste, le benêt!

Sganarelle

Comment, le benêt?

Dom Juan

Quoi! tu prends pour de bon argent ce que je viens de dire, et tu crois que ma bouche était d'accord avec mon coeur?

Sganarelle

Quoi! ce n'est pas... Vous ne... Votre... (*A part.*) Oh! quel homme! quel homme! quel homme! (307)

And to make doubly sure there is no mistaking his real intent, Dom Juan goes on to deliver the long, extraordinarily angry tirade in which, glad to have "un témoin du fond de mon âme," he unfolds the "true motives" behind the adoption of the aptly named "profession of a hypocrite":

> Il n'y a plus de honte maintenant à cela, l'hypocrisie est un vice à la mode, et tous les vices à la mode passent pour des vertus. Le personnage d'homme de bien est le meilleur de tous les personnages qu'on puisse jouer aujourd'hui, et la profession d'hypocrite a de merveilleux avantages. C'est un art de qui l'imposture est toujours respectée; et, quoiqu'on la découvre, on n'ose rien dire contre elle. Tous les autres vices des hommes sont exposés à la censure, et chacun a la liberté de les attaquer hautement; mais l'hypocrisie est un vice privilégié qui, de sa main, ferme la bouche à tout le monde, et jouit en repos d'une impunité souveraine... Combien crois-tu que j'en connaisse qui, par ce stratagème, ont rhabillé adroitement les désordres de leur jeunesse, qui se sont fait un bouclier du manteau de la religion, et, sous cet habit respecté, ont la permission d'être les plus méchants hommes du monde? On a beau savoir leurs intrigues, et les connaître pour ce qu'ils sont, ils ne laissent pas pour cela d'être en crédit parmi les gens et quelque baissement de tête, un soupir mortifié, et deux roulements d'yeux, rajustent dans le monde tout ce qu'ils peuvent faire... Que si je viens à être découvert, je verrai, sans me remuer, prendre mes intérêts à toute la cabale, et je serai défendu par elle envers et contre tous... (307-308)

By the time Dom Juan addresses his deceitful speech to Dom Carlos in 5.3, we already *know* he is a hypocrite; the stage direction is entirely redundant. Nor moreover is Dom Carlos fooled; unlike Dom Louis, he sees through Dom Juan's professions as readily as his sister did in 1.3. In the earlier scene indeed, Done Elvire responds to her lover's claim to have been driven from her arms by a sudden attack of "scruples" by delivering the speech she had expected to hear, a wonderfully recursive gesture in which she utters the words both she and her seducer recognize the circumstances call for:

> Ah! que vous savez mal vous défendre pour un homme de cour, et qui doit être accoutumé à ces sortes de choses! J'ai pitié de vous voir la confusion que vous avez. Que ne vous armez-vous le front d'une noble effronterie? Que ne me jurez-vous que vous êtes toujours dans les mêmes sentiments pour moi, que vous m'aimez toujours avec une ardeur sans égale, et que rien n'est capable de vous détacher de moi que la mort? Que ne me dites-vous que des affaires de la dernière conséquence vous ont obligé de partir sans m'en donner avis; qu'il faut que, malgré vous, vous demeuriez ici quelque temps, et que je n'ai qu'à m'en retourner d'où je viens, assurée que vous suivrez mes pas le plus tôt qu'il vous sera possible; qu'il est certain que vous brûlez de me rejoindre, et qu'éloigné de moi vous souffrez ce que souffre un corps qui est séparé de son âme? Voilà comme il faut vous défendre, et non pas être interdit comme vous êtes. (289)

Just so, in 5.3, goaded by Dom Juan's repeated, insolently empty invocations of "le ciel" ("Eh bien! toujours le ciel!"), her brother haughtily refuses to let his adversary "dazzle" him, rejects being "paid with words," and breaks off the exchange with a mordant "Il suffit, dom Juan; je vous entends." (309) Far from signaling a hidden meaning, the direction cues a performance enraging for its utter *transparency*. Just because there is no mistaking his intent, the speech provokes a duel that, given the martial prowess certified by the killing of the Commander and the rescue of Dom Carlos from the robbers who beset him in 3.3, Dom Juan is certain to win.

This brings us to a first point about the guidance the direction gives. Assuming (as we cannot here) that the point of hypocrisy is to convince its target of the sincerity of our proffered words, a

302   INDISCERNIBLE COUNTERPARTS

"hypocritical tone" is logically indistinguishable from the one it
mimics. Like the counterfeit coin Dom Juan invokes in disabusing
Sganarelle's false interpretation of his earlier, successfully hypocritical performance for his father, it would circulate freely precisely because no one could tell it from the real thing. A truly hypocritical
tone is the indiscernible counterpart of the quite *other* tone the situation demands: in the present case, the regret, remorse, and new-
found piety Dom Juan's words expressly endorse. But Dom Juan's
aim here is *not* to be believed. In its very literalness, cuing a performance that is meant to be recognized as hypocritical by its victim
as well as the public, the direction underscores just what Dom Juan
claims in his explanatory speech to Sganarelle in 5.2: less the fact of
wearing a mask than the *impunity* it grants, an impunity so great he
does not even bother to conceal his true sentiments.

Dom Juan's reprise of the role of Tartuffe takes up the theme of
hypocrisy where the other play leaves off. As noted earlier, were it
not for the miraculous arrival of the *exempt*, *Tartuffe*'s internal logic
would assure the impostor's triumph and the ensuing destitution of
his deluded host. It is only thanks to the act of faith the happy ending ritually enacts that Orgon's ruin finds a remedy. But the act of
faith that saves Orgon is now *revoked*: the "cabale" Dom Juan expressly cites in describing his hypocritical profession retains the
impunity he rubs in Dom Carlos's face. And this in turn provokes a
crisis it takes God himself to solve in the animate statue that carries
the villain off to the accompaniment of thunder, lightning, and the
hellfire erupting from the trap through which Dom Juan falls.

We should stress the *extremity* this divine intercession signals.
True, like *Tartuffe*'s, the dénouement is preprogrammed. An important part of the legend the play draws on, the hero's damnation provides an alibi for the story's underlying immoralism. Already in Tirso de Molina's *Burlador de Sevilla* of 1630, and still more explicitly
in the Italians by whom Tirso's invention is directly transmitted to
the French stage, the trickster-seducer embodies a cheerful lawlessness whose power to enfranchise as well as frighten is magnified by
the intellectual scope Molière gives it. [50] This is one aspect of

---

[50] See Couton's "notice," Pléiade *Œuvres complètes* 2.12-13. See too Leo Weinstein, *The Metamorphoses of Don Juan* (Stanford: Stanford University Press, 1959)
24-26.

Sganarelle's otherwise inexplicable loyalty to a master he so vehemently claims to abhor. Sganarelle is rightly scared of him, and also needs the wages he vainly hopes to be paid. But a noble whose social status grants his actions a freedom and consequence denied his servant, and a villain as enviably glib as he is unscrupulous, Dom Juan shares the energy, venality, self-centered realism, and crafty role-playing Sganarelle exhibits in the plays in which he stars, and notably in the next season's *Médecin malgré lui*.

Still, enviable and even admirable as Dom Juan's lawlessness may be, he poses a threat whose measure is just the exorbitant means required to eliminate it. In Tirso, the justice seekers who besiege the King in the final scenes supply an informal census of the entire social order, allying humble farm- and fisherfolk with the dishonored noble families that people the royal court. This registers the limitless scale of the seducer's sexual appetite; but it also indexes the anarchic desires he unleashes in others: an assault on social coherence epitomized by the ludicrously misnamed Aminta, a stridently non-pastoral peasant intent on redeeming the outrageous pledge of ennoblement to which the don's promise of marriage entitles her. This prompts the audible sigh of relief when the prince learns of the don's supernatural fate, untangling a political knot it is beyond even his royal power to untie.[51] Molière is hardly so frank. Though he changes the father's name from Tirso's generic "Diego" to the resonantly topical "Louis," making him moreover an explicit surrogate of the sovereign with whom he threatens his son during their angry meeting in act 4,[52] he does not adduce the King himself even in the transposed person of an *exempt*. But like Tirso's before him, Molière's seducer penetrates all sectors of society, nobles and peasants, beggars and bandits, and even the commercial sphere represented by M. Dimanche, a creditor swindled of the money he is owed by Dom Juan's fast-talking flattery (4.3). And like Tirso's,

---

[51] For the assembly of suppliant subjects, see Tirso de Molina, *El Burlador de Sevilla y convidado de piedra*, ed. James A. Parr (Binghampton: Medieval & Renaissance Texts & Studies, 1994), Jornada tercera, 2485-2634. For the anticlimactic finale, ibid. 2783-2870.

[52] "De quel œil, à votre avis, pensez-vous que je puisse voir cet amas d'actions indignes, dont on a peine, aux yeux du monde, d'adoucir le mauvais visage; cette suite continuelle de méchantes affaires, qui nous réduisent à toute heure à lasser les bontés du souverain, et qui ont épuisé auprès de lui le mérite de mes services et le crédit de mes amis?" (304).

Molière's don inspires deluded social aspirations as ominous as they are comic–a major theme in act 2, where the seduction of the peasants Charlotte and Mathurine turns on the social merit Dom Juan assigns their beauty: "Quoi! une personne comme vous serait la femme d'un simple paysan!" (293) All of this explains why, in the savage complaint with which the final curtain falls, Sganarelle brings the whole society in for the kill:

> Voilà, par sa mort, un chacun satisfait. Ciel offensé, lois violées, filles séduites, familles déshonorées, parents outragés, femmes mises à mal, maris poussés à bout, tout le monde est content; il n'y a que moi seul de malheureux, qui, après tant d'années de service, n'ai d'autre récompense que de voir à mes yeux l'impiété de mon maître punie par le plus épouvantable châtiment du monde. (310)

The furious contrast between the universal content his master's damnation procures and the penury to which this reduces him maps the cosmic scheme his master's immolation restores.

The impunity underscored by Dom Juan's both redundant and self-contradictory "ton hypocrite" thus creates a menace so pervasive and profound that God alone can counter it. But more menacing than this impunity is its *source* and what that source reveals about the world the finale's supernatural agency rescues. For if, as a fact of Molière's own experience, Dom Juan's "cabale" incontestably triumphs, it is because its sinister members understand that what their dupes regard as the natural order hypocrisy violates is merely a *mirage*: a godless amalgam of convention and appearance, fear and superstition, habit, prejudice, ignorance, and veiled self-interest whose hold on reality extends no further than our naïve readiness to believe in it.

Nowhere is nature's nature as mirage more consistently developed than in the title role. Dom Juan's performance as a hypocrite is only one of the many parts he plays. The comedy is traditionally seen as a prolonged experiment exposing the chameleonlike substance of Dom Juan's personality to varying social, rhetorical, and psychological conditions in an effort to elicit a coherent set of properties that, in fixing his identity, enable us to judge who he "really" is. Such is the view Lionel Gossman elaborates in order to reconcile the essentialist presumptions on which he bases a forceful condemnation of Dom Juan's moral character with his otherwise acute insights into the alienating wearing of masks that forms his overarching theme.[53]

Thus, in act 1, the play presents the restless libertine whose insatiable sexual appetites lead him to scorn ordinary moral scruples as weightless superstition and shameful *ridicule*. In act 2, we get the nimble trickster, Tirso's "burlador," working on the misguided vanity and social ambition of the peasants Charlotte and Mathurine, and the base ingrate who repays Pierrot for saving him from drowning by seducing his fiancée. Act 3 exposes the cynical atheist whose callous disregard for others emerges in the "scène du pauvre," where he exploits a beggar's penury to try to induce him to blaspheme in exchange for money, and in the sarcasms addressed to the statue of the Commander during the visit to his tomb: "Parbleu! le voilà bon, avec son habit d'empereur romain!" (301) Act 4 exhibits Dom Juan in a diversity of lights: as the aristocratic bully who threatens his moralizing servant with a flogging; as the foxy scam artist conning the slow-witted M. Dimanche out of the money he is owed; as the *fils ingrat* who scorns his father's appeal to his sense of honor and to the duties attending his privileged birth; as the sensualist perversely aroused by the spectacle of a veiled Done Elvire taking religious vows in hopes of stirring him to repentance; then as the arrogant *homme de cœur* refusing to be intimidated when the stone image invites him to the fatal feast. Thus are we supposed to be brought by successive stages to the very *heart* of the man, stripped of the disguises that conceal his true nature. Or rather is it that, flushed from covert by the gathering consequences of his crimes, Dom Juan discloses his true face at last in the ironic likeness of the hypocrite's mask.

There is much to recommend this reading. Appealing as the *donjuanisme* descending from Mozart and Da Ponte through Byron

---

[53] Gossman argues that, for Molière, morality (or the *necessity* of morality) is a kind of Kantian reflex of the inescapable fact of wearing of masks. Everything in life (our own delinquent psyches as well as the coercions of social existence and personal relationships) forces us to conceal our true identities. Yet to the precise extent that the fact of concealment reveals the logically prior fact of the truth we conceal, the only alternative to moral commitment is the cynically self-exculpatory egoism Gossman's Dom Juan incarnates. Note that Weinstein shares Gossman's view of Molière's moral judgment of his title character. However, committed (like Felman) to an *heroic* sense of the Don Juan legend, this leads him to bemoan not only a loss of excitement, but also a loss of stature on the part of Molière's "hero." See *Metamorphoses* 34.

and Pushkin to Camus may be, producing the intellectual genealogy by which the Lacanian Felman has plainly been seduced, Molière's character is distinctly unpleasant. For all his elegance, intelligence, and charm, his actions reveal a quite breathtaking meanness and vulgarity. This yields his shock at receiving a visit from his jilted mistress in inappropriate dress ("Est-elle folle, de n'avoir pas changé d'habit, et de venir en ce lieu-ci avec son équipage de campagne?") (289), the cheap face-saving line with which he tosses the beggar his coin despite the latter's mulish refusal to blaspheme ("Va, va, je te le donne pour l'amour de l'humanité") (299), or his petulant insistence on seigneurial right in his dealings with his servant–"Ecoute. Si tu m'importunes davantage de tes sottes moralités, si tu me dis encore le moindre mot là-dessus, je vais appeler quelqu'un, demander un nerf de bœuf, te faire tenir par trois ou quatre, et te rouer de mille coups. M'entends-tu bien?" (302) And yet perhaps the strangest and most unpalatable thing about him, tempering not only the admiration the legend's posterity tempts us to read back into Molière, but also the moralism that, in Gossman, takes comfort in whatever confirms his villainy, is his curious moral *absence*, the creeping sense that he is never properly there at all.

It is remarkable that, with the exception of the mock heroic encomium of amorous conquest in 1.2 and the diatribe on hypocrisy in 5.2, everything Dom Juan says reacts to, and to this extent is *screened* by, the immediate circumstances of its utterance. Nor is he granted a single soliloquy, not once appearing alone on stage. He is of course always in Sganarelle's company, and usually that of some third party: Done Elvire, the peasants of act 2, the beggar, Dom Carlos, his father, M. Dimanche, the statue of the Commander, or the Specter sent as a divine ultimatum just before his climactic descent to hell. With Sganarelle moreover he mainly plays the straight-man, feeding cues for his servant's burlesque defenses of morality, medicine, belief in spirits and the afterlife, the existence of God, or the innate dignity of the human soul.

For the rest, he is confined to mordant one-liners underlining the farcical incompetence of Sganarelle's apologetics. In 3.1, we get a pocket satire occasioned by his servant's not very serious misgivings about prescribing cures for people who consult him owing to the physician's robe he dons as a disguise when master and man flee from anonymous riders intent on revenge:

Et pourquoi non? Par quelle raison n'aurais-tu pas les mêmes privilèges qu'ont tous les autres médecins? Ils n'ont pas plus de part que toi aux guérisons des malades, et tout leur art est pure grimace. Ils ne font rien que recevoir la gloire des heureux succès; et tu peux profiter, comme eux, du bonheur du malade, et voir attribuer à tes remèdes tout ce qui peut venir des faveurs du hasard et des forces de la nature. (297)

But the immediate point of this remark is to provoke a discussion in which Dom Juan's role is entirely limited to providing linkage and ironic filler:

Sganarelle

Comment, monsieur, vous êtes aussi impie en médecine?

Dom Juan

C'est une des plus grandes erreurs qui soient parmi les hommes.

Sganarelle

Quoi! vous ne croyez pas au séné, ni à la casse, ni au vin émétique?

Dom Juan

Et pourquoi veux-tu que j'y croie?

Sganarelle

Vous avez l'âme bien mécréante. Cependant, vous voyez, depuis un temps, le vin émétique fait bruire ses fuseaux. Ses miracles ont converti les plus incrédules esprits; et il n'y a pas trois semaines que j'en ai vu, moi qui vous parle, un effet merveilleux.

Dom Juan

Et quel?

Sganarelle

Il y avait un homme qui, depuis six jours, était à l'agonie; on ne savait plus que lui ordonner, et tous les remèdes ne faisaient rien; on s'avisa à la fin de lui donner de l'émétique.

Dom Juan

Il réchappa, n'est-ce pas?

Sganarelle

Non, il mourut.

Dom Juan

L'effet est admirable.

Sganarelle

Comment! il y avait six jours entiers qu'il ne pouvait mourir et cela le fit mourir tout d'un coup. Voulez-vous rien de plus efficace? (297)

Similarly, when, later in the scene, they move from medicine to broader articles of faith, Dom Juan delivers a one-sentence credo enfolding a bargain-basement materialism worthy of *film noir*. Having elicited his master's disbelief in heaven ("Laissons cela"), hell ("Eh!"), the devil ("Oui, oui"), the afterlife ("Ah! ah! ah!"), and, in a touch the *dévots* found especially offensive, the "moine bourru" ("La peste soit du fat!"),[54] Sganarelle insists that he *must* nonetheless believe in *something*:

Sganarelle

Qu'est-ce donc que vous croyez?

Dom Juan

Ce que je crois?

Sganarelle

Oui.

Dom Juan

Je crois que deux et deux sont quatre, Sganarelle; et que quatre et quatre sont huit. (297)

---

[54] For a representative howl of sanctimonious indignation, see note 1 above.

But even this chiefly stimulates what follows. Appalled to discover that his master's faith amounts to little more than "arithmetic," Sganarelle launches into a burlesque "proof by design," a torrent of scrambled platitudes, garbled echoes of half-digested theological authorities, and tortured logic to which Dom Juan's replies with insidious *silence*:

Sganarelle

Oh! dame, interrompez-moi donc, si vous voulez. Je ne saurais disputer, si l'on ne m'interrompt pas. Vous vous taisez exprès, et me laissez parler par belle malice.

Dom Juan

J'attends que ton raisonnement soit fini.

Sganarelle

Mon raisonnement est qu'il y a quelque chose d'admirable dans l'homme, quoi que vous puissiez dire, que tous les savants ne sauraient expliquer. Cela n'est-il pas merveilleux que me voilà ici, et que j'aie quelque chose dans la tête qui pense cent choses différentes en un moment, et fait de mon corps tout ce qu'elle veut? Je veux frapper des mains, hausser le bras, lever les yeux au ciel, baisser la tête, remuer les pieds, aller à droite, à gauche, en avant, en arrière, tourner... (*Il se laisse tomber en tournant.*)

Dom Juan

Bon! Voilà ton raisonnement qui a le nez cassé! (297-98)

Dom Juan does come to life when third parties enter the stage: in the elegant *passage d'armes* with his jilted mistress in 1.3, the verbal dance in which he juggles Charlotte and Mathurine in 2.4, the toying encounter with the haughty Dom Carlos in 3.3, the sarcastic bearding of the Commander's statue in 3.5, or the ingratiating patter in which he entangles the luckless M. Dimanche in 4.3. But whenever Dom Juan becomes a vivid vocal presence, his invariable purpose is to deceive. We get indeed a *false* presence: in place of the don himself whatever disguise the occasion requires–that, or a certain sardonic *reserve* whose most devastating expression comes in 4.4, when the ungrateful son derails his father's windy sermon on the duties of noble birth by interrupting him with a single insolent sentence of glacial *politesse*: "Monsieur, si vous étiez assis, vous seriez mieux pour parler." (305)

Molière's Don Juan thus stands to one side of the world to which the other characters earnestly belong. This helps explain the curious skepticism with which he receives the otherwise dramatically unequivocal warning the Specter delivers in 5.4: "Si le ciel veut me donner un avis, il faut qu'il parle un peu plus clairement, s'il veut que je l'entende." (309) Whatever appears on stage, however solid or explicit, is for him by definition suspect; his true business is always *elsewhere*, in the infernal regions to which he seemingly *wills* that he be brought. If we succumb to the illusion that Dom Juan has a consistent personality, it is chiefly on the strength of the two speeches mentioned a moment ago, speeches placed at each end of the play to frame the elusive appearances in between. Yet, on closer scrutiny, neither speech turns out to be quite the unambiguous expression of who the don is this framing function suggests.

The first presents Dom Juan's eloquent defense of his faithless conduct in matters of the heart. The opening scene lays the foundation in the elaborate portrait Sganarelle paints for Done Elvire's bewildered valet Gusman:

> [T]u vois en dom Juan mon maître, le plus grand scélérat que la terre ait jamais porté, un enragé, un chien, un diable, un Turc, un hérétique, qui ne croit ni ciel, ni enfer, ni loup-garou; qui passe cette vie en véritable bête brute; un pourceau d'Epicure, un vrai Sardanapale, qui ferme l'oreille à toutes les remontrances chrétiennes qu'on lui peut faire, et traite de billevesées tout ce que nous croyons. Tu me dis qu'il a épousé ta maîtresse; crois qu'il aurait plus fait pour sa passion, et qu'avec elle il aurait encore épousé, toi, son chien, et son chat. Un mariage ne lui coûte rien à contracter; il ne se sert point d'autres pièges pour attraper les belles; et c'est un épouseur à toutes mains. Dame, demoiselle, bourgeoise, paysanne, il ne trouve rien de trop chaud ni de trop froid pour lui; et, si je te disais le nom de toutes celles qu'il a épousées en divers lieux, ce serait un chapitre à durer jusqu'au soir. (286)

By the time the don himself speaks, we have been primed for a direct and thus truthful account of the lawless erotic drives legend ascribes him. And in keeping with the poetics of the *comédie de caractère* Molière is in the process of perfecting, the speech Dom Juan now delivers is a masterpiece of self-betraying doubletalk. Alongside gratuitous sneers at the scruples that bind other people ("la constance," for example, "n'est bonne que pour des ridicules") is the striking disproportion between the venereal adventures of which Dom Juan boasts and the martial conquests of Alexander with which it flatters him to compare them in the speech's coda:

> Enfin, il n'est rien de si doux que de triompher de la résistance d'une belle personne; et j'au, sur ce sujet, l'ambition des conquérants, qui volent perpétuellement de victoire en victoire, et ne peuvent se résoudre à borner leurs souhaits. Il n'est rien qui puisse arrêter l'impétuosité de mes désirs; je me sens un cœur à aimer toute la terre; et, comme Alexandre, je souhaiterais qu'il y eût d'autres mondes, pour y pouvoir étendre mes conquêtes amoureuses. (287-88)

More subtle is the ironic inversion by which the archseducer absolves himself of mere demotic faithlessness by blaming his victims. Far from arising from inner weakness or depravity, his infidelities are induced by external compulsion, the irresistible "charms" to which successive mistresses expose him: "Pour moi, la beauté me ravit partout où je la trouve, et je cède facilement à cette douce violence dont elle nous entraîne." (287) This is followed by the maneuver of turning faithlessness into purest *equity*, the fair acknowledgement of the "just pretensions" all beautiful women "have on our hearts":

> toutes les belles ont droit de nous charmer, et l'avantage d'être rencontrée la première ne doit point dérober aux autres les justes prétentions qu'elles ont sur nos cœurs... J'ai beau être engagé, l'amour que j'ai pour une belle n'engage point mon âme à faire injustice aux autres; je conserve des yeux pour voir le mérite de toutes, et rends à chacune les hommages et les tributs où la nature nous oblige. (287)

Molière adds one final self-incriminating irony. Asserting the equal right every woman possesses as the beautiful individual she is, the don abolishes the individuality thus honored. Since each deserves

our love, *all* do so without distinction, dissolving them in the theoretical indifference the universality of their right implies.[55] This gesture is linked to another feature of Dom Juan's erotic discourse, encoded in the coda's heroic simile on Alexander, namely, the *violence*
characterizing the *art d'amour* exhibited in donjuanesque seduction:

> Les inclinations naissantes, après tout, ont des charmes inexplic-
> ables, et tout le plaisir de l'amour est dans le changement. On
> goûte une douceur extrême à réduire, par cent hommages, le
> cœur d'une jeune beauté, à voir de jour en jour les petits progrès
> qu'on y fait, à combattre, par des transports, par des larmes et
> des soupirs, l'innocente pudeur d'une âme qui a peine à rendre
> les armes; à forcer pied à pied toutes les petites résistances
> qu'elle nous oppose, à vaincre les scrupules dont elle se fait un
> honneur, et la mener doucement où nous avons envie de la faire
> venir. (287)

Seduction is a militant enterprise, investing, besieging, "reducing"
what it craves; it consumes and finally destroys a being whose very
nature is made to depend on the desire that, in fixing on, constitutes it as the desirable thing it ceases to be the moment it has been
won.

On the surface then Dom Juan's speech in 1.2 looks truthful not
only because it seems to come from the speaker's heart, but in the
way its characterological ironies expose the gap between the self-
image Dom Juan entertains and the image of self he unwittingly
presents. This is of course a technique on which the *comédie de caractère* generically trades: the essence of the classical *caractère* consists in an abject failure to see around the corners of one's own self-

---

[55] The maneuver here is pertinent to Lacan. Thus, in "Sosie," Lacan suggests
that, by virtue of the symbolic order on which "marriage" construed as the normative expression of "love" is based, "love" (and thus one of the English language's
senses of "truth") is a form of faith (*fides*) whose parties (let us say "I" and "thou")
are ultimately *transcendental*, and to that extent unreal. (See Janet Lungstrum, "A
Transcendental Infidelity: Kleist, Lacan and *Amphitryon*," *Modern Language Notes*
22.4 [Fall 1992] 67-75.) This points in Lacan (as, too, in Felman) to a hard fact: we
are not the autonomous "individuals" we imagine, endowed with the rights as well
as identities that status accords. But it also fingers a certain *escamotage*: though we
may not *be* the individuals we imagine, that is nonetheless how we *suffer*, as suffer
we do. Infidelity hurts no less concretely for being "transcendental."

deluding pretensions. Classical comic characters compulsively give themselves away, producing a satirical portrait (the "caractère," precisely) in the form of the comic *self*-portrait their butts perform unawares.

In *Le Misanthrope*, for example, we have the self-denouncing inconsequence of Alceste, and in particular the ironic way in which the "sincerity" he demands of other people converges on their idolatrous acknowledgement of what he takes to be his own compelling virtues. As he puts it to Philinte at 1.1.63, "je veux qu'on me distingue," a remark that at once echoes and vitiates the "je veux qu'on soit sincère" pronounced 28 lines earlier. But the mechanism of unconscious self-portraiture also surfaces to spectacular effect in the gallery of *caractères* with which Célimène delights visitors to her *salon*. Thus, invited to draw the likeness of "Damon le raisonneur," Célimène replies,

> C'est un parleur étrange, et qui trouve toujours
> L'art de ne vous rien dire avec de grands discours:
> Dans les propos qu'il tient on ne voit jamais goutte,
> Et ce n'est que du bruit que tout ce qu'on écoute.
> (2.4.579-82)

Reminded that "Timante, encor, madame, est un bon caractère," she observes:

> C'est de la tête au pieds un homme tout mystère,
> Qui vous jette, en passant, un coup d'œil égaré,
> Et, sans aucune affaire, est toujours affairé.
> Tout ce qu'il vous débite en grimaces abonde;
> A force de façons, il assomme le monde;
> Sans cesse il a tout bas, pour rompre l'entretien,
> Un secret à vous dire, et ce secret n'est rien;
> De la moindre vétille il fait une merveille,
> Et jusques au bonjour, il dit tout à l'oreille.
> (2.4.586-94)

If the word "character" denotes both a satirical portrait and its target, it is because the target draws the portrait at its own expense as a reflex of the disparity between self-imagination and the conduct that self's imaginariness engenders.

Yet it would be naïve to think that Dom Juan inhabits his own character in the way Alceste does. It is possible, for instance, to read the ironic contradictions in his speeches as calculated insincerities, as hyperboles and misdirections consciously savored by the speaker himself. The divorce between the willful nature of his infidelities and the external constraints or considerations of equity he ironically alleges as their source would only characterize him if he *meant* them. But if anything characterizes Dom Juan, it is that he never unambiguously means *anything* he says. Whence Sganarelle's telling reaction to the speech: "Vertu de ma vie! comme vous débitez! Il semble que vous avez appris cela par cœur, et vous parlez comme un livre." (288) Far from compulsively divulging a true character that eludes his own conscious scrutiny, he exploits the psychic distance an actor enjoys, reciting his responses "by heart" from the "book" or script (*livre* or *livret*) prescribed by the legend that defines his role.

We meet similar difficulties when we turn to the second speech. The temptation to believe that Dom Juan inhabits the character the tirade on hypocrisy ascribes him is stronger on several counts. Where the earlier speech presents the legendary seducer whose ludic insincerity is a matter of public record, the new one proposes a hypocrite intent on "professing" his insincerity in something like deadly earnest. Insincerity here is no longer a game; it is a "policy," a "useful stratagem" designed to ward off the real consequences of his deeds. Then too, as noted earlier, Dom Juan himself encourages us to read the speech *à la lettre* by confessing his relief at having "a witness to the bottom of my soul and the true motives that oblige me to do these things." The first speech is got "by heart," a recital of the traditional script that lays down the character he plays. In the second however, where Molière exceeds his writ, adding a novelty to the legend on which he draws, the speaker seems animated by a curious horror at what he himself now proposes to become, at the *fate*, even, he now willingly embraces: that of being permanently and systematically mistaken for a "true" hypocrite in Diderot's Neveu's sense.

Yet a feature of this speech is how it questions its own source. Certainly, in what looks like an attempt to cleanse himself of the infamy attaching even in his own eyes to the vile policy he adopts, Dom Juan strings exculpatory arguments together based on the pervasiveness of the practice he adopts. In this sense, the speech constitutes a *doubly* hypocritical act in which, even while confessing the opprobrium rightly assigned his latest vice, he discharges himself of responsibility, or at least mitigates the fault, by laying it at society's door. But the very pervasiveness of the sin, engendering a perverse parody of the argument from "universal consent" that early-modern theologians used to defend "natural religion," underscores the tirade's dominant tone: a barely controlled anger whose autobiographical resonance is unmistakable. Dom Juan is not alone in speaking here; indeed, what cause has *he* to be so angry about the vicious "profession" by which he now intends to profit? The speech belongs above all to *Molière*, who seizes the occasion of the title character's confession to confront his enemies face to face.

As Uranie's "public mirror" defense of comic satire in the *Critique de l'Ecole des femmes* reminds is, comic portraits "tombent directement sur les mœurs, et ne frappent les personnes que par réflexion." (207) This Horatian model defines Molière's normal comic procedure, providing among other things the wiggle room that allows spectators to imagine that the foibles and vices he exposes belong to someone else. Nor is this mere public etiquette; it deflects the kind of violent response fear of which leads Sganarelle to chide his master's "libertinage" under cover of addressing not Dom Juan himself, but some suppositious "other" master unmitigated by the virtues he pretends to believe his real one possesses:

> Je ne parle pas aussi à vous, Dieu m'en garde! Vous savez ce que vous faites, vous; et, si vous ne croyez rien, vous avez vos raisons: mais il y a de certains petits impertinents dans le monde qui sont libertins sans savoir pourquoi, qui font les esprits forts, parce qu'ils croient que cela leur sied bien; et si j'avais un maître comme cela, je lui dirais fort nettement, le regardant en face: "Osez-vous bien ainsi vous jouer du ciel, et ne tremblez-vous point de vous moquer comme vous faites des choses les plus saintes? C'est bien à vous, petit ver de terre, petit mirmidon que vous êtes (je parle au maître que j'ai dit), c'est bien à vous à vouloir vous mêler de tourner en raillerie ce que tous les hommes révèrent? Pensez-vous que pour être de qualité, pour avoir une perruque blonde et bien frisée, des plumes à votre chapeau, un habit doré, et des rubans couleur de feu (ce n'est pas à vous que je parle, c'est à l'autre), pensez-vous, dis-je, que vous soyez plus

habile homme, que tout vous soit permis, et qu'on n'ose vous
dire vos vérités? (288)

This time, however, there is no pseudo-distinction between "true"
and "false" of the sort *Tartuffe* lives by: Dom Juan's tirade on
hypocrisy eschews alibi, denouncing the "cabale" *by name*. But who
in fact speaks here? The denunciation of hypocrisy is itself the ultimate hypocrisy; in revealing what lies at the "bottom of [his]
heart," Dom Juan reveals *nothing* for, in human terms, *nothing is
what he is*. Pointing to the mask behind which he proposes for ever
to vanish, he performs an act of absolute self-erasure, an ontological
suicide that measures the savagery of the portrait his author paints.
But what prompts the savagery is the anguish inspired by the conviction that the maneuver will *succeed*. Dom Juan's sneering nega-
tion of his own humanity thus encompasses ours as well precisely
insofar as it negates all meaningful human truth.

Unlike everyone else in the play, Dom Juan is a rhetorical place-
holder rather than a consistent person. This is partly because he absorbs such identifying color as he has from those on whom he
works–and we note another dark parody of theological precedent:
the seducer, swindler, actor, and hypocrite satanically mimics the St.
Paul of 1 Corinthians 9.22 in being "all things to all men." [56] But
there is more: possessed of no native color of his own, he uncannily
mirrors his environment back on itself. The infinitely adaptable because empty blankness he shares with mirrors images the unconscious emptiness of the society before which he stands.

What makes Dom Juan's role-playing possible is that the rote
performance of roles is what the world *calls for*. Such is Done
Elvire's testimony in 1.3, when she delivers the excuses Dom Juan
ought to have supplied in place of the insultingly transparent "scruples" he invokes. Elvire's speech betokens of course her intelligence
and pride; but it also reveals that the identities the confrontation requires read "like a book," as the set text the scene demands. Or
take Dom Louis's speech in 4.4. The father's harangue has a certain
affecting nobility; the portrait of heroic worth he draws challenges

---

[56] However, this latent parody should be put in context with the controversies
surrounding this and other accommodating Pauline utterances like it. See Zagorin,
Ways of Lying 15-20.

his wayward son's sense of honor the more pertinaciously for acknowledging the performative grounds of the "quality" granted by aristocratic birth:

> Ne rougissez-vous point de mériter si peu votre naissance? Etes-vous en droit, dites-moi, d'en tirer quelque vanité? Et qu'avez-vous fait dans le monde pour être gentilhomme? Croyez-vous qu'il suffise d'en porter le nom et les armes, et que ce nous soit une gloire d'être sorti d'un sang noble, lorsque nous vivons en infâmes? Non, non, la naissance n'est rien où la vertu n'est pas. Aussi, nous n'avons part à la gloire de nos ancêtres qu'autant que nous nous efforçons de leur ressembler; et cet éclat de leurs actions qu'ils répandent sur nous nous impose un engagement de leur faire le même honneur, de suivre les pas qu'ils nous tracent, et de ne point dégénérer de leurs vertus, si nous voulons être estimés leurs véritables descendants. Ainsi, vous descendez en vain des aïeux dont vous êtes né; ils vous désavouent pour leur sang, et tout ce qu'ils ont fait d'illustre ne vous donne aucun avantage; au contraire, l'éclat n'en rejaillit sur vous qu'à votre déshonneur, et leur gloire est un lambeau qui éclaire aux yeux d'un chacun la honte de vos actions. (304)

Yet affecting as it may be, the speech is pure boilerplate, the automatized rehearsal of the hoary platitudes dictated by the *part* Dom Louis plays. This gives bite not only to the insolent *politesse* with which the son interrupts the old man's sermon, but to the bored irritation provoked by news of his approach: "Ah! me voici bien! Il me fallait cette visite pour me faire enrager." (304) The mere fact of his father's visit dictates the whole content of the speech he will infallibly deliver, reproducing the script in which society composes the roles less cynical performers mistake for authentic selves.

What is true of Done Elvire or Dom Louis is also true of Sganarelle, to whom it falls to defend the cause of religion in the face of his master's atheism. What is both funny and scandalous in Sganarelle's apologies for the faith–the absurd "proof by design" that ends in the pratfall with which theological reasoning "breaks its nose"; the grotesque string of mangled proverbs, parables, emblems, biblical loci, philosophical allusions, and exegetical tropes with which he reproves his master's profession of hypocrisy–is that they are parodies. But of course parody demands a *model* if the audience is to recognize and savor the deformation that makes the parody both funny and telling:

> Sachez, monsieur, que tant va la cruche à l'eau, qu'enfin elle se brise; et, comme dit fort bien cet auteur que je ne connais pas, l'homme est, en ce monde, ainsi que l'oiseau sur la branche; la branche est attachée à l'arbre; qui s'attache à l'arbre suit de bons préceptes; les bons préceptes valent mieux que les belles paroles; les belles paroles se trouvent à la cour; à la cour sont les courtisans; les courtisans suivent la mode; la mode vient de la fantaisie; la fantaisie est une faculté de l'âme; l'âme est ce qui nous donne la vie; la vie finit par la mort; la mort nous fait penser au ciel; le ciel est au-dessus de la terre; la terre n'est point la mer; la mer est sujette aux orages; les orages tourmentent les vaisseaux; les vaisseaux ont besoin d'un bon pilote; un bon pilote a de la prudence; la prudence n'est pas dans les jeunes gens; les jeunes gens doivent obéissance aux vieux; les vieux aiment les richesses; les richesses font les riches; les riches ne sont pas pauvres; les pauvres ont de la nécessité; la nécessité n'a point de loi; qui n'a pas de loi vit en bête brute; et, par conséquent, vous serez damné à tous les diables. (308)

The arguments Sganarelle at once deploys and distorts are all readymades plucked from the *magasin des accessoires* of prevailing culture as surely as the doctor's gown he wears in act 3.

The theme of performance accounts at last for what is so frightening as well as enticing in the mirrorlike blankness Molière gives his version of the don. Dom Juan is a vacancy conjured up as the angry index of the moral vacuum that creates him. This surfaces as early as scene 1, when Sganarelle explains to a horrified Gusman why he remains in service to such a villain: "un grand seigneur méchant homme est une terrible chose." (286) The obvious implication here is *force*: it is a "terrible thing" when a "great lord" turns out to be a "wicked man" because the right of violence society confers on him enables him to escape the penalty for his crimes. But just because the conduct of a "grand seigneur méchant homme" reduces obedience to the threat of physical force that is his empty birthright, Dom Juan exposes the very condition he exploits: the social order is a mirage that at once justifies and masks the violence that spawns it. What makes Dom Juan "terrible" is not only his freedom from constraint, but the revelation of the naked social fiction that grants that freedom.

This insight travels in all directions. It informs the critique of medicine in act 3. When Dom Juan mocks the pretensions of physicians by attributing their ostensible successes to the play of "chance" and the self-serving "grimaces" that cover their ignorance, he implicitly invokes the reductive topography of the new mechanistic science. The patent symptoms doctors observe and treat are in themselves nothing but empty appearances, contingent empirical "vestiges" of the hidden causal processes that produce them.[57] Contemporary medicine thus offers explanatory fantasies in lieu of causal etiologies beyond their power precisely for want of the sort of intuition Dom Juan's example encodes in the dimension of social order: what meets the eye is always the mystified expression of underlying forces that systematically determine the mere surface phenomena people take for the thing itself. Similarly, religion is equated with "superstition" because both share a common root in the fear induced by ignorance of the ultimate "reason" of things. When it is not mere prejudice or hypocrisy, faith is a consoling fiction (Sganarelle's undigested trinity: "ciel," "enfer," "loup-garou") covering our enslavement to material processes we cannot fathom. And then there is *money*, invoked in the image of the counterfeit. The anxiety counterfeit causes springs from an inability to distinguish between genuine coin and its diabolical replica. But at a deeper level lies the acknowledgement of the degree to which economic values and relations are mere blind *credit*, an act of faith that assigns worth as a function not of substance, but of perception, habit, convention, and desire. Gold has no more intrinsic meaning than the words with which Dom Juan pays the hapless M. Di-

---

[57] This essentially deconstructive procedure is what Bacon describes as the "interpretation" (as opposed to "observation") of nature. See my commentary in "The Vindication of Susanna." In a different vein, see the discussion in Patrick Dandrey's massive 2-vol. study, *La médecine et la maladie dans le théâtre de Molière* (Paris: Klincksieck, 1998), vol. 1, *Sganarelle et la médecine, ou de la mélancolie érotique*, pt. 1, chap. 3, "Dom Juan et l'éloge paradoxal de la médecine," 265-324. I believe my sense of the epistemological grounds of *Dom Juan*'s critique cuts deeper than Dandrey's *rapprochement* with the tradition of "éloges paradoxaux" of which Erasmus's *Praise of Folly* is the paradigm.

manche or his credulous father. Money is a collective delusion whose currency stems from unthinking trust.[58]

All of this finds its way into the spectacle Sganarelle makes of himself in the furious speech denouncing Dom Juan's profession of hypocrisy. The servant is beside himself with indignation, anguish, and horror. But so is the author Molière. Molière indeed, *playing* Sganarelle, listens to a cynical speech he himself has penned that voices the rage the ongoing "querelle du *Tartuffe*" inspires. Then, still in the role of Sganarelle, he risks incurring the further wrath of the cabal Dom Juan now personates in order to say point blank what anger dictates. The result however, as noted a moment ago, is only another parody; the helpless outrage both servant and poet feel disgorges a flood of garbled platitudes that reduces reason itself to ludicrous stammering. This yields the force of Dom Juan's typically sardonic rejoinder: "O le beau raisonnement!" (308) Molière makes yet another joke in Sganarelle's fatuous reply: "Après cela, si vous ne vous rendez, tant pis pour vous." But the question remains: on what *true* rather than merely parodic grounds can morality, justice, or truth be said to stand in the wake of Dom Juan's cynical demonstrations?

The immediate upshot is the set of paradoxes in the dénouement. On one hand is the villain's willful refusal to heed the multiple portents of the fate in store for him, culminating in the airborne Specter of 5.5 that, entering as a "veiled woman," is suddenly transformed into Time itself, typological scythe in hand. But the machinery involved merely points to the fact that both the portents and the spectacular descent to hell they forecast are mere *theater*, a further instance of the illusory power of belief. When, unmoved by its warning, Dom Juan strikes at the Specter with his sword "pour éprouver... si c'est un corps ou un esprit," the player inside the contraption prudently "s'envole dans le temps que dom Juan veut le frapper." (309) Similarly, the gate to hell through which the villain falls is a trapdoor, and the thunder, lightning, and erupting flames pure scenic flummery. The play undermines its own moral at

---

[58] See Apostolidès, *Le prince sacrifié*, chap. 5, "L'univers quotidien," esp. the sections on *L'Avare* ("L'échange d'argent," 154-61) and *Dom Juan* ("L'échange universel," 161-73), and Harrison, *Pistoles/Paroles* 7-11. More generally, see Marc Shell, *Money, Language, and Thought: Literary and Philosophic Economies from the Medieval to the Modern Era* (Berkeley: University of California Press, 1982).

every point, eliminating hope of redemptive faith. Whence the furious inconsequence of its closing lines, to which I now restore the framing lament for lost wages omitted the first time it was quoted:

> Ah! mes gages! Mes gages! Voilà, par sa mort, un chacun satisfait. Ciel offensé, lois violées, filles séduites, familles déshonorées, parents outragés, femmes mises à mal, maris poussés à bout, tout le monde est content; il n'y a que moi seul de malheureux, qui, après tant d'années de service, n'ai d'autre récompense que de voir à mes yeux l'impiété de mon maître punie par le plus épouvantable châtiment du monde. Mes gages, mes gages, mes gages! (310)

As silence falls on the echo of Sganarelle's mercenary plaints, Dom Juan's damnation turns on the society whose interest his immolation serves.

It is nevertheless important that we do not necessarily meet here with a conscious *intent* on Molière's part. The whole complex performance may be likened to the dynamic structure of act 3, combining the symbolic scenic multiplicity that characterizes the entire play with the fierce energy that drives the protagonists from one episode to the next. When the act begins, master and man have taken in disguise to the open road, fleeing anonymous riders through a forest. The openness of the road and the change of character implied by the change of costumes encourage Sganarelle to debate the great thematic issues the play joins. But these discussions do not bring them nearer to the truth; rather, it induces a state of distraction in which the travelers *lose their way*: "Mais," Dom Juan drily observes, "tout en raisonnant, je crois que nous nous sommes égarés." (298) Many things follow from this: the enigmatic encounter with the beggar at the crossroads; Dom Carlos's rescue from robbers; the exchange of compliments and threats reflecting seigneurial codes of honor; the first visit to the tomb of the Commander. But what all of them point to is the central fact of going astray. And what is that if not the very form of social experience and the historical process whose blind design it follows?

CHAPTER 6

MEDEA'S POISON: THE WORK OF HISTORY
IN THE TEXT OF RACINE'S *PHEDRE*

THE presiding theme of the book now approaching an end is
what I have called the "invention" of the text in French classical drama. The great dramatists of seventeenth-century France
forge what remains the fundamental model of French literary grandeur. But in doing so, they simultaneously frame and discover what
contemporary theory terms "the text." To read the plays of classical
France is to stand in the presence of deliberate monuments intended to serve as incontrovertible paradigms of the greatness they embody. But the very texts by which these paradigms commit themselves to posterity teach us to detect, as it were *behind* the imposing
monuments that meet us at first glance, the critical double formed
by the historical coercions that attend their creation. The dramatic
masterpieces the *grand siècle* has left us thus become their own
"indiscernible counterparts," inscribing the documentary ruin to
which the revisionist canons of latterday cultural theory consign
them. Nor is it simply that the monuments of classical drama concede a condition endemic to cultural artifacts as such. As a reflex of
the unprecedented literary ambitions that, at another level, man-
date the concealment of the historical contingencies that shape
their historical moment, they consciously *engage* the documentary
ironies to which history consigns them.

Corneille's *Le Cid* doubles as its own "new historicist" critique.
But it does so precisely because the hubristic assertion of its author's transcendent immortality as a Poet puts him in conflict with
the royal sovereign and the canny minister in whom he perceives
both rivals and prototypes. This in turn engenders the "poetics of

322

equivocation" sustaining the artful ambiguities *Horace, Cinna,* and *Rodogune* explore. In his contentious dealings with an emergent state whose authority he simultaneously mimics and challenges, Corneille discovers ("invents") the Derridean *différance* inherent to drama's dual status as poem and play. Source of a theatrical spectacle designed to preempt the critical detachment needed to sort its true motives out, drama is also at once the product and vehicle of the concerted act of *writing* that makes those motives legible. Corneille exploits the potential for temporizing doublespeak at the root of dramatic art, transforming it into a medium of poetic self-assertion the more unanswerable for its enigmatic evasiveness. And yet the result is just the text of his art's documentary deconstruction; or rather, the monument Corneille erects *just is* the critical document in whose light we dismantle it.

Similarly, the project of self-authorization enshrined in the name the humble drapier's son Jean-Baptiste Poquelin makes for himself as "Molière" highlights the constraining social conditions it aims to surmount. An index of Molière's dilemma is the *mise en abyme* by which the comic twins of *Amphitryon* enact the tension between the demands of classical "imitation" the conventions of French classicism prescribe and the originality supporting his claims to independent authorship. In the process, however, Molière's predicament as an author becomes an emblem of the alienating "interpellation" and "méconnaissance" to which society subjects its members as an ineluctable condition of identity. This in turn is why, in the violent controversies of which *L'Ecole des femmes, Tartuffe,* and *Dom Juan* arise as both objects and episodes, Molière's ambitions as a poet fuse with the ironic demonstration of their own impossibility. *L'Ecole des femmes* stages a proto-Lacanian "comedy of the subject" in which, by identifying the authorial project with its parodic counterpart in Arnolphe's self-promoting schemes, the comic text transforms the apotheosis of poetic mastery into a symptomatic allegory of the poet's defeat. But in exposing the defeat his ambitions undergo, Molière lays bare the self-defeating performativeness theater shares with the society it mirrors. In responding to the violent public outcry *L'Ecole's* critique of the "subject" provokes, *Tartuffe* and *Dom Juan* not only denounce, but *reproduce* the multiple "hypocrisies" that form the very fabric of social truth.

What is true of Corneille and Molière is, if anything, still more true of Racine, the poet who, in building on their accomplishments, supersedes them, absorbing them into his own unique literary substance. In the "Paradoxe sur le comédien," Diderot's first speaker remarks at one point that "il n'y a presque rien de commun entre la manière d'écrire la comédie et la tragédie en Angleterre et la manière dont on écrit ces poèmes en France." One result of this lack of common ground is an unbridgeable difference in national acting styles that makes it impossible for actors on one side of the channel to perform plays composed on the other:

> [C]elui qui sait rendre parfaitement une scène de Shakespeare ne connaît pas le premier accent de la déclamation d'une scène de Racine; puisque enlacé par les vers harmonieux de ce dernier, comme par autant de serpents dont les replis lui étreignent la tête, les pieds, les mains, les jambes et les bras, son action en perdrait toute sa liberté. [1]

The Laokoon-like picture of the English actor helplessly entangled in the harmonious toils of Racinian numbers is a defamiliarizing device designed to illustrate a point the dialogue urges from the start: that what theater audiences take for "nature" is in fact mere sublimated artifice, an idealized "second" nature that only becomes visible when we try to pass from one cultural community to another. But behind the immediate thought lies its corollary, closely tied to the revisionist theses regarding the character and use of the French classics (and among them of course Racine) Diderot develops in the *Neveu de Rameau*. What we take for nature *in general,* for that encompassing order of things of which theater is the putative portrait or mirror, is itself mere artifice–is indeed "de la comédie," pure illusion, fiction, pretense, subject as such to the paradoxes acting exhibits.

In England, the preeminent source of the illusion behind the presiding sense of nature goes by the name of "Shakespeare"; the "freedom" or *naturel* the English actor loses when he attempts to declaim Racinian verse is his indiscernible bondage to the verse forms the Bard bequeaths his nation. In France, the equivalent is

---

[1] Diderot, "Paradoxe sur le comédien," 126-27.

"Racine." Racine amounts to something like a national *fate*. Like the serpents from Virgil's *Aeneid* throttling the lone Trojan clairvoyant enough to recognize the Greek gift for what it is, Racine's alexandrines weave the invisible ligatures that bind actors, poets, and audiences alike, forging chains the more unbreakable for being unseen, defining the rhythms, postures, and *démarches* that form the very element of theatrical expression. To mirror nature is to do theater; but to do theater is to do Racine, an endless repetition enforced by the fact of walking in the giant shadow the Racinian monument casts over French literature to this day. Whence the compulsion Diderot images, and more precisely the *history* of which he presents himself as the Laokoonian captive, bound in serpentine knots from which he vainly struggles to escape. [2] After Racine, everything is "after" Racine, the belated echo of the Big Bang that he begot.

We began this book where the golden age of French classicism did, with Corneille's *Le Cid* and the resulting quarrel in which French classical culture first set out to define itself. We now end it with Racine's *Phèdre*, a play whose most striking feature is the lu-

---

[2] The Laokoon analogy is tantalizingly topical. The sculptural group emerges as a focus of interest in Johann Joachim Winckelmann's *Reflections on the Imitation of Greek Works in Painting and Sculpture* (1755), German text & parallel trans. Elfriede Heyer & Roger C. Norton (La Salle: Open Court, 1987), chap. 4, where it illustrates the "noble simplicity" and "quiet grandeur" by which, surpassing mere natural beauty, Greek art instructs modern epigones in the highest demands of their calling. Winckelmann's *Reflections* then provoke Lessing's *Laokoon* (1766), challenging not only the earlier writer's assessment of the Laokoon group itself, but above all the underlying aesthetic system encoded in the term "imitation," i.e., the doctrine *ut pictura poesis* prescribing classical art as a model for poets as well as sculptors and painters. Thus, in contesting Winckelmann's interpretation of the Laokoon group by asserting the proper "limits" defining visual and verbal art, Lessing does two closely related things of great interest to Diderot: he argues for a rigorous separation of aesthetic forms and he rejects the imitation of classical example as the essential school of art. See Gotthold Ephraim Lessing, *Laocoon: An Essay on the Limits of Painting and Poetry*, ed. & trans. Edward Allen McCormick (Indianapolis: Bobbs-Merrill, 1962). Meanwhile, though we cannot place the composition of the "Paradoxe" precisely, Diderot refers to it in a letter to his German correspondent Grimm dated 14 November 1769 (see the editor's "notice" in Diderot, *Paradoxe sur le comédien, précédé des Entretiens sur le Fils naturel* 119). This suggests a date in the late 1760's, making it more than possible that both Winckelmann's *Reflections* and Lessing's critique were in his mind when he chose his serpentine metaphor to describe Racinian verse.

cidity with which, in the theatrical death of its eponymous queen, it deliberately *makes* the end we find in it. Indeed, in the deep silence that falls with the heroine's death, *Phèdre* transmits itself to us *as* that end, the simultaneous consummation and abridgement of the classical legacy. In making an end, *Phèdre* makes *history*, closing out the classical era in such a way as to nominate itself as constituting its in every sense ultimate embodiment. It is nevertheless in the nature of the self-nominating end by which *Phèdre* makes the historical epoch it at once terminates and epitomizes that its very success should prove its undoing. In giving itself to be read as the end, *Phèdre* gives itself, verbatim, *to be read*. The ironic consequence of Racine's achievement is to have inaugurated the sequence of historical metamorphoses that comprises its history *as a text*. And yet if *Phèdre* succeeds in making history, it is because it opens itself *to* history, incorporating (and thereby forestalling) the historical ruin Diderot tries to inflict. Even the ironies to which the play is exposed magnify its greatness since even its ironies turn out to inhabit the text its author contrived to write.

That Racine and, more specifically, the Racine of *Phèdre* should occupy this curiously double place as the repository of the historical ironies of which he is the compulsory butt reflects to begin with the studied *perfection* he brings to his art. The tragedies of Racine are in the strongest possible sense great works of art, displaying the precision and balance, the self-disciplined autonomy and reasoned self-containment classical doctrine prescribes. There is something almost autistic about Racinian tragedy, a magnificent if at times monstrous solipsism comparable to nothing so much as the hermetic self-involvement of its leading characters. Racinian "love" is fundamentally self-directed, a psychomoral pathology rather than an erotic relation whose paradigmatic symptom is the poet's predilection for the intransitive form of the relevant verb. The quintessential expression of amorous inclination–Phèdre's "J'aime!" at 2.5.673, for instance, a complete sentence without a direct object–has no external referent, turning instead toward an image thrown up on the inner screen of erotized consciousness itself. But Racinian love is but one symptom of a more pervasive narcissistic bondage. *Andromaque* closes with the reeling exit of the mad Oreste pursued by vengeful phantoms lodged in his own brain. In *Bérénice*, the eponymous heroine superbly turns her back on both of her disappointed lovers, withdrawing into the autarchic redoubt of her private kingdom far from the messy publicity of Republican Rome. And what ultimately enlists Phèdre's complicity in the calumny with which her servant Œnone accuses Hippolyte of the incestuous passion of which his father's queen is guilty is wounded vanity. The trigger of Phèdre's final and, given its fatal outcome, most irrevocable crime is the intolerable mental picture not only of the younger Aricie's success, but of her own abjection as "le seul objet" the disputed boy cannot bring himself to desire:

> Hippolyte est sensible, et ne sent rien pour moi!
> Aricie a son cœur! Aricie a sa foi!
> Ah, dieux! lorsqu'à mes yeux l'ingrat inexorable
> S'armait d'un œil si fier, d'un front si redoutable,
> Je pensais qu'à l'amour son cœur toujours fermé
> Fût contre tout mon sexe également armé:
> Une autre cependant a fléchi son audace;
> Devant ses yeux cruels une autre a trouvé grâce.
> Peut-être a-t-il un cœur facile à attendrir:
> Je suis le seul objet qu'il ne saurait souffrir.
>
> (4.5.1203-12)

It is important that Phèdre's fascination with this tormenting image does find an objective echo in the at once vainglorious and sadistic satisfaction her rival derives from overcoming Hippolyte's resistance to her charms. Confiding to Ismène what she desires in Thésée's son, Aricie explicitly triumphs over the aging queen:

> J'aime, je prise en lui de plus nobles richesses,
> Les vertus de son père, et non point les faiblesses;
> J'aime, je l'avouerai, cet orgueil généreux
> Qui jamais n'a fléchi sous le joug amoureux.
> Phèdre en vain s'honorait des soupirs de Thésée:
> Pour moi, je suis plus fière, et fuis la gloire aisée
> D'arracher un hommage a mille autres offert,
> Et d'entrer dans un cœur de toutes parts ouvert.
> Mais de faire fléchir un courage inflexible,
> De porter la douleur dans une âme insensible,

D'enchaîner un captif de ses fers étonné,
Contre un joug qui lui plaît vainement mutiné;
C'est là ce que je veux, c'est là ce qui m'irrite.
(2.1.441-53)[3]

Yet it is remarkable that, despite their intense awareness of each other, Phèdre and Aricie never appear on stage at the same time. Phèdre never therefore actually *witnesses* Hippolyte's *fléchissement*, the pliant bend beneath the "amorous yoke" her rival plants on his neck, the ambiguous erotic "pain" she inflicts, the "irons" in which she shackles a "captive" dumbstruck (*étonné*) to discover the irons he bears. Nor consequently does Phèdre witness Aricie's triumph at her expense. The vision is thus strictly and entirely *imaginary*, a Lacanian mirage spawned by the obsessive *amour-propre* that alienates her from real relation. Just so, to the degree that Racine's plays reach and touch us, it is because they *absorb* us, establishing only so much reference to the world we inhabit as they need to overcome resistance to their coercive self-regard. Like poor Hippolyte himself, we become helpless captives of a foreign power to whose extortionate demands we yield in dumbstruck wonder.

The chief formal source of this monumental self-containment is Racine's systematic adherence to the principle of immanence underlying the classical theory of dramatic mimesis. Given the role dramatic monologue plays in this development, a particularly striking index of Racinian practice is the strict limit he sets on traditional soliloquy. Mindful of the convention's unnatural basis as highlighted by the parodic one-way dialogue in Molière's *L'Ecole des femmes* 4.2, where a distracted Arnolphe utters private thoughts out loud in the presence of a notary who responds as though they were addressed to him, Racine favors the device of the confidant. The public expression of private passion is motivated and justified as an intimate confidence to the trusted companion whose anxious questions elicit it. Such exceptions as we meet confirm the rule in that they arise at just those moments when their speakers reach an

---

[3] Note that, though both uses of the verb "aimer" in this speech have a direct object, in each case the text inserts a delaying syntactical distance: "J'aime, je prise en lui de plus nobles richesses" and "J'aime, je l'avouerai, cet orgueil inflexible." The naming of *what* the speaker loves is marked by a failure (perhaps even incapacity) to carry straight on from verb to object.

extremity of pain, rage, or tormented hallucination. Thésée's soliloquy in the immediate aftermath of the angry encounter with his son precipitated by Œnone's accusation of attempted rape is clinically insane. It is not just that, crazed by a frantic compound of jealousy, injured vanity, and a conviction that he has been betrayed ("Qui m'a trahi!") (3.5.980) all the more invincible for mirroring his own sexual faithlessness, he presents the spectacle of a man talking to himself out loud. The pathology is certified by the tirade's central figure. Like the demented Oreste of *Andromaque* shouting at visions of a dead Pyrrhus, a dead Hermione, and the furious Nemeses come to punish the matricide with which he avenged his father Agamemnon's murder, Thésée gives himself up to *apostrophe*. In an irony pointed by what the audience knows to be the negative answers to the rhetorical questions with which the speech concludes, he harangues an Hippolyte who is no longer there–indeed, a *guilty* Hippolyte who never existed at all:

> Misérable, tu cours à ta perte infaillible!
> Neptune, par le fleuve aux dieux mêmes terrible,
> M'a donné sa parole, et va l'exécuter.
> Un dieu vengeur te suit, tu ne peux l'éviter.
> Je t'aimais; et je sens que, malgré ton offense,
> Mes entrailles pour toi se troublent par avance.
> Mais à te condamner tu m'as trop engagé:
> Jamais père, en effet, fut-il plus outragé?
> Justes dieux qui voyez la douleur qui m'accable,
> Ai-je pu mettre au jour un enfant si coupable?
>
> (4.3.1157-66)

But Racine's commitment to the economy of immanence emerges above all in his exact conformity to the classical unities. Perfect unity of place is achieved by confining the action to a single set whose dimensions coincide with those of the stage itself: in *Andromaque*, a public reception room (*une salle*) in Pyrrhus' palace; in *Brittanicus*, an inner chamber in the imperial abode; in *Bérénice*, a "cabinet" between the private apartments of the emperor Titus and the Palestinian queen whose regal title so offends the Roman people; in *Bajazet*, a room in the harem of the sultan Amurat; in *Athalie*, a vestibule in the Temple of Jerusalem. Racinian theater fuses the space of events with the space of their representation: dramatized world and dramatic work arise as one and the same, producing a claustrophobic closure the scenic counterpart of the characters' quasi-autistic introvertedness.

Similarly, perfect unity of time is attained through the theatrical equivalent of the "pregnant moment" in the parallel art of history painting. The curtain rises at a point of gathering crisis typically focused on the *decision* circumstances compel the central protagonists to make: a dilemma whose pressure at once elicits the spontaneous rehearsal of the play's dramatic antecedents and triggers the tragic *péripéties*, the series of reversals and recognitions that drive the unfolding plot. In *Andromaque*, Pyrrhus' choice between the Greek demand that he kill the Trojan Hector's son Astyanax and his overmastering desire for Hector's widow both brings the tragic personnel to the stage (Andromaque is his prisoner; Oreste arrives as the Greeks' messenger; Hermione is sent as the bride Greek policy offers in compensation for Astyanax's execution) and sets a limit on the time in which a dramatic issue must be found. In *Bajazet*, the interval in which the protagonists seek to resolve the triangle formed by the title character, his mistress Atalide, and the tyrannical Amurat's favorite concubine Roxane is framed by the time it takes to learn the outcome of the sultan's conflict with the distant kingdom of Babylon and the bare hour left once news arrives with Amurat's murderous slave Orcan. And in *Phèdre*, the time of the action is delimited by Thésée's erroneously reported death in the underworld and his ensuing resurrection and return, ensnaring the principals in the consequences of his queen's avowal of her adulterous passion for his son.

But the ultimate expression of Racinian dramatic practice is the relentless unity of the tragic action itself. The initial crisis provokes a train of violent confrontations steering the characters toward a mortal close. Racine works indeed to a rigorous formula whereby, precisely midway through the third of his five acts, the protagonists commit themselves to an irretrievably tragic end. In *Andromaque*, the action passes failsafe in the run of scenes (3.4-7) in which, by refusing to intervene on behalf of her rival's son, the vindictive Hermione leaves Andromaque no alternative but capitulation to Pyrrhus' blackmailing promise to spare Astyanax in exchange for her hand in marriage. In *Bajazet*, the tragic threshold is crossed in

3.4-5, where despite his mistress's plea that he save his life by yielding to Roxane's predatory passion, the hero rejects his brother's concubine, compounding the injury to Roxane's pride with foolish appeals to sentiments of honor and the sanctity of true love. In *Phèdre*, the characters' fates are also sealed in 3.4-5 when Phèdre and Hippolyte's refusal to name the source of the mysterious disturbance that greets Thésée's homecoming kindles the jealous suspicions Œnone's calumny stirs up into a lethal rage that, in causing the innocent son to be torn to pieces by the sea monster Neptune sends in answer to Thésée's misguided prayer, brings on the queen's climactic suicide. The actors' independent decisions, unmediated by authorial commentary, thus converge on a calculated tragic fulcrum round which the dramatic masses wheel toward inexorable ruin.

The monumental self-containment of Racinian tragedy is further accentuated by its self-referential character. In *Bajazet*, for example, the rigorous observation of the unity of time and the related clockwork precision of the plot become a *theme*. Temporal allusions, figures, and indicators hammer a beat that culminates in the famous "Sortez" (5.4.1564) with which Roxane despatches the hero to the death that awaits his climactic exit:

Un long chemin sépare et le camp et Byzance;
Mille obstacles divers m'ont même traversé:
Et je puis ignorer tout ce qui s'est passé.
(1.1.26-28)

Prince, l'heure fatale est enfin arrivée
Qu'à votre liberté le ciel a réservée.
Rien ne me retient plus; et je puis, dès ce jour,
Accomplir le dessein qu'à formé mon amour.
(2.1.421-24)

Bajazet, écoutez; je sens que je vous aime:
Vous vous perdez. Gardez de me laisser sortir:
Le chemin est encore ouvert au repentir.
(2.1.538-40)

Venez, seigneur, venez: il est temps de paraître,
Et que tout le serail reconnaisse son maître.
(3.5.1013-14)

> Le temps presse. Que faire en ce doute funeste?
> Allons, employons bien le moment qui nous reste.
>
> (3.8.1117-18)

> D'ailleurs, l'ordre, l'esclave, et le visir me presse.
> Il faut prendre parti: l'on m'attend.
>
> (4.4.1234-35)

> Je ne vous ferai point des reproches frivoles:
> Les moments sont trop chers pour les perdre en paroles.
>
> (5.4.1469-70)

But a more subtle expression of the same self-referentiality is the undertow of poetic emulation shaping not only the Roman play *Bérénice*, composed and staged in direct competition with the venerable Corneille's version of the same story, but Racine's two model Greek tragedies, *Andromaque* and his last tragedy proper, *Phèdre*.

All of the major protagonists in *Andromaque* are haunted by their captivity to the heroic generation of the Trojan War. Hermione is Helen's daughter, a fact that embitters the wound inflicted by Pyrrhus' rejection of her charms, escaping the erotic thrall in which her mother's beauty held an entire world. Tormented by the furies unleashed by his retributive murder of his mother Clytemnestra, a crime dictated by his filial debt to his butchered father Agamemnon, Oreste seeks salvation in the abject passion for Hermione that Helen's child manipulates in her powerplay with the insensible Pyrrhus. Andromaque meanwhile is entirely consumed by her identity as Hector's widow and the mother of Hector's son, the faithful bearer of the legacy the Greeks mean to annihilate. As befits besides his own identity as Achilles' son, Pyrrhus alone pursues an autonomous path. Motivated by what Roland Barthes has called the "refus d'hériter," the defiant refusal of the role inherited from his heroic progenitor, [4] he doggedly rejects the duty his great father's ghost enjoins; and he does so all the more emphatically by replacing it with love for the wife of Achilles' paradigmatic adversary. But he is also motivated by an underlying *ressentiment*. Though in on the

---

[4] Barthes, *Sur Racine* 50-52. What we have already seen of *Phèdre*'s Hippolyte shows him to be a major exemplar of this trait. See too Apostolidès, "La tragédie des fils: 'Andromaque'," in *Le prince sacrifié*, chap. 4, "L'univers tragique," 94-101.

kill at Troy, the frenzied acts of butchery he performed are eclipsed by the authentic heroism that distinguishes his father even in death, exhausting all possibility of independent accomplishment. He is then the mere *émule*, the diminished epigone of the manly grandeur achieved by the true heroes of Troy.

Andromaque specifically touches this nerve when, withholding the love Pyrrhus demands in exchange for Astyanax's life, she tells him that braving Greek anger on her son's behalf without hope of reward is itself an heroic feat comparable to any his dead father performed: "voilà des soins dignes du fils d'Achille" (1.4.310). But the first exchange between Pyrhhus and Oreste makes the same point more subtly. Speaking as Greek ambassador, Oreste opens the scene thus:

> Avant que tous les Grecs vous parlent par ma voix,
> Souffrez que j'ose ici me flatter de leur choix,
> Et qu'à vos yeux, seigneur, je montre quelque joie
> De voir le fils d'Achille et le vainqueur de Troie.
>
> (1.2.143-46)

Since we know from 1.1 that Oreste hates Pyrrhus as his rival for Hermione and that his ambassadorial mission is prompted by Pyrrhus' refusal to comply with Greek demands for Astyanax's death, Oreste's insincerity is patent. But so is the accuracy with which his malice hits home. Pyrrhus' designation as "le fils d'Achille" delivers an ironic thrust pointed by its recipient's failure to live up to the name Oreste gives him. And that Pyrrhus takes the barb in this spirit is confirmed in the upshot, when he replies with a glacial *politesse* whose ironic subtext is even more insulting:

> La Grèce en ma faveur est trop inquiétée:
> De soins plus importants je l'ai crue agitée,
> Seigneur; et, sur le nom de son ambassadeur,
> J'avais dans ses projets conçu plus de grandeur.
> Qui croirait en effet qu'une telle entreprise
> Du fils d'Agamemnon méritât l'entremise;
> Qu'un peuple tout entier, tant de fois triomphant,
> N'eût daigné conspirer que la mort d'un enfant?
>
> (1.2.173-80)

Pyrrhus lands a double blow. First, there is reproach at the unseemly disproportion between the ambassador's noble identity and the squalid task the Greeks have assigned him. But, second, there is the implied sarcasm in addressing Oreste as "fils d'Agamemnon," that is, as the son of a man butchered in his bath by the wife who cuckolded him with his own cousin. The wounding symmetry of Pyrrhus' rejoinder thus underscores the pertinacity of its provocation.

Just so, in *Phèdre*, in addition to having to live down the bad example of his father's notorious amours, Hippolyte must contend with the noble model Thésée's heroic exertions set. When the play begins, we learn that, despite his "proud" resolve to foreswear sexual entanglement, remaining forever chaste in order to expunge the ignominy inherited as his faithless father's son, he has fallen in love with the captive Aricie. But what makes this passion intolerable is not merely the embarrassment involved in yielding to amorous temptation; it is his incapacity to atone for his venereal sins in the way his father does since Thésée has already slain all the monsters and brigands in whose blood a compensatory heroic identity could be forged:

> Et moi-même, à mon tour, je me verrais lié!
> Et les dieux jusque-là m'auraient humilié!
> Dans mes lâches soupirs d'autant plus méprisable,
> Qu'un long amas d'honneurs rend Thésée excusable.
> Qu'aucuns monstres par moi domptés jusqu'aujourd'hui
> Ne m'ont acquis le droit de faillir comme lui!
>
> (1.1.95-100)

Yet what is the complex belatedness of Racine's major characters if not a displaced image of his own situation relative to the great epic and tragic poets of antiquity? As we saw in chapter 3 with reference to Plautus' *Amphitruo*, even comic dramatists learn their trade in the school of classical imitation, manufacturing vernacular verse out of ancient precedent. What is true of Rotrou or Molière is all the more so of tragic poets like Racine. Great tragedy requires great tragic *subjects*, and for the classical age, these are by definition the ones embodied in the classical tradition on which the

Greek Racine consistently draws. [5] The second-generation heroes Pyrrhus and Hippolyte live in the shadow of the paradigmatic fathers from whom they inherit the moral dilemmas circumstances oblige them to resolve while simultaneously denying them the means to do so. But Racine shares their derivative stature, writing in the afterglow not only of what Thomas Greene has aptly styled the heroic "light in Troy," but of the aged Corneille whose sublime example he is condemned to imitate. [6]

Racine's tragedies are then not only great works of art, but bristle with the *consciousness* of their workly greatness and the artful means required to achieve it. Such is, besides, the testimony of his prefaces, betokening both the pride with which he improves on ancient models and his obsession with demonstrating his superiority to Corneille. [7] Racinian tragedy means to be in every sense exemplary, a deliberate paragon of the monumental perfection the ideal of tragic drama enjoins. Nevertheless, self-engendering, self-announcing, and to that degree transcendent though we must acknowledge them to be, the monuments of Racinian art are also historical *documents*. For all their perfection, they bear incidental witness to the underlying mentalities, the ruling "discourse," "imaginary," and taste that made them possible.

---

[5] See, e.g., La Mesnardière, *Poëtique* 1.5, "La Composition du Sujet, Premiere Partie de la Tragédie," and d'Aubignac, *Pratique du théâtre* 2.1, "Du Sujet."

[6] See Greene, *The Light in Troy* and Quint, *Origin and Originality in Renaissance Literature*.

[7] See, e.g., the preface to *Brittanicus*, where Racine responds to criticism of Junie's return on stage following Brittanicus' murder on the grounds that the action is properly complete with the hero's death by launching a violent attack on Cornelian dramaturgie: "Que faudrait-il faire pour contenter des juges si difficiles? La chose serait aisée, pour peu qu'on voulût trahir le bon sens. Il ne faudrait que s'écarter du naturel pour se jeter dans l'extraordinaire. Au lieu d'une action simple, chargée de peu de matière, telle que doit être une action qui se passe en un seul jour, et qui, s'avançant par degrés vers sa fin, n'est soutenue que par les intérêts, les sentiments et les passions des personnages, il faudrait remplir cette même action de quantité d'incidents qui ne se pourraient passer qu'en un mois, d'un grand nombre de jeux de théâtre d'autant plus surprenants qu'ils seraient moins vraisemblables, d'une infinité de déclamations où l'on ferait dire aux acteurs tout le contraire de ce qu'ils devraient dire. Il faudrait, par exemple, représenter quelque héros ivre, qui se voudrait faire haïr de sa maîtresse de gaîté de coeur, un Lacédémonien grand parleur, un conquérant qui ne débiterait que des maximes d'amour, une femme qui donnerait des leçons de fierté à des conquérants. Voilà sans doute de quoi faire récrier tous ces messieurs." (143) A measure of Racine's touchiness is the fact that the attack on Corneille has no bearing on the point at issue.

To be sure, unlike the baroque Corneille, defiantly rejecting the classical programme dictated by Richelieu's Académie, or the still more bitterly embattled Molière, whose plays so often directly engage their political as well as cultural context, Racine draws firm lines between poetry and polemic. Neither his ferocious response to the Jansenist Pierre Nicole's denunciation of dramatic poets as poisoners of public morals nor his largely tacit engagement in the *querelle des anciens et des modernes* find anything like overt expression in his dramas per se.[8] Moreover, despite dedicating *Alexandre le grand* to the king in an epistle drawing ingratiating parallels between the young Louis XIV and the Macedonian hero he takes as his theme, he sets a high barrier between the tragic works on which he stakes his reputation and the absolutist panegyric that enables him to make his way at court. Like the slavish Perrault whose *Siècle de Louis le grand* is occasioned by the monarch's happy escape from a protracted fever, Racine writes an ode to celebrate the sovereign's recovery from illness; and in his later capacity as court historiographer, he will write chronicles of royal affairs that shamelessly praise what stricter canons of historiographical veracity would bid him blame.[9] Still, the dramatic poems that earned him his fame are carefully insulated from the topical issues of the day.

---

[8] The distant occasion of the "affaire des Visionnaires" or, as it is also called, "affaire des Imaginaires" was Nicole's defense of Jansenism against charges of heresy in *Les Imaginaires, ou Lettres sur l'hérésie imaginaire*, an epistolary series modeled on Pascal's *Provinciales* begun in 1664. However, the immediate spur was *Les Visionnaires, ou seconde partie des Lettres sur l'hérésie imaginaire* (1667), responding to an anti-Jansenist pamphlet by Desmarets de Saint-Sorlin, in which Nicole challenges Desmarets's right to pronounce on matters of faith in that, as a novelist and dramatist, he is himself a poisoner of public morals. For the text of Racine's reaction to this charge, together with the preface written for a projected (but, thanks to Boileau's intercession, unpublished) edition of both his first public letter and a still more violent second one, see *Œuvres complètes* 307-14. For Racine's sole public contribution to the gathering *querelle des anciens et des modernes*, see his preface to *Iphigénie* (225), defending Euripides against "modern" criticisms.

[9] See "Sur la convalescence du roi," *Œuvres complètes* 443-44. Beyond the belated apology on behalf of his Jansenist upbringers, the *Abrégé de l'histoire de Port-Royal* (315-61), Racine's chief historical works are the long fragments, *Précis historique des campagnes de Louis XIV depuis 1672 jusqu'en 1678* (387-400) and the *Relation de ce qui s'est passé au siège de Namur* (400-20). That Racine was perfectly aware of the difference between the kind of history he wrote and the kind of thing history should properly be is attested by his extracts from Lucian's essay on historiography. We shall return to these later.

Further, where the unfortunate Molière continues to act and direct as well as write quite literally to the hour of his death, Racine maintains a prudent distance from the morally and socially compromising world of the stage. He writes for the theater, and even on at least one occasion is known to have rehearsed an actress in her role. Yet Racine's scandals, and in particular the allegation that he poisoned his mistress la Du Parc, leading lady of the theatrical company installed in the Hôtel de Bourgogne, do not directly implicate his dramatic career as such. [10] It is telling indeed that, the dedication to *Alexandre* apart, the exceptions to this rule are the comic *Plaideurs* and the two Roman plays, *Brittanicus* and *Bérénice*: the one a satire on lawyers, the others tragedies staged in direct competition with Corneille. But the *Plaideurs* was an experiment never to be repeated: it constitutes Racine's sole foray in the inevitably topical genre of comedy; and set in "la basse Normandie," its action unfolds at a careful distance from the capital. And the point of the two Roman tragedies is to beat his aging predecessor at his own game, showcasing his specifically *artistic* superiority independent of all topical resonance.

Even so, the broader social, political, and ideological forces that shape the age also shape the tragedies of its foremost poet. As early as 1948, Paul Bénichou's *Morales du grand siècle* situates Racine in the demoralized context of the triumph of Ludovican absolutism sealed with the defeat of the Frondes and the ensuing personal seizure of power concluded with the incarceration of the century's last great private adventurer, the minister Fouquet. The self-consuming solipsism of Racine's major protagonists is thus seen to reflect the more general sardonic inwardness to which political defeat drove the generation of La Rochefoucauld, Pascal, and La Bruyère, writers whose psychological pessimism contrasts sharply with the heroic *élan* characterizing the generations of Descartes, Balzac, Corneille, and Rotrou. [11]

---

[10] On Racine rehearsing his then leading actress La Champmeslé in her role for *Mithridate*, see Viala, *Racine* 152. On the accusation (leveled long after the alleged fact, during the notorious "affaire des poisons") of having poisoned la Du Parc, ibid. 213-14.

[11] See Paul Bénichou, *Morales du grand siècle*. For an interesting English parallel, see Christopher Hill, *The Experience of Defeat: Milton and Some Contemporaries* (New York: Viking, 1984).

Bénichou's book is followed a decade later by Lucien Goldmann's *Le Dieu caché*, with its famous thesis concerning Racinian
tragedy's socio-historical testimony as a byproduct of seventeenth-
century class warfare. What makes tragedy possible (and it is a
tribute to Goldmann's genuinely dialectical insight that he follows
Georg Lukács's example by grounding his social argument in
analysis of the inner logic of the tragic genre as such) is the
uncompromising vision of the world's irrevocable fallenness and
the self-accusing crimes lightless human error breeds. But this vision is the product of the specific social environment formed by the
religious community of Port-Royal in which the orphaned Racine
was raised. Racine's portrayal of the predestined yet inexpiably
guilty nature of human conduct reproduces the Augustinian austerity of his Jansenist upbringing: the tragic poet becomes the dramatic counterpart of Pascal's "hidden God," witness and judge of the
self-defeating ironies of human delusion, vanity, and desire. But
Jansenism is itself the product of an alienated professional, legal,
and administrative caste increasingly excluded from its customary
access to power by the consolidation of the absolutist state. The
tragic vision infusing Racinian tragedy is a reflex of the widening
control exerted by royal ministries and commissions, transforming
the ambitious intellectuals installed in parliaments and law courts
into helpless bystanders. Racine's tragedies reflect a social response
to arbitrary authority for which Jansenism supplies the metaphysical expression. [12]

Bénichou and Goldmann lay out a general interpretive stance
that has been systematically refined ever since. Barthes's analysis of
the archetypal Racinian being (*l'homme racinien*) as a focus of insatiable narcissistic appetite echoes Bénichou's interpretation of classical psychology; and his related picture of the Racinian stage as the
"antechamber" of paternal Power transforms Goldmann's "hidden
God" into a version of the Lacanian Gaze from whose pitiless solar
orbit there is all the less chance of escape in that it has been systematically internalized. [13] Alain Viala's more recent investigations of

---

[12] Lucien Goldmann, *Le Dieu caché*. For Goldmann's chief source on the constitutive "vision" of tragedy, see the pre-Marxist Georg Lukács's Hegelian *Soul and
Form*, trans. Anna Bostock (Cambridge, Mass.: MIT Press, 1974).

[13] See Barthes, *Sur Racine*, essay 1, "L'Homme racinien." On the "antechamber" and the related theme of the gazing eye of paternal power, 9-11. Though muted

the social standing of *gens de lettres* in the classical era enable us to interpret Racinian aesthetic grandeur as an allegory of the emerging social institution of literary Authorship itself; [14] and Viala's *Stratégie du caméléon* goes on to rewrite Racine's entire career as a lurid compound of cynical opportunism and shameless adaptation to evolving public taste. [15] Crossed with Julia Kristeva's account of "abjection" and Hans Blumenberg's analysis of the neo-Gnostic impulse animating early modern renewals of St. Augustine's austere insistence on fallen humanity's predestined corruption, Goldmann's characterization of the Jansenist ground of Racinian tragedy has inspired Marie-Florine Bruneau's exploration of the "melancholy" shaping Racine's experience of historical "modernity." [16] But especially as sharpened by Barthes's *Sur Racine*, the Bénichou-Goldmann position has also provided the general framework for Mitchell Greenberg's psychoanalytic approach to the simultaneously moral and ontological roots of the psycho-politics endemic to the culture of absolutist France. [17] Marc Fumaroli's *Héros et orateurs* lends Bénichou and Goldmann's insights greater philological precision by relating them to contemporary literary and rhetorical as well as theological schemes of education, sharpening our sense of the Jansenist contribution by deepening the contrast with the heroic sensibility enshrined in the Jesuit *ratio studiorum* in which Corneille was trained. [18] To all of which may be added analyses of the at once social and metaphysical thrust of Racine's involvement

---

by a dearth of explicit references to earlier critical studies, Barthes's debt to Goldmann is obvious, as is his debt to Starobinski's "Racine et la poétique du regard" in *L'Œil vivant* 73-92.

[14] Viala, *Naissance de l'écrivain*.

[15] This is the major theme of Viala's *Racine*. But see too Rohou, *Jean Racine*, which pursues a similar line, albeit with greater sympathy toward the poet than Viala shows.

[16] See Bruneau, *Racine: Le jansénisme et la modernité*.

[17] See Greenberg, *Subjectivity and Subjugation*, chap. 6, "Racine's Children," where Freud's insights are intensified by the author's enlistment of the work of Lacan and Irigaray. Thus Greenberg analyzes the denaturing consequences of the role gender plays in the constitution of the absolutist "subject," a figure grounded in the alienating repression of the "feminine" conceived as the embodiment of the political as well as psychological chaos classical culture identifies as its at once instigating and legitimizing Other.

[18] See Fumaroli, *Héros et orateurs*, parts 2, "Corneille et la Société de Jésus," and 4, "Corneille et la rhétorique de l'humanisme chrétien."

in the *querelle des anciens et des modernes* as chronicled by Marc
Soriano and Joan DeJean. [19]

To the extent moreover that Racine's tragedies serve as historical documents, they become "texts" in the tellingly polemical
sense defined in Barthes's famous essays, "La mort de l'auteur" and
"De l'œuvre au texte." [20] With the demise of the in every sense
"classic" figure of the author notoriously announced in the first of
these essays, the monumental Work is transformed into what the
second calls the "methodological field" defined by the questions,
interests, and preconceptions readers bring to it. In defiance of the
ideology of transcendent authorship to which the inherent grandeur of Racinian tragedy aspires, the work answers not only to the
conscious and (in an insight whose rigorous formulation is but one
of the fruits of our later age) *un*-conscious motives grounded in
Racine's historical era; it also responds to the critical acts of explanation and understanding by which we form the documentary
record of History itself. Whence indeed the guiding thesis stated in
the foreword to Barthes's *Sur Racine*. Racine's "actualité," his ongoing interest for readers today, springs from "un art inégalé de la dis-
ponibilité, qui lui permet de se maintenir éternellement dans le
champ de n'importe quel langage critique." But the source of this

---

[19] See DeJean, *Ancients against moderns*. DeJean does not, however, single
Racine out, focusing instead on a general critique of "fin-de-siècle" ancients and
moderns alike in which the tragic poet takes his lumps along with everyone else. Soriano's *La Brosse à reluire* takes a more indirect tack by concentrating on the merciless sarcasm to which the "ancients" Boileau and Racine subject the inept
"flagornerie" disfiguring the "modern" Perrault's dedicatory epistle presenting the
Dictionnaire de l'Académie Française to Louis XIV. Both Perrault's *épître* and
Boileau and Racine's critique appear in *Œuvres complètes*, the first at 422-23, the
second, at merciless length, at 423-27.

[20] Barthes, "La mort de l'auteur" and "De l'œuvre au texte." See too his book-
length anticipation of these views in what, since Fish, we would call the "conven-
tionalist" or "constructivist" theses informing *Critique et vérité*, his response to the
intemperate attacks on *Sur Racine* launched by Raymond Picard, author of *La Carrière de Jean Racine* (Paris: Gallimard, 1956). Picard's *Nouvelle critique ou nouvelle
imposture* (Paris: Pauvert, 1965) touched off the general debate between French
"new criticism" and traditional, university-based modes of interpretation to which
Critique et vérité contributed. One of the many ironies surrounding the controversy
is that, for all Picard couches his attacks in terms of both historical and philological
accuracy, Barthes's context-free reader-based criticism contributed far more to the
later historical methods of writers like Marin and Apostolidès than did his adversary's essentially hagiographic approach. *La Carrière* is a dead letter; *Sur Racine*
is not.

availability is less what Racine puts into his texts than what he leaves out, namely, the *meaning* we assign them:

> Ecrire, c'est ébranler le sens du monde, y disposer une interroga-tion *indirecte*, à la quelle l'écrivain, par un dernier suspens, s'abstient de répondre. La réponse, c'est chacun de nous qui la donne, y apportant son histoire, son langage, sa liberté; mais comme histoire, langage et liberté changent infiniment, la ré-ponse du monde à l'écrivain est infinie: on ne cesse jamais de répondre à ce qui a été écrit hors de toute réponse: affirmés, mis en rivalité, puis remplacés, les sens passent, la question demeure.[21]

Over against the normalizing tautology "Racine, c'est Racine" satirized in his earlier *Mythologies*,[22] Barthes sets the "denaturaliz-ing" because *historicizing* assertion of "Racine aujourd'hui." He thereby anticipates the point the epistemologist and aesthetician Joseph Margolis recently makes in what amounts to a philosophical systematization of the reader-response doctrine distilled in Stanley Fish's notorious rhetorical question, "Is there a text in this class?" As Margolis puts it, texts "have a history," by which he means not only the historical conditions governing their composition, the range of intentions possible at the moment of their original produc-tion, but the evolving "career" they enjoy as a reflex of their evolv-ing reception.[23] The entity we designate (we imagine tautologically) as "Racinian tragedy" is an artifact of what, in a phrase whose am-biguity speaks to the heart of the case, we *make of it*. It answers not only to the deep structure of the historical moment–the assertion of such a structure being a critical move that itself typifies the process in question–but to changing styles of interpretation and the "inter-pretive communities" whose models, assumptions, preoccupations, and interests determine (by *over*-determining) what appears.[24] The

---

[21] Barthes, *Sur Racine* 7.

[22] Roland Barthes, "Racine est Racine," in *Mythologies* (Paris: Seuil, 1957; "Points" paper ed.) 96-98.

[23] See Stanley E. Fish, *Is There a Text in This Class? The Authority of Interpre-tive Communities* (Cambridge, Mass.: Harvard University Press, 1980), and Margo-lis, *Interpretation Radical but Not Unruly*, esp. the intro. and chap. 3, "Prospects for a Theory of Radical History."

[24] See Harold Bloom's opening statement in *A Map of Misreading* (Oxford: Ox-

very value Racine's tragedies possess as historical documents reflects their sensitivity to an evolving historical uptake.

However, it is too simple to shrug our shoulders and go with the
in any case irresistible cultural flow. [25] Though all works are surely
"historical" in Margolis's sense, that is, Barthesian "texts" we
"make" in the process of "making something" of them by reading
them, it is never quite in the same way. Barthes indeed suggests as
much when he claims that the interpretive "availability" writing imparts to texts *in general* is nonetheless especially in evidence in the
work of Racine *in particular* as a poet he does not hesitate to call "le
plus grand écrivain français." [26] Racine's historical destiny and witness remain *different*, retaining the indigestible integrity Barthes in
other moods opposes to the fundamental "indifference" of his own
theoretical positions. [27] And what makes the historical difference
constitutive of Racinian tragedy is the degree to which, beyond
merely documenting, it actively accommodates the historical fate
that determines our sense of its origin and meaning.

I come at this reading through the exemplary historical difficulties surrounding the interpretation of *Phèdre* 5.7.1638 proposed by
Fumaroli. Having confessed the incestuous secret behind her stepson's mysterious reticence and her confidante's suicide following his
terrible end, Racine's heroine announces her own self-inflicted
death from "un poison que Médée apporta dans Athènes." Fumaroli proposes that we take this as a *mise en abyme*. On one hand,
Phèdre's citation of the infernal sorceress and infanticide, Jason's
wife, closes the string of relentless mythological allusions binding
her identity and fate. It is to this extent the last and for that reason
most decisive reference by which, at once descendant of the Apol-

---

ford University Press, 1975) 3: "Reading, as my title indicates, is a belated and all-
but-impossible act, and if strong is always a misreading. Literary meaning tends to
become more under-determined even as literary language becomes more over-de-
termined. Criticism may not always be an act of judging, but it is always an act of
deciding, and what it tries to decide is meaning."

[25] This is the gesture Fish makes in *Doing What Comes Naturally: Change,
Rhetoric, and the Practice of Theory in Literary and Legal Studies* (Durham, NC:
Duke University Press, 1989). Fish's major contention here is that, in light of the
"authority of interpretive communities" *Is There a Text* explores, "theory" cannot
make the difference it arrogantly claims since "theory" is merely a belated (and often self-deluding) rationale for what the reader already does.

[26] Barthes, *Sur Racine* 7.

[27] See Roland Barthes, *S/Z* (Paris: Seuil, 1970) 9-10.

Ionian Sun and Pasiphaë's passionate daughter, "fille de Minos"
and thus child of the Labyrinth, yet enemy of Venus through her luminous root in sunlike Phoebus, Phèdre is brought to an impasse
whose only issue is self-murder. But, on the other hand, the reference also points back to Corneille's *Médée* of 1634: the tragedy with
which Racine's great predecessor, model, and rival inaugurates at
once his own career as a tragic poet and the apogee of the genre in
seventeenth-century France. On the eve of the twelve-year cessation
of Racine's activity as a playwright, the verse enacts its author's
notoriously ambivalent relation to "le grand Corneille" and his
equally notorious ambivalence toward the art they share. For Fumaroli, then, Phèdre's suicide becomes the deliberate "mise à mort"
of the tragic genre Racine inherits from Corneille: a recursive gesture in which the silence that falls with the self-inflicted death of
the incestuous queen coincides with to the point of *being* the silence that overtakes the era's preeminent tragic author. [28]

A first problem with this reading is that it fails to show that
Racine actually meant what it alleges–that the construction placed
on the verse, what indeed Fumaroli *makes* of it, answers to the authorial intent he assigns. Fumaroli marshals a good deal of corrobo-
rative detail in its defense–enough circumstantial evidence to make
a *prima facie* case for his interpretation. Thus he links *mise en
abyme* in general, as a formal device at Racine's disposal, to the
comparably self-referential form of classical allegory. [29] The prevailing "allegorism" of classical taste and sensibility is reinforced by

---

[28] Fumaroli, "De *Médée* à *Phèdre*: naissance et mise à mort de la tragédie
cornélienne," in *Héros et orateurs* 493-518. For the reading of the incriminated
verse, 512-13. But see Amy Wygant, "Medea, Poison, and the Epistemology of Error in *Phèdre*," *Modern Language Review* 95.1 (January 2000) 62-71. In addition to
providing a helpful "genealogy" for Fumaroli's reading that firmly places it in the
tradition of psychoanalytic interpretations of Racinian tragedy as a function of its
relation to the paternal Corneille, Wygant challenges that tradition by suggesting
that the verse's, if not "true," at any rate more topical aim is "triumphantly to conclude the *Querelle des Imaginaires*" (69) by "taking a detour to truth via an errant
poison"–a detour for which Pascal's polemical "Entretien avec M. De Saci" is a
model.
[29] "Une des clefs qui se proposent à l'exploration de cet 'espace du dedans'
propre au chef-d'oeuvre, c'est évidemment l'allégorisme." *Héros et orateurs* 495.
Fumaroli then refers to an earlier piece, "Rhétorique, dramaturgie et critique littéraire: le recours à l'allégorie dans les querelles littéraires," republished in *Critique
et création littéraire au XVIIe siècle* (Paris: C.N.R.S., 1977) 53-72.

Fumaroli's readings of parallel *mises en abyme* evidenced by Alcandre's systematic rhetorical manipulation of the paternal spectator
Pridamant in *L'Illusion comique* or by the anagrammatic Elmire's
performance in *Tartuffe*'s second seduction scene. [30] To which we
should add the overwhelming self-consciousness of classical drama
generally as evinced by Georges Forestier's exhaustive documenta-
tion of the *théâtre dans le théâtre*–the massive incidence of "plays
within plays" instanced not only by *L'Illusion* or *Tartuffe*, but by
Scudéry's *Comédie des comédiens*, Rotrou's *Le Véritable Saint-Genest*, or, to cite more indirect examples explored earlier in the present book, the scene of judgment featured in the finale of *Le Cid*,
the pointed regularity of *Horace*, or Molière's play on the theme of
authoritative names in *L'Ecole des femmes*. [31]

But Fumaroli also identifies a powerful *personal* motive for *Phèdre*'s *mise en abyme* in the resurgent *querelle de la moralité du
théâtre*. [32] To develop Fumaroli's idea further than he himself does,
Phèdre's death by poison is surely overdetermined, a component of
the play's Euripidean fable magnified by Nicole's characterization
of dramatic poets as poisoners of public morals in *Les Visionnaires*.
Racine's well-documented sense of having betrayed his Jansenist
upbringing induced his morbid sensitivity to Nicole's text, explaining among other things why he was so quick to read himself into a
charge whose explicit target was in fact the "modern" Desmarets
rather than Racine himself. [33] Even after the ten-year interval between "l'affaire des Imaginaires" (1666-67) and *Phèdre*'s premiere
(1 January 1677), the choice of poison testifies to a jealous self-regard whose measure is not only the acuity with which Racine portrays the sinful passions that drive his tragic personnel, but whatever it was in his character and conduct that gave color to the rumors
concerning the poisoning of la Du Parc.

Still, in the absence of direct evidence of Racine's intent, Fumaroli cannot bridge the gap between conjecture and certainty. The

---

[30] See Fumaroli, *Héros et orateurs* 261-87 and 488-91.
[31] See Georges Forestier, *Le Théâtre dans le théâtre sur la scène française du
XVII* siècle, 2ⁿᵈ, enlarged ed. (Geneva: Droz, 1996).
[32] Fumaroli, *Héros et orateurs* 506-13. Note too that the last chapter in the
book, "De *Médée* à *Phèdre*" follows "*Sacerdos sive rhetor, orator sive histrio*," the
one specifically devoted to the *querelle*.
[33] See note 8 above.

closest we come to a complete statement is the preface to the printed text. But the preface is in the main an apology defending the
choice and treatment of the incestuous plot. In addition to citing
his classical precedent in Euripides, Racine emphasizes his efforts
to mitigate the fable. Though he admits that his heroine is not "tout
à fait innocente" inasmuch as she surrenders to unnatural love for
Thésée's son, neither is she "tout à fait coupable":

> elle est engagée, par sa destinée et par la colère des dieux, dans
> une passion illégitime dont elle a horreur toute la première: elle
> fait tous ses efforts pour la surmonter; elle aime mieux se laisser
> mourir que de la déclarer à personne, et lorsqu'elle est forcée de
> la découvrir, elle en parle avec une confusion qui fait bien voir
> que son crime est plutôt une punition des dieux qu'un mouve-
> ment de sa volonté. (246)

Nor are Racine's attempts to diminish the opprobrium inevitably attached to Phèdre's character confined to underscoring her desperate efforts to overcome a passion ordained by the gods:

> J'ai même pris soin de la rendre un peu moins odieuse qu'elle
> n'est dans les tragédies des anciens [Euripides, and Seneca after
> him], où elle se résout d'elle-même à accuser Hippolyte. J'ai cru
> que la calomnie avait quelque chose de trop bas et de trop noir
> pour la mettre dans la bouche d'une princesse qui a d'ailleurs
> des sentiments si nobles et si vertueux. Cette bassesse m'a paru
> plus convenable à une nourrice, qui pouvait avoir des inclina-
> tions plus serviles, et qui néanmoins n'entreprend cette fausse
> accusation que pour sauver la vie et l'honneur de sa maîtresse.
> (246-47)

He even takes steps to soften the calumny itself. Where, in Euripides and Seneca, Hippolyte is accused "d'avoir en effet violé sa
belle-mère," in his own play Œnone accuses him only "d'en avoir
eu le dessein"–an attenuation that, in reducing the heinousness of
the crime, also spares Hippolyte's royal father Thésée "une confusion qui l'aurait pu rendre moins agréable aux spectateurs." (247)
So while Racine has much of interest to say regarding the problems
of morality, decorum, and taste latent in his subject, he remains
silent on the issues Fumaroli raises.

But graver than the lack of direct evidence in support of Fumaroli's hypothesis is its *anachronism*. In arguing that Phèdre's suicide enacts the symbolic execution of the "Cornelian" tragedy
Racine inherits, Fumaroli supposes on the poet's part an awareness
of the genre's subsequent history he could not have had. He attributes him indeed a perspective that, informed by foreknowledge
both of his own career and of the future evolution of French literature, transcends the immediate historical moment, infusing Racine's
text with insights available only to our later, far different vantage
point on the history we construct to explain and interpret it. Even
assuming that Racine did in fact will the end of tragedy as Fumaroli
alleges, he was not placed to judge his own success.

And yet the convergence of perspectives Fumaroli's recursive allegory of the death of tragedy invokes feels compelling just the
same. Though Racine could not have known it, the tragic genre
Corneille invents does in fact die with *Phèdre*. Racine will of course
finally break his twelve-year silence as a dramatist at the bidding of
Mme de Maintenon. But what emerges is a pair of "tragedies drawn
from Holy Scripture" radically different from the tragedies proper
abandoned in 1677. To be sure, with the triumph of its heartless
fanatic high priest, the ominous future of the young king anointed
in Athalie's blood, and the tortured inwardness of the eponymous
queen herself, pursued even in her dreams by the play's pitiless jealous God, *Athalie* exhibits the dark Jansenist bite we associate with
Racinian tragedy. [34] Moreover, in the rosier *Esther*'s Aman, a
courtier whose secret acknowledgement of the true God compli-
cates the politic cynicism with which he pursues the extinction of
God's chosen people, it is tempting to see a displaced self-portrait–Racine's belated confession of the apostasy implicit in his pursuit of worldly fame. [35] Yet at least at the conscious surface, both

---

[34] For the dream, see *Athalie* 2.5.490-514. For powerful commentaries both on
the dream itself and on sinful humanity's relation to an implacable God, see, in addition to Goldmann's *Dieu caché*, Barthes, *Sur Racine* 48-49 and 120-26, Apostolidès, *Le prince sacrifié* 127-31, Bruneau, *Racine*, chap. 8, "Athalie 'surhomme': La
mort de Dieu," and Greenberg, *Subjectivity and Subjugation*, chap. 6, "Racine's
Children."

[35] Here too, of course, the evidence is both external and circumstancial, con-
sisting chiefly of Racine's belated reconciliation with Port-Royal following the abandonment of theater in 1677 and his marriage later that same year, and the late
Abrégé de l'histoire de Port-Royal (1697).

plays embrace a theodicical perspective the antithesis of the bleak vision that constitutes the Racinian norm: their very source in holy writ affirms the possibility of a redemption Racine's profane tragedies preclude.[36] And while Racine has in fact many successors, from his immediate contemporaries and rivals, Thomas Corneille, Quinault, and Pradon, to the Voltaire of *Œdipe*, *Mariamne*, *La Mort de César*, and *Zaïre*, all unmistakably bear the shackles of the Racinian measures Diderot treats to ironic revision in the "Paradoxe."[37]

Further, tragedy does in fact die of the toxic substance Fumaroli incriminates. That the great age of French classical tragedy should turn out to have begun with Corneille's *Médée* proves in retrospect as appropriate as that it should have ended with Racine's *Phèdre*. The play's at once magnificently self-dramatizing and terrifyingly transgressive queen precociously embodies everything most infernal as well as heroic in Cornelian drama. The passions that drive her are monstrous. Within the confines of the play itself, we encounter the horrific murder of Créuse and her father Créon, burned alive by the poisoned wedding dress Médée deviously gives Jason's new bride with ironic as well as vengeful intent; a crime later compounded by the still more horrific infanticide with which, in killing her own children, Médée destroys the dynastic hopes for whose sake Jason sets her aside. But we also have the antecedent action in which sexual passion leads her to betray father, brothers, and native land to help Jason obtain the Golden Fleece.

Médée's crimes lend color to Greenberg's characterization of Corneille's witch as a proto-Irigarian "speculum de l'Autre femme," the lawless female whose boundless feral will overwhelms the classical male ego, the frail Cartesian vessel official culture floats on the vast ocean of incipient chaos its own fabrication posits.[38] Médée combines indeed a medley of symbolically dangerous roles.

---

[36] George Steiner, *The Death of Tragedy* (New York: Knopf, 1961). See, e.g., 324, where the fundamentally optimistic soteriological perspective of Christian faith paradoxically lands it in the same bag as a putatively diametrically opposite eschatological creed: "The metaphysics of Christianity and Marxism are anti-tragic."

[37] Let us note in passing that Voltaire's conformity to the classical model is systematic, covering all four major tragic fields: Greek (*Œdipe*), Roman (*La Mort de César*), religious (the martyr play, *Mariamne*), and Oriental (*Zaïre*).

[38] See Greenberg, *Corneille*, chap. 1, "Mythifying matrix: Corneille's *Médée* and the birth of tragedy."

Her identity as a wife and mother prescribes the passive pliancy of a broodmare, bearing the children on which Jason bases the dynastic ambitions that lead him to abandon her in favor of the younger second wife from whom he may claim the kingdom he intends to leave his heir. But Médée is also both a foreigner and a sorceress, the potent alien witch from the non-Greek world of Asia. She thus embodies and, what is more, prestigiously *speaks for* the properly uncanny powers of disorder, resentment, and anarchic desire against which official classical culture sets its face, forcing them to the margins of social discourse. And in so doing, she provides a blueprint for the succession of powerful, castrating women that dominate the Cornelian stage. The invocation of the swarming hosts of hell that forms the central burden of the spectacular Senecan soliloquy she delivers in her furious entrée in 1.3 lays down a pattern of both noble and demonic feminine speech to which Corneille reverts throughout his career. The resentful Lyse of *L'Illusion comique* 3.6, angrily stifling her love for the faithless Clindor in the service of heroic revenge; the resolute Emilie who opens *Cinna* with the enraged adjuration of her own multiple motives for bending the title character's love for her to the cause of regicide; the Cléopâtre of *Rodogune* 2.1, apostrophizing the devious lies and politic masks and devices that, in cloaking her true intent, have brought her to the threshold of absolute power; the evil Arsinoé of *Nicomède* 1.5, gloating over the subtle trap she sets for her noble stepson—all conform to the model Médée incarnates from the very start.

But the strain of wicked Medean might is finally (if ambiguously) indissociable from the Muse by which Corneille claims to have been inspired and by which, first in the "Excuse à Ariste" and then in the deeply ironic dedication of *Horace*, we have seen him assert his own autonomous grandeur in haughty contrast to the ignoble compromises made by his poetic rivals, Mairet, d'Aubignac, Chapelain, or Desmarets. The arrogant boast launched in the "Excuse," "Je ne dois qu'à moy seul toute ma Renommée,"[39] echoes in the atavistically feudal sense of personal right that shapes his militant villainesses. Nor are their anarchic ambitions, desires, or claims to honor ever simply or straightforwardly evil. It is not just that

---

[39] Gasté, *La Querelle du Cid* 64.

Lyse, Emilie, or Cléopâtre have ample cause for revenge or that, however vile the expedients to which she resorts, Arsinoé's promotion of her own son's interests at Nicomède's expense is a thoroughly natural one. Corneille's incontestably noble women, *Le Cid*'s Chimène, *Horace*'s Camille, *Polyeucte*'s Pauline, the eponymous heroine of *Rodogune*, or, to cite a late Carthaginian example whose ambiguous, quasi-bigamous defiance of Scipionic Rome in no way diminishes the heroic nature of her resistance, the *Sophonisbe* of 1663, all conform to the same pattern. What changes are the circumstances under which female heroism manifests itself. Nor should we overlook how often it is *women* who drive Cornelian action, reducing their male counterparts to the state of passive instruments or showing them to be monstrous automata in the image of the heartless Horace or the vampire-like paternal *revenants*, Don Gomès and Nicanor.

To the extent then that, as Fumaroli suggests, classical tragedy not only begins with Corneille, but is in its very essence an ambiguous Cornelian compound of good and evil, sexual passion and noble idealism, ambition and merit, stiff-necked pride and heroic self-assertion, we readily understand why, in the overdetermined light of his own character and upbringing, Racine was destined to respond to it with self-punishing ambivalence. It is a commonplace of the critical literature that Racine is the reincarnation of Corneille shorn of the alibis of heroic self-overcoming. [40] In Corneille, as Médée or Cléopâtre show, even treason, patricide, or child murder can express an exaltation of personal force and self-mastery that is inherently noble. In Racine by contrast, the indisputably noble figures (Iphigénie, Andromaque, Brittanicus and Junie, Bajazet and Atalide, Hippolyte, Esther) are all characterized by weakness. As a rule, events crush the good in Racine. If Iphigénie survives, it is because Eriphile is sacrificed in her place; and Hippolyte is literally torn to pieces by the sea monster his father's overreaching prayer conjures up. But even when good prevails, the triumph is linked to total self-abnegation. Andromaque's authority derives entirely from her systematic subsumption in the shade of her dead husband and in the future of the son in whom she hopes the father may live

---

[40] For an early, authoritative statement, see Bénichou, *Morales du grand siècle* 180-94.

again; and Esther's victory over the scheming Aman is triggered by the fainting fit that reveals to the astonished Assuérus how, in decreeing death for the Jews, he has condemned his own bride. [41]

Above all we have the testimony of Racinian love. In Corneille, love invariably inspires what is best in human nature: the improbable parallel self-sacrifice of *Le Cid*'s Rodrigue and Chimène is the romantic paradigm to which all Cornelian lovers conform. [42] By contrast, in Racine, where love (as, for instance, between Brittanicus and Junie or Bajazet and Atalide) is not merely a pretty toy the plays' monsters smash in fulfilling their evil natures, it is an unholy amalgam of vanity and violence whose deepest spring is a predatory wanting that destroys what it desires. Perhaps the most outspoken expression of the phenomenon belongs to *Phèdre*'s Aricie in the speech from 2.1 cited earlier comparing her lucky love for Thésée's son with Phèdre's unhappy marriage with his faithless father. The central principle of the speech is a sadism evinced in part by her vulgar crowing at the aging queen's expense, but chiefly directed at Hippolyte himself. Aricie speaks here exactly like the heartless seducer of Molière's *Dom Juan*. True, her talk of "bending" Hippolyte's stiff-necked pride (his "orgueil généreux") beneath the "yoke" of amorous surrender, of her power to "extort" (*arracher*) a plaintive lover's "homage" from his breast, of causing "pain" in an otherwise "insensible soul," of "enchaining" her "captive" in "irons" from which he vainly struggles to escape is at one level pure erotic boilerplate. To this extent, the speech recycles stock figures drawn from the fund Petrarch bequeaths the main tradition of Western amorous verse. But whereas this language conventionally fills the lover's mouth as self-description, Racine renews its force by reas-

---

[41] *Athalie* is a special case. Though the good triumphs to the extent that the idolatrous daughter of Ahab and Jezebel is destroyed for Judah's sake, it is far from clear that either Judah or the fanatic priest who promotes him are worthy. But the exception points the irony of the Racinian rule as stated by Barthes: "Il existe chez Racine, on le sait, une contradiction entre son éthique et son esthétique: le Bien, qu'il choisit, est chez lui une abstraction, mêlée de conformisme, ses personnages apparemment positifs sont des personnages ennuyeux, des sortes de grands masques vides; le Mal, qu'il condamne, est vivant; sous la noirceur apparente, des nuances, des tentations, des regrets s'agitent, comme si dans le héros noir venait se déposer le noyau même de la subjectivité racinienne." *Sur Racine* 123.

[42] Fumaroli, "Du *Cid* à *Polyeucte*: une dramaturgie du couple," in *Héros et orateurs* 399-413.

signing it to the normally speechless mistress of whom the lover complains. The tired metaphors of Petrarchan love poetry acquire a fresh and sinister energy that climaxes in the delicious maddening itch with which Aricie turns the pain the lover *receives* into the pain his beloved takes calculated pleasure in *inflicting*–"C'est là ce que je veux, c'est là ce qui m'irrite."

But the cruelty characteristic of Racinian love is not confined to the dramatic personnel; it infects the nature of tragic spectacle as such, and thus the public whose ambiguous taste it satisfies. Such is the testimony of a celebrated passage from *Brittanicus*. The infamous emperor Néron recounts the sudden, wholly unexpected inception of his ultimately murderous passion for the mistress of the play's eponymous hero and sacrificial victim–and we note that, in addition to being Néron's rival for the beautiful Junie, Brittanicus is also his cousin, his adoptive brother, and the rightful claimant to the imperial throne Néron occupies. In a telling switch whose motive seems to lie not only in the theme of courtly treachery, but in the relevant character's resonant name, Néron describes the moment not to his own tutor and confidant Burrhus, but to Brittanicus', Narcisse. The result however is less an explanation necessary for the audience's comprehension of the tragic action than what amounts to an etiology of tragedy itself:

> Excité d'un désir curieux,
> Cette nuit je l'ai vue arriver en ces lieux,
> Triste, levant au ciel ses yeux mouillés de larmes,
> Qui brillaient au travers des flambeaux et des armes;
> Belle sans ornements, dans le simple appareil
> D'une beauté qu'on vient d'arracher au sommeil.
> Que veux-tu? Je ne sais si cette négligence,
> Les ombres, les flambeaux, les cris et le silence,
> Et le farouche aspect de ses fiers ravisseurs,
> Relevaient de ses yeux les timides douceurs.
> Quoi qu'il en soit, ravi d'une si belle vue,
> J'ai voulu lui parler, et ma voix s'est perdue:
> Immobile, saisi d'un long étonnement,
> Je l'ai laissé passer dans son apartement.
> J'ai passé dans le mien. C'est là que, solitaire,
> De son image en vain j'ai voulu me distraire.
> Trop présente à mes yeux je croyais lui parler;

J'aimais jusqu'à ses pleurs que je faisais couler.
Quelquefois, mais trop tard, je lui demandais grâce:
J'employais les soupirs, et même la menace.
Voilà comme, occupé de mon nouvel amour,
Mes yeux, sans se fermer, ont attendu le jour.

(2.2.385-406)

Néron's love is triggered less by the person on whom his gaze alights, a woman with whom he does not speak till the next scene, than by what he himself calls an "image." Junie's tearful and terrified arrival in the imperial palace, seized by armed guards in the middle of the night as a hostage in the ongoing struggle for the throne, is narrated rather than shown. Still, the central theme of the narration is the spectacle Néron paints for the audience in describing what he witnessed of the scene–as indeed he puts it to Narcisse a moment later, "Mais je m'en fais peut-être une trop belle image." (2.2.407) The emperor relates what he saw from covert, spying on Junie's entry from behind a curtain; and the result is the ekphrastic counterpart of a painting like Rubens's *Andromeda* (fig. 7), portraying a helpless female discovered in arousing *déshabille*, at the mercy of a monstrous power that threatens physical and, by implication, sexual violence. The verbal picture Néron paints is the quasi-pornographic portrayal of a rape licensed by the fact that the rape does not happen. In Rubens, the spectators can imaginatively luxuriate in the violent promise of Andromeda's helpless exposure to the precise extent that they know that, in the continuation, Perseus will ride to the rescue. So here, thanks to Néron's narrative, Racine's audience savors the image of the half-naked female prey decorum forbids the play to present on stage, secure in the assurance of her subsequent withdrawal to the relative safety of the private apartment the emperor has assigned her.

As Néron's narrative proceeds, its focus turns from the instigating event to its mental repercussions. In moving from the covert station from which he witnessed Junie's arrival to the private chamber where he plays the spectacle over in his mind, the scene Néron describes shifts from the external world to the sleepless emperor's febrile imagination. What begins as recounted action becomes a mesmerizing mental fetish, precisely comparable to a private pornographic picture, before which Néron plants himself in "soli-

Figure 7. Rubens workshop, *Perseus and Andromeda*. Oil on canvas. Staatliche Museen zu Berlin–Preussischer Kulturbesitz, Gemäldegalerie. Photo: Jörg P. Anders

tary" onanistic thrall. The play as a whole of course rehearses the well-known story of Néron's descent into the horrific sadism and depravity for which he is proverbial. This indeed defines the dramatic tension out of which Racine fashions the taut unity of his plot. The drama unfolds in the brief interval that remains for appeal to the emperor's better nature, the last glimmer of humanity kindled by the very passion that ultimately pushes him into the abyss. The image thereby prepares the way for what we know must follow by identifying the central issue on which the action revolves. But it does so in the character of a *symptom*. Coupled with Néron's desperate efforts to escape the encroaching mother whose crimes on his behalf, spelled out in 4.2, have literally made him what he is, it diagnoses the evil whose historical outbreak it simultaneously foreshadows and forestalls.

But the image also functions as a *mise en abyme*. As suggested both by Néron's repeated use of the term "image" and by the dramatic as well as informative role the speech plays, enabling the audience to see something the reigning decorum does not allow us to witness directly, the "curious desire" that led him to spy on Junie's arrival in the palace mirrors the equally "curious" urge that brings spectators to the theater. Precisely because Racine's source in Tacitus tells us who Néron is, we savor how the very love that offers hope of salvation must in the end precipitate the monstrous metamorphosis all of the protagonists, Junie, Brittanicus, Néron's otherwise odious mother Agrippine, his tutor Burrhus, and even Néron himself struggle to avert. The tragic irony on which the play's impact depends, and thus the peculiar *pleasure* the unfolding spectacle affords, is conditioned by foreknowledge of the vicious beast Néron is historically fated to become. But this same foreknowledge furnishes the ambiguous incitement to attend the play: we do not come to *learn* who Néron is; we come rather in the prurient hope of *seeing him in action*. And what is this if not just the concupiscence to which Nicole's *Visionnaires* claims theater ministers all along?

All of this goes to show that, even if Racine did not specifically intend Phèdre's death in the way Fumaroli alleges, his reading works just the same: the complex symptomatic act by which *Brittanicus* converts Néron's onanistic fetish into an image of theater itself points to a potential in *Phèdre*'s finale that demands just Fumaroli's hypothesis to come to light. But this in turn defines our fundamental question. How are we to reconcile our knowledge of Racine *in* history with the Racine who is the artifact of the later reading that history's subsequent evolution licenses?

A first stage in formulating an answer is to interrogate more closely what we mean by "Racine." At the most basic level, the name specifies a particular historical personage: the empirical author and accomplished dramatist who, though absent from the text inasmuch as his characters speak in their own tormented voices as an expression of their engagement in the action of which they are victims, nevertheless composed the words they say. In this sense, "Racine" denotes the generically sublated authorial "I," the (in Kant's strict technical sense) "transcendental" intention and will of which even the preeminent response theorist Fish acknowledges texts are read as correlates.[43] A play, after all, is not a naturally occurring fact; it is an *artwork*, the product of designs, choices, and desires of which reading is the distant and distorting echo. This determines the finally inescapable pertinence of biography, sociology, or history itself–the indelible place of context and of the methods by which contexts are brought to bear in lessons we can neither ignore nor forget except by the kind of formalist fiat in which New Criticism abounds in both its French and Anglo-American avatars.[44]

But closer scrutiny of interpretive usage reveals a further sense of the authorial name. In addition to identifying the empirical author, "Racine" designates the corpus of writings relative to which

---

[43] This does not however invalidate Fish's core arguments. The fact that "intention" forms a dimension of what we read or listen for in a text or utterance reflects merely the kind of thing we take a text or utterance to be qua artifact: making sense of it requires making sense of it as bearing the sense someone means to convey by it. But this does not mean that the sense we make is or can be rigorously *controlled* by the intended one, or even that we may successfully determine what the intended sense was. Nor, further, can it rule out the many cases in which (a) we assume intent where there is none (when, e.g., someone talks in her/his sleep or without thinking) or (b) perceive an intent other than the one the speaker consciously acknowledges–a procedure central to a great many contemporary methodologies.

[44] For France, see in particular the texts by Barthes identified in note 20 and Jacques Derrida, "signature événement contexte." The major English-language statement is William K. Wimsatt & Monroe C. Beardsley, *The Verbal Icon: Studies in the Meaning of Poetry* (Lexington, KY: University of Kentucky Press, 1954), a work whose chapter on the "intentional fallacy" remains authoritative to this day.

we note and value the empirical man. To this extent, the name serves as a convenient label for a sprawling monument we would otherwise be obliged to itemize at length. But the name also encodes a Foucaldian "author function," the methodological fiction used to concentrate, shape, and control the body of work *for* which but also *by* which its author has come to be known and in whose name we interpret it. [45] "Racine" is then the focus of the inevitably intentionalized meanings that we impute the empirical author as a means of organizing the objects of our interpretations. It denotes the *œuvre* as both the expression and correlate, the circular monument and document, of our own critical uptake.

This bears on the deepest, but also the least noted and least understood of the "doctrines" laid out in J.L. Austin's *How to Do Things with Words*: the theory of "perlocutions," of what a speaker does not only *in* saying something (the "*il*-locution"), but *by* saying saying it (the "*per*-locution"). [46] At one level, the theory of perlocutions makes room for the question of ulterior motives. It addresses the furthest aim a given speech act sets itself as defined by the particular *effect* the performance intends to produce beyond both sense and force–the words the speaker uses and the specific context-bound act the uttering of those words performs. But the theory of perlocutions further acknowledges the effects an utterance may produce *independent* of its intent, as a function of how it *chances to be taken*–of what hearers or readers make of it as a reflex of their own context-bound expectations, motives, or interests.

In writing a play like *Phèdre*, Racine ("Racine") has many more or less conscious (as, too, many more or less *un*-conscious) ends in view. Some of these ends are immediately literary–for example, to cite a goal Forestier has emphasized with great *éclat*, to impart a certain kind of pleasure, the peculiar *frisson* associated with the

---

[45] Michel Foucault, "Qu'est-ce qu'un auteur?" in *Dits et écrits, 1954-1988*, ed. Daniel Defert & Françoise Ewald (Paris: Gallimard, 1994) 1.789-821.
[46] Austin, *How to Do Things with Words*, lectures 8-10. Much of the debate initiated by Derrida's "signature événement contexte" is conditioned (if not determined) by a failure on both sides to recognize the doctrine's importance. For the exchange between Searle and Derrida, see *Glyph* 1-2 (1977). Derrida subsequently reprinted his first two responses to Searle, together with a third, in *Limited Inc* (Evanston: Northwestern University Press, 1988). See also Stanley Cavell, "What Did Derrida Want of Austin?" in *Philosophical Passages: Wittgenstein, Emerson, Austin, Derrida* (Oxford: Blackwell, 1995) 42-65.

tragic emotions of "pity" and "fear." [47] If all goes well, the audience will then respond in a particular way: gasping, weeping, and applauding at all the right places; listening to the verses in rapt silence, or emitting the murmurs of approval, rising at times to outright exclamation, the era called "le brouhaha." [48] And it is also hoped that theater goers will turn up in satisfying numbers, generating revenues through ticket and, once the published text appears, book sales. Other aims reflect the complex politics animating the institution of literature. In addition to advancing Racine's ongoing effort to displace Corneille as the preeminent practitioner of classical tragedy, *Phèdre* is calculated to demonstrate its author's superiority to the rival Pradon, whose *Phèdre et Hippolyte* (1677) was meant to do to Racine what Racine's own *Bérénice* (1670) had done to the Corneille of *Tite et Bérénice* seven years before. [49] To these we may further add Racine's *social* ambitions: the desire, notably, so to impress both the king and his minister Colbert as to secure, beyond his earlier election to the Académie Française (1672), the post of royal historiographer granted in October of the year in which *Phèdre* appeared.

But the multifarious effects Racine consciously aimed at in composing and staging *Phèdre* by no means preclude but, on the contrary, directly occasion an infinite series of quite other effects that, for all they may be unintended, nevertheless belong to Racine. The tragic *frisson* whose ambiguous delights earn the applause the king eventually translates into a royal pension and commission provokes a storm of envy and recrimination from which the poet never escapes. Racine's success thus earns him the vicious assaults Corneille and Molière suffered before him, and for the same reasons. But it also inspires the uninterrupted series of interpretive *readings* that, for all they fulfil Racine's ambition to take a place among the heroes of the French Parnassus, put his plays at the mercy of a critical readership whose insights as well as misprisions he could never

---

[47] See Forestier, *Essai de génétique théâtrale* and *Corneille: le sens d'une dramaturgie*.

[48] For period use of the term "brouhaha," see Molière's *Impromptu de Versailles* 216.

[49] On the "cabale de *Phèdre*," see Viala, *Racine* 188-92 and Rohou, *Jean Racine* 311-19. The rivalry with Corneille is a constant of both books, as it was of Racine's entire career.

have precisely imagined let alone controlled. To the extent moreover that, as Austin's meditations on the perlocutionary suggest, the
Racinian text is not merely the instrument or occasion, but the
product of its own effects, a monument of the meanings generations
of scholars have taken it to document, "Racine" is the name for
what we make of him in the process of construing his work.

But "Racine" points to yet a third thing, associated with what
period rhetoric would have called the originating faculty of "invention" or "design," the underlying intelligence, distinguishable from
if nonetheless systematically coordinate with the work that manifests its authority and power. As we have seen with reference to the
episode of the "cinq auteurs," the group of poets charged with
the *mise en vers* of plot outlines entrusted to them by Richelieu, the
true author of a play is not necessarily identified with the dramatic
text as it meets us on the page. [50] The author is rather a "genius"
whose existence and character, whose temper, will, and intent must
be *inferred* from the text in the manner of the teleological "primary" causes that, in seventeenth-century metaphysics, condition the
"secondary" causes whose reductive operations are observed in
physical nature.

The figure of "genius" as the inferential source of the dramatic
poem's instigating invention finds a telling echo in latterday critical
debates. In particular, it speaks to the curious fusion of formalism
and historicism that characterizes much contemporary critical
thought. [51] To be sure, we tend today to regard talk of "genius" as
hopelessly retrograde and jejune, a myth historical skepticism has
exploded once and for all. And yet, though emptied of the ideological content both classical and Romantic aesthetics assigned it, the
basic semantic *structure* on which notions of "genius" rely remains
in force. In this perspective, "Racine" is the name reserved less for
the autonomous intentional origin of Racinian tragedy than for a latent conscious inhabitant of the Racinian text itself envisaged as
both independent of and logically prior to any conscious act or intention on the author's part.

---

[50] On the "cinq auteurs," see Couton's "notice" to *La Comédie des Tuileries* in
Corneille, *Œuvres complètes* 1.1406-14, and the later account in *Richelieu* 25-31.
[51] For a stimulating discussion of the fusion of "formalism" and "historicism,"
see the intro. to Lezra's *Unspeakable Subjects*.

This is of course a view championed by New Criticism in both its French and Anglo-American versions. Though the French version speaks in more dramatic terms of the polemical "death" of author and work alike, it shares its Anglo-American counterpart's fundamental axiom–the denunciation of what Wimsatt and Beardsley call the "intentional fallacy" of traditional literary history and literary "appreciation." [52] A consequence of the axiom is the notion that a text's intrinsic formal properties make for their own intelligence. Whatever the contingent conditions surrounding its genesis may be, the text itself, construed now as New Critical "work," now as a Barthesian "methodological field," announces its nature, and thus its true meaning, only *after the fact*–once rigorous "practical criticism" takes it up as an object in its own right. There are many rival theories defining what counts as a text's "true" nature and meaning. Formalism borrows from a variety of disciplines to frame the intrinsic formal properties on which it works: linguistics and semiotics; narratology and the structural analysis of discursive genres; analytic philosophy of language and the Austinian theory of speech acts; but also psychoanalysis, a theory whose ongoing prestige in literary circles has much to do with the authoritative terms in which it preempts traditional canons of conscious authorial intent in the service of a radically decontextualized interpretation.

But the same general view informs what at first glance looks like formalism's highly contextualized opposite: the historicism for which the text is a more or less mystified precipitate of an underlying social or ideological discourse and the system of determinant socio-economic relations and conditions of which it presents the legible symptoms. We see the symmetry of formalist and historicist theses in the universal relevance of what Althusser calls the "topological" metaphors guiding the simultaneously *deconstructive* and *reconstructive* modes of interpretation our century has inherited from the nineteenth. [53] Marx's classic contrast between the socio-economic "infrastructure" or "base" of which cultural (ideological) phenomena constitute the mere "superstructural" expression or "reflection" joins with Freud's equally classic fixation on the system of unconscious drives and desires that determine the "manifest"

---

[52] For Wimsatt & Beardsley, see note 44.
[53] Althusser, *Positions* 138-40.

content of dream, repetition syndromes, or the work of art to form
the dominant model of both the literary text and the procedures required to interpret it. Nor have more recent theories like Derridean
"grammatology" or the closely related notions of "allegory" and
"rhetoric" in Paul de Man changed this basic picture. Direct descendants of the hermetic formalism shaping Anglo-American
"practical criticism" and the traditional French *explication de texte*,
Derrida and de Man sever the bond between text and context to reveal the infinite undecidability of the signifying process. Reading
thus becomes the art of discovering uncontainable difference where
context-bound methods seek the metaphysical "reassurance" of
"the same." But the net effect of this shift of emphasis is merely to
replace one set of metaphysical postulates with another. The text
becomes the surface correlate of its own differential undecidability.
The radical "difference" from which Derrida's grammatology or de
Manian rhetoric proceed assume the character of an ontological
condition exactly parallel to those in whose light Marxism and psychoanalysis affirm their historical etiologies. The reader's task remains what it always was: to unearth and reinstate an underlying dimension of *being* no less invariant for donning the mask of infinite
différance.[54]

By "Racine" then critics increasingly mean less the docu-
mentable historical person to whom the text owes its proximate
empirical occasion than an intention and meaning immanent to the
text itself: a latent purposiveness and significance, an automatized
"reproduction" or "repetition" that arise as a reflex of a formal
history (formalism and historicism fused in a quasi-Lacanian
"unconscious") our readings simultaneously confect and feast on.

[54] The metaphysical hypostasis of difference in Derrida and de Man is evinced
less by their theoretical utterances per se than by their characteristic readings. See,
e.g., Derrida on the repression of writing in Saussure, Rousseau, and Lévi-Strauss in
De la grammatologie; or de Man on the Romantic repression of allegory in "The
Rhetoric of Temporality," *Blindness and Insight: Essays in the Rhetoric of Contemporary Criticism*, 2nd ed. (Minneapolis: University of Minnesota Press, 1983) 187-
228 or on the repression of the undecidable nature of tropes in "Semiology and
Rhetoric," in *Allegories of Reading: Figural Language in Rousseau, Nietzsche, Rilke,
and Proust* (New Haven: Yale University Press, 1979) 3-19. Reading becomes what,
developing the amalgam of Marxism and psychoanalysis he inherits from Althusser,
Macherey, and Balibar, Lezra's *Unspeakable Subjects* calls an "etiology" that, as
such, posits both an underlying pathogen and the system of causal regularities that
license its inferential identification.

"Racine" is the name we give the autonomous historico-formal "subject" of his own texts: an impersonal place-holding precipitate determined by the coercive structure of the historical, differential, discursive, or ideological conditions from which we derive what we take to be its expression.[55] Nor is this just "theoretical," the work of the deconstructive "demon" of motiveless *différance* that Antoine Compagnon has recently tried to exorcise.[56] Consider a parallel text by Racine's great friend and ally Boileau: a fellow "ancien" whose testimony is all the more valuable for the authority he has earned as the preeminent spokesman for the classical "clarity" and "distinctness" by which contemporary interpretive darkness was methodically opposed. The text in question is the eighth of Boileau's verse epistles, addressed to the king, which opens as follows:

> Grand roi, cesse de vaincre, ou je cesse d'écrire.
> Tu sais bien que mon style est né pour la satire;
> Mais mon esprit, contraint de la désavouer,
> Sous ton règne étonnant ne veut plus que louer.
> Tantôt, dans les ardeurs de ce zèle incommode,
> Je songe à mesurer les syllabes d'une ode;
> Tantôt d'une Enéide auteur ambitieux,
> Je m'en forme déjà le plan audacieux:
> Ainsi, toujours flatté d'une douce manie,
> Je sens de jour en jour dépérir mon génie;
> Et mes vers en ce style, ennuyeux, sans appas,
> Déshonorent ma plume, et ne t'honorent pas.[57]

At an immediate level, Boileau's overture is a witty tour de force, a "belle trouvaille" or ingenious "invention" designed to

---

[55] This presumption is reflected in an enduring vogue of book titles: Philippe Lacoue-Labarthe, *Le sujet de la philosophie* (Paris: Aubier-Flammarion, 1979), Kaja Silverman, *The Subject of Semiotics* (Oxford: Oxford University Press, 1983), Catherine Belsey, *The Subject of Tragedy* (London: Methuen, 1985), Anthony J. Cascardi, *The Subject of Modernity* (Cambridge: Cambridge University Press, 1992), Peter Haidu, *The Subject of Violence* (Bloomington: Indiana University Press, 1993), Tony E. Jackson, *The Subject of Modernism* (Ann Arbor: University of Michigan Press, 1994), Deborah Lesko Baker, *The Subject of Desire* (West Lafayette: Purdue University Press, 1996).

[56] Antoine Compagnon, *Le démon de la théorie: Littérature et sens commun* (Paris: Seuil, 1998).

[57] Boileau, Epître VIII, "Au Roi," 1-12.

solve the basic rhetorical dilemma endemic to royal panegyric. As Boileau reminds his contemporaries in the final movement of *L'Art poétique*, the verse treatise on the art of poetry that supplies the most authoritative statement of classical doctrine the era produced, the fundamental business of French poets is to sing the monarch's praises:

> Auteurs, pour les chanter, redoublez vos transports:
> Le sujet ne veut pas de vulgaires efforts. [58]

The problem however is that, precisely because panegyric is not only obligatory, but ceaseless, an endless inflationary recycling of a message that is always the same, it becomes increasingly difficult for poets to achieve the distinctive difference, the inimitable *originality*, required to single themselves out from the adulatory crowd. As attested by the parallel conventions of love lyric, there is nothing so stereotyped as the language of praise. [59] While ridicule and blame profit from the seemingly inexhaustible diversity and concreteness of human folly, weakness, and vice, praise inevitably idealizes; and the ideal is inherently limited by its own rarity, perfection, and price. What is true of praise in general is all the more so when its object is not only the source of a social and material beneficence more enduring than sexual favors or the critical approbation that is sex's literary counterpart, but the embodiment of a political power like that of Ludovican absolutism—a coercive force beyond the reach of public irony.

Royal panegyric of the sort Boileau both will and *must* go on to offer in the epistle's continuation thus reproduces in intensified miniature the condition Barthes has diagnosed as constitutive of lit-

---

[58] Boileau, *L'Art poétique* 4.221-22.
[59] This is one of the many issues raised in the intro. to Fineman, *Shakespeare's Perjured Eye*. To the extent that, as Fineman argues, the Petrarchan poetics of praise of the beloved is a conventional pretext for self-advertising epideictic verse, an "invention" by means of which lyric (and thus the lyric "subject") assumes authoritative form, the poets who practise it are committed to a dialectic of difference in which they simultaneously locate themselves in and distinguish themselves from the conventions that make lyric writing possible. In this sense, even the anti-Petrarchism of, say, Shakespeare's sonnet 18 ("Shall I compare thee to a summer's day?") or sonnet 130 ("My mistress' eyes are nothing like the sun") function like Boileau's disclaimer of his competence to praise as versions of what they revise.

erary originality at large. As La Bruyère famously puts it at the very
start of the book on which he laid his own claim to literary fame,
"Tout est dit, et l'on vient trop tard depuis plus de sept mille ans
qu'il y a des hommes, et qui pensent." [60] What the poet means to
write has already been written, creating a situation Barthes characterizes by inverting the terms of a central axiom inherited from the
Romantics:

> On entend souvent dire que l'art a pour charge d'*exprimer l'in-
> exprimable*: c'est le contraire qu'il faut dire (sans nulle intention
> de paradoxe): toute la tâche de l'art est d'*inexprimer l'expri-
> mable*, d'enlever à la langue du monde, qui est la pauvre et puis-
> sante langue des passions, une parole *autre*, une parole *exacte*. [61]

It is here that we find at once the spur and spring framing the
conceit by which Boileau puts his novel spin on the mandatory idiom of praise. The opening gambit plays on his own notorious
generic standing as a *satirist*. What has earned him a public name,
and thus the right to compose panegyric verses not only addressed
to the king, but read to him in the presence of his court, is his earlier work as a writer of the comic poetry of blame. What will distinguish Boileau's praise from the unworthy productions (the "vulgai-
res efforts") of rivals like the "modern" Charles Perrault, to whose
inept panegyrics Boileau and Racine devoted joyfully malicious
commentary, [62] is the ironic confession of his incompetence. To do
justice to Louis's character and deeds demands not merely epideictic skills Boileau does not possess, but an epic vein entirely beyond
his reach. Needless to say, this opening gesture motivates precisely
what the framing invention pretends the poet cannot give: the full-
some recital of the sovereign's glorious accomplishments that forms
the epistle's burden. But it also sets up the poem's ingenious close
when, unnerved by the ludicrous spectacle he makes of himself in
the very act of explaining the kind of verse he cannot but is compelled to write, the satirist hears the voice of a judicious reader urging him to break off a performance that can only embarrass him:

---

[60] Jean de La Bruyère, *Les Caractères* 1.1.
[61] Roland Barthes, *Essais critiques* (Paris: Seuil, 1964) 15.
[62] For Soriano's account of this episode, see note 19.

> Au récit que pour toi je suis prêt d'entreprendre,
> Je crois voir les rochers accourir pour m'entendre;
> Et déjà mon vers coule à flots précipités,
> Quand j'entends le lecteur qui me crie: Arrêtez.
> Horace eut cent talents; mais la nature avare
> Ne vous a rien donné qu'un peu d'humeur bizarre.
> Vous passez en audace et Perse et Juvénal:
> Mais sur le ton flatteur Pinchesne est votre égal.
> A ce discours, grand roi, que pourrais-je répondre?
> Je me sens sur ce point trop facile à confondre;
> Et, sans trop relever des reproches si vrais,
> Je m'arrête à l'instant, j'admire et je me tais.
>
> (97-108)

But now we meet a deeper irony that overtakes the surface jest of Boileau's *trouvaille*. For a major long-term effect of the praise that the epistle pretends to give at its author's expense is the success of the social ambition that is one of its most obvious if unacknowledged objectives. Like his friend Racine, Boileau was in the end not only elected to the Académie, but received the commission of court historiographer, an office that, in accordance with the dictates of Ludovican absolutism, requires nothing less than ceaseless panegyric. A court historiographer is indeed no impartial chronicler of events; he is a propagandist charged with converting even blundering disaster into praise. What is more, a strict condition of Boileau's employment in the king's service was the abandonment of all publication unconnected with his royal function. Thus, albeit in a sense Boileau surely never considered, the king does in fact continue to triumph, and the result of this triumph is just what the poet warns: Boileau *ceases to write*, foreswearing his independent career as a satirist for his victorious sovereign's sake. [63] The ultimate effect of the ambition of which the epistle's royal panegyric is the tool is ex-

---

[63] On the conditions of Boileau's commission, conditions shared with Racine, see Rohou, *Jean Racine* 338. The most explicit documentary source is a letter by Mme de Sévigné dated 13 October 1677, where she reports that "Le Roi a donné deux mille écus à Racine et à Despréaux, en leur commandant de tout quitter pour travailler à son histoire." But we also have the more indirect testimony of Boileau's preface to the *Œuvres diverses* of 1683, where he boasts of the "glorieux emploi qui m'a tiré du métier de poésie." For a sense of the contemporary meaning of the "silence" Boileau and Racine's appointment as court historiographers entailed, see Rohou's judicious discussion, ibid. 329-40.

actly what the reflexive form of the poem's closing verb inscribes *à son insu*, yet no less truly for that: "j'admire" and, reduced to the awestruck silence admiration imposes, "je me tais." Boileau falls silent, the victim of a finally self-administered silence precisely comparable to the one to which, following Phèdre's self-administered death, Racine succumbs, foreswearing drama for the sake of the office of court historian he shares with his satiric friend.

All of this helps identify what Fumaroli responds to in proposing his reading of *Phèdre* 5.7.1638. The verse is at once the site and product of a double inscription, a palimpsest in which the dead hand of the historical author is written over by the living hand of subsequent readers to reveal a meaning other than the one consciously intended. But we are now also in a position to identify the *trap* Fumaroli falls into–or rather (*pace* Compagnon) the trap he sets for himself in the terms in which he poses the dilemma. Fumaroli fails to authenticate his interpretation of Phèdre's dying verse not because he is in any simple sense wrong, but because he assigns the historical Racine a meaning only *history* could write in the form of the text we attribute him–in the form of the text we call "Racine." And Fumaroli does so moreover for revealing if largely unconscious historical reasons. The misreading is a testament to the success of the classical enterprise, creating the secular cult of the transubstantial heroes of French literature we call the "grands classiques."

Whence the implicit axiom informing Fumaroli's commentary: what it is now possible to read *in* Racine must at some level be imputable *to* him, if need be in the form of an allegory of just the sort Fumaroli adduces. [64] The period precedent will be obvious: the exegetical practices of early modern scriptural commentary. As a reflex of holy scripture's putatively sacred source in an act of divine

---

[64] Note however, in fairness to Fumaroli, that allegories of this sort are the literary critic's stock in trade, and perhaps nowhere more emphatically than in the Marxist, psychoanalytic, and deconstructive modes of interpretation from which Fumaroli's erudite philological humanism distinguishes itself. Such is, e.g., the quite conscious testimony of de Man's *Allegories of Reading*, as, more remarkably still, of Frederic Jameson in *The Political Unconscious: Narrative as a Socially Symbolic Act* (Ithaca, NY: Cornell University Press, 1981) 28-33, where he evokes the fourfold system of medieval Christian allegoresis as a model for the application of the psychoanalytic Marxism he derives from Althusser.

authorship, everything in the text is not only significant, but *intend-ed*–and never more so than in those cases where the text contradicts itself, making the attribution of a single, unified authorial intention problematic. In scriptural commentary, this yields a "figural" or "typological" hermeneutics of the sort Pascal's unfinished *Apologie de la religion chrétienne* was meant to highlight. [65] The so-called "old" testament, a term mandated by the advent of the "new" one enshrined in the Gospels and Paul's epistles, was inevitably found to differ from the later text by which it was held to have been at once completed, illumined, and superseded. Like the "new," it remained of divine origin–divinely inspired, divinely ordained, and thus divinely *intended*. At the very least, as a sacred history serving as a repository of paradigmatic stories more prestigious even than those inherited from classical poetry, legend, and myth, it offered a pattern for human self-understanding, available at the "moral" level of Aquinas' fourfold exegetical scheme. [66] This defines indeed the relevance of the Hebrew stories of Esther and Athaliah to which Racine turns after the twelve-year silence begun with *Phèdre*. But this moral relevance cannot dispel the scandal the old testament represents for Christian exegetes. Accordingly, St. Paul rewrites the cosmic war of light and darkness, spirit and flesh, heavenly truth and deluded worldly illusion, as a contest between the dead letter of Hebrew scripture and the living spirit of Christian grace: a rivalry St. Augustine in turn expresses in the doctrine of allegorical "charity" that converts the paternal other of Jewish law into the filial identity born in the incarnate Word of the belated son. [67]

---

[65] For an introduction to Pascalian typology, see Erec R. Koch, *Pascal and Rhetoric: Figural and Persuasive Language in the Scientific Treatises, the Provinciales, and the Pensées* (Charlottesville: Rookwood Press, 1997).

[66] See Jameson, *The Political Unconscious* 29-31. Jameson draws heavily on Henri de Lubac, *Exégèse médiévale* (Paris: Aubier, 1959-64) 1.139-69 and 200-207. The other three levels of interpretation are the "literal" (where reading begins), the "metaphorical" (where Holy Scripture is shown to refer to other things by analogy), and the "anagogical" (where it reveals its ultimate meanings in the understanding of God's providential plan). The "moral," in this scheme, marks the moment, midway between the "metaphorical" and the "anagogical," when we learn to apply the text's meaning to our own immediate actions and concerns.

[67] On "figura," "typology," and the founding "scandal" of Christianity's debt to Judaism, see the classic studies by Erich Auerbach, "Figura," in *Scenes from the Drama of European Literature* (New York: Meridian Books, 1959) 11-76 and Jean Daniélou, *Sacramentum futuri: Etudes sur les origines de la typologie biblique* (Paris: Beauchesne, 1950).

This gives us the figural reading of which Pascal is a topical exemplar. Pascal devotes many of the notes assembled for the *Apologie* to readings of the Hebrew prophets as foreshadowing the later Christian revelation in whose light the earlier texts' allegorically "true" as opposed to mere literally "apparent" sense is at last disclosed, explained, and consecrated. One of the passages to which Pascal was drawn was Daniel 2, in which the prophet interprets Nebuchadnezzar's dream, and in particular what Pascal calls the "petite pierre," the little stone "cut out by no human hand" that smites the feet of clay on which the "great image" of gold, silver, brass, and iron stands, breaking it to pieces scattered in the wind "like the chaff of the summer threshing-floors." (Daniel 2.31-35) [68] The stone's significance is already allegorical in Daniel itself. The prophet demonstrates the divine origin of his wisdom and testimony not only by recounting the king's dream to him, but by decrypting it as a prefiguration of the successive kingdoms by which, following the impending collapse of Nebuchadnezzar's own age of gold, God will at last destroy *all* earthly kingdoms for the sake of a divine order that "shall stand for ever." (Daniel 2.36-45) But, for Pascal, the iconoclastic allegory into which the prophet transforms Nebuchadnezzar's dream prefigures a new one keyed to the paronomastic stone (*pierre*; the Vulgate's *petrus*) that works the image's ruin. The "petite pierre" becomes the Rock of Faith (*petrus*, but of course also St. Peter) on which Christ establishes his new dispensation among the ruins of the Jewish law it supersedes.

Such is, besides, the kind of reading Racine officially undertakes in the late "tragédies religieuses" performed by the inmates of the Collège de St.-Cyr at Mme de Maintenon's behest. The self-sacrificial heroine of *Esther* and, in a more complex, ambivalent form, the later *Athalie*'s zealot high priest blindly yet infallibly foreshadow the Christian truth–Christ's redemptive passion and resurrection; the destruction of Jewish as well as pagan idolatry–that the Hebrew histories simultaneously promise and veil in anticipation of the coming revelation. Whence the double meaning of the day on which *Athalie* unfolds. As Racine reports in his preface, scripture does not specify the date of Athaliah's downfall. It is therefore his own decision to choose Pentecost, "l'une des trois grandes fêtes des Juifs,"

---

[68] Pascal, *Pensées*, fragments 329, 485, 487 (Lafuma); 361, 456, 458 (Sellier).

celebrating "la mémoire de la publication de la loi sur le mont de Sinaï" (284). But with the advent of Christianity, Pentecost marks the descent of the Holy Spirit on the Apostles after Christ's resurrection, consummating the metamorphosis of Judaic law into Christian grace and love. To be sure, as the role of *Esther*'s Aman reinforced by *Athalie*'s murderously fanatical Joad suggests, both plays may be taken as allegories of the absolutist court, characterized by the unholy combination of political unscrupulousness and religious intolerance that mark the later reign of Louis XIV. To this extent, the figure of Pentecost is susceptible to an ironic interpretation. A liturgical date meant *en bonne doctrine* to commemorate the transformation of tribal and sectarian hate into the spirit of universal Christian love ends in a massacre we may readily construe as a covert denunciation of the rigid (and profoundly stupid) Ludovican piety exhibited in the revocation of the Edict of Nantes or the closure of the Jansenist community at Port-Royal. But the model remains that of Christian exegesis, positing in the text a belated figural reading supernaturally intended from the start.

What is true of the divine author of holy writ is equally true of Fumaroli's Racine. The historical ironies that overtake *Phèdre* are adduced to Racine himself, a poet we receive not only as an empirical representative of the historical past, but as a transcendental intelligence free of the constraints of historical time and space. Racine is not just one writer among others; he is a landmark that serves as a fixed point of orientation by which literary history itself is organized. He is seen therefore in a circular retrospect in which literary history *already is* what, *as* history, it will only later *become*. The irony to which he is subject in the sense of being its victim is transformed into an irony of which he is the subject in the sense of being its conscious origin, thereby enabling the name "Racine" to foreshadow its own place in the historical record of which it constitutes a critical ordering principle.

Fumaroli's error is an artifact of reading and the axioms on which that reading is based as an expression of his subscription to the authorial myth, that is, to the central *literary* myth, of Racine's "classical age" and the historic consecration that age confers. But in saying this, I do not merely want to write Fumaroli's reading off as a byproduct of a certain literary historical servitude and idolatry, the hypnotic illusion of transcendence our various "new historicisms" have systematically discredited. I want rather to suggest that the artifact adheres to the Racinian text itself, an insight immanent to it even if it is only now that we are in a position to make it out at its author's expense. Consider once more the precedent afforded by the ironic fate not only in store for, but *inscribed* in Boileau's witty frame to his royal panegyric. Just as Boileau's frame performatively encodes the ironies to which its author's subsequent career shows it to be subject, so does our verse from *Phèdre*. In Boileau, satire is extinguished by the panegyric to which the satirist is reduced by his satires' success in promoting the poet's social as well as literary ambitions. But so too is tragedy in a play in which the last voice to speak is that of a king whose ironically self-defeating prayer brings about the series of deaths that mark the close of Racine's career as a tragedian.

But Racine's text goes much further in this than Boileau's. The silence that falls over the satirist's eighth epistle is merely his own, a proleptic echo of the ironic defeat that attends his social triumph. By contrast, the silence that falls at the end of *Phèdre* is universal. This universality is in one sense fortuitous since it proves contingent on the fact that it comes in a tragic *play* rather than a courtly performance. It is a reflex of its social occasion and an accident of genre. Reciting a verse epistle to the king to whom it is publicly addressed in the presence of his assembled courtiers, Boileau provokes admiring laughter at the pretty conceit with which his performance ends by wittily voicing the silence in which it *must* end. Triggering the *brouhaha* of delighted surprise at the self-enacting cleverness of the close, the silence is thus Boileau's alone. The silence with which the tragedy closes, on the other hand, is meant to silence the audience as well, enforcing a deep attention for which, on the marquis-infested stage of seventeenth-century France, total silence is the only true measure. The silence at the end of *Phèdre* is *sublime*, translating the sublimity of the tragic poem. But it is also the medium in which the audience is brought to hear a further, deeper silence: that of the gods whose ironic fulfilment of Thésée's precipitous prayer, granting the paranoid wish as a reward for his heroic past, provokes the deaths that are the tragedy's final cause.

Yet the very pertinacity of the accidents of occasion and genre underscores the point I want to make: the uncanny way in which Racine's text accommodates its own unconscious ironies. Mind you, it is not just in his capacity as a *poet* that, an unwitting empirical instrument in history's hand, Racine inscribes the ironies of which he is the historical butt. He also does so as an *historiographer*, the office to which, in Boileau's company, he is paradoxically reduced by the worldly success he too craved. We see this, for instance, in the conflict between what his extracts from Lucan's treatise on history writing suggest he knew history to be and the propagandizing image subtending the panegyric record of the reign of Louis XIV he consented to compose in its place. The first three points retained from Lucan are these:

> L'éloge et l'histoire sont éloignés infiniment, et comme disent les musiciens, *dis dia pason*: c'est-à-dire, que ce sont les deux extrémités.
>
> Il n'y a guère moins de différence entre l'histoire et la poésie. Le poète a besoin de tous les dieux quand il veut peindre Agamemnon. Il lui faut la tête et les yeux de Jupiter, la poitrine de Neptune, et le bouclier de Mars. Mais l'historien peint Philippe borgne, comme il était.
>
> L'utilité est le principal objet de l'histoire. Le plaisir suit l'utilité, comme la beauté suit d'ordinaire la santé. (368)

This at once critical and utilitarian spirit informs some of the historical fragments Racine has left: the portraits of personalities from the reign of Louis XIII and the regency of Anne d'Autriche; his notes on the foreign powers with which Louis XIV contended, the Holland of De Witt, the Ottoman empire, Germany, England; or his archival investigations of the dubious dynastic and territorial claims made by the Bouillon family, his enemies and Pradon's allies in the "querelle de *Phèdre.*" However, the public works he produced–the *Précis historique des campagnes de Louis XIV depuis 1672 jusqu'en 1678* or the *Relation de ce qui s'est passé au siège de Namur*–intend, and can *only* intend, to trumpet the monarch's wisdom, justice, prudence, and fortitude. To cite the fourth point Racine cons from Lucan, "L'historien a pour juges des lecteurs malins, qui ne demandent pas mieux que de le reprendre, et qui l'examinent avec la même rigueur qu'un changeur examine la monnaie." (368) The intrinsic worth of some of the components of Racinian historiography cannot conceal what the ill-intentioned cunning of later readers reveals, namely, the *counterfeit* into which he turns them.

It is nevertheless only in the tragedies, *because* they are tragedies, that the irony fully reaches us. It will help here to return to what we saw earlier concerning the solipsism of Racinian characters, the quasi-autistic self-regard expressed by desires whose intransitive nature mirrors the monumental autarchy of the tragic work. What determines the tragic action, producing the logical necessity of a well-conducted plot rather than a mere ad hoc congeries of independent deeds, is a fearful synergy beyond the participants' ken. When she enters in act 1, Phèdre is dying of the unspeakable passion she bears, a passion whose crushing weight is redoubled by the at once social and mythological identity symbolized by her royal garments:

> Que ces vains ornements, que ces voiles me pèsent!
> Quelle importune main, en formant tous ces nœuds,
> A pris soin sur mon front, d'assembler mes cheveux?
> Tout m'afflige et me nuit, et conspire à me nuire.
>
> (1.3.158-61)

Following on the loaded reference to the sun whose light the suffering queen cannot bear to look upon (1.3.155), this complaint inaugurates the chain of mythological allusions, identifications, and parallels that sound throughout: her lineal descent from Helios, god of the sun, but also a double of Phoebus Apollo, god of language, reason, and poetry; her father Minos, Zeus' son and lord of the Labyrinth whose coils echo in the heavy "knots" piled on Phèdre's head; her mother Pasiphaë, daughter of Helios and thus child of light whose bestial desires nevertheless drove her to couple with the bull that sired the Minotaur on her, the monster Minos placed at the heart of the Labyrinth to devour the sacrificial youths demanded in tribute from Athens; her sister Ariadne, whose guiding thread (this too echoed in the wearisome ornaments on Phèdre's head) enabled their common lover Theseus to escape the Labyrinth after killing the monster at its heart; the inimical Aphrodite ("C'est Vénus tout entière à sa proie attachée") (1.3.306) whose hostile perversity has already surfaced in Pasiphaë's bestial passion; and finally her cousin Medea, from whom she inherits the poison with which she brings both her life and the play to an end. All of this–including a possible allusion to Medusa, this too bound up in the knots on the heroine's head, seconded by the petrifying confession she is about to make and the image of feminine desire it reveals to her confidante and her horrified step-son–specifies who Phèdre is and what this identity enjoins. In particular, it places her at the junction of the warring cosmic principles of passionate darkness and penetrating light, of enslavement and freedom, bodily desire and accusing mind, whose implacable conflict will finally kill her.

But the spectacle of the weary, self-loathing queen triggers Œnone's desire to learn the mortal secret her mistress conceals: a desire all the more insistent, erotic, and cruel in that the love that motivates it is complicated by the alienation Phèdre's confidante endures. For not only is Œnone the nurse who received Phèdre into the world; as she reminds her mistress at 1.3.235-36, she is also a sacrificial victim in her own right, having lost everything ("pays," "enfants") in becoming a slave in Minos' royal house. The two characters thus magnify each other's motives, committing them both to deeds neither alone would have performed whose consequences elude them the more utterly for the darkness in which they grope.

The way in which, in 1.3, Phèdre and Œnone amplify each other's actions supplies a model for the conduct of all of the major protagonists. The Hippolyte of the play's opening scene has a secret of his own: the passion for his father's prisoner Aricie that conflicts with the celibacy on which he resolves in reaction to Thésée's degrading sexual adventures. This inner conflict defines at once the son's identity and his psychic predicament. It thereby determines the fatal silence with which he both greets his father's return from the underworld and leaves Phèdre in the dark about his love for Aricie–a fact whose belated discovery prompts the rejected queen to authorize Œnone's calumnious account of what happened in Thésée's absence. Then comes the proud Aricie, a sexual predator whose unscrupulous urges not only bend the unlucky Hippolyte to her will, but provoke the jealous spasm that drives her rival to vengeance following the humiliating rejection she suffers as a reward for the equally humiliating confession of incestuous passion Œnone extracts with the news of Thésée's apparent death (1.5.350).

All of these entanglements are finally dominated by Thésée himself. Thus his image haunts Phèdre even at the very height of her
passion for his son:

> Oui, Prince, je languis, je brûle pour Thésée.
> Je l'aime, non point tel que l'ont vu les enfers,
> Volage adorateur de mille objets divers,
> Qui va du Dieu des morts déshonorer la couche;
> Mais fidèle, mais fier, et même un peu farouche,
> Charmant, jeune, traînant tous les cœurs après soi,
> Tel qu'on dépeint nos Dieux, ou tel que je vous voi.
>
> (2.5.634-40)

True, as Gilles Declerq acutely observes, the imposition of the father's image on the son constitutes a *détour galant*.[69] It not only intimates a passion Phèdre cannot bring herself to name, hoping instead that Hippolyte will divine it for himself, as indeed he does; it
is a *tease*, enabling her to approach his erotized body under cover
of displacement–"Il avait votre port, vos yeux, votre langage, /
Cette noble pudeur colorait son visage." (2.5.641-42) Yet though
designed to titillate and seduce, Phèdre's detour also spares her the
spectacle of her own abjection in her interlocutor's eyes, veiling her
intent in order to put off the moment of absolute self-disclosure in
hopes of securing a favorable reception she rightly fears she cannot
obtain. Further, the projection of Thésée's image on his son suggests the *delusion* to which she succumbs. It is not Hippolyte himself she sees, but a phantom engendered by her desire for what she
takes him for. Moreover, in the process, she subjects the beloved
object to the emasculating identification he has fruitlessly tried to
escape, producing a double projection in which the two participants' inverse imaginaries coalesce in the person of the doubly
alienated boy.

But Thésée is also the play's only true agent–the only character
who communicates with the outside world, beyond the exiguous
precincts of the palace in which all of the others are held hostage to

---

[69] Gilles Declerq, lecture delivered to the 1999 conference of the North American Society for Seventeenth-Century French Literature held at the University of
California at Santa Barbara. The text of the lecture is to appear in a forthcoming
volume of conference proceedings.

his selfish will. Indeed, he is the only character capable of making something *happen*, a power exercised in the prayer that, in taking Hippolyte's life, forces all secrets from covert. But as a reflex of the nature of his agency, and above all as an ironic consequence of his symbolically supercharged position as father, husband, legendary hero, and king, Thésée is also condemned to act in the dark. His lawless erotic impulses commit his wounded son and embittered queen to the lethal *méprise* in which they ensnare each other; and his equally lawless hubris leads him to enter the underworld in order to "déshonorer la couche" of the god of the dead (2.5.637), thereby lending color to the rumored death whose fatal consequence is the avowal of passion it appears to license. The same hubris inspires the jealous suspicions that induce him not only to assume the worst from the moment he returns home, but to believe the calumny directed at his son. Just as Phèdre projects on Hippolyte the image of the father with whom she originally fell in love, so Thésée projects his own appetites on him, killing the boy for crimes that are his alone. Above all, there is the deluded arrogance of his fatal prayer, claiming his right to the unnatural murder by which Neptune's debt to him is liquidated in the blood of his heir.

The action is thus an intricate dance to a music the dancers cannot hear, criss-crossing steps by which they maneuver each other toward a tragic fate no one wills or foresees. This constitutes of course a properly *tragic* irony, the dark rite of tragic "recognition," of Oedipal *anagnorisis*, on which the genre turns. But the irony here is brought to a perfection all the more poignant in that it mirrors the *historical* irony that overtakes its author. *Phèdre* is a consummate work of art, and nowhere more obviously than in its masterly handling of tragic irony. But the ultimate fruit of this mastery is to have earned its poet the ironic fate he shares with Boileau, a fate in turn reflected in the ironic self-betrayal shaping the historiography to which dramatic poetry gave way. If our verse from *Phèdre* encodes an ironic consciousness that, in retrospect, proves just and true in a way beyond its historical agent's reach, it is because the central trope reproduces the ironic self-betrayals that define the poet's historical condition.

History and tragedy coincide in the ironic intelligence we call "Racine." But this in turn means that history is not merely a set of constraining conditions or the empirical legacy conveyed by the documentary record the historical Racine leaves in his wake. It is the ironic difference between intent and act, choice and conse- quence, conscious aim and finished artifact that, *in* our evolving readings, finally *constitutes* that record to form the perlocutionary text we call by its author's name. Which brings us to one final *mise en abyme*, this too inscribed in the figures the tragic queen deploys on making her first entrance:

> Que ces vains ornements, que ces voiles me pèsent!
> Quelle importune main, en formant tous ces nœuds,
> A pris soin sur mon front, d'assembler mes cheveux?
> Tout m'afflige et me nuit, et conspire à me nuire.

As noted earlier, the ornaments, the veils, the knotted tresses that weigh so heavily on the guilty queen initiate the intricate sys- tem of echoes and allusions that define Phèdre's tragic identity. But in the light of Fumaroli's perlocutionary reading of the origin of the poison that kills her following her climactic entrance in act 5, these figures of her at once royal and mythological state also serve as em- blems of verse itself, and thus of the Medean art of tragedy whose suicide Phèdre enacts. As a tragic heroine, and for all her palpable reality, Phèdre is ultimately a mere creature of words, a trompe- l'oeil bearing witness to the hallucinatory power of the veiled indirections and carefully crafted plot whose interwoven strands "conspire" to cause her anguish and death. Above all, she is the fic- tive victim of the "importunate" authorial "hand" that, in penning the words she speaks, ties the dramatic "knots" that determine the action against whose binding necessity she struggles from the start. And yet she is also more than that since, even as a mere thing of words, it is her fate to be half conscious of the artifice that makes her act and live only to suffer and die. If the Phèdre who ingests Medea's poison personifies a tragic art that accomplishes its own deliberate *mise à mort* in the self-inflicted death assigned her role, the Phèdre who enters in act 1 embodies the sickness unto death that *makes* her die: a sickness indissociable from the consciousness she speaks and from the unknown hand that writes the verses she recites in order to speak it. Poetry is vanity, a worldly fiction all the more mortal for the deceitful "veils" and "ornaments" with which, in accordance with the conventional idiom of the day, it at once dis-

guises and indicts its own true nature and designs. Indeed, as embodied by the actors and actresses who declaim their conscious sufferings on stage, poetry is the indiscernible counterpart of mortality
itself.

Whence at last Racine's inimitable greatness, and the *invention*
on which that greatness depends: to have found a means of transforming the dramatic poem into the agent of its own critical undoing. The text of Racine's *Phèdre* turns out from the start to have
been the text of what Margolis calls the "career" it at once endures
and endorses both *in* and *as* the history of reading. And yet just because the measure of Racine's greatness is the elegant recursiveness
with which the *mises en abyme* that frame his final tragedy consummate the epoch they bring to an end, he merely epitomizes a practice Corneille and Molière undertake before him. As Diderot's
"Paradox" suggests, after Racine, everything is "after" Racine; and
if this is so, it is because he prospectively exhausts the vein he
works. But though Racine may exhaust it, he did not *open* it. His
greatness lies rather in perfecting the instrument Corneille and
Molière put in his hand–the text itself conceived as the thing he
wrote that we might read.

BIBLIOGRAPHY

Adam, Antoine. *L'Age classique* (Paris: Arthaud, 1968-71).

Alberti, Leon Battista. *On Painting*, ed. & parallel trans., Cecil Grayson (London: Phaidon, 1972).

Allier, Raoul. *La Cabale des dévots* (1902; rpt. Geneva: Slatkine, 1970).

Alpers, Svetlana. "Interpretation without Representation," *Representations* 1 (1983) 31-42.

———. *Rembrandt's Enterprise: The Studio and the Market* (Chicago: University of Chicago Press, 1988).

Althusser, Louis. *Positions (1964-1975)* (Paris: Editions sociales, 1976).

Altman, Janet Gurkin. *Epistolarity: Approaches to a Form* (Columbus: Ohio State University Press, 1982).

Apostolidès, Jean-Marie. *Le roi-machine: spectacle et politique au temps de Louis XIV* (Paris: Minuit, 1981).

———. *Le prince sacrifié: théâtre et politique au temps de Louis XIV* (Paris: Minuit, 1985).

Aristotle. *Poetics*, trans. James Hutton (New York: Norton, 1982).

———. *Rhetoric*, trans. W. Rhys Roberts, in *The Rhetoric and the Poetics of Aristotle* (New York: Modern Library, 1954).

Arnauld, Antoine & Pierre Nicole. *L'Art de penser*, ed. Bruno Baron von Freytag Löringhoff & Herbert E. Brekle (Stuttgart-Bad Cannstatt: Friedrich Frommann Verlag, 1967).

Ascoli, Albert Russell & Victoria Kahn (eds.), *Machiavelli and the Discourse of Literature* (Ithaca, NY: Cornell University Press, 1993).

Auerbach, Erich. "Figura," in *Scenes from the Drama of European Literature* (New York: Meridian Books, 1959) 11-76.

Austin, J.L. *Philosophical Papers*, 2nd ed. J.O. Urmson & G.J. Warnock (Oxford: Oxford University Press, 1970).

———. *How to Do Things with Words*, 2nd ed. J.O. Urmson and Marina Sbisà (Cambridge, Mass.: Harvard University Press, 1975).

Baby, Hélène & Alain Viala. "L'essor de la vie théâtrale," in Viala (ed.), *Le théâtre en France* 156-59.

———. "Naissance de la modernité théâtrale (1600-1650)," Ibid. 177-93.

Bacon, Francis. *The New Organon and Related Writings*, ed. Fulton H. Anderson (Indianapolis: Bobbs-Merrill, 1960).

Bacon, Francis. *A Selection of His Works*, ed. Sidney Warhaft (London: Macmillan, 1965).

Bairoch, Paul. *Cities and Economic Development: From the Dawn of History to the Present*, trans. Christopher Braider (Chicago: University of Chicago Press, 1988).

Bal, Mieke. *Reading Rembrandt: Beyond the Word-Image Opposition* (Cambridge: Cambridge University Press, 1991).

Barish, Jonas A. *The Antitheatrical Prejudice* (Berkeley: University of California Press, 1981).

Barthes, Roland. *Mythologies* (Paris: Seuil, 1957).

———. *Sur Racine* (Paris: Seuil, 1963; "Points" paper ed.).

———. *Essais critiques* (Paris: Seuil, 1964).

———. *Critique et vérité* (Paris: Seuil, 1966).

———. "La mort de l'auteur," in *Le bruissement de la langue* (Paris: Seuil, 1984) 71-80.

———. "De l'œuvre au texte," ibid. 81-85.

Baxandall, Michael. *Painting and Experience in Fifteenth-Century Italy* (Oxford: Oxford University Press, 1972; 2nd ed., 1988).

———. *Patterns of Intention: On the Historical Explanation of Pictures* (New Haven: Yale University Press, 1985).

Bénichou, Paul. *Morales du grand siècle* (Paris: Gallimard, 1948).

———. *Le Sacre de l'écrivain, 1750-1830: essai sur l'avènement d'un pouvoir spirituel laïque dans la France moderne* (Paris: José Corti, 1973).

Benjamin, Walter. *The Origin of German Tragic Drama*, trans. John Osborne (London: New Left Books, 1977; Verso paper ed., 1985).

Biet, Christian. "Plaisirs et dangers de l'admiration," *Littératures classiques* 32 (January 1998) 121-34.

Blumenberg, Hans. *The Legitimacy of the Modern Age*, trans. Robert M. Wallace (Cambridge, MA: MIT Press, 1983).

Boileau, Nicolas Despréaux. *Satires, Epîtres, Art poétique*, ed. Jean-Pierre Collinet (Paris: Gallimard, 1985).

Bold, Stephen C. "Ma(s)king a Name: Onomastics in Rotrou's Theater," *French Forum* 20.3 (September 1995) 279-97.

Bossuet, Jacques-Bénigne. *Maximes et réflexions sur la comédie*, ed. Guy Soury (Paris: A. Hatier, 1925).

———. *Discours sur l'histoire universelle*, ed. Jacques Truchet (Paris: Garnier-Flammarion, 1966).

Bourdieu, Pierre. *La distinction: critique sociale du jugement* (Paris: Minuit, 1979).

———. *Ce que parler veut dire: L'Economie des échanges linguistiques* (Paris: Fayard, 1982).

———. *Les règles de l'art: genèse et structure du champ littéraire* (Paris: Seuil, 1992).

Braider, Christopher. "The Vindication of Susanna: Femininity and Truth in Early Modern Science and Art," in *Yearbook of Comparative and General Literature* 40 (1992) 41-58.

———. *Refiguring the Real: Picture and Modernity in Word and Image, 1400-1700* (Princeton: Princeton University Press, 1993).

Brown, Jonathan. *Velázquez: Painter and Courtier* (New Haven: Yale University Press, 1986).

Bruneau, Marie-Florine. *Racine: Le jansénisme et la modernité* (Paris: Corti, 1986).

Bryson, Norman. *Word and Image: French Painting of the Ancien Régime* (Cambridge: Cambridge University Press, 1981).

Buci-Glucksmann, Christine. *La folie du voir: le baroque* (Paris: Galilée, 1986).

Burke, Peter. *The Fabrication of Louis XIV* (New Haven: Yale University Press, 1992).

Campbell, Mary Baine Campbell. *Wonder & Science: Imagining Worlds in Early Modern Europe* (Ithaca, NY: Cornell University Press, 1999).

Carlson, Marvin. *Theories of the Theatre: A Historical and Critical Survey, from the Greeks to the Present* (Ithaca, N.Y.: Cornell University Press, 1984).

Cascardi, Anthony J. *The Limits of Illusion: A Critical Study of Calderón* (Ithaca, NY: Cornell University Press, 1984).

Cassirer, Ernst. *The Individual and the Cosmos in Renaissance Philosophy*, trans. Mario Domandi (New York: Barnes & Noble, 1963).

Cavell, Stanley. "What Did Derrida Want of Austin?" in *Philosophical Passages: Wittgenstein, Emerson, Austin, Derrida* (Oxford: Blackwell, 1995) 42-65.

Chapelain, Jean. *Sentiments de l'Académie.*

———. *Sentiments* (draft), ed. Georges Collas (Geneva: Slatkine, 1968).

Charpentrat, Pierre. *Le mirage baroque* (Paris: Minuit, 1967).

Chedozeau, Bernard. *Le Baroque* (Paris: Nathan, 1989).

Church, William Farr. *Richelieu and Reason of State* (Princeton: Princeton University Press, 1973).

Cicero, *De partitione oratoria*, Loeb Classical Library, ed. & trans. H. Rackham (Cambridge, Mass.: Harvard University Press, 1942).

Compagnon, Antoine. *Le démon de la théorie: Littérature et sens commun* (Paris: Seuil, 1998).

Coogan, Robert. *Erasmus, Lee and the Correction of the Vulgate: The Shaking of the Foundations* (Geneva: Droz, 1992).

Corneille, Pierre. *Œuvres complètes*, ed. Georges Couton (Paris: Gallimard, 1980-87).

Couton, Georges. *Richelieu et le théâtre* (Lyon: Presses universitaires de Lyon, 1986).

Dandrey, Patrick. *La médecine et la maladie dans le théâtre de Molière* (Paris: Klincksieck, 1998).

Daniell, David. *William Tyndale: A Biography* (New Haven: Yale University Press, 1994).

Daniélou, Jean. *Sacramentum futuri: Etudes sur les origines de la typologie biblique* (Paris: Beauchesne, 1950).

Danto, Arthur. *The Transfiguration of the Commonplace: A Philosophy of Art* (Cambridge, Mass.: Harvard University Press, 1981).

D'Aubignac, François Hédelin, abbé. *La Pratique du théâtre*, facsimile of the Amsterdam edition of 1715 (Munich: Wilhelm Fink Verlag, 1971).

Defaux, Gérard. *Molière, ou les métamorphoses du comique: De la comédie morale au triomphe de la folie* (Lexington, KY: French Forum, 1980).

DeJean, Joan. *Tender Geographies: Women and the Origins of the Novel in France* (New York: Columbia University Press, 1991).

———. *Ancients against Moderns: Culture Wars and the Making of a Fin de Siècle* (Chicago: University of Chicago Press, 1997).

de Man, Paul. "The Rhetoric of Temporality," in *Blindness and Insight: Essays in the Rhetoric of Contemporary Criticism*, 2nd, revised ed. (Minneapolis: University of Minnesota Press, 1983) 187-228.

———. *Allegories of Reading: Figural Language in Rousseau, Nietzsche, Rilke, and Proust* (New Haven: Yale University Press, 1979).

Derrida, Jacques. "Cogito et histoire de la folie," in *L'écriture et la différence* (Paris: Seuil, 1967; Points paper ed.) 51-97.

Derrida, Jacques. *De la grammatologie* (Paris: Minuit, 1967).

———. "La pharmacie de Platon," in *La dissémination* (Paris: Seuil, 1972) 69-198.

———. *Marges de la philosophie* (Paris: Minuit, 1972).

———. *Limited Inc* (Evanston: Northwestern University Press, 1988).

Descartes, René. *Œuvres philosophiques*, 3 vols., ed. Ferdinand Alquié (Paris: Garnier, 1988-92).

Descombes, Vincent. *L'Inconscient malgré lui* (Paris: Minuit, 1977).

Diderot, Denis. *Paradoxe sur le comédien, précédé des Entretiens sur le Fils naturel*, ed. Raymond Laubreaux (Paris: Flammarion, 1981).

———. *Le Neveu de Rameau*, ed. Jean-Claude Bonnet (Paris: Flammarion, 1983).

Dock, Stephen Varick. *Costume & Fashion in the Plays of Jean-Baptiste Poquelin Molière: A Seventeenth-Century Perspective* (Geneva: Slatkine, 1992).

Dollimore, Jonathan. *Radical Tragedy: Religion, Ideology and Power in the Drama of Shakespeare and his Contemporaries* (Chicago: University of Chicago Press, 1984).

Doubrovsky, Serge. *Corneille et la dialectique du héros* (Paris: Gallimard, 1963).

Drake, Maurice & Wilfred. *Saints and Their Emblems* (1916; rpt. Detroit: Gale Research Co., 1971).

Eagleton, Terry. *The Ideology of the Aesthetic* (Oxford: Blackwell, 1990).

Elias, Norbert. *The Civilizing Process*, trans. Edmund Jephcott (New York: Pantheon, 1982).

Felman, Shoshana. *Le scandale du corps parlant: Don Juan avec Austin, ou la séduction en deux langues* (Paris: Seuil, 1980).

Fineman, Joel. *Shakespeare's Perjured Eye: The Invention of Poetic Subjectivity in the Sonnets* (Berkeley: University of California Press, 1986).

Fish, Stanley E. *Self-Consuming Artifacts: The Experience of Seventeenth-Century Literature* (Berkeley: University of California Press, 1972).

———. *Is There a Text in This Class? The Authority of Interpretive Communities* (Cambridge, Mass.: Harvard University Press, 1980).

———. *Doing What Comes Naturally: Change, Rhetoric, and the Practice of Theory in Literary and Legal Studies* (Durham, NC: Duke University Press, 1989).

Force, Pierre. *Molière ou Le Prix des choses: morale, économie et comédie* (Paris: Nathan, 1994).

Forestier, Georges. *Esthétique de l'identité dans le théâtre français (1550-1680): Le déguisement et ses avatars* (Geneva: Droz, 1988).

———. *Le Théâtre dans le théâtre sur la scène française du XVIIe siècle*, 2nd, enlarged ed. (Geneva: Droz, 1996).

———. *Essai de génétique théâtrale: Corneille à l'oeuvre* (Paris: Klincksieck, 1996).

———. *Corneille: Le sens d'une dramaturgie* (Paris: SEDES, 1998).

———. "Politique et tragédie chez Corneille, ou de la 'broderie'," *Littératures classiques* 32 [January 1998] 63-74.

Foucault, Michel. *Histoire de la folie à l'âge classique* (1961; rpt. Paris: Gallimard, 1972).

———. *Les mots et les choses: une archéologie des sciences humaines* (Paris: Gallimard, 1966).

———. *L'archéologie du savoir* (Paris: Gallimard, 1969).

———. *Surveiller et punir: naissance de la prison* (Paris: Gallimard, 1975).

———. *Dits et écrits, 1954-1988*, ed. Daniel Defert & Françoise Ewald (Paris: Gallimard, 1994).

Freedberg, David. *The Power of Images: Studies in the History and Theory of Response* (Chicago: University of Chicago Press, 1989).

Freud, Sigmund. "The 'Uncanny'," in *The Standard Edition of the Complete Psychological Works*, ed. & trans. James Strachey, in collaboration with Anna Freud & assisted by Alix Strachey & Alan Tyson (London: Hogarth, 1953-74), vol. 17, 219-56.

Fumaroli, Marc. *Critique et création littéraire au XVIIe siècle* (Paris: C.N.R.S., 1977).

———. *Héros et orateurs: rhétorique et dramaturgie cornéliennes* (Geneva: Droz, 1990).

———. *Le Poète et le Roi: Jean de La Fontaine en son siècle* (Paris: Fallois, 1997).

———. & Jacqueline Hellegouarch (eds.). *L'Art de la conversation* (Paris: Classiques Garnier, 1997).

Gasté, Armand (ed.). *La Querelle du Cid: Pièces et pamphlets* (Paris: H. Welter, 1899).

Gaukroger, Stephen. *Descartes: an intellectual biography* (Oxford: Oxford University Press, 1995).

Gendre, André. "Le Jupiter de Rotrou et Molière ou le scandale justifié," in *La Mythologie au XVIIe siècle* 177-85.

Genette, Gérard. "Vraisemblance et motivation," in *Figures II* (Paris: Seuil, 1969) 71-99.

Gilman, Ernest B. *The Curious Perspective: Literary and Pictorial Wit in the Seventeenth Century* (New Haven: Yale University Press, 1978).

———. *Iconoclasm and Poetry in the English Reformation: Dagon Went Down* (Chicago: University of Chicago Press, 1986).

Girard, René. *La Violence et le sacré* (Paris: Grasset, 1972).

———. *Le Bouc émissaire* (Paris: Grasset, 1982).

Goldmann, Lucien. *Le Dieu caché: Etude sur la vision tragique dans les Pensées de Pascal et dans le théâtre de Racine* (Paris: Gallimard, 1959).

Goodkin, Richard. *Birth Marks: The Tragedy of Primogeniture in Pierre Corneille, Thomas Corneille, and Jean Racine* (Philadelphia: University of Pennsylvania Press, 2000).

Gossman, Lionel. *Men and Masks: A Study of Molière* (Baltimore: The Johns Hopkins University Press, 1963).

Grafton, Anthony. *Joseph Scaliger: A Study in the History of Classical Scholarship* (Oxford: Clarendon Press, 1983-93).

———. *Commerce with the Classics: Ancient Books and Renaissance Readers* (Ann Arbor: University of Michigan Press, 1997).

———. with April Shelford & Nancy Siraisi. *New Worlds, Ancient Texts: The Power of Tradition and the Shock of Discovery* (Cambridge, MA: Harvard University Press, 1992).

Graves, Robert. *The Greek Myths* (Baltimore: Penguin Books, 1955).

Greenberg, Mitchell. *Detours of Desire: Readings in the French Baroque* (Columbus, Ohio: Ohio State University Press, 1984).

———. *Corneille, Classicism, and the Ruses of Symmetry* (Cambridge: Cambridge University Press, 1986).

———. *Subjectivity and Subjugation in Seventeenth-Century French Drama and Prose: The Family Romance of French Classicism* (Cambridge: Cambridge University Press, 1992).

———. *Canonical States, Canonical Stages: Oedipus, Othering, and Seventeenth-Century Drama* (Minneapolis: University of Minnesota Press, 1994).

Greenblatt, Stephen. *Renaissance Self-Fashioning: From More to Shakespeare* (Chicago: University of Chicago Press, 1980).

Greenblatt, Stephen. *Learning to Curse: Essays in Early Modern Culture* (New York: Routledge, 1990).
———. *Marvelous Possessions: The Wonder of the New World* (Chicago: University of Chicago Press, 1991).
Greene, Roland. *Unrequited Conquests: Love and Empire in the Colonial Americas* (Chicago: University of Chicago Press, 1999).
Greene, Thomas M. *The Light in Troy: Imitation and Discovery in Renaissance Poetry* (New Haven: Yale University Press, 1982).
Grimm, Jürgen. *Molière en son temps* (Paris: Biblio 17, 1993).
Guicharnaud, Jacques. *Molière, une aventure théâtrale: Tartuffe, Dom Juan, Le Misanthrope* (Paris: Gallimard, 1963).
Guillory, John. *Cultural Capital: The Problem of Literary Canon Formation* (Chicago: University of Chicago Press, 1993).
Hagstrum, Jean. *The Sister Arts: The Tradition of Literary Pictorialism and English Poetry from Dryden to Gray* (Chicago: University of Chicago Press, 1958).
Hall, Hugh Gaston. *Comedy in Context: Essays on Molière* (Jackson: University of Mississippi Press, 1984).
Hampton, Timothy. *Writing from History: The Rhetoric of Exemplarity in Renaissance Literature* (Ithaca, NY: Cornell University Press, 1990).
Hardy, Alexandre. *Scédase, ou l'hospitalité violée*, in *Théâtre du XVIIᵉ siècle*, ed. Jacques Schérer (Paris: Gallimard, 1975) 1. 85-129.
Harrison, Helen. *Pistoles/Paroles: Money and Language in Seventeenth-Century French Comedy* (Charlottesville, VA: Rookwood Press, 1996).
Harth, Erica. *Cyrano de Bergerac and the Polemics of Modernity* (New York: Columbia University Press, 1970).
———. *Ideology and Culture in Seventeenth-Century France* (Ithaca, NY: Cornell University Press, 1982).
———. *Cartesian Women: Versions and Subversions of Rational Discourse in the Old Régime* (Ithaca, NY: Cornell University Press, 1992).
Hazard, Paul. *Crise de la conscience européenne, 1680-1715* (Paris: Arthème Fayard, 1961).
Hegel, Georg Wilhelm Friedrich. *The Phenomenology of Mind*, trans. George Lichtheim (New York: Harper & Row, 1967).
———. *Introductory Lectures on Aesthetics*, trans. Bernard Bosanquet, ed. Michael Inwood (London: Penguin Books, 1993).
Hill, Christopher. *The World Turned Upside Down: Radical Ideas in the English Revolution* (London: Maurice Temple Smith, 1972).
———. *The Experience of Defeat: Milton and Some Contemporaries* (New York: Viking, 1984).
Hobbes, Thomas. *Leviathan* (London: Everyman, 1914).
Howarth, W.D. *Molière: A Playwright and His Audience* (Cambridge: Cambridge University Press, 1982).
Hubert, J.D. *Molière and the Comedy of Intellect* (Berkeley: University of California Press, 1962).
Hunt, Alan. *Governance of the Consuming Passions: A History of Sumptuary Law* (New York: St. Martin's Press, 1996).
Jameson, Frederic. *The Political Unconscious: Narrative as a Socially Symbolic Act* (Ithaca, NY: Cornell University Press, 1981).
Jodelle, Etienne. *Didon se sacrifiant*, in Donald Stone, Jr. (ed.), *Four Renaissance Tragedies* (Cambridge, MA: Harvard University Press, 1966).
Jonson, Ben. *Bartholomew Fair*, in *Five Plays*, ed. G.A. Wilkes (Oxford: Oxford University Press, 1981; World Classics paper ed., 1988).

BIBLIOGRAPHY 383

Jouhaud, Christian. *Mazarinades: La Fronde des mots* (Paris: Aubier, 1985).
——. *La Main de Richelieu, ou le pouvoir cardinal* (Paris: Gallimard, 1990).
——. "Power and Literature: The Terms of the Exchange 1624-42," in Richard Burt (ed.), *The Administration of Aesthetics: Censorship, Political Criticism, and the Public Sphere* (Minneapolis: University of Minnesota Press, 1994) 34-82.
Judovitz, Dalia. *The Culture of the Body: Genealogies of Modernity* (Ann Arbor: University of Michigan Press, 2001).
Kahn, Victoria. *Rhetoric, Prudence, and Skepticism in the Renaissance* (Ithaca, NY: Cornell University Press, 1985).
Kant, Immanuel. *Critique of Judgment*, ed. & trans. Werner S. Pluhar (Indianapolis: Hackett, 1987).
Kantorowicz, Ernst H. *The King's Two Bodies* (Princeton: Princeton University Press, 1957).
Kermanac'h, Yves. *Molière ou la double tentation* (Paris: Galilée, 1980).
Koch, Erec R. *Pascal and Rhetoric: Figural and Persuasive Language in the Scientific Treatises, the* Provinciales, *and the* Pensées (Charlottesville: Rookwood Press, 1997).
Kogan, Stephen. *The Hieroglyphic King: Wisdom and Idolatry in the Seventeenth-Century Masque* (Rutherford, NJ: Fairleigh Dickinson University Press, 1986).
Kuhn, Thomas S. *The Copernican Revolution: Planetary Astronomy in the Development of Western Thought* (Cambridge, MA: Harvard University Press, 1957).
La Bruyère, Jean de. *Les Caractères ou les moeurs de ce siècle*, ed. Julien Benda (Paris: Gallimard, 1951).
Lacan, Jacques. *Ecrits* 1 (Paris: Seuil, 1966).
——. *Les Ecrits techniques de Freud (1953-54), Le Séminaire de Jacques Lacan*, bk. 1, ed. Jacques-Alain Miller (Paris: Seuil, 1975).
——. *Le Moi dans la théorie de Freud et dans la technique de la psychanalyse (1954-55), Le Séminaire de Jacques Lacan*, bk. 2, ed. Jacques-Alain Miller (Paris: Seuil, 1978).
——. *Les quatre concepts fondamentaux de la psychanalyse, Le séminaire de Jacques Lacan*, bk. 11, ed. Jacques-Alain Miller (Paris: Seuil, 1973.).
La Mesnardière, Jean de. *La Poëtique* (Paris: Antoine Sommaville, 1640).
La Rochefoucauld, François de. *Maximes*, ed. Pierre Kuentz (Paris: Bordas, 1966).
Lasserre, François. *Corneille de 1638 à 1642: La crise technique d'Horace, Cinna et Polyeucte* (Paris: Biblio 17, 1990).
Lawrenson, T.E. *French Stage and Playhouse in the XVIIth Century* (New York: AMS Press, 1986).
Lennon, Thomas M. *Reading Bayle* (Toronto: University of Toronto Press, 1999).
Lessing, Gotthold Ephraim. *Laocoon: An Essay on the Limits of Painting and Poetry*, ed. & trans. Edward Allen McCormick (Indianapolis: Bobbs-Merrill, 1962).
Lezra, Jacques. *Unspeakable Subjects: The Genealogy of the Event in Early Modern Europe* (Stanford: Stanford University Press, 1997).
(Pseudo-)Longinus. *On Great Writing (On the Sublime)*, trans. G.M.A. Grube (Indianapolis: Hackett, 1957).
Lubac, Henri de. *Exégèse médiévale* (Paris: Aubier, 1959-64).
Lukács, Georg. *Soul and Form*, trans. Anna Bostock (Cambridge, Mass.: MIT Press, 1974).
Lungstrum, Janet. "A Transcendental Infidelity: Kleist, Lacan and *Amphitryon*," *Modern Language Notes* 22.4 (Fall 1992) 67-75.
Lyons, John D. *A Theatre of Disguise: Studies in French Baroque Drama* (Columbia, SC: French Literature Publications, 1978).

Lyons, John D. *Exemplum: The Rhetoric of Example in Early Modern France and Italy* (Princeton: Princeton University Press, 1989).

——. *The Tragedy of Origins: Pierre Corneille and Historical Perspective* (Stanford: Stanford University Press, 1996).

——. *Kingdom of Disorder: The Theory of Tragedy in Classical France* (West Lafayette: Purdue University Press, 1999).

Maillard, Jean-François. *Essai sur l'esprit du héros baroque (1580-1640): le même et l'autre* (Paris: Nizet, 1973).

Mairet, Jean. "L'Autheur du vray Cid Espagnol à son Traducteur François," in Armand Gasté (ed.), *La Querelle du Cid: Pièces et pamphlets* (Paris: H. Welter, 1899) 67-68.

Mallet, Francine. *Molière* (Paris: Grasset, 1986).

Margival, Henri. *Essai sur Richard Simon et la critique biblique au 17ᵉ siècle* (1900; rpt. Geneva: Slatkine, 1970).

Margolis, Joseph. *Interpretation Radical but Not Unruly: The New Puzzle of the Arts and History* (Berkeley: University of California Press, 1995).

Marin, Louis. *La Critique du discours: sur la "Logique de Port-Royal" et les "Pensées" de Pascal* (Paris: Minuit, 1975).

——. *Le portrait du roi* (Paris: Minuit, 1981).

——. *La parole mangée et autres essais théologico-politiques* (Paris: Meridiens Klincksieck, 1986).

McGregor, Gordon D. "*Rodogune, Nicomède,* and the Status of History in Corneille," *Stanford French Review* 11 (Summer 1987) 133-55.

Meinecke, Friedrich. *Machiavellianism, the Doctrine of Raison d'Etat and Its Place in Modern History,* trans. Douglas Scott (New Haven: Yale University Press, 1957).

Merlin, Hélène. *Littérature et public en France au XVIIᵉ siècle* (Paris: Les Belles lettres, 1994).

——. "*Cinna, Rodogune, Nicomède*: Le Roi et le moi," *Littératures* 37 (Fall 1997) 67-86.

——. "Corneille et la politique dans *Cinna, Rodogune* et *Nicomède,*" *Littératures classiques* 32 (January, 1998) 41-61.

Mitchell, W.J.T. *Iconology: Image, Text, Ideology* (Chicago: University of Chicago Press, 1986).

Molière (Jean-Baptiste Poquelin). *Œuvres complètes* (Paris: Seuil, 1962).

——. Pléiade *Œuvres complètes,* ed. Georges Couton (Paris: Gallimard, 1971).

Molina, Tirso de. *El Burlador de Sevilla y convidado de piedra,* ed. James A. Parr (Binghampton: Medieval & Renaissance Texts & Studies, 1994).

Mongrédien, Georges. *La Vie quotidienne des comédiens au temps de Molière* (Paris: Hachette, 1966).

——. *La Querelle de l'Ecole des femmes* (Paris: Marcel Didier, 1971).

——. *Comédies et pamphlets sur Molière* (Paris: Nizet, 1986).

Montaigne, Michel de. *Essais* (Paris: Garnier-Flammarion, 1969).

Montrose, Louis. "'Eliza, Queene of Shepheardes' and the Pastoral of Power," *English Literary Renaissance* 10 (1980) 153-82.

Moore, Timothy J. *The Theater of Plautus: Playing to the Audience* (Austin: University of Texas Press, 1998).

Morello, Joseph. *Jean Rotrou* (Boston: Twayne, 1980).

Moriarty, Michael. *Taste and Ideology in Seventeenth-Century France* (Cambridge: Cambridge University Press, 1988).

Murray, Timothy. *Theatrical Legitimation: Allegories of Genius in Seventeenth-Century England and France* (Oxford: Oxford University Press, 1987).

Naudé, Gabriel. *Considérations politiques sur les coups d'Etat*, ed. Frédérique Marin & Marie-Odile Perulli (Paris: Editions de Paris, 1988).

Nicole, Pierre. *Traité de la comédie*, ed. Georges Couton (Paris: Les Belles lettres, 1961).

Nicoll, Allardyce. *The Development of the Theatre*, 5th ed. (New York: Harcourt, Brace, and World, 1966).

Norman, Larry J. *The Public Mirror: Molière and the Social Commerce of Depiction* (Chicago: University of Chicago Press, 1999).

Nurse, Peter Hampshire. *Molière and the Comic Spirit* (Geneva: Droz, 1991).

Nussbaum, Martha. *The Fragility of Goodness: Luck and Ethics in Greek Tragedy and Philosophy* (Cambridge: Cambridge University Press, 1986).

Orgel, Stephen. *The Illusion of Power: Political Theater in the English Renaissance* (Berkeley: University of California Press, 1975).

———. "The Example of Hercules," in Walther Killy (ed.), *Mythographie der frühen Neuzeit: Ihre Anwendung in den Künsten* (Wiesbaden: O. Harrassowitz, 1984) 25-47.

Panofsky, Erwin. "The History of Art as a Humanistic Discipline," in *Meaning in the Visual Arts* (Chicago: University of Chicago Press, 1955; Phoenix paper ed.) 1-25.

Pascal, Blaise. *Pensées*, ed. Louis Lafuma (Paris: Seuil, 1962).

———. *Pensées*, ed. Philippe Sellier (Paris: Classiques Garnier, 1991).

Passage, Charles E. & James H. Mantinband. *Amphitryon: The Legend and Three Plays (Plautus, Molière, Kleist)* (Chapel Hill: University of North Carolina Press, 1974).

Perrault, Charles. *Parallèle des anciens et des modernes*, ed. Hans Robert Jauss (Munich: W. Fink, 1964).

Picard, Raymond. *La Carrière de Jean Racine* (Paris: Gallimard, 1956).

———. *Nouvelle critique ou nouvelle imposture* (Paris: Pauvert, 1965).

Plato. *The Symposium*, trans. Walter Hamilton (Harmondsworth: Penguin, 1951).

Plautus, *Amphitruo*, in *Complete Works*, Loeb Classical Library, ed. Paul Nixon (Cambridge, Mass.: Harvard University Press, 1937), vol. 1.

Popkin, Richard H. *The History of Scepticism from Erasmus to Spinoza*, rev. ed. (Berkeley: University of California Press, 1979).

Prigent, Michel. *Le Héros et l'Etat dans la tragédie de Pierre Corneille* (Paris: Presses universitaires de France, 1986).

Quint, David. *Origin and Originality in Renaissance Literature: Versions of the Source* (New Haven: Yale University Press, 1983).

Quintilian, *Institutio oratoria*, Loeb Classical Library, ed. & trans. H.E. Butler (Cambridge, Mass.: Harvard University Press, 1986).

Racine, Jean. *Œuvres complètes* (Paris: Seuil, 1962).

Reiss, Timothy J. "Descartes, the Palatinate, and the Thirty Years War: Political Theory and Political Practice" in *Baroque Topographies: Literature/History/Philosophy*, ed. Timothy Hampton, *Yale French Studies* 80 (New Haven: Yale University Press, 1991) 108-45.

Rigolot, François. *Poétique et Onomastique: l'exemple de la Renaissance* (Geneva: Droz, 1977).

Rohou, Jean. *Jean Racine entre sa carrière, son oeuvre et son Dieu* (Paris: Fayard, 1992).

Rotrou, Jean. *Les Sosies*, ed. Damien Charron (Geneva: Droz, 1980).

Rousset, Jean. *La Littérature de l'âge baroque en France: Circe et le paon* (Paris: Corti, 1954).

Schérer, Jacques. *La Dramaturgie classique en France* (1950; rpt. Paris: Nizet, 1986).

Scudéry, Georges de. *Observations sur Le Cid*, in Armand Gasté (ed.), *La Querelle du Cid: Pièces et pamphlets* (Paris: H. Welter, 1899).

Searle, John. "Las Meninas and the Paradoxes of Pictorial Representation," *Critical Inquiry* 6 (1980) 477-88.

Serres, Michel. *La Naissance de la physique dans le texte de Lucrèce: Fleuves et turbulences* (Paris: Minuit, 1977).

Shapin, Steven. *A Social History of Truth: Civility and Science in Seventeenth-Century England* (Chicago: University of Chicago Press, 1994).

Shell, Marc. *Money, Language, and Thought: Literary and Philosophic Economies from the Medieval to the Modern Era* (Berkeley: University of California Press, 1982).

Slater, Niall W. *Plautus in Performance: The Theatre of the Mind*, 2nd ed. (Amsterdam: Harwood Academic Publishers, 2000).

Snyder, Joel. "Las Meninas and the Mirror of the Prince," *Critical Inquiry* 11 (1985) 539-72.

Snyder, Joel & Ted Cohen. "Reflections on Las Meninas: Paradox Lost," *Critical Inquiry* 7 (1980) 429-47.

Soriano, Marc. *La brosse à reluire sous Louis XIV: "L'Epître au roi" de Perrault, annotée par Racine et Boileau* (Paris: Nizet, 1989).

Stanton, Domna C. *The Aristocrat as Art: A Study of the Honnête Homme and the Dandy in Seventeenth- and Nineteenth-Century France* (New York: Columbia University Press, 1980).

Starobinski, Jean. *L'Oeil vivant* (1961; enlarged ed., Paris: Gallimard, 1999).

Steinberg, Leo. "Velasquez' *Las Meninas*," *October* 19 (1981) 45-54.

Steiner, George. *The Death of Tragedy* (New York: Knopf, 1961).

Stewart, Zeph. "The 'Amphitruo' of Plautus and Euripides' 'Bacchae'," *Transactions of the American Philological Association* 89 (1958) 348-73.

Stone, Harriet Amy. *Royal DisClosure: Problematics of Representation in French Classical Tragedy* (Birmingham, AL: Summa Publications, 1987).

———. *The Classical Model: Literature and Knowledge in Seventeenth-Century France* (Ithaca, NY: Cornell University Press, 1996).

Strauss, Leo. *Persecution and the Art of Writing* (Glencoe: The Free Press, 1952).

———. *Spinoza's Critique of Religion*, trans. E.M. Sinclair (New York: Schocken, 1965).

Sweetser, Marie-Odile. "La conversion du Prince: réflexions sur la tragédie providentielle," *Papers on French Seventeenth-Century Literature* 10.19 (1983) 497-510.

———. "Tragic Situation and Providential Intervention: The Case for a New Concept of Tragedy in the XVIIth Century," *Seventeenth-Century French Studies* 7 (1985) 97-107.

Tapié, Victor-Lucien. *Baroque et classicisme* (Paris: Plon, 1957).

———. *Le baroque* (Paris: Presses universitaires de France, 1961).

Thuau, Etienne. *Raison d'Etat et pensée politique à l'époque de Richelieu* (Paris: Armand Colin, 1966).

Todorov, Tzvetan. *Littérature et signification* (Paris: Larousse, 1967).

Ubersfeld, Anne. "Le double dans l'*Amphitryon* de Molière," in *Dramaturgie, langages dramatiques: Mélanges pour Jacques Schérer* (Paris: Nizet, 1986) 235-44.

Viala, Alain. *Naissance de l'écrivain: sociologie de la littérature à l'âge classique* (Paris: Minuit, 1985).
——. *Racine: La Stratégie du caméléon* (Paris: Seghers, 1990).
—— (ed.). *Le théâtre en France des origines à nos jours* (Paris: Presses Universitaires de France, 1997).
Voragine, Jacques de. *La Légende dorée*, ed. & trans. J.-B. M. Roze (Paris: Edouard Rouveyre, 1902).
Vuillemin, Jean-Claude. *Baroquisme et théâtralité: le théâtre de Jean Rotrou* (Paris: Papers on French Seventeenth-Century Literature, 1994).
Weinstein, Leo. *The Metamorphoses of Don Juan* (Stanford: Stanford University Press, 1959).
Whelan, Ruth. *The Anatomy of Superstition: A Study of the Historical Theory and Practice of Pierre Bayle* (Oxford: Voltaire Foundation, 1989).
Wimsatt, William K. & Monroe C. Beardsley. *The Verbal Icon: Studies in the Meaning of Poetry* (Lexington, KY: University of Kentucky Press, 1954).
Winckelmann, Johann Joachim. *Reflections on the Imitation of Greek Works in Painting and Sculpture*, German text & parallel trans. Elfriede Heyer & Roger C. Norton (La Salle: Open Court, 1987).
Wygant, Amy. "Medea, Poison, and the Epistemology of Error in *Phèdre*," *Modern Language Review* 95.1 (January 2000) 62-71.
Yovel, Yirmiyahu. *Spinoza and Other Heretics* (Princeton: Princeton University Press, 1989), vol. 1, *The Marrano of Reason*.
Zagorin, Perez. *Ways of Lying: Dissimulation, Persecution, and Conformity in Early Modern Europe* (Cambridge, MA: Harvard University Press, 1990).
Zanger, Abby E. "Paralyzing Performance: Sacrificing Theater on the Altar of Publication," *Stanford French Review* 12.2-3 (Fall/Winter 1988) 169-85.
——. "Classical Anxiety: Performance, Perfection, and the Issue of Identity," in David Trott & Nicole Boursier (eds.), *L'Age du théâtre en France/The Age of Theatre in France* (Edmonton: Academic Printing & Publishing, 1988) 327-39.
——. *Scenes from the Marriage of Louis XIV: Nuptial Fictions and the Making of Absolutist Power* (Stanford: Stanford University Press, 1997).
Zebouni, Selma. "*L'Amphitryon* de Molière ou l'autre du sujet," in Ralph Heyndels & Barbara Woshinsky (eds.), *L'autre au XVIIe siècle* (Tübingen: Biblio 17, 1999) 347-55.

NORTH CAROLINA STUDIES IN THE ROMANCE LANGUAGES AND LITERATURES

I.S.B.N. Prefix 0-8078-

Recent Titles

THE POETICS OF INCONSTANCY, ETIENNE DURAND AND THE END OF RENAISSANCE VERSE, by Hoyt Rogers. 1998. (No. 256). *-9260-2.*

RONSARD'S CONTENTIOUS SISTERS: THE PARAGONE BETWEEN POETRY AND PAINTING IN THE WORKS OF PIERRE DE RONSARD, by Roberto E. Campo. 1998. (No. 257). *-9261-0.*

THE RAVISHMENT OF PERSEPHONE: EPISTOLARY LYRIC IN THE *SIÈCLE DES LUMIÈRES,* by Julia K. De Pree. 1998. (No. 258). *-9262-9.*

CONVERTING FICTION: COUNTER REFORMATIONAL CLOSURE IN THE SECULAR LITERATURE OF GOLDEN AGE SPAIN, by David H. Darst. 1998. (No. 259). *-9263-7.*

GALDÓS'S *SEGUNDA MANERA:* RHETORICAL STRATEGIES AND AFFECTIVE RESPONSE, by Linda M. Willem. 1998. (No. 260). *-9264-5.*

A MEDIEVAL PILGRIM'S COMPANION. REASSESSING *EL LIBRO DE LOS HUÉSPEDES* (ESCORIAL MS. h.I.13), by Thomas D. Spaccarelli. 1998. (No. 261). *-9265-3.*

'PUEBLOS ENFERMOS': THE DISCOURSE OF ILLNESS IN THE TURN-OF-THE-CENTURY SPANISH AND LATIN AMERICAN ESSAY, by Michael Aronna. 1999. (No. 262). *-9266-1.*

RESONANT THEMES. LITERATURE, HISTORY, AND THE ARTS IN NINETEENTH- AND TWENTIETH-CENTURY EUROPE. ESSAYS IN HONOR OF VICTOR BROMBERT, by Stirling Haig. 1999. (No. 263). *-9267-X.*

RAZA, GÉNERO E HIBRIDEZ EN *EL LAZARILLO DE CIEGOS CAMINANTES,* por Mariselle Meléndez. 1999. (No. 264). *-9268-8.*

DEL ESCENARIO A LA PANTALLA: LA ADAPTACIÓN CINEMATOGRÁFICA DEL TEATRO ESPAÑOL, por María Asunción Gómez. 2000. (No. 265). *-9269-6.*

THE LEPER IN BLUE: COERCIVE PERFORMANCE AND THE CONTEMPORARY LATIN AMERICAN THEATER, by Amalia Gladhart. 2000. (No. 266). *-9270-X.*

THE CHARM OF CATASTROPHE: A STUDY OF RABELAIS'S *QUART LIVRE,* by Alice Fiola Berry. 2000. (No. 267). *-9271-8.*

PUERTO RICAN CULTURAL IDENTITY AND THE WORK OF LUIS RAFAEL SÁNCHEZ, by John Dimitri Perivolaris. 2000. (No. 268). *-9272-6.*

MANNERISM AND BAROQUE IN SEVENTEENTH-CENTURY FRENCH POETRY: THE EXAMPLE OF TRISTAN L'HERMITE, by James Crenshaw Shepard. 2001. (No. 269). *-9273-4.*

RECLAIMING THE BODY: MARÍA DE ZAYA'S EARLY MODERN FEMINISM, by Lisa Vollendorf. 2001. (No. 270). *-9274-2.*

FORGED GENEALOGIES: SAINT-JOHN PERSE'S CONVERSATIONS WITH CULTURE, by Carol Rigolot. 2001. (No. 271). *-9275-0.*

VISIONES DE ESTEREOSCOPIO (PARADIGMA DE HIBRIDACIÓN EN EL ARTE Y LA NARRATIVA DE LA VANGUARDIA ESPAÑOLA), por María Soledad Fernández Utrera. 2001. (No. 272). *-9276-9.*

TRANSPOSING ART INTO TEXTS IN FRENCH ROMANTIC LITERATURE, by Henry F. Majewski. 2002. (No. 273). *-9277-7.*

IMAGES IN MIND: LOVESICKNESS, SPANISH SENTIMENTAL FICTION AND *DON QUIJOTE,* by Robert Folger. 2002. (No. 274). *-9278-5.*

INDISCERNIBLE COUNTERPARTS: THE INVENTION OF THE TEXT IN FRENCH CLASSICAL DRAMA, by Christopher Braider. 2002. (No. 275). *-9279-3.*

When ordering please cite the *ISBN Prefix* plus the last four digits for each title.

Send orders to: University of North Carolina Press
P.O. Box 2288
Chapel Hill, NC 27515-2288
U.S.A.
www.uncpress.unc.edu
FAX: 919 966-3829